D0492247

The Organization of Business

University of Huddersfield Learning Centre,
Queensgate, Huddersfield, HD13DH

407570

University of
HUDDERSFIELD
LIBRARY SERVICES

Telephone:
Renewals   01484-472045
Learning Centre   01484-473888

Class No: 658. 00941

Suffix: ACKROYD, S

This book is to be returned on or before
the last date stamped below

The Organization of Business

Applying organizational theory to contemporary change

Stephen Ackroyd

University of Lancaster

OXFORD

UNIVERSITY PRESS

OXFORD
UNIVERSITY PRESS

Great Clarendon Street, Oxford OX2 6DP

Oxford University Press is a department of the University of Oxford.
It furthers the University's objective of excellence in research, scholarship,
and education by publishing worldwide in

Oxford New York

Auckland Bangkok Buenos Aires Cape Town Chennai
Dar es Salaam Delhi Hong Kong Istanbul Karachi Kolkata
Kuala Lumpur Madrid Melbourne Mexico City Mumbai Nairobi
São Paulo Shanghai Singapore Taipei Tokyo Toronto

with an associated company in Berlin

Oxford is a registered trade mark of Oxford University Press
in the UK and in certain other countries

Published in the United States
by Oxford University Press Inc., New York

© Stephen Ackroyd, 2002

The moral rights of the author have been asserted
Database right Oxford University Press (maker)

First published 2002

All rights reserved. No part of this publication may be reproduced,
stored in a retrieval system, or transmitted, in any form or by any means,
without the prior permission in writing of Oxford University Press,
or as expressly permitted by law, or under terms agreed with the appropriate
reprographics rights organizations. Enquiries concerning reproduction
outside the scope of the above should be sent to the Rights Department,
Oxford University Press, at the address above

You must not circulate this book in any other binding or cover
and you must impose this same condition on any acquirer

British Library Cataloguing in Publication Data
Data available

Library of Congress Cataloging in Publication Data
Data available
ISBN 0–19–874269–X

Typeset in Minion and Argo
by RefineCatch Limited, Bungay, Suffolk
Printed in Great Britain by
Biddles Ltd, Guildford, Surrey

UNIVERSITY
LIBRARY
0 9 DEC 2002
59 069 70109
HUDDERSFIELD

In memory of Robert Ackroyd
1951–1998

A good man—a great loss

Preface

A great Nation, which possess the instinct for great things. The soul of Shakespeare lives in it.

Hector Berlioz on a visit to London in 1851

Today it is common to divide academic books into two kinds: textbooks and monographs. A textbook is a summation of the research and knowledge available in a particular field; and it is an attempt to give an overview or summary of an entire academic field. A monograph is a specialist work of scholarship, in which particular areas of thought and/or research are given sustained attention. The best monographs are highly influential and may acquire a considerable readership amongst academic colleagues and advanced students, but they are not usually thought of as covering whole academic fields. This book has many of the attributes of a textbook in the emerging academic field of organization studies: there is the inclusion of much basic material about the constitution of companies, for example, as well as many descriptions and models of organizational designs. Readers will also find in this book discussions of much work that has been highly influential in the development of the discipline of organization studies, especially that which has systematic empirical reference. In these ways this book is like a standard textbook.

On the other hand, there is no assumption here that everything conceivably relevant to the study of business organizations should be included. There has been deliberate selection of the material to discuss and the ways to handle it. There is more focus on particular subjects and extended treatment of the ideas of particular authors than is common in many textbooks. As well as the inclusion of historical and culturally diverse illustrative materials, there is much emphasis on the contemporary relevance of theories and ideas. There is also emphasis on making theoretically informed connections between areas within the subject. In these ways there has been a choice both in favour of depth and relevance to understanding contemporary change in the book. Thus the book hopefully avoids the blandness and superficiality that are attributes of some textbooks.

By drawing selectively from the subject matter of organization studies, then, this book also has some of the features of the monograph. It certainly aims to argue a distinctive thesis. As well as avoiding superficiality, it is also important to avoid any implication that the field of study addressed by this book can be seen as exclusively containing reliable or in some sense established knowledge, an impression that many textbook writers clearly wish to give. On the contrary, although there has been much work undertaken, and there is much that is intellectually stimulating and provocative, there is actually little that can be accepted as reliable knowledge and even less on which it might be possible to base policy. The impression that organization studies is a field of established knowledge is only achieved at the cost of authors reducing to superficiality what are often highly challenging and discrepant findings and points of view. As more advanced students of organization well know, this is a field that is riven with controversy. Nevertheless, this book selects from the total contributions to organization studies a subset of ideas and findings, arguing for its relevance to understanding contemporary change and its reliability as a guide to action.

The thesis argued in this book is that organization studies can be usefully approached by analysing (and studying empirically) the structural properties of groups, organizations, and the social contexts in which these are embedded. Interest in these matters has a long history, but, clearly, it is not shared by all who study organizations today. Some colleagues are attempting to make what they call 'post-structural' organization studies: they see their project precisely in terms of abandoning the very concepts that are central to the kind of study which this book promotes. It is an illustration of the controversy pervading this subject area how far practitioners in this field differ on the importance of a structural emphasis in the analysis of organizations and related phenomena. It is difficult to imagine a deeper controversy in a putative intellectual field. It should be quite clear that this book takes one side in this stand-off. It features the consideration of structure centrally; and, as explained more fully in Chapter 1, it is suggested that this sort of theoretical emphasis should be consolidated by connecting with (and building on) a highly traditional approach to the subject in this respect. It is argued both explicitly and implicitly that this kind of approach to the subject still has an important contribution to make.

The motivation to write this book is, therefore, very much a reaction to the controversy in this field of study. It is part of an intellectual movement which aims at reasserting the value of specific traditions in scholarship, and argues in favour of a particular approach to organization studies. This movement may be described as philosophically realist as well as theoretically structuralist. In intention at least, it aims to analyse organizations objectively, and assumes that, by doing so, key characteristics of organizations can be identified that will allow us to make accurate descriptions of them and the way they work. The aspiration is to begin to construct precise and accurate knowledge of organizations which points to the relevance of policies that can be used to direct the development of economic institutions. Key sources of inspiration, surprising though it may seem, are the ideas of thinkers who are primarily classified as theorists. The most important single figure here is the great German analyst, Max Weber. It is often forgotten that Weber, as most of the classical writers on social affairs, was also greatly interested in problems of policy and interested in making contributions in this sphere. Weber was a founder member of the influential German policy 'think tank', the *Verein fur Sozialpolitik*.

Grandiose though it may sound in these days of pervasive post-modernism, in which the best work in many areas of scholarship aspires to be nothing more significant than seriously playful, this book was written with a sense of deepening conviction that the task of developing sound knowledge of organizations is urgent. When the research of academics from a range of specialist areas (such as economic history, political economy, economic, and sociological institutionalism) is stitched together with some basic ideas from structuralist organizational studies, as is done here, a diagnosis of the present situation can be produced that has considerable intellectual support and grim implications. As is argued here, there are many reasons to think that the economic strength in the institutional core of the economy of Britain is finally draining away, leaving society not only economically but culturally impoverished. The problem is not just that capital is being exported in large amounts by our major corporations, leaving little serious or valued work for the majority of the people to do; but that such actions are held up as morally justifiable, indeed are taken as the very model of appropriate behaviour.

Such comments may lead the reader to decide that there is also a moralizing undertone in the background to the assessment of the evidence and argument arrayed in this book. It is there, but, hopefully, it is not obvious or intrusive in the text itself. Yet it does merit some acknowledgement in a preface. In essence this moral thread runs as follows: profit maximization, without some other broader cultural or intellectual justification is, paradoxically but inevitably, impoverishing. It is not clear that Berlioz, resurrected and returned to London 150 years after the visit which provoked the admiring comments quoted above, would recognize the 'soul of Shakespeare' in our society and people today.

There are some obvious cultural continuities in the ideas that motivated many of the adventurers who took the first steps towards creating the British Empire and the contemporary businessmen who run our large corporations. To put the matter very bluntly, they share the desire to make the largest possible profit in a short period of time. Of the many differences between these groups, however, one is that, in the first group, the desire for economic advantage was not the only motivation. For the British freebooters and adventurers—the embodiments of entrepreneurial impulse in the seventeenth and early eighteenth centuries—the pursuit of economic gain was not separated from other ideas: there was, often, a peculiar semi-secularized set of Christian religious convictions for example, and a form of nationalism that combined the desire to acquire capital with the idea that British institutions and civilization were being advanced in the process. Today, by contrast, the desire to realize huge profits in the shortest possible time stands alone as, seemingly, the only motivation of those who occupy the commanding heights of our corporations. This motivation, clearly, has the virtue of simplicity (which removes the need for any difficult moral choices). These days there can be no excuse for failure arising because, at a critical juncture, a decision-maker is caught between the cross-cutting loyalties of personal gain and the interests of the state, or those of patriotism and common decency.

Much of the time today, scholars seem generally unable to muster the ability to comment on the general trend of events. Academia, especially that branch devoted to the study of business, is set on a trajectory of increasing specialization that at best produces a Balkanization of research communities and interests, which is inimical to the development of anything approaching a comprehensive, not to mention complete, assessment of the trajectory of change in society. As this preface is being written, the staff in my institution are this week being invited to attend two talks: the first of these applies Markov's mathematical models to the prediction of returns from investments in futures markets and the second is an application of the ideas of a French post-structuralist thinker to the 'governability' of a hospital. Both of these talks will be given by academics in the forefront of research in their respective fields, as is necessary and appropriate for a leading school of management. Both of these talks are likely to be very interesting to their audiences. I propose to be present at least at one of them. The suspicion is, however, that if someone were to attend both these talks, and perhaps dozens of others of a similar level of abstraction and specialization, it would not be possible for them to begin to construct a reliable overall assessment of the prospects for the economy and society of Britain. In a curious way, the specialization of academic life, which involves, *inter alia*, the exclusion of any general evaluation of the trend of events, mimics the specialization occurring in business, which also concentrates on its maximizing returns from its specialist areas of activity and excludes anything approximating a general development strategy, or commitment to the home economy. Arguably, the time has come for some business academics to reassert the value of general analysis and policy-related assessments. The reader will have to judge the value of this limited attempt to produce an overall assessment.

As is often remarked, writing a book incurs debts. There are those who are close who have been neglected and who deserved better treatment. I owe large debts to my family, for the time I was not able to spend with them, and their tolerance of the preoccupied frame of mind I was habitually in when I did take some time off. During some of the time I was writing this book, for example, my wife, Pam, who is herself a senior manager, was having to work

extremely hard to retain agreement about the appropriate strategic direction
for her organization (not to mention the commitment of some of her colleagues to basic day-to-day operational integrity) and she could have done
with more support than I was able to give her. Despite the pressing claims on
her attention, she has always managed to find the time to read successive
drafts of this book and to correct many mistakes. Some people are simply
more capable than others—both morally and intellectually. I do realize that
another book on my shelf and in the library is hardly likely to be adequate
compensation for what occurred, Pam; but, for the moment, it will have to do.
Our two children, Jon and Emily, might also charge me with serious neglect.
Once again it was they who found the time to help me, by being generally
appreciative of my activities. After his graduation, Jon found the time to fix
my computer and help me with the bibliography and other final preparations
for the publication of this book. (We will gloss over the fact that I had to offer
a hefty bribe to get him to do it.) Since both children were full-time students
for most of the time I was writing this book, it is not clear that they would
have welcomed parental attention to their welfare anyway. I am only vindi-
cated by the fact that both have succeeded wonderfully well in spite of serious
paternal neglect.

I have also been very lucky with my students. The book was written with my
undergraduate students very much in mind and they have been very tolerant
of my working through this material with them over the last few years. They
have, on many occasions, offered insightful comments, both written and ver-
bal, on my ideas. In the last two years, I have tested out drafts of the chapters
on them as tutorial readings and had the benefit of their comments on the
text. These have no doubt made a contribution to improving the readability of
the text, if not the acceptability of the argument. My post-graduate students
have also been subjected to selections from this material. MBA students, to
whom I have also given this sort of material, have been helpful in insisting that
I connect what I have been saying with examples of corporate behaviour and
they have provided me with many additional illustrations to the points I have
been making. In recent years, I have also been blessed with some brilliant and
largely self-motivating doctoral students. Although they have made little direct contribution to this project, most of them have continued with their
research without the need for major remedial inputs—intellectual or
psychological—from me. I would therefore like to thank Daniel Muzio, Fari-
dah Shamsudin, and Terri O'Brien, in particular, for being committed to their
scholarly projects, and for undertaking their work with such a high level of
professionalism.

I also owe a considerable debt to departmental colleagues. Frank Blackler,
Mike Reed, Colin Brown, Brain Bloomfield, Norman Crump, Martin
Brigham, Bogdan Costea, Niall Hayes, and Lucas Introna have been the kind

of colleagues anyone would wish for: continually supportive and, when the occasion arises, rigorous in their critique and stimulating in their comments. There are also many colleagues in the Social Science faculty at Lancaster to acknowledge and to thank, whose work has been a continual source of inspir- ation to me in different ways. I must mention Andrew Sayer, Bob Jessop, John Urry, John Hughes, and Keith Soothill. It is a privilege to work in the same institution as such colleagues as these, even though, academic rate-busters all, they do often leave one with a feeling of inadequacy. I also acknowledge the help of scholars, some of whom I do not know very well, and with whom I have never worked, but whose research and thinking has been a particular source of inspiration. Here I would like to mention the following: Margaret Archer, Peter Armstrong, Rick Delbridge, Paul Edwards, Gerry Hanlon, Christel Lane, Karen Legge, Glenn Morgan, John Purcell, Jill Rubery, Chris Smith and Tony Elger, Paul Stewart, Tony Tinker, Barrie Wilkinson, Karel Williams and Colin Haslam, Richard Whitley, and Richard Whittington.

Our departmental secretary, Jean Yates, will no doubt be glad this book is finished, if only because I no longer have the excuse that I am writing it as a reason for staying away, and not doing as much as I should in my department. I single out for special thanks and appreciation two of my departmental colleagues: Sharon Bolton and Steve Fleetwood, with whom I have undertaken joint projects, and who have made the (sometimes tedious) business of aca- demic research and writing as painless an experience as it can be. As always, the *lack* of complete intellectual agreement has been part of the recipe for creative collaboration, and has never been a problem, only a source of stimula- tion. The same can be said for the range of other colleagues outside my institution with whom I have had fruitful collaborations. I must mention here, in particular, Steve Procter, Paul Thompson, and David Lawrenson. Steve Procter has been kind enough to let me use what is really jointly produced material in Chapter 5, though he disassociates himself with some of my con- clusions. The ideas and research work I have completed with Paul and Dave have less overlap with the present work than that undertaken with Steve, but I am nonetheless clearly deeply indebted to both for ideas and ways of thinking about problems. Ian Kirkpatrick is to be thanked for keeping another, and largely unrelated, project going; and putting up with my reluctance to turn my energies to working with him as opposed to continuing with this project. Well that period is over now.

Finally, I have to thank various people on the publishing side: Angela Grif- fin, Patrick Brindle, and David Musson were always helpful and supportive. I owe a large debt to John Scott who, as a series editor for Oxford University Press, originally commissioned a book on this subject area from me. He showed great tolerance when the MS did not turn up precisely on time and, when it did appear, of the fact that it had much more in it than the contents we had originally agreed. What he could have done, and indeed what I expected him to do, was suggest that I slim down the MS as submitted, in short to write the book I contracted to write. Instead, he suggested it would be a waste to simplify my MS and that I should indeed extend the book further. The result is that the book I have now written is much more ambitious than the one he contracted with me. I cannot decide which is the more wonderful about John, the quality and range of his (unremitting) intellectual output—or his tolerance and respect for colleagues; but I am sure that he is a prince amongst men, and I am proud to count him among my friends.

S. A.

Lancaster, 2002

Acknowledgements

The author and the publisher wish to thank the following people and organizations for the use of copyright material. Every effort has been made to trace all the copyright holders of material appearing in this book and if any have been inadvertently overlooked, the publishers and the author will be pleased to respond if duly notified.

Blackwell Publishing is thanked for permission to reproduce material from *The Culture of Technology* by Arnold Pacey, 1983 (pp. 18–19) and by Ash Amin, the editor of *Post Fordism: a Reader* 1994 (pp. 7 and 136–7) and for other material in the same volume, viz from the chapter 'Searching for a New Institutional Fix' by J. Peck and A. Tickell (p. 307) and from the chapter by B. Jessop 'Post Fordism and the State', p. 260. Blackwell are also the publishers of *The British Journal of Management*, and we thank them for permission to quote from a paper in Vol .7 (1996) by D.W. Cravens, N.F. Piercy and S.H. Shipp, 'Organisational Forms for Competing in Highly Dynamic Environments: The Network Paradigm' (p. 303). B.T Batsford and Chrysalis Books are thanked for permission to publish short extracts from D. Watterson, *The Gods of Ancient Egypt* 1993 (pp. 44, 45, and 46). The Perseus Books Group of New York are thanked for material from *The Second Industrial Divide: Possibilities for Prosperity*, by M. Piore and Charles Sabel (pp. 28–31). Harper-Collins are thanked for permission to reproduce a section from F.Braudel's book *The Wheels of Commerce* which is volume II of the larger study, *Civilisation and Capitalism*, orginally published in London by William Collins. Oxford University Press is thanked for material from *Corporate Business and the Capitalist Classes*, by John Scott, 1997 (pp. 80 and 84); from *Keeping Good Company: A study of Corporate Governance in Five Countries*, by J. Charkham, 1994 (pp. 340 and 341); from *Life on the Line in Contemporary Manufacturing*, by R. Delbridge, 1998 (pp. 52–53); from *The Decline of the British Economy* by B. Elbaum and W. Lazonick, 1986 (p. 7) and from *Divergent Capitalisms*, by R. Whitley, 1999 (p. 129). Oxford University Press is also to be thanked for material from the chapter 'The International Diffusion of Knowledge' by O. Solvell and I. Zander, in *The Dynamic Firm: The Role of Technology, Strategy, Organisation and Regions* edited by A. Chandler, P. Hagstrom and O. Zander 1998 (p. 411) and for a quotation from 'The New Unionism' by E. Heery, in *Contemporary Industrial Relations: A Critical Analysis* edited by I. Beardwell, 1996, (p. 196). Sage Publications and Gareth Morgan are thanked for permission to publish material from *Creative Organisation Theory*, by G. Morgan,

1989, (p. 65) and for material from *Consumption and Identity at Work*, by P. Du Gay, 1996, (pp. 102–3). Routledge, a member of the Taylor and Francis Group of Companies, is thanked for material from Chapter 12 of *Understanding Business Organisations*, edited Graeme Salaman entitled 'The End of Classical Organisational Forms?' by C. Mabey, G. Salaman and J. Storey, 2001, (p. 181); and material from from Chapter 3 of *Changing Forms of Employment* edited by R. Compton, D. Gallie and K. Purcell, 1996, entitled 'Towards the Transnational Company?' by P.K. Edwards, P. Armstrong, P. Marginson and J. Purcell (pp. 40–42); and from 'Trapped in Their Wave', by M. Kipping, from *Critical Consulting: New Perspectives on the Management Advice Industry*, by T. Clark and R. Fincham, 2001, (abstracted from pp. 34 and 36). Routledge are also publishers of *Economy and Society* and we thank them for permission to quote from a paper in Vol 27 (1998) by C. Lane, 'Between Globalisation and Localisation: A comparison of the Internationalisation Strategies of British and German MNCs' (pp. 462 and 485). Carfax Publishing, also a member of the Taylor and Francis group, is the publisher of the journal Policy Studies and is thanked for permission to publish an extract from a paper by R.P. Dore, entitled: 'Financial Structures and the Long-Term View' in *Policy Studies*, 1985 (p. 13). John Atkinson and The Institute of Employment Studies of the University of Sussex (formerly the Institute for Manpower Studies) are thanked for permission to reproduce a diagram from the research paper 'Flexibility, Uncertainty and Manpower Management' by J. Atkinson (1984) Institute for Employment Studies, Report No 89. Thomson Business Press is thanked for *Corporate Realities: Dynamics of large and small organisations*, by R. Goffee and R. Scase, 1995, (p. 11). I.F.S. Publishing (Bedford) are thanked for permission to reproduce a diagram from Robots at Work: A practical guide for engineers and managers, by J. Hartley, 1983 (p. 125). David Buchanan, Andrzej Huczynski, and Pearson Education Limited are thanked for their permission to reproduce a summary of Weber's model of bureaucracy from *Organisational Behaviour an Introductory Text*, by A. Huczynski and D. Buchanan, 2001, (p. 489), based on *The Theory of Social and Economic Organisations*, by Max Weber, 1947, (pp. 328–37). The Telegraph Group Ltd for permission to quote from the following articles in the *Daily Telegraph*: by Dominic White on 14th July, 2001; by Kate Rankine on 17th March, 2001, by A. Cave on 28th July, 2001 and by Dan Sabbagh on 8th September, 2001. News International Newspapers Ltd for permission to quote from an article in the *Sunday Times* by John O'Donnell on 11th March, 2001 © John O'Donnell/Times Newspapers Ltd (2001). The Financial Times Ltd for material from Tony Jackson's 'Comment and Analysis' column 15th December, 1998 and from and extended interview with Sir Geoffrey Mulcahy published on 15th September, 2001. Palgrave Macmillan and Paul Thompson and David McHugh are thanked for permission to reproduce a version of figure 11.2: A Post-Bureaucratic Organisation? from page 155 of the third edition of Work Organisations: A Critical Introduction, 2001.

Contents

structure-

List of Figures

List of Tables

Abbreviations

AGM	annual general meeting
AMT	advanced manufacturing technology
AMU	agriculture, mining, and utilities
AR	accumulation regime
AS	accumulation system
B.Ae	British Aerospace
BCG	Boston Consulting Group
BIM	British Institute of Management
CAD	computer aided design
CBI	Confederation of British Industry
CEF	capital extensive firm
CEO	chief executive officer
CIM	computer-integrated manufacturing
CIPP	Centre for Industrial Policy and Performance, University of Leeds
CNC	computer numerical control
C-SCEF	commercial services capital extensive firm
EC	European Community
EDI	electronic data interchange
ERPS	enterprise resource planning systems
ESS	executive support system
FDI	foreign direct investment
FMS	flexible manufacturing system
FPBS	finance, property, and business services
FS	flexible specialization
GBAF	global industry advisory firms
GDP	gross domestic product
GGNP	global gross national product
GM	General Motors
GNP	gross national product
GWP	gross world product
HR/HRM	human resources/human resource management
HSF	high surveillance firm
ILO	International Labour Office
IT	information technology
JIT	just in time
KIF	knowledge-intensive firm
MBA	Master of Business Administration

MIS	management information system
MNC	multinational corporation
MR	mode of social regulation
M-TCEF	manufacturing-trading capital-extensive firm
NACAB	National Association of Citizens' Advice Bureaux
NC	numeric control
NEDO	National Economic Development Office
NFF	new flexible firm
R&D	research and development
SME	small–medium enterprise
TNC	trans-national corporation
TQM	total quality management
TUC	Trade Union Congress
WTO	World Trade Organization

1

Introduction

1.1 The approach to organization

During the last two decades, there has been an avalanche of changes in the institutions that make up the British economy. This book aims to cast light on these changes by considering organizational aspects of economic development. The main thrust of the discussion is concerned with clarifying what has happened to organizational structures and discussing the new patterns of relationships between them. As it unfolds, the argument is also concerned with analysing the reasons for organizational change and considering the implications of change for policy.

To advance the argument, the intellectual resources of a relatively new discipline to be taught in business schools are utilized. Models, theories, and ideas are drawn from the discipline, variously known as organizational behaviour, organizational analysis, or organization theory, but which is referred to here simply as organization studies. Taken as a whole, organization studies is constituted by the academic work that takes any sort of interest in organizations. This is to designate a broad field; and scholars working in this area are varied in their interest in and approach to this subject. Not all practitioners in this field are interested in the structural analysis which features centrally in this book, or are moved to consider the causes and consequences of structural change.

Many of the academics in organization studies today are focused on individual and small group behaviour, for example, being interested in questions concerning the motivation of individuals and or the interactive dynamics of small groups. These researchers draw their inspiration from the discipline of psychology and study behaviour in a quite detailed way. Another influential branch of this discipline is essentially a theoretical enterprise and its exponents play with different ways of conceiving organizations. Many recent contributions from scholars have featured the applicability of the ideas of the French philosophers Michel Foucault and Jacques Derrida to the study of organizations. By contrast, this book draws on—and attempts to develop from—a particular tradition in the approach to organization studies. The approach here considers models and theories referring to organizational structures—and also interorganizational structures. It considers the reasons for the development of particular kinds of organizations, the reasons for change in structures, and the consequences of the existence of organizations with particular kinds of structure.

The concept of structure is analysed at various points in what follows—Chapters 3 and 4 contain extended considerations of structures—but a working definition of it is necessary at this point. Briefly put, we may define the structure of an organization as the recurrent pattern of relationships through which authority is exercised and through which organizational activities are coordinated and controlled. An organizational chart that depicts the levels of management and indicates their functions, such as might be produced by the management of a firm, is often a good basic depiction of an organization's structure. It is possible to produce more adequate views of organizational structure than this; but, for many purposes, the accounts offered in the books are not much advance on these charts. Some of the value of structural analysis comes not from the concept of structure itself, so much as the generalizations that can be made about structures and what can be inferred from these generalizations. However, the basic ideas about structure in use here are connected with ideas drawn from social theory, and, in later stages of the book, when emergent interorganizational relationships are considered, conceptually more sophisticated uses of structure are developed.

Academic analysts use the basic idea of organizational structure differently from the manager who produces an organizational chart. Analysts are interested in producing general depictions or 'models' of structures. Analysts produce and argue about what they propose are general models of distinctive organizational 'types'. These generic organizational types have the purpose of describing—and to some extent explaining—distinct forms of organizations. Organizational analysts also produce contrasting sets of these abstract general models of structural types, usually called 'typologies' of organizational structures. Mintzberg's set of five organizational models is an interesting recent example of the practice (Mintzberg 1979; 1993). Mintzberg distinguishes what he calls the simple functional organization from the bureaucracy, the professional bureaucracy and two other types, the multidivisional organization and 'the adhocracy'. Mintzberg, among other organizational analysts, makes the claim that such an abstract general understanding of structures secures a knowledge of the principles that supposedly underlie organizational structures. They use the term 'organizational designs' to describe the different structures they have identified (Khandwalla 1977; Mintzberg 1993). The implication of this, of course, is that professors in business schools are able to teach business executives and others how to organize their businesses; that is, how to design them to best effect. How reliable such claims are is open to argument. It is certainly true there is much organizational innovation taking place today that is not depicted in many of the current textbooks.

The approach to organizations used here does draw on ideas about organizations developed initially by sociologists. The most important figure here is the German sociologist Max Weber (1864–1920) who, more than any other single person, pioneered the analysis of organizational and social structures. Weber is best known in organization studies for clarifying an idealized model (what he called an 'ideal type') of the modern Western bureaucracy; but, as will be suggested later, concentrating on this alone is to overlook much of importance in Weber's work. Since Weber formulated his model of bureaucracy in the early years of the last century, there have been many generations of structural analysts. Following Weber, the most significant contribution came from the Columbia School which Robert Merton (1910) founded at Columbia University in New York in the 1930s (Merton 1949). The Columbia writers Peter Blau (1955), Philip Selznick (1949), and Alvin Gouldner (1954, 1955), to name only a few, developed a highly effective mode of case study research into the working of organizations. Since then there have been numerous other schools of structural analysts. One might cite the celebrated (or infamous, depending on your point of view) Aston School—which tried to convert structural analysis into an exact science and which was particularly active in Britain in the 1970s (Pugh and Hickson 1976; Pugh and Hinnings 1976). Today there are numerous groups of writers on organizational structure.

This study, then, stands in a long tradition of academic work. However, as will be argued here, the book also attempts to reorientate structural analysis, seeing it as a species of applied sociology rather than a branch of empirical science, and locating its roots in the work of sociologists like Max Weber and the Columbia School. It is also argued that there is much work to do for such a discipline. The last twenty years have witnessed some dramatic developments in organizations and the relations between them. There have been few periods of history that compare to the present for the rapidity and scale of organizational change, though the period 1760 to 1830 in Britain (when the Industrial Revolution occurred and during which numerous small manufacturing workshops were set up), or the period 1890 to 1920 in the North-Eastern USA (the period of the development of modern mass production) are probably comparable. As with the earlier periods of dynamic change, the introduction of new technology, the development of new organizational forms, and new social structures are bound up together.

For some teachers and students in this field, a book written mainly about organizational structures will be a restricted (and restrictive) view of the field. Not only are small groups and much of the theory left out of the account, but there is a lack of consideration of many aspects of contemporary organizations. Such an approach is seemingly content to leave out such appealing topics as behaviour in organizations and organizational culture, subjects that are often thought of as being of great interest in themselves but also as being central to mainstream organizational studies. Moreover, ideas about culture, belief, and identity are interesting to new students. Teaching organization studies in a British university today leaves the practitioner in no doubt of the appeal of knowledge about the normative dimensions of organizations. The topic of organizational culture has in many areas swept all before it: much of the substantive discussion in organization studies today concerns this aspect of organizations; and there seems to be widespread use of the idea of culture in politics and educated debate. By concentrating on structures to the exclusion of other aspects of organizations this book is rendered somewhat unfashionable.

There are several things that could be said in criticism of the subjectivist and normative tendencies of much contemporary organizational studies; but suffice it to say that the choice to overlook culture and concentrate on structure was quite deliberate. Culture is a much more complicated subject than it may at first appear: it is notoriously difficult to conceive of adequately and the analysis of culture does not readily yield effective tools for the academic or the practitioner. By contrast, the applications of structural ideas seem to be legion and the approach is unfairly undervalued. Business executives are under no such illusions. They know quite well that one of the most effective things they can do is reorganize the formal structure of a business. They readily readjust the structures of the organizations they control. Indeed they have been doing so at an astonishing rate—and to an unprecedented extent—in recent decades. Business executives have not waited for academics to tell them what to do.

Although it is unfashionable, the analysis of organizational structures connects with the realist tradition of organizational analysis and social thought in social science which has a long history in Western social science (Ackroyd and Fleetwood 2000). Hopefully it will become clear from reading this book that applying structural analysis to contemporary organizations covers a great deal of material and throws up a very large number of insights. These are quite enough to fill a textbook of this kind, which is mainly aimed at advanced undergraduates or postgraduates and MBA students wishing to know more about this subject. A great deal more could have been written on this same subject; only limitations of space preventing it. Hence, although a large number of models and theories concerning contemporary organizations and their patterns of organization are presented, the study is by no means definitive. It has been expedient to concentrate on a selection of authors. Thus attention is focused on the ideas that have provoked debate and which are thought to be particularly insightful or interesting.

There is a good deal of discussion of work published during the last twenty years concerning contemporary organizational structures—the particular forms they are now adopting and the reasons for their structural transformation. One reason for reading the book is to obtain an introduction to the most interesting ideas that try to account for new organizational types and organizational change. But this is not all there is in the book. There is also consideration of the question of how to understand change from a theoretical point of view and, at the last, an attempt to revive the question of industrial policy. Thus, attention is paid to aspects of the institutional context of British firms, and how these have developed historically and shaped the typical structures to be observed today. The approach is significantly broader than some treatments of organizational structure. But before saying exactly why and how the treatment is different from traditional accounts, an overview of all that the book contains follows.

1.2 The organization of the book

Starting point: the need for an analysis of structures

The first task undertaken in the book is to establish the need for a reanalysis of organizations in terms of their structure. In the next chapter, some of the available government statistics concerning contemporary organizations in Britain are reviewed. On the basis of these data, it is clear there is a lot of change going on, but what these changes are and what is causing them is far from clear. The book thus begins by looking at some of the available facts and figures and, through the consideration of these, argues that considerable change in the organization of business is occurring.

Some of the features of the reorganization of business are well known: that large-scale, hierarchical, and bureaucratic organizations are being disassembled, and smaller team-based and informal organizations are being put in their place, for example. It is now rare to find a factory (or, for that matter other kinds of workplace) in Britain employing more than 1500 people. Twenty-five years ago, by contrast, a place employing 1500 would have been quite small and those employing 5000 people were not particularly remarkable (Lash and Urry 1987: 102–4). What underlies these sorts of changes is less well understood. A key point to note is that almost all kinds of business have been reorganizing themselves to do more with less.

Change in the size of organizations is not to be equated with a shift from large business to small business. The economy has not regenerated itself from the bottom up by the spontaneous creation of many new small businesses, as is sometimes assumed. In fact, the policies and activities of large businesses lie behind the movement to smaller organizations. Big businesses are heading the movement of reorganization by reconstituting themselves as constellations of small and semi-independent business units. Considered as aggregates of their many parts, big businesses are even larger and more influential today than they have been in the past. This is not only because they own many small business units, but because they are key actors in complex cooperative networks of organizations, many of which they do not own, but which they control by their activities.

There is a complex process of disaggregation and internationalization taking place, in which British businesses are deconstructing themselves into constellations of smaller units and exporting more of their capacity and assets overseas. In addition, the domestic economy is being increasingly penetrated by multinationals based in foreign countries. There has been much change in small businesses too, but much of this is to be explained as accommodation to changes initiated elsewhere. Many small businesses have been reconstituting themselves to cooperate more effectively with disaggregated large businesses, both British and foreign. It would be a substantial mistake to think that there are only small companies left in the economy, and that the main task for the organizational analyst is to produce realistic models of small, flexible organizations, as some analysts seem to have conceived of their task (Volberda 1998).

It soon becomes clear from this examination that organizations—as distinct from companies—are becoming more numerous and smaller, and this sort of process has gone quite far in some sectors of the economy. Further, it seems also that there are many fewer employees in some sectors of the economy today than there were twenty years ago. However, the wealth created by the fewer people employed—to judge by such things as company profits—is not less. Hence, a reduction in the numbers of organizations, and/or a decline in the numbers employed in a particular sector, cannot be regarded as evidence of a decline in that area of economic activity. If this were so, it could well be argued that the British economy is in general decline as the numbers of organizations in most sectors of the economy is in decline. Although there is a question mark over the continued success of the institutions of the British economy—especially in some areas of which manufacturing is the most important example—it does not seem any longer that what is needed is an explanation of the reasons for British failure. There is a question, however, about the general direction of change in the British economy, and the first chapter of the book concludes with some popular views on this question.

The uses of organization theory

To understand and explain organizational change, one of the sources of insight is organization theory. Organizational theory includes many ideas about organizational structure. It is a natural choice, therefore, to look in Chapters 3 and 4 at what organizational theory has to offer in the explanation of organizational structures. The orthodox approach to structure is explored in Chapter 3, and a more innovative type of conflict theory is introduced in Chapter 4. The orthodox approach to organization theory—which is given various names, structural functional theory and contingency theory amongst them—does offer a useful starting point for the study of structures. It allows some basic models of organizational structures to be considered together with some standard explanations of why they exist.

However, orthodox organizational theory turns out to be not very helpful in explaining contemporary organizational change. In contingency theory it is held that there is a small number of types of organizational structures. These are alleged to be highly adapted to (and functional within) certain environmental circumstances. The contingencies to which organizations adapt are features of the environment, and organizations tend to adopt structures that allow them to perform. However, there is some evidence to suggest that many organizations are changing in similar ways today; so, unless the circumstances of many organizations are changing in a similar way, there must be a question about the validity of this explanation. Contingency theory recognizes only a small number of organizational types, most of which are variations on the standard 'unitary' or 'U' organizational form (Williamson 1975), which is a simple hierarchy with a single apex. Other commentators have given this basic type other names. Chandler prefers the label 'F' form or 'functional form' (Chandler 1962). Mintzberg, whose work offers an accessible account of the contingency approach, calls the basic model the simple structure (1979, 1993). Four of Mintzberg's five types of organizations are developments of the 'U' form or simple structure. However, many organizational analysts today think that this organizational form, particularly the large version of it—known as the bureaucracy—either no longer exists or is under serious threat of 'implosion'. Contingency theory does not adequately explain why this might be nor does it envisage some of the new forms of organizations that are currently observed. The models proposed by contingency theorists remain useful as reference points, even if there is a question mark over their relevance today.

If contingency theory cannot be accepted, the next logical task is to attempt a modest reconstruction of organization theory, and this is undertaken in Chapter 4. Here it is argued that the explanation for organizational structure embodied in contingency theory needs to be modified. The explanatory idea of contingency theory is that structures exist because they are functional for the organization. They allow the organization to perform—to produce goods or provide services, for example—efficiently and effectively. It is argued in Chapter 4 that, although organizational structures must be functional to some degree, organizations are also an alliance of groups with different contributions to make and expecting different rewards from participation. The organizational structure—which is a set of authority relations—is an arrangement for ensuring the cooperation and coordination of the conduct of different groups. In fact, the structure is an expression of the relative powers of the groups of people in an organization. Although this is implied by many of the contingency theorists, who acknowledge that structure is concerned with authority (authority being legitimate or accepted power), for them this is not the main point.

The approach to structure in this book makes authority more important than function. There can be organizations that are manifestly not functional, and, in particular, which do not perform effectively, but which nonetheless continue to exist (Meyer and Zucker 1989). Thus, in Chapter 4, the organization is considered as a set of relationships between groups of actors. From this viewpoint, the powers and resources that groups within organizations have decide their relative importance in shaping organizational outcomes and defining the rewards that they get from participation. This is not all there is to the forces producing structures. There are certain forces holding the organization in a particular pattern of relations and ensuring that the politics of the organization do not pull it apart. The most basic point is that authority tends to produce conformity. This is not primarily because authority involves sanctions that can be applied to the disobedient, but because authority is power that is accepted as legitimate and so it produces conformity.

There are other forces causing organizations to retain their shape—to retain recognizable patterns of structure. One such force is custom and tradition. All institutions are set ways of doing things—which tend to persist even beyond the point where there is further need for them. Another similar force for conformity is that organizations more or less model themselves on each other by copying what is considered to be best practice. This point has been noticed by many observers, some of whom make it an important reason for the perpetuation of particular organizational forms. Institutional analysts call this sort of effect 'isomorphism' (Powell and DiMaggio 1991; Scott and Meyer 1994). Also, there is the influence of the surrounding organizations which transact business with an organization. Another theorist has labelled similar effects in social organization more generally as 'mediate' and 'proximate' structuration (Giddens 1979). Surrounding organizations also have expectations about appropriate forms of organization and so exert some pressure towards the adoption of a set pattern of relations.

On this account of structure, however, although there is a range of factors producing conformity to set patterns for organizations, the exercise of authority is basic; it is this that keeps the conflict between the groups within it—which are constantly contesting with each other over their relative contribution and rewards—within bounds. However, authority can also work the other way round. Instead of being used to ensure conformity, it can be used to secure change. Thus the basic importance of power is suggested by the fact that if it is decided by those controlling the use of resources, that a new arrangement in the organization is necessary, it is done. Usually the outcome of change is more or less as those in authority decide it will be. In many periods of history, the containing forces—as outlined above—exceed the dynamic forces arising from the activities of groups. In periods of dynamic change—as during the last two decades in most developed countries—the innovative forces have exceeded the containing ones. If this view is true, then some changes in the balance of power are at the bottom of the widespread changes in organizational structure.

New resources create an opportunity

A core proposition of the organizational theory proposed in this book is that structural change does not happen automatically as organizational circumstances change, as contingency theorists often suggest. On the contrary, it comes about only when initiated by some identifiable group or groups, and then only when their power is sufficient to overcome the opposition of other groups and the inertial drag of existing procedures and practices. Today, change is being undertaken by the managers of firms—and those controlling very large firms have been the most important agents of change. This group has chosen to exercise their power to change their own organizational structures, and their relations with other firms. The choice has been made to exercise latent power, but it is also necessary to note that some things have happened to alter the resources available to such people. In this case, to put the matter starkly, there are three factors that can be readily identified which have radically altered the balance of power within organizations and which have made possible—indeed inevitable and widespread—change in organizational forms and structures.

These factors are the availability of new technology, the liberalization of access finance, and the relaxation of government and other controls on business activities. These three factors have increased the resources available to business executives and, in particular, offer new opportunities for those controlling large businesses. They have allowed dramatic changes in the structures of organizations to be undertaken. Of the three however, the availability of new technology is by far the most important. In all sectors of the economy, the impact of new technology on productivity has been considerable. The availability of integrated management information systems (MIS), has allowed the reduction, if not the removal, of middle management and the effective coordination of otherwise physically remote plants and offices. New technology has made possible not only new patterns for production but their articulation within much more complex networks of cooperation between business units.

It is particularly true that the largest firms operating in manufacturing and commerce have been able to make extensive changes as a result of having new management information systems available to them. With IT, there is the possibility of much more effective programming of business information, making for much more efficient management with fewer people, and for cheap and effective communications over long distances. These new technical capacities, combined with the reconfiguration of organizations and the extensive redeployment of human resources, have made new kinds of strategic managerial plans possible. Hence, large firms have not only been able to reorganize themselves but, through their chosen strategies of development, they have been able to change the relations between themselves and other companies. They have therefore become key sources of more general change in the economy.

In the rest of the book, the approach to organizational structures developed in the early chapters is used to assess proposals about organizational change and their likely applicability in Britain today. New technology, and the other factors that have been identified, allow corporate controllers new scope for action. New technology in particular puts into the hands of corporate managers a resource that allows them to undertake the wholesale reorganization of their businesses.

The relevance of history

It has to be recognized that these new opportunities cannot be acted on in ways that are unconstrained. British businesses—large and small—already exist in particular forms and patterns. Business leaders are therefore constrained by working with existing structures and within existing patterns of relationships with other institutions. What strategies of change and development business leaders undertake therefore start from a given point; that is, from a given organization with a given structure and institutional context. To present the thesis developed in this book, therefore, it seemed logical to give an account of the typical organizational structures of both small and large businesses as they have been formed historically. This then allows the consideration of processes of change initiated within this particular setting.

Because of the context in which British business has operated historically, the business organizations found in Britain today have some distinctive patterns. Analysing traditional organizations in this way is seen to be necessary before beginning to consider the way opportunities for change have been perceived and acted on by those controlling the business organizations originating in this country. Hence in Chapters 5 and 6, an account of the particular situation of British companies is set out. In these accounts it is argued that British businesses—because of their historical configuration and institutional circumstances—have adopted some very distinctive structures. These chapters do not ignore the changed circumstances in which business leaders now act, but they do put forward the proposition that innovation has occurred—and corporate managers have been constrained to act—within particular contexts.

In Chapter 5 a historically based account of small and medium-sized business in Britain is set out. This sees them as being historically burdened by a lack of adequate finance, and this is associated with chronic underinvestment in efficient technology. Underinvestment leads to a characteristic style in the management of labour. The same features of the environment of small business have made them relatively weak and vulnerable to takeover. Despite a recurrent tendency for commentators to think that contemporary organizational change is a phenomenon driven by the re-emergence of effective small business, on the basis of the understanding of change developed here, it is possible to show convincingly that this sort of scenario is implausible to say the least. The levels of investment in productive technology are too low and the availability of new information technology does nothing to solve this. Hence, for many small businesses, the availability of cheap and effective information technology has not solved the underlying problem of inadequate capital and the consequent overreliance on labour to produce; but it has allowed them to be more responsive and to cooperate more fully with other firms. It has often allowed the reconfiguration of the productive technology of businesses but in ways that have, at best, merely allowed continued survival of business units in a new context. Thus, the thrust of the analysis in Chapter 5 is to show that the distinctive new patterns of organization that are emerging are special to the British context. Indeed, the new forms of flexible organization reflect the continuing weakness and vulnerability of small businesses.

This unpromising picture is by no means replicated by the situation of large businesses, as discussed in Chapter 6. They too have experienced problems of access to capital, but this has not prevented them from pioneering organizational forms that are distinctive and effective. If the indictment of British business handed out by some American scholars was correct (Elbaum and Lazonick 1986; Chandler 1990), it is in some ways surprising to find any significant British business surviving into the twenty-first century. But the fact is that, although the pattern of activities of British businesses has changed a good deal, they have pioneered structures that have allowed innovative patterns of activity and allowed the development of strategies that serve them adequately in the new context in which they now conduct business. Thus although there are some weaknesses still evident in the organization of the largest British businesses that have made them weaker than the comparable businesses of other countries, they have nonetheless become adept at being mobile and reorganizing their activities. It is British large companies that show most tendency to be 'footloose', that is to escape from their country of origin and operate independently in many countries of the world.

Evaluating proposals about new organizational forms

The historically based accounts of British organization and their characteristic structures set out in Chapters 5 and 6 are followed by an evaluation of the models of new organizations and the accounts of change that are often put forward in organization studies. The logic here is that only when a better picture has been established, of the pressures acting on British firms which have led them to adopt particular traditional organizational forms, does it seem appropriate to consider how the executives controlling them are likely to act. In Chapter 7 a start is made in considering some of the more interesting models of new organizational forms that have been put forward. Approaches to organizational change which put forward a simple but general new model for organizations are considered first. There are a number of writers who propose new generic models for the organization to replace the bureaucracy. Even the more sophisticated of these—such as the post-bureaucracy proposed by Heckscher and Donnellon (1994)—are rejected as too general.

It is surprising how often the causes of organizational change are misdiagnosed. Some studies of organizations do identify the importance of IT—though it is usually in amongst a host of other points. The basic point to notice is that corporate executives choose to adopt IT, to change their strategy and to adapt their structures accordingly. Unless they do this, no change will occur. Thus IT alone is a necessary but not a sufficient condition for change, and professors in business schools have taken the opportunity to advise business leaders to use it in particular ways. IT is widely available and in many applications, but not all organizations avail themselves of the opportunities it provides to the same degree. Even in parts of the IT industry itself there are some highly orthodox organizations. IT, plus some motive to innovate—pressure on profit margins, for example or the search for new markets—is required to point the relevance of innovation. It is argued here that it is because they are often forced to seek high profits in the short term that British businesses have usually moved further and faster in IT innovations—and in the adoption of associated organizational changes—than the comparable businesses of other countries.

Despite the acknowledgement that IT can be used to reorganize work and work organizations, there is a persistent tendency to argue that the new organizational forms are preferred primarily because of the cooperativeness that they feature. This sort of proposition has the causal sequence the wrong way round. The need for cooperation is a requirement of adopting advanced technical systems. New technology allows the number of staff employed to be cut; and this is widely undertaken. In the process, in many organizations today, the human organization structure has become attenuated. This is possible because so much information is now carried by technology rather than human connections. The people augment the technical system rather than the other way round. In these circumstances, those employees that remain have to fill in the gaps left by IT systems. To function effectively as an employee requires a high level of awareness and concern about business processes and willingness to cooperate on a wide variety of tasks when necessary. Surprisingly, this also means that employers are in some ways highly dependent in various ways on their remaining staff.

In Chapter 7 there is also discussion of some of the more interesting proposals for new corporate forms which refer to what is happening to large companies. This is very much the heart of the matter—if this analysis of organizational change is correct. The best known of the models of the major corporation—the so-called 'N' form of organization proposed by Hedlund (Hedlund and Ridderstrale 1992; Hedlund 1994) is discussed, as is the wonderful invention of Charles Sabel, which he calls the Moebius strip organization (Sabel 1991). Both are plausible descriptions of some of the aspects of the reconfigured large British organizations. However, the last third of this chapter is reserved for setting out and criticizing much that has been written about the idea of the network. In this analysis, the success of business is seen to be predicated on the discovery of new patterns of interorganizational cooperation in which the dominance of the major companies is not only preserved but developed.

National and wider patterns of change

Chapter 8 adopts a broader perspective and considers theories which attempt to account for the emergence of new organizational structures and which concentrate on explaining change within particular societies. In this chapter institutional analyses are considered. These suggest that a country like Britain has a particular set of socio-economic institutions that tend to fix the patterns of business relationships. The exponents of this thinking go to great lengths to show that institutions conform to the patterns they describe, and come up with persuasive characterizations of the British system of institutions. Some of these studies have great value for the ways they describe how the institutions of the economy and society interlock. But these studies of institutional systems are better at accounting for continuity than change. Although they can explain why it is that some national systems will be likely to change (or not), they have no very developed view of why it is that there are periodicities in change. As has been argued here, at some times the pace of change is slow and limited in scope, while at other times, such as today, it is rapid and extensive. Institutional theory does not explain well the sudden onset of extensive change—what we should call epochal change.

For this reason, in subsequent sections of Chapter 8 theories of change which do feature and try to explain epochal changes are considered. The neo-liberal analysis of change contained in the work of Piore and Sabel (1984)—and the neo-Marxist work of the so-called regulationist school (Aglietta 1979; Boyer 1988; Peck 1998)—take the explanation of epochal change much more seriously, and are, for this reason, given much more extended consideration in this book. Both these approaches are helpful in identifying change as originating for particular reasons. The one is recognizably liberal—identifying the origin of change in the invention of new techniques that are crystallized in particular institutional circumstances. The other looks to the internal problems of the capitalist mode of production to explain the need for change and the kinds of changes that occur in response. Both approaches have some value, but both have the drawback that they work best when applied to the patterns of institutions found within national economies, and much economic development today seems to be associated with the internationalization of big businesses.

In Chapter 9, the context for the evaluation of structural changes in the organizations of the British economy is set most broadly of all. Some of the interesting recent writing suggesting that it is economic globalization that explains both the fact of change—and many of its characteristic features—is considered. It can be argued that it is not the configuration of the domestic economy, and its fit with other domestic institutions, that have to be analysed if we wish to account for change, so much as the new-found capacity of business to break out of these confines and to participate in the growth of the world economy. The national economy is arguably not the most important context for the consideration of corporate business. In this part of the book the question of the extent to which organizations are involved in a process of globalization is considered. This is of course a large subject, not only because of its frame of reference, but because there is a huge literature surrounding it. In this account of globalization, emphasis is laid on the limited extent of economic globalization. Following Hirst and Thompson (1999), it is argued that what is happening is not globalization but a limited form of internationalization and, in this, the role of the multinational businesses is pivotal. Once more the role of large business seems to be basic to contemporary organizational change.

And finally: the problem of policy

In Chapter 10, some of the salient features of the argument which have relevance for industrial policy are pulled together. What actions government should consider taking in respect of the organizational changes examined in the book and their economic and social consequences are now set out. The discussion of policy ideas is not taken as far as the importance of the subject matter merits. Moreover for many reasons the topic of industrial policy is not likely to get a very sympathetic hearing from policy-makers. The whole subject is deeply unfashionable. Even left-leaning and social democratic governments shrink from having any point of view on the subject. There are signs that some policy-makers in the European community have grasped something of the importance of this subject, but, even in that context, awareness is not universal. However, part of the rationale for trying to revive an interest in structures has to do with trying to find policy relevance for social science once more.

As can be seen from the outline summary of this book, the subject of structural organizational studies is defined quite widely. The subject need not be about such limited matters as trying to describe the new varieties of organization that are appearing, or of trying to persuade students that one form of organizational structure would be better than another. The subject may be defined as being about understanding the causes and evaluating the effects of the activities and policies of corporations. At the moment people seem to be only dimly aware—if they are at all—that large companies are exporting more and more of their productive capacity. This means that they are exporting capital and employment in pursuit of profitability. The dire effects of this are not perceived for a variety of reasons, not least of which is that the message itself is unpalatable, and while there are some obvious policy solutions, they are far from being very palatable in the present climate of rampant enthusiasm for capitalism. Meanwhile, the ability to raise taxation is under severe pressure and the levels of expenditure on social services in Britain are among the lowest of any European country.

1.3 Back to basics

The relevance to policy that has been outlined is at least similar in aspiration to the original Weberian approach to social science. Perhaps because Weber produced a seminal model of the dominant organizational form at the time he was writing—the bureaucracy—there is a tendency for him to be remembered for this and this alone. Khandwalla, whose tome on organizational design (1977) has been seen by many as the main authoritative guide to organizational analysis, treats Weber in this way. According to Khandwalla and many other authors, Weber is just one of a legion of writers on organizations, memorable for his clarification of the nature of bureaucracy, but that is all. It is true that Weber's analysis of bureaucracy was an astonishing act of intellectual clarification; it is a model as neat and compact and valuable as the idea of the perfect market. Few models have been so widely used or proved so durable as Weber's ideal type. But, clearly, the thrust of Weber's work is much broader than this; and the traditional structural analysis of organizations potentially is so too. Weber saw organizational structures as part of a broader pattern of institutions, and as a structure which is capable of having a quite different relationship with the society of which it is part.

An institution like modern bureaucracy had been brought into being in other locations than the contemporary West, according to Weber; but it had existed in a quite different relation to the wider society in other places. Chinese patrimonial society was served by a highly developed state bureaucracy, for example. However, the Chinese institutional order existed—in roughly the same form—for millennia: much longer than any other in the history of the world. Indeed, Chinese traditional society exhibited extraordinary continuity which was produced by the bureaucracy among other causes. So machine-like and impersonal was it that, although ruling dynasties fell as a result of invasions from the outside or, less frequently, because of internal insurrections, the bureaucracy continued providing reliable administration. Because of its bureaucratic features—such as the system for the selection of officials by examination and its rigorous segregation of the bureaucratic hierarchy from the structures of kinship—the state bureaucracy could remain untouched by changes of dynasty and provide the core of a durable society. Bureaucracy held the huge Chinese Empire together and provided for its enormous continuity. For Weber, then, interest in bureaucracy extends beyond establishing the place of it in one society.

Although the modern Western bureaucracy had some similar features to the Chinese—the impersonality of its selection processes, for example—it does not work in the same sort of way in relation to the wider society. Rather than being contained by the society and stabilizing it, bureaucracy in the West was dynamic and invasive. The main feature of Western bureaucracy for Weber was its rational design, which enabled it to undertake any task effectively and to deliver on any objective without consideration of its character. Because of its obvious efficiency by comparison with traditional patterns of organizing, Weber argued, the bureaucratic form had a tendency to be applied

---

BOX 1.1 **Western bureaucracy is not unique**

Historical examples of relatively clearly developed and quantitatively large bureaucracies are: (a) Egypt, during the period of the New Kingdom, although with strong patrimonial elements; (b) the later Roman Principate, and especially the Diocletian monarchy and the Byzantine polity which developed out of it; these, too, contained strong feudal and patrimonial admixtures; (c) the Roman Catholic Church, increasingly so since the end of the thirteenth century; (d) China, from the time of Shi Hwangti until the present, but with strong patrimonial and prebendal elements; (e) in ever purer forms, the modern European states and, increasingly, all public bodies since the time of princely absolutism; and (f) the large modern capitalist enterprise, proportional to its size and complexity.

Max Weber (1968)

---

to every social objective. Thus, it would not only drive out other types of institutions and modes of organizing, but it would end up taking over everything and competing with itself, so producing what might be described as an institutional logjam. The medium-term tendency would be for the rational pursuit of particular ends to collide with each other and the end would, paradoxically, involve the loss of any overall benefit, or what Weber called the loss of 'substantive rationality'.

Although Weber was right to identify bureaucracy as the most important social invention of the modern period, and right again to say that its relation to society was not passive but transformative, he overlooked other forces that would limit its growth and influence. By creating the conditions of economic stability and by producing goods in abundance, bureaucracies created a market society and in this and other ways undermined the conditions necessary for their continued existence. But there is no doubt of the importance of the broad speculation concerning the relationships of organizations to society which Weber's work initiates. There is a clear suggestion here, anyway, that following Weber's general sociological approach will bring into the subject matter of organization studies questions and issues that analysts have a tendency to overlook and exclude. It is contended here that organizational change is not something that should be studied in a narrow way—simply by examining what contribution organizational change is likely to make to industrial efficiency. Economic change has also had a series of ramifying effects on British society and the experience of life for many British people, and these effects should be considered by anyone interested in what has been happening in the economy.

As with most epochal change, at the time, the causes are not so much complicated as difficult to discern. By contrast, the changes to be observed in organizations are numerous and can be directly observed: hence description wins out over explanation. A key idea motivating this book is that if the essential nature of the new organizational structures can be effectively clarified, then looking backwards for causes and forwards for effects is, to a considerable degree, simplified. As will be argued, the new organizations that various writers have recognized and struggled to identify, describe, and analyse, are best understood as involving the emergence of a new institutional order. At the root of change is the activity of particular social groups who have found new bases for effective action through organizations and who have become the substantial beneficiaries of the new order. By implication, there are other groups which are substantially excluded from benefit and are, comparatively speaking, substantial losers as a result of the changes that are occurring.

In this book, the question of what the important contemporary organizational changes actually are taken to be is central to the analysis; but the related questions of what has caused these changes and what their full effects might be are also given consideration. The key point to note is that this account comes to the conclusion that new structures are the outcome of the intentional activity of identifiable groups of people and that their activity introduces and consolidates new ways of generating and distributing wealth. The new organizations themselves comprise new and highly effective relationships of control and subordination, and it is this that enables them to be the machinery of accumulation and distribution. Hence, the search is not only to clarify what the new structures are, but also to bring into focus and to develop an account of their causes and consequences.

2

The need for an analysis of structures

2.1 How many organizations and what do they do?

Texts in organization studies do not typically begin by considering the number of organizations in Britain and what they do. And yet by looking at figures relating to these matters—especially the trends established in recent years—it should be possible to see if change is going on and whether it is widespread. There will not be much consideration of statistics in this book, and no very great quantitative skill will be needed to assess the evidence that is presented, but the consideration of quantitative data is helpful now and then to get a handle on the trend of events.

The figures given in Table 2.1 offer a general categorization of types of organizations by groups of industrial sectors derived from the index of industrial classification. They show the changing numbers of organizations over the last twenty years of the twentieth century. The figures themselves are provided by the government, in a publication which is called *Size Analysis of United Kingdom Businesses*, issued by the Office for National Statistics. Some of the historical data for the table have been constructed from other government data. Consideration of data of the general sort, given in Table 2.1, is about as far as the discussion of empirical data usually gets in organization studies. What, if anything, can be gleaned from it?

Table 2.1 suggests, firstly, that there were in total more than 1.66 million British organizations in 1999. The figure possibly understates the numbers of very small organizations—although it does include sole traders. Since the employed population for the same year was about 27 million, the average size of these organizations must be about fifteen employees, a figure which is much higher than for many other developed countries. Moreover, from the table it seems that there has been buoyant growth in the numbers of

Table 2.1 Classification of organizations in Britain by industrial sector for selected years: 1980–1999.

	1980		1985		1990		1995		1999	
	Actual	%	Actual	%	Actual	%	Actual	%	Actual	%
Production	525 210	38.0	563 589	37.2	626 090	35.5	515 760	32.1	503 999	30.3
Commerce	449 935	32.6	469 582	31.0	487 605	27.6	416 817	26.0	390 335	23.5
Infrastructure	59 555	4.3	66 101	4.4	80 904	4.6	71 230	4.4	69 556	4.2
Services	346 246	25.1	414 650	27.4	570 579	23.3	602 260	37.5	698 305	42.0
Total	1 380 946	100	1 513 922	100	1 765 178	100	1 606 067	100	1 662 195	100

Sources: Size Analysis of United Kingdom Businesses, 1999; Business Monitor for various years and other statistics issued by the Office for National Statistics

organizations in recent years. Between 1980 and 1990, numbers grew sharply, only contracting slightly in the last decade. Yet, these figures still show a net increase of more than 20 per cent, over the whole period 1980–99.

This table also suggests that in several general areas of the economy—namely, 'production', 'commerce', and 'infrastructure'—organizations have been declining in absolute numbers since 1990. More significantly, organizations of these types have been declining as a proportion of the total of all organizations throughout the twenty years covered by Table 2.1. Production organizations in particular are sharply down: they have fallen by nearly 10 per cent as a proportion of the total population of organizations. By contrast, all the growth and development has been concentrated in the area of services. At the start of the period covered by Table 2.1, nearly 40 per cent of organizations were in the production sector, while around 16.5 per cent only were in services. At the end of the century, twenty years later, this order of priority has been all but totally reversed. According to this evidence, the largest category of organizations is now services, this category having nearly doubled in numbers.

Such general statistics have fuelled some debate in the field the reader is about to enter. Data of this sort have been taken by some as indicating fundamental change in the nature of the British economy. Considered in isolation, it does look like evidence for the continuing decline of production and the inexorable rise of the service economy, the emergence of which was forecast for some years. Since the 1970s, in fact, commentators were forecasting the inevitable rise of the service economy (Touraine, 1974; Bell 1976; cf. Gershunny 1978; Gershunny and Miles 1983). Without further investigation, there would seem to be evidence here for the emphasis on consumption found in contemporary social science writing (Urry 1990; Casey 1995; Du Gay 1996). But what does this evidence allow us to say? Certainly not that theme parks and amusement arcades are the typical organizations of the late twentieth century or that production organizations are no longer important. It will be argued here that any such conclusion is substantially wrong. Production and commerce remain important to any modern economy, and Britain is not an exception. The rise of the services sector is not what it seems.

An expanded version of Table 2.1 is given in Table 2.2. The category labelled 'production' in Table 2.1 can now be considered in terms of the contribution of three subcategories of organizations. In addition to the production of goods—which is what manufacturing is—there is also 'construction' (i.e. building and civil engineering) and the diverse category of 'agriculture, mining, and utilities' (AMU). It is in these areas rather than manufacturing that there has been the most marked reduction in the number of organizations. In agriculture, which contributes the vast majority of organizations in the AMU category, there has been a good deal of simple contraction as farms have gone out of business and farmland is given over to residential and other non-productive uses. Hence, a good deal of the decline in the numbers of firms in agriculture—and in AMU more generally—can be understood as the removal of capacity. On this evidence, however, manufacturing organizations are still about 10 per cent of the total, indeed in absolute numbers there are about 15 per cent more of them than there were in 1980. Manufacturing has in fact experienced dramatic change over the last twenty years, but the nature of it is not revealed by these figures.

The additional data of Table 2.2 suggest more things that are not as many people expect, such as what is happening within the general category of 'infra-structure'. Despite the huge growth in telecommunications, and a tenfold increase in the numbers of firms, organization numbers in this sector are tiny. There are unexpected things in the general category labelled here as 'commerce', which we may think of as buying, selling, and distribution. These data suggest that the numbers of organizations operating in the retail sector has been declining rapidly. This is against the common experience that the variety of goods available to buy is now huge and the numbers of outlets from which they can be bought are many. Du Gay has argued for the importance of retailing as the paradigmatic industry of our age (1996: 97–118). If this is so, it is against the background of the numbers of retailing organizations being sharply in decline. If retailing is as important as Du Gay suggests it is, it must be for other reasons than the number of firms in the sector or, for that matter, the numbers employed there, which he does acknowledge (Du Gay 1996: 102–3). By these measures it could well be thought that the retail sector is in decline.

The biggest surprises are to be found in 'services'. Despite the huge growth of catering outlets and hotel capacity in the last twenty years, according to these figures there has been an actual decline in the numbers of organizations providing them. This is due to the increasing involvement of very large firms in these sectors. As can now be seen also, a substantial proportion of services are involved in providing health, education, and other public services. These are hardly providing anything very novel or new. Organizations of this type were substantially reduced in numbers in the 1980s, but are now back to the same levels of the 1970s. As can be seen from Table 2.2 as well, the largest division within the services category is 'finance, property, and business services'(FPBS). It is this category of organizations, and this alone, that has experienced explosive growth. Indeed, if the category FPBS were broken down further, it could be shown that *business* services are by far the largest category under this heading, and that it is organizations of this type that have contributed almost all of the growth seen in the category of FPBS organizations. There is other evidence to indicate the phenomenal growth in this type of organization. Today, more than 30 per cent of all British companies are business services companies of one kind or another.

Table 2.2 Classification of organizations in Britain by industrial sector and segment for selected years: 1980–1999.

	1980 Actual	1980 %	1985 Actual	1985 %	1990 Actual	1990 %	1995 Actual	1995 %	1999 Actual	1999 %
Agriculture/mining/utilities	182 136	13.2	184 669	12.2	177 914	10.1	169 178	10.5	159 883	9.6
Manufacture	144 038	10.4	155 540	10.3	171 471	9.7	157 967	9.8	165 669	10.0
Construction	199 036	14.4	223 380	14.8	276 705	15.7	188 615	11.7	178 447	10.7
Production (subtotal)	525 210	38.0	563 589	37.2	626 090	35.5	515 760	32.1	503 999	30.3
Wholesale	103 258	7.5	124 244	8.2	135 886	7.7	130 513	8.1	125 197	7.5
Retail	273 733	19.8	268 567	17.7	267 986	15.2	214 848	13.4	196 877	11.8
Motor trades	72 944	5.3	76 771	5.1	83 733	4.7	71 456	4.4	68 261	4.1
Commerce (subtotal)	449 935	32.6	469 582	31.1	487 605	27.6	416 817	26.0	390 335	23.5
Transport	59 555	4.3	65 638	4.3	79 417	4.5	68 523	4.3	64 203	3.9
Post/telecoms	—	—	463	<0.1	1 487	0.1	2 707	0.1	5 353	0.2
Infrastructure (subtotal)	59 555	4.3	66 101	4.4	80 904	4.6	71 230	4.4	69 556	4.2
Hotel/catering	120 872	8.8	124 655	8.2	131 471	7.4	113 210	7.0	112 590	6.8
Finance/property/business services	91 068	6.6	187 831	12.4	296 788	16.8	341 637	21.3	439 460	26.4
Public admin social other services	134 306	9.7	102 164	6.7	142 320	8.1	147 413	9.2	146 255	8.8
Services (subtotal)	346 246	25.1	414 650	27.4	570 579	32.3	602 260	37.5	698 305	42.0
Grand Total	1 380 946	100	1 513 922	100	1 765 178	100	1 606 067	100	1 662 195	100

Hence, it can be argued on the basis of this evidence that the typical British company these days is not a production or a retailing company, but a *business services* organization; and it is perhaps this sort of organization we should be thinking of if we want to produce a model of the typical organization of today. The numbers of British factories went down considerably and their average size fell sharply in the period 1970–99. It is now not possible (if other government figures are a reliable guide) to find a single organization in the manufacturing sector with more than 1500 employees. Yet, during the same time, we have witnessed the development of some large business services groups, with hundreds and sometimes thousands of employees. Business

---

BOX 2.1 Growth of business consultancy firms

In some recent research it was estimated that there were more than 120 000 business consultants working in the UK in 1998, and the firms in which they worked employed many more people than just these principals themselves. But what is perhaps as interesting as the large number of people now doing these jobs is the types of organization delivering these services.

There are large numbers of very small businesses in this sector, with the vast majority of firms having only one or two consultants working for them, and, although they may subcontract their work to other firms, they are not otherwise capable of undertaking large scale projects. At the other end of the scale, however, there are some very large firms with very large numbers of consultants employed in them. In this 'super-heavy' category, which includes firms employing 1000 consultants or more, the very big accountancy firms are strongly represented. As is well known, these firms have diversified into business consultancy and related services in recent decades. It is also well known that there have been structural tensions between the accountancy and consultancy operations of some of these firms leading to splits. Rose and Hinings (1999) call the largest of these firms global business advisory firms (or GBAFs). Surprisingly perhaps, the 'super-heavy' category as a whole—in all nine firms—constitutes significantly less than 20 per cent of the UK population of consultants.

Between the very small and the very large, it is interesting to note the emergence of the multi-functional business consultancy business, with firms employing between 20 and 100 consultants being increasingly prevalent and increasingly important in the amount of business they do. There are numerous firms now—the number was estimated at about 40—that have between one hundred and one thousand consultants on their payroll. These firms have enough consultants to be able to work with the largest of firms on significant business projects. The largest of these firms can, of course, run large numbers of projects simultaneously. By the standards of the times, these are large firms employing very large numbers of people, even if we do not take into account the clerical and other supporting staff employed in them. As little as twenty years ago the occupation of business consultant was very rare; and the idea that there might be firms employing thousands of consultants would have been thought very unlikely indeed.

Extracted from Ackroyd (2000)

consultancies, which are an important kind of new business services firm, also include numerous companies with more than 1000 employees each. These organizations are orientated towards business rather than leisure and tourism. Indeed, many of these business services companies are in fact business consultancies. As such, they are heavily involved in the management of production and commercial companies on a continuing basis. For these reasons we should be very careful about interpreting figures concerning services companies as evidence for a move away from production, or as evidence for a fundamental change in the character of the economy.

2.2 What is happening?

Data of the kind provided in Tables 2.1 and 2.2 must be carefully assessed. It needs to be intelligently considered in conjunction with other indicators. It is easy to misunderstand what is happening if we do not look in enough detail; and even then we may well be misled if we are not also willing to think carefully about the likely processes that underlie observable measures of change. In this case we should ideally consider the numbers of organizations in relation to the numbers employed in them and if possible also look at measures of output. However, if they are carefully interpreted, even indicators as crude as the numbers cited in Tables 2.1 and 2.2 are helpful.

It should be clear by now that the number of organizations in a sector, even if accurately measured, may indicate little of significance by itself. Only rarely is it safe to infer that there are some simple processes at work that are straightforwardly reflected in the figures of the numbers of organizations. An example of where this is the case is the agricultural sector. Here the falling numbers of organizations goes along with falling employment and, in some areas of production, capacity. In this area, the fall in the number of organizations is mainly accounted for by contraction within the industry. Hence, in agriculture, the falling numbers of organizations *does* indicate significant contraction.

On the other hand there are many situations where the numbers of organizations are also falling, but where it would be wrong to infer significant contraction or decline. For example, it has been common enough in the past for economic growth to be led by the emergence of a few giant companies. For many commentators, in fact, the development of monopoly—as the domination of a single larger producer is called—is the expected tendency of economic development in the West. The early American car industry between 1910 and 1930 was a spectacular example of this. Here the number of organizations in the sector went down dramatically as the Ford Motor Company demolished or bought out its rivals, and the General Motors group emerged as Ford's only significant competitor. At the same time, the numbers employed in the industry went up equally dramatically, as did turnover in the industry. At its height in the 1930s the Ford Motor Company employed hundreds of thousands of people, a high proportion of whom worked at the main plant of the company at River Rouge in Michigan. In some sectors of the contemporary British economy there are trends somewhat like this lying behind the figures of Tables 2.1 and 2.2. In several sectors, there has been some consolidation. In a few cases, as the result of takeovers and mergers, there are fewer firms operating whilst the employment in the sector has not changed much or has marginally increased. The civil engineering industry, which comes under the general area of 'construction', for example, has shown this pattern amongst its larger firms for some of the period under consideration. So it is that the declining numbers of firms in the construction sector should not be understood as indicating contraction.

Over the last twenty years, a different pattern seems to have predominated in core areas of the British economy, especially in manufacturing and commerce. In these areas there has been consolidation amongst the largest companies, combined with a radical reduction of the scale of their activities at particular sites. Closely related to this, there has been a tendency for such firms to outsource for many of their needs, encouraging the development of small satellite companies to work with them. In the process large companies have fewer of their assets in any one place, and are able to move into more locations and countries. The net effect of this is for the number of organizations involved in a sector in the country to remain pretty much the same, but for the total level of employment to fall. In short, in many sectors there has been industrial consolidation combined with rationalization and more interdependence. In these circumstances, even falling numbers of organizations, combined with falling numbers employed, is not associated with the absolute decline of a sector as measured by productivity or profitability. Clearly, in some sectors of the economy, there has been increasing capacity with the same—or even lower—levels of inputs. Businesses have found ways of making unexpected efficiency gains with the same levels or even reduced resources.

It is true that, generally, firms have been reorganizing themselves in order to do more with less; and especially fewer people. The largest firms in the core areas of the economy are in the forefront of these developments. The availability of new information technology (IT) has provided enormous opportunities for reorganization so that firms are able to produce or deliver with more effectiveness. With new IT systems it is usually emphasized that there is the possibility of cheap and effective particular applications of IT within firms or business units, and such systems do provide opportunities for any business or business unit to work with less staff. However, IT has also provided the possibility for cheap and effective communication between business units over long distances. The capacity for system integration, in which the local data from business units are integrated by effective corporate-wide business information systems is thus the key development in explaining a good deal about contemporary corporate transformation. Large firms can now coordinate their activities between sites more effectively, and the fact that they may be separated by large distances has become a matter of much less importance.

New technical capacity allows managers to know what precisely has been produced, in what numbers, and at what cost; how much stock is being held, where it is located; how much product is being sold and at what profit, and so on: all at the touch of a button. These are important developments. They allow for more efficient control of organizations, whether they be small businesses or multinational conglomerates made up of hundreds of constituent business units.

This does not mean that corporate and organizational change is simply caused by the availability of new technical means. On the contrary, it is best to see IT and other developments in technology as a necessary but not a sufficient condition of reorganization. What produces change is the aim to achieve increased efficiency and/or profitability. This the development of IT systems now allows. In this sense, IT has provided the opportunity for corporate managers to rethink their strategies and to contrive extensive reorganization of firms and organizations to meet new business objectives. The amount of innovation and change will vary a lot from sector to sector, as managers decide what changes are necessary. Along with all this talk of change, we should not forget, of course, that managers tend to undertake change only to the extent they feel is necessary. Change takes effort and is costly. Hence, there will be, if only for this reason, significant continuity as well as change in organizations. What is interesting to observe is how far the extent of change varies within and between different sectors of the economy. As Paul Thompson never tires of pointing out, the extent of continuity in organizational arrangements is significant and the extent of change can easily be overstated (Thompson and McHugh 2001).

Be that as it may, such things as the availability of new technical means in IT, and the discovery of new organizational forms to accommodate it, means that falling numbers of organizations combined with falling numbers employed in them may not be an indication of decline in that industry. If we take the data cited in Table 2.2 in conjunction with data on employment, it seems clear that, in several sectors of the economy, we are looking at the reduction in the numbers of organizations *and, at the same time*, a reduction in the levels of employment. However, it would be wrong to identify this as contraction and decline. These trends are often associated with significant growth in productivity and the development of significantly increased

---

BOX 2.2 Corporate restructuring and IT consultancies

From the late 1970s onwards, the large diversified corporations which had marked economic activities in the previous decades, came increasingly under pressure. This was partially the result of changes in the environment, particularly the repeated oil price shocks, and also the arrival of new competitors from Japan and other Asian countries with leaner and more focused structures. Some of the financially weakened conglomerates fell victim to corporate raiders who sold off their different businesses separately. Subsequently, the increasingly global financial markets have continued to pressure companies to concentrate on their core competencies and adopt leaner management structures. As a result, the co-ordination of activities both within companies and with suppliers and customers has become a crucial competitive advantage. The role of managers has changed as a result, focusing less on corporate organization and strategy and more on the management of the value chain as well as internal and external relationships. At the same time, the development of information technology has enabled managers to obtain the necessary data to maintain control over such a networked organisation. . . .

Much of the consulting revenue of . . . . IT related consultancy firms resulted from assisting in the implementation of new company-wide software. Especially prominent in this respect has been the installation of so-called enterprise resource planning systems (ERPSs), such as SAP/R3, which help to integrate data flow and access to information over the whole range of a company's activities. Consulting services centred on the need to adjust the organization to the requirements of the ERPS and to train its users. These projects very often last one, two or more years and involve large teams of consultants. Revenue growth from ERP-related consulting projects has slowed recently, because their installation has reached saturation point, especially in the United States. But they are more than replaced by consulting projects related to the creation of company intranets and electronic commerce, both business to business and customer interfaces.

Abstracted from Kipping (2001: 34 and 36)

---

industrial capacity. Several areas of the economy are being extensively reorganized in this way (Allen and Massey 1989).

Retailing is a spectacular example. Here there has been a contraction both in the numbers of organizations and in the numbers employed in the sector; but, at one and the same time, there has been an explosive growth in goods sold and in the levels of corporate profitability. The discovery of new ways of organizing a highly traditional activity is the key to understanding what has been happening. Traditional high-street stores, especially those small businesses owned and run by local proprietors, have faced stiff competition of various kinds and many have gone out of business. We have exchanged the locally based small business in the high street for the syndicated chain and franchise operation. (The Wal-Mart organization is a giant retail chain that has become the fourth largest company in the world. It depends for its success on the strategy of buying in bulk and undercutting the prices of other suppliers.) In addition to this sort of strategy, however, new and even more effective ways of retailing at cheaper and cheaper overhead costs have been developed. There has been the invention of the catalogue and mail order company, followed by the telephone sales organization. The most recent in a long line of innovations is the development of the e-commerce sales operation, which potentially can supply a world market with very few staff.

Hence Du Gay (1996) does have a point about the importance of retailing, but it is one that can only be made by looking at the sales end of the business (which has grown hugely) and disregarding the organizations and the people in them (which have marginally contracted). His argument for the importance of the sector is drawn partly in terms of the increasing power retailers are alleged to have over producers, and partly in terms of the increasing dominance that the cultural values of consumerism are alleged to be achieving. In this account, by contrast, the changes in retailing are seen to be part of a broader pattern of change; and it is argued that there are similar effects to be observed in other sectors of the economy as well. Although manufacturing has concentrated and diversified, it has by no means entirely disappeared, as we shall see. In manufacturing as in retailing, the scale of operations as measured by sales and profits has moved dramatically up, so the resources committed to businesses (as a proportion of the value of the items sold), has gone down. There are now, as can be seen from Table 2.2, many fewer organizations in the retailing sector; but nobody would pretend that this sector is of declining significance.

In manufacturing, there has also been quite a lot of reorganization. All firms operating in this sector, especially the largest, have undergone almost continuous change since 1980. It is true that the success of this change in the longer term is much less clear than in retailing and other areas of commerce. In the decade 1980 to 1990, there was considerable loss of employment and capacity in manufacturing. As with retailing, many small firms went out of business and larger firms dispensed with unprofitable lines of activity and undertook considerable geographical relocation (Ackroyd and Whitaker 1990). At the same time, the numbers of people employed in the sector fell from around 30 per cent of the working population to under 20 per cent. Numbers employed in manufacturing are still much larger than the numbers of organizations in the sector would lead us to expect, in that manufacturing organizations are only around 10 per cent of the total of organizations, but employ just short of 20 per cent of the working population.

In manufacturing there has been the discovery of new and more effective means of organizing for production in addition to the adoption of IT systems for business information. New ways of organizing production have been devised which allow production to take place in greater variety, at higher

---

BOX 2.3 **Concentration in retailing**

The scale of change in UK retailing can be assessed by the evidence from the 1950 census of distribution which suggests that there were 583 000 shops in the country at that time. Since then, somewhere in the region of 250 000 retail outlets have disappeared. Overall, the retail sector can be seen to be shrinking in terms of the number of outlets, businesses and number of employees, although not in terms of volume, while the sector as a whole has become increasingly dominated and controlled by large companies. The large multiples gain competitive advantage over the independents mainly from economies of scale and economies of replication. As they have grown larger, the multiples have been able to gain from their size in terms of their buying power from suppliers and from administrative centralization. Thus the process of concentration also entails a parallel move towards greater centralization of control.

This huge change in retailing size has been associated with considerable mutations in structure and organizational type. The major development has been the rapid growth of the multiples at the expense of the traditional independent retailer and the cooperative retail sector. In 1980, for example, the large retail multiples (those with 10 or more outlets) accounted for 54 per cent of all retail trade through 1 300 outlets. By 1986, the multiples were achieving a 60 per cent share through less than 900 stores. Expansion into new areas (diversification) is also easier due to the size of the enterprise. These types of benefit have also pertained from economies of replication in which a standard, or relatively standard, retail outlet or procedure can be duplicated across a large number of sites. This brings cost savings through conformity of operation, in price systems, for example. Both of these procedures have been aided by the introduction of new technology , a point to which I will return. These sorts of advantage are available to the multiples, while independents and fragmented cooperatives are often unable to benefit in the same way.

The process of concentration has passed through several stages. First, there was the local general store; then in towns and town centres, speciality stores—butchers, greengrocers, haberdashers etc. The innovation of the department store was to locate a number of speciality stores under one roof—to concentrate these specialisms spatially. The discount store sought to undercut the department store by stocking fewer lines, offering less direct service and cutting prices to increase turnover on lower margins. The development of supermarkets and superstores was based in part on an expanded selection of speciality goods in a central location. Finally, shopping malls, hypermarkets and gallerias function in a similar way to the earlier department stores in that they concentrate speciality shops.

Paul Du Gay (1996: 102-3)

---

quality, and at lower costs than were possible hitherto. One such set of techniques goes under the general name of 'lean production' (Womack *et al.* 1990). This was pioneered and developed by the Japanese in Japan, and has since been exported by them all over the world. Many Japanese and other foreign firms in Britain operate on a version of lean production. Car manufacture in Britain—now mostly owned by foreign companies—is almost all undertaken using versions of this set of production techniques (Williams *et al.* 1992; Wickens 1996). There are many other technical and organizational developments—just-in-time, business process re-engineering, agile production—which managers can use to contribute to more efficient organization at the same or lower input cost. The result is fewer large organizations, less employment but greater output.

In the last decade, the scale of contraction in the sector has levelled off. There remain many large firms still involved in manufacturing in the UK. However, a high proportion of these have drastically changed the extent of their manufacturing operations and what activities they will undertake for themselves. Many things that companies would have done for themselves in the past—both in manufacturing itself and in administration—are now outsourced. Manufacturing firms have gone as far as any in subcontracting— even subcontracting some management functions. Such changes have helped to foster the development of management consultancies and business services groups whose emergence was noted earlier. New forms of organization for profitable manufacture have been developed which depend on the close cooperation between numbers of businesses. What these are will be considered again in Chapter 4. However, the extent to which the new forms of organization will prove effective in the longer term, and form a basis on which manufacture might regain some of its former economic importance, remains doubtful.

It is appropriate to end this section with the observation that the changes underlying the figures of Table 2.2 are complicated. It is necessary to consider a great deal more than simply the numbers of organizations in sectors, in order to begin to understand what is happening in this field. There are clearly some important conceptual issues with which we shall have to grapple as well as matters of fact.

2.3 The importance of firms and business groups

In the foregoing discussion of the changes lying behind the figures with which we began, it has been helpful to think in terms of firms (and what their managements are up to), the patterns of relationships between firms, and so on. Indeed, in the above discussion, we have not been discussing firms and there has been slippage between the concepts 'organizations' and 'firms'. We began by discussing 'organizations', because that is what the available data describe. However, in trying to understand changes indicated by the figures, it was more useful and realistic to discuss firms, and to consider their opportunities and activities. It has also proved helpful to begin to think in terms of patterns of development involving the different kinds of firms in a given sector.

It is an important limitation of the figures in Tables 2.1 and 2.2 that they record the number of organizations and not the numbers of firms. Hence,

---

BOX 2.4 Changes in the engineering sector

Britain still leads the world in motor engineering, epitomised by the nation's success in Formula One. But very large engineering companies are becoming rather few in the British economy. Aerospace and defence engineering still provide the FTSE 100 with BAE Systems, Smiths Group and Rolls-Royce, but these are now increasingly focused and specialist companies. There have been significant losses as large British companies have restructured. Rover group has passed into and out of German ownership being hugely reduced in size and potential in the process. LucasVarity and Turner and Newell were taken over by the Americans.

GEC, GKN and Invensys are the only firms among Britain's top 100 quoted companies with significant traditional engineering activities. GEC itself is much smaller that it was under the Chairmanship of Lord Weinstock, whose final act before retirement was to split up the company. GKN, although a significant engineering company which owns, among subsidiaries, the Westland helicopter maker, is planning a demerger. This will leave a group that will be too small to feature in the top FTSE 100. In effect, Invensys is the only very large diversified British engineering company that is left.

Invensys itself was formed by a merger in 1999—against the trend of change elsewhere in the sector. This was between BTR a highly diversified and ailing engineering group and Siebe a company with a similar past. Siebe had made its name in marine engineering but had become large group. In 1963, Barrie Stephens became chief executive and began transforming the business, slashing costs, sacking half the workforce and turning Siebe into a focused industrial controls company. It swallowed up rivals, cut costs and building margins. Its shares performed fabulously. Then it merged with BTR.

BTR (formerly British Tyres and Rubber) has its own place in the pantheon of British engineering. Its architect, Sir Owen Green, became managing director in 1965. Among the many firms bought by BTR were Thomas Tilling and aeroplane maker Hawker-Siddeley. Green stepped down in 1993, but his successors struggled to replicate his success. Their weak management was not helped by the rapid changes in the industrial world.

Now the problem remains of how to combine these two very large businesses into one effective whole. An industry commentator said recently: 'The rationale from Siebe's viewpoint for the BTR deal was to give it a total solutions capability. Maybe the reality is that this was not what the marketplace actually required.' It is a big job to bring the two companies together and there is doubt as to whether the company is viable. In the eyes of stock market commentators that there is a big management issue. There is likely to be drastic surgery from a team of company managers headed by new chief executive Rick Haythornthwaite.

Compiled from various sources including especially an article by
A. Cave in the *Daily Telegraph*, 28th July 2001

counting separate organizations is only one way of trying to understand change in the economy—and one which has some inbuilt biases. Data about firms might have been more useful as a place to start. Really what is needed is to compare changes in the number of firms and the number of separate firms. A problem with this is that firms are usually classified in terms of their legal type. Hence they are classified whether they are partnerships, companies or public corporations. Large companies are not all PLCs, that is companies whose shares are publicly traded. There are some very large and powerful private companies and some huge partnerships such as the global business advisory firms identified by Rose and Hinings (1999). There are some government figures which use the category 'enterprises' which takes the number of legally separate entities, and these figures are helpful—especially when considered in conjunction with other data.

What we need really, however, are measures which allow us to assess organizations according to their economic and political importance—that is, in terms of the resources they have at their disposal and whether they control and direct the activity of other entities as well as their own. The data we have been examining so far are a very unreliable guide to this. Indeed, in some ways the data seem to have been calculated in such a way as to give us the wrong impression. Large firms will often account for themselves as a number of separate sites—each of which counts as a separate organization. This gives the impression that businesses are getting smaller and generally are becoming organized on a more human scale. If we were to divide the total number of people employed in a sector by the numbers of organizations given in Tables 2.1 and 2.2, to calculate the average size of organization in each sector, for example, the available data would give an even stronger impression of reduction in the typical scale of operations of organizations. By this sort of measure, the average size of organizations is moving inexorably in one direction—it is coming downwards.

There is a reality to this that we should recognize. It is a common pattern for large firms these days to be organized as a large number of geographically separate sites in which different activities take place, and which, for many purposes are separate entities. For some purposes, such as the consideration of much of the behaviour exhibited in organizations, they can be considered as separate organizations with no detriment. On the other hand, it would be a mistake to think there are no big businesses any more, or that such entities are no longer important. Firms are by no means all getting smaller. Just think of Ford, Wal-Mart or McDonald's. (It is interesting that British-owned major companies that might be considered the equivalent of these—B.Ae Systems, Kingfisher Group, and Allied Domecq, for example—have less visibility and notoriety.) Be that as it may, clearly, large firms can be very big entities indeed.

The largest companies these days are larger than whole countries

Table 2.3 Sectoral classification of the 200 largest British firms by market capitalization, 1996.

	Number	%	Capital ization (£bn.)	%	Ave. size (£bn.)
1. Extraction and oil	7	3.5	87.9	10.9	12.6
2. Chemicals and pharmaceuticals	9	4.5	85.9	10.7	9.5
3. Telecommunications	5	2.5	44.9	5.6	9.0
4. Finance and property	35	17.5	173.1	21.5	5.0
5. Media	19	9.5	65.4	8.1	3.4
6. Commerce and retail	23	11.5	74.7	9.2	3.2
7. Manufacuring	64	32.0	186.7	23.2	2.9
8. Utilities	21	10.5	52.8	6.6	2.5
9. Transport and services	17	8.5	34.2	4.2	2.0
Totals	200	100	805.6	100	4.0

Source: Lancaster Archive of Large British Companies

BOX 2.5 **The powers of giant firms**

Giant firms are the principal drivers of the global economy. Their decisions shape the lives of most of the world's people and the directions of every national economy. They produce most of the world's goods and services, finance that production, and trade more and more of it across borders. In turn they have steered the agendas of most governments at every level and have twisted the operations of the institutions set up to govern the global economy in their interests.

Anderson and Cavanagh (2000: 65)

---

considered in terms of their assets and their turnover (Anderson and Cavanagh 2000). They may be, indeed, they often are, constituted by hundreds of organizations defined in the terms used to compile Tables 2.1 and 2.2. But this should not lead us to think large companies can be ignored because as entities they do have a significant influence on events. Although they are made up of a large number of quite small parts, and are, apparently, becoming more decentralized rather than less, they are clearly highly significant centres of power. They control directly the activities of the firms they own and indirectly the activities of companies with which they have significant business.

Large organizations do not have the powers of states. They do not, legally at any rate, exercise force as states do. However, they are, in many ways, equally if not more powerful than states. What they do influences the prosperity of industries and regions. The kinds of people they choose to employ can have important effects on the prosperity of individuals and whole classes of people. How they choose to realize their profits can undermine economic policies and affect the stability of governments. Nor do large businesses have to be bound by the desires and interests of their employees as states are bound by the needs and aspirations of citizens. This is not crudely apparent, of course. Gone are the days when large organizations openly dictated regional and national policy, but large organizations remain very important in the thinking of governments. Modern states—and Britain is no exception here—are under no illusions about the power and influence of large businesses. A good part of British economic policy is planned bearing in mind the need to induce multinational corporations to locate their plants and facilities here rather than abroad.

Considered in this way, a different picture emerges from that encouraged by a cursory viewing of Tables 2.1 and 2.2. Viewed from the perspective that firms are the significant point of reference, it would seem that, in many sectors, the size of the typical *constituent parts* of a large firm is going down—especially as measured by the numbers of people employed at a particular site. Let us call the organizations that are parts belonging to large firms their *business units*. At the same time, *considered as wholes, the size and the profitability of the firms are going up*. This is more obvious if size is measured in terms of total assets rather than employment. Small and independent firms not owned by any other business or business group do exist. But small firms that are really independent are few and far between. As we shall see, the small firm sector has been weak in Britain for a long time. Small firms are increasingly today tied into long-term relations with larger companies, when they are not owned by them. These firms may be described as affiliated with larger companies. The recent surge in the numbers of small firms during the 1980s and early 1990s—which is reflected in the growing numbers of organizations shown in the data of Tables 2.1 and 2.2—has occurred as part of the general reorganization of business in this country, which has, in turn, been driven by the policies of big business groups.

In short, big business is still very much a salient feature of our time, even though the scale of the constituent organizations that make up firms is itself moving in the other direction. It is argued in this book that it is not only important to consider change in organizations at the level of the plant or office, but also the connections between firms. Hence it is important to consider what is happening to business groups and other groupings larger than the firm. Much of the analysis in this book considers firms and their activities rather than individual business units of organizations. We must also ask how is the economy—which is an entity much broader than any one firm or even sector—actually connected. What is its character considered as a whole?

2.4 **Three possibilities concerning the economy**

To conclude, we have to acknowledge that that our knowledge of what is happening in the economy—so far as its organizational base is concerned—is deficient. It does seem clear that there are major changes under way in Britain, although the full extent of them and the reasons why they are occurring have not yet been fully established. Also, we do not have much grip on what the full social and economic consequences are. This has not prevented various commentators from sketching out different possibilities for the development of the economy. A need for this level of analysis has been brought to our attention from the apparently mundane factual issues with which this chapter began.

In the remaining few pages of this chapter, three possibilities about the shape of the British economy and the way it might develop are articulated. The different possibilities imply quite different scenarios concerning socio-economic development. The plausibility of these possible developments and their implications are questions with which some academics in the field of organization studies are currently grappling. In this book a sustained argument in favour of one of these possibilities and against the others will be undertaken. However, it should be made clear that although each has been strongly argued for by different writers, the argument is far from being finally resolved. The debate is interesting because it draws attention to the question of the general direction in which the economy is heading—it also helps to clarify the kinds of evidence that will have a bearing on the question.

The three different possibilities that will now be considered are that the economy will become (a) a service economy, dominated by the provision of services by services companies, or (b) a knowledge economy regulated by the activity of companies' command expertise, or (c) that the economy continues to be an economy based on manufacturing and production. In each of these arguments it is suggested that a certain area of the economy should be considered the leading one and, thus, the most important. What happens in the leading sector is to be given most attention for this will decide the fate of the other areas of the economy. Such arguments do not really affect points made in the last section of this chapter about the importance of big business. Speculation at this level can, however, indicate in which sectors of the modern economy large business and business activity will grow.

The service economy

Even if we question the rate of increase in services during the last twenty years, it still should be obvious that leisure industries are now very important in the economy. In addition, some writers argue that many of the organizations included under the category of infrastructure in Tables 2.1 and 2.2 above, should actually be considered to be providing services. The services sector then is made up of producer services, distribution services, and personal and social services. Viewed in this way the service sectors of the economy may be seen as approaching 50 per cent of organizations and 60 per cent of employment at the end of the last century. There is also the contribution of financial services to added-value and the balance of international payments to be considered.

In support of this thesis orthodox economists have long argued that it does not much matter whether an economy produces goods or not, so long as there is a profitable market for what is offered for sale. Services are, on this view, as good as manufactured goods when it comes to people earning a living and keeping the national accounts in balance. Certainly, despite the size of the country's manufacturing sector until recent times, Britain has seldom been in surplus as a result of its productive activities. In economists' language, the balance of *trade* (i.e. the value of *goods* bought and sold internationally) has often been adverse, but the balance of international payments has been kept in the black (and the British economy has generally remained solvent) as a result of payments to the City of London for financial services. Historically, the levels of services provided in the economy have been high, and current levels of service provision represent a return to the levels experienced in Victorian times when personal services were widespread in the shape of people in domestic service (Gershunny and Miles 1992).

But the importance of services is not founded simply on the actual prevalence of service work and the numbers of people working in services alone. For many sociologists in particular, it is the impact of service work on social values, and ways of thinking and behaving, that makes these activities important, rather than their economic importance as such. The idea that we are now a society in which consumption is more important than production is significant because of the effects of this on culture and values. Just as the core of the British economy has moved away from production and manufacturing so the basis of our sensibility has moved from a concern to produce to a concern to consume. The avant-garde sociologists, Lash and Urry, conceive of contemporary societies as having economies of signs. It is the dynamic relationship between symbols (signs) and the distribution of organizations in spaces that are the keys to understanding the economic development of economies (Lash and Urry 1994).

To state the case polemically: the whole subject area of organization and management studies is 'productionist' in outlook if it continues to be pre-occupied with manufacture. By this is meant that the subject is biased towards the consideration of production to the extent that a disproportionate and unjustifiable amount of attention is paid to this area of economic activity. Production in general and manufacturing in particular are rapidly dwindling in importance, and should be displaced from centrality in the concerns of organizational researchers. For some writers, then, modern economies have fundamentally changed so that they are now symbolically rather than materially constituted.

The knowledge economy

Secondly, there is the thesis of the emerging knowledge economy. Again these arguments are not new (Touraine 1974; Bell 1976). Sometimes it is simply asserted that it is obvious that knowledge is making an increasing contribution to value-added in the most advanced economies, but the most sophisticated arguments along these lines suggest that changes in the basis of manufacturing are making knowledge more important (Reich 1992; Castells 1996).

The argument runs along the following lines. So extensive and sophisticated have been the improvements in the techniques of manufacture that it is now no longer possible to squeeze more efficiency out of it except by employing the cheapest possible labour. For this reason manufacturing operations are often relocated in underdeveloped parts of the world in order to reduce the costs of production in the wages paid to labour. By doing this, firms, if they are willing to invest and have the energy to keep relocating every ten years, can continue to make a profit by exploiting new pools of inexperienced labour and opening up new markets in the Third World. At this stage in the developed world, it is only possible to make serious profit out of services. In the manufacturing sphere, value is added by improvements in design aesthetics. If this is the case, we can expect that goods are increasingly assembled from parts produced at numerous points around the world. According to this argument, the appropriate model for the future is the production of information technology rather than cars.

In future profits will be secured not only by technical innovations which will continue to reduce the costs of parts, but also by final assembly being located in the cheapest place. As the problems of efficient production are solved, so there is a diminishing amount of extra productivity to be wrung out of it, so the key to profitability becomes innovative thinking: how to find new applications for existing technology, and so sell more units; how to create market advantage by good design and exclusivity; how to increase sales by differentiating products and clever marketing.

According to this argument, economic survival will come from know-how rather than investment. Today, many British companies are involved in the design, specification, and procurement of manufactured goods; but, increasingly, the manufacture of these goods is undertaken overseas by companies that contract to manufacture goods to given specifications. Hence, many goods that appear to be of British manufacture are not, though they may carry the names and badges of British companies. As there are no longer firms making cathode ray tubes and other key electronic components in British ownership, there can be no such thing as a British television set in the sense of one made up entirely of parts made in this country. Today, however, even the assembly of televisions by British firms from foreign-made parts has ceased. The televisions we buy in our shops, and watch in our homes, are either assembled by foreign companies operating in this country (Japanese, Korean, or Chinese most of them) from parts made throughout the world or they are imported, ready made, from the Far East. If such sets carry the name of a British company or a British trademark, they are not of British manufacture. Increasingly, goods can be and are procured from many different parts of the world and simply badged with the trademarks and logos of British companies. Amstrad computers and Fidelity televisions, for example, are manufactured by foreign companies to the specifications determined by the owners of these trade names. In the traditional meaning of the term, they are not British goods.

If we accept this argument, there is no economic disaster implied by the decline of the productive economy. Because of relative costs of production, there is in fact no real future for manufacturing and production in the advanced world. It would thus be foolish to try to turn the clock back and to re-establish Britain as the workshop of the world. The point is for Britain to participate in the world economy by adapting its institutions to allow them to deal in knowledge rather than production. On this account, we have to become a knowledge economy and to make money out of such knowledge skills.

The changing economy of manufacture

The literature in the area of organization and management studies pays a great deal of attention to what is happening in manufacturing; and arguably much more so than is justified on the basis of the size of this sector considered in isolation. When there is discussion of forms of organization or management structures, the examples used tend to be concerned, implicitly or explicitly, with the production of goods. In much of the material we shall be considering in later chapters it is implied (when it is not explicitly stated) that production of some sort or, to a lesser extent, the commercial trading of goods, is really what ought to be the centre of our concern. Much of the discussion about change in the likely pattern of new institutions is still taken up with how to organize manufacturing so that it can be made profitable and effective. There is a strong implication that the economy should be rebuilt on the basis of a reorganized manufacturing base.

In support of this it can be argued that manufacturing is the most import-ant source of value creation. Manufactured goods—made out of raw materials having little intrinsic value—directly increase the stock of physical assets available in a community. In other words, manufacture increases the stock of material wealth in a way that no other kind of activity does. When cars or other consumer durables are made and distributed, the standard of living increases in a community. Now it is clearly the case that the productivity of modern manufacturing plants is high. Goods are abundant in the developed world—more abundant than at any other time in history. Yet this is achieved with a smaller and smaller proportion of the population being involved in making things. Hence, considered in terms of the number of people employed the manufacturing sector of any advanced country will be quite small. How-ever, it remains absolutely indispensable to continued prosperity. Manufacture must be undertaken if we wish to maintain our present high standards of material well-being. If a country does not make things for itself, then it is forced into selling something else—raw materials or services for example—in order to make the cash with which to purchase goods.

We are thinking wrongly if we conclude that the manufacturing sector is unimportant because it is small. Rather, we should be asking: is the manu-facturing sector really too small for the job of wealth creation that we expect of it? Many British commentators, including some economists, have argued that the British economy is weak precisely because its productive sector is too small and undercapitalized. Again these positions are long-standing (Bacon and Eltis 1976; Blackaby 1979; Pollard 1982, 1992; Owen 1999). There has been a recurrent concern about the disproportionate loss of manufacturing capacity from the economy (Hirst and Zeitlin 1988; Allen and Massey 1989; Ackroyd and Whitaker 1990; Williams *et al.* 1990*b*). In support of this argu-ment, the larger and most economically advanced economic powers in the world—the United States, Japan, and Germany—all have more highly developed manufacturing industries than Britain. As developing countries have proved again and again, the most direct route to economic development has been through building up a domestic manufacturing industry. It is in fact difficult to envisage a country that is (or aspires to be) a major world power that does not have a significant manufacturing sector. In Britain, we seem to value our military capability and our politicians seem to see us as contributing significantly to the self-imposed task of policing the globe. Certainly, the perceived need to be self-sufficient in arms has led the British government to continue to favour British companies for the production of weapons and weapons systems.

In addition, manufacture and commerce are much more important to the economy than the number of organizations in these sectors would imply. While, as we have seen, only around 10 per cent of all organizations are involved in manufacturing, their contribution to the total of people in employment is nearly double this. Indeed, these days, because of the out-sourcing and subcontracting that are now prevalent, there are a good number of organizations (and associated employment) which directly support manu-facturing, in the shape of business services companies. Such companies have taken over functions that, in the recent past, would have been undertaken by manufacturing companies themselves, and represent a displacement of manu-facturing jobs which are now counted as jobs in the services sector. A recent estimate suggests that 1.2 million jobs were created in business services since 1970. The growth of business services precisely corresponds with the period of reorganization of manufacturing in this country. As we have seen, the much vaunted growth of the services sector seems to have been mainly caused by a huge growth in business services. Now we can add to this the idea that much of the growth in business services is itself associated with changes in the organization of production and commerce in which activities formally under-taken in-house are now outsourced. Hence, the shift towards services as a whole is much more apparent than real. We ought to consider also the many other jobs that indirectly depend on the continued vitality of the manufactur-ing sector. Unless goods are produced the commercial sector cannot distribute them or make profits from their sale. Thus the manufacturing sector contributes to the vitality and profitability of the commercial sector.

True, manufacturing activities have been much more important historically than they are today, considered particularly in terms of the number of people employed. Government figures suggest that until 1960 or so, nearly 40 per cent of the employed population worked in manufacturing industry. As we know, the figure today is less than 20 per cent. This decline appears not simply to arise from the substitution of machinery and equipment for labour.

In answer to this point, those who argue that production should be con-sidered as the core of the economy usually argue on the basis of what should be rather than what is. The point is that the British economy is suffering because of the rapid decline of the production sector and because a dis-proportionate number of British multinationals, formerly involved in produc-tion in the UK, have relocated a good proportion of their capacity abroad. The problem is not so much that production is not important as that an appropriate level of manufacturing apparently cannot be sustained by the British econ-omy. It is now difficult to find British companies that take on the task of producing complex and high value-added manufactured products. Things like

BOX 2.6 **The eclipse of manufacturing?**

Several factors—among them intensifying competition between producers—have helped to give impetus to some revolutionary changes in manufacturing.

The first development was called 'lean production'. Pioneered in Japan in the post-war years and transferred to the US in the 1980s, this involved a massive reduction of waste through eliminating defects, slashing inventories and making production lines more adaptable. Equally important were the changes attributable to information technology. Computers were used to standardise and codify processes. Combined with the opening of world markets, this was explosive. Output could be more readily shifted, since production processes could be replicated. And since those processes were increasingly standardised, technical advances were swiftly copied by competitors.

Today, some claim, another change is transforming industry: this is so-called 'agile manufacturing'. The thesis is set out by Mansoar Sarhedi of Brunel University: 'Lean manufacturing represents a big step in productivity, as did the switch from craft to mass manufacture in the early years of the century. But lean manufacturing is in one sense inflexible. Because the individual lean firm carries no spare inventory, it cannot respond extremely quickly to surges in demand. Hence, the idea of agile manufacturing, developed first under US government prompting in the early 1990s. In essence, agile production involves using information technology to stitch lean enterprises into alliances. This will be, its proponents argue, the future of manufacturing itself. They point to a large number of examples such as Airbus, an alliance of companies that now seems to be outperforming its conventionally structured competitors.'

The implication is that as it develops, agile production will provide a new lease of life for manufacturing as a whole. All the time though, the pace of evolution is quickening. . . . Through plant flexibility and networking each maker helps out shortfalls in the others' production. These producers are already agile and it does them little good. In such cases declining profit margins initiate a process of manufacturing migration. The logic suggests that the production of things like TV sets will have to migrate to cheaper and cheaper countries. For these reasons, the long run outlook for makers of undifferentiated goods, memory chips, microwave ovens as well as TVs and perhaps also utility cars is distinctly unpromising . . . in the advanced economies.

Extracted from Tony Jackson's 'Comment and Analysis' column, *FT*, 15 December 1998

machine tools, industrial and consumer durable products, and domestic electronics are either not produced by British companies at all or such companies only produce some parts of such products. There is almost no significant British-owned manufacturing of electronic goods, optical goods such as cameras and video equipment, or almost any consumer durables. The last British volume carmaker, Rover Group, fell into German ownership in 1994, only to be abandoned a few years later when it could not be made financially viable. Rolls-Royce, the aerospace group, which produces jet engines amongst other things, is one of very few surviving British companies capable of high value-added manufacturing. Where firms producing complex products can be found, they almost invariably have some kind of connection with defence procurement by the state (Williams *et al.* 1983). There is nothing like the range and variety of industrial organizations found in major competitor nations such as Germany and Japan.

Central to these changes has been the systematic withdrawal from involvement in manufacturing activities in this country by many large British companies. There are some significant British businesses still involved in manufacturing, including sixty companies with more than a billion pounds of equity which manufacture on a significant scale (Ackroyd and Procter 1998). British businesses are not, however, undertaking manufacturing activities in Britain on the scale they once were. Many of them have moved a large proportion of their manufacturing activities overseas. The things that even large businesses do produce here tend to be low value-added products such as bricks or washing powder and food. There are, as we will see, many British factories (some of which are owned by very large companies) making parts and components to order. They contribute to what are called the component supply chains for complex manufactured goods; but it is clear that they do not have a large-scale or long-term commitment to this type of activity.

In support of a productionist emphasis in organization and business studies, it is the case that recent change in the activities of businesses, and in particular the movement away from traditional manufacturing, has had a series of identifiable, serious effects in other areas of the economy and society. As industry has declined, and its willingness to employ skilled manual workers in large numbers has declined, so the balance of power has shifted between men and women and the traditional nuclear family has been destabilized. Much that has happened in social change in modern Britain can be traced to the changed patterns of activities of the big businesses involved in manufacturing over the last twenty or so years. Hence, in much of the rest of the book, attention is paid to such questions as how to organize for production: at the level of the firm and at the level of the business group or at the level of the economy and society. In this sense the book shares the productionist emphasis of much traditional work in this area.

3
The orthodox account of structure

The last chapter suggests that there is a need for insightful ways of thinking about the forms of organization adopted by businesses, and to understand what causes them to change. Hence, it is appropriate to consider the branch of organizational studies that deals with organizational structures and offers explanations for the variations in them. In this chapter the established approach to organizations—variously labelled the structural-functional approach and contingency theory—will be examined and the explanation it offers for variations in structure will be reviewed.

It will be concluded that the orthodox approach to structure does not provide a satisfactory basis for understanding, especially contemporary patterns of organizational change. The ideas turn out to be flawed and it is argued here that they should be discarded. In the next chapter, an alternative perspective on organizational structure, which implies a more adequate explanation of current changes, is proposed. Hence, the question might well be posed: why look at the material covered in the present chapter? The answer is that the orthodox approach constitutes a starting point from which a more adequate account of structure can be developed. Also, writers with this outlook have described some historically important organizational types. They do not explain these types adequately, but the models they propose—the small unitary firm, the bureaucracy, the multidivisional firm, and the holding company or conglomerate—provide some useful points of reference. It is valuable to know what these things are, even though it is fairly certain they are not viable forms of organization any more.

Organizational analysts habitually discuss idealized models. These are things which do not exist in the tidy forms set out by analysts anywhere in reality; but the models allow us to think about organizations—and their attributes and characteristics—effectively. There is no objection to this way of working. This book includes the discussion of many models of structures; though it suggests and promotes a different way of analysing structures and of understanding their relationship with what lies outside of them.

3.1 The functional/contingency approach to organizations

This approach was in general use for more than thirty years after the Second World War, and, up until 1980 or so, was widely accepted as correct. For some observers, indeed, these ideas were thought by many to be scientifically established (Donaldson 1985). There is a considerable body of work in this tradition (Woodward 1958; Burns and Stalker 1961; Pugh and Hickson 1976; Pugh and Hinings 1976). Even today, for some researchers, these ideas, or developed and modified versions of them, are still sound (Miller and Friesen 1982; Aldrich 1992; Brock *et al.* 1999). Many commentators have recognized the limitations of the approach and have tried to modify it (Child 1984; Mintzberg 1993). However, there are some stalwarts who are still strongly promoting the approach. Lex Donaldson, who first attempted to stem the tide of criticism in 1985, is still arguing for the validity of a version of these ideas (Donaldson 1995, 1996).

Although there are many exponents of the orthodox approach to structure, there are some common features. Those who follow this approach assert that organizations have structures, but also that the existence of structures and the forms structures take are explained by the functions they perform. They also share a holistic idea about organizations: they hold that organizations should be analysed as totalities. The organization is a set of relationships that must be understood as a system: you cannot understand an organization by looking at parts of it. The organizational structure is a basic part of the system of relations and contributes to its effective functioning. Both of these points—structures are functional and organizations are systems—contain some truth, but need to be qualified.

Writers in the tradition of thought with which we are now concerned, draw on and use an idea of structure that is familiar to many people. The basic notion of structure is used in a similar way to illuminate a wide variety of subjects and not only organizations. In architecture, for example, the structure of a building makes sense as an idea about the principal components of a building. The structure of a house is constituted by such things as the rafters, trusses, and beams (purlins) that bear the weight of the roof, the load-bearing walls which transmit the weight to the ground, such things as the beams over the doors and windows (lintels), and the foundations that stop the building from sinking. Similarly, the basic structure of the human body is provided by the skeleton and musculature. Without the bones of the skeleton, the body would not be strong enough to stand, without the muscles it could not move about. In essence, the idea of structure is that there are basic features of things that allow them to cohere and to function.

In the study of organizations it is contended that organizations have a structure in a similar way. Organizational structure is the basic arrangement of an organization's main parts and positions. Textbooks in organizational behaviour define organizational structure somewhat differently, but most include the idea that a structure is essentially recurrent features of the relationships within an organization. In books which draw heavily on the functional tradition of thinking, it is emphasized that the recurrent relationships of interest are those that allow the organization to function. In organizational analysis then, as with architecture and anatomy, structure can be defined in functional terms. In a similar way that a body without a skeleton would not work or a house without foundations and walls would not stand, so it is suggested that an organization without structure would not be at all effective either.

Dimensions of structure

There are two aspects of organizational structure that are usually distinguished and are sometimes referred to as 'dimensions' of structure. The first involves vertical distinctions, usually thought of as *levels of hierarchy*. The second is horizontal distinctions, and can be thought of in terms of specialization of activities. The general term usually used to describe this is the *span of control*.

BOX 3.1 Functional structures

'Structure is a means for obtaining the objectives and goals of an institution.'

P. Drucker, *Harvard Business Review*, 1974: 52, quoted approvingly by J. Child: *Organisations: A Guide to Problems and Practice*.

Child adds:

'As Drucker points out the function of an organisational structure is to assist the attainment of objectives.' (1977: 8).

He also suggests:

'The allocation of responsibilities, the grouping of functions, decision-making, co-ordination and control—all these are fundamental requirements for the continued operation of an organisation. The quality of an organisation's structure will affect how well these requirements are met.'

(Child 1977: 9 and 1984: 4)

Both dimensions of structure can be easily illustrated. It is traditional, for example, to distinguish three different levels of authority. Management is conventionally divided into senior management (usually including the directors of a company and its senior executives), middle management (which organizes and coordinates the internal working of a business), and supervision (which concentrates on overseeing the work activity of ordinary employees). These levels of the management structure direct the activities of the main group of employees. In practice there can be many or few levels. Historically, large organizations have typically had many levels of hierarchy. These days, there is a tendency to try to organize with as few levels of formal hierarchy as possible.

In addition there is a horizontal dimension of structure. There can be high levels of differentiation of activities in an organization or a lack of such specialization. In the recent past, there has been a tendency for extreme specialization in the division of labour. Factories included many shops and departments undertaking highly specialized activities—such as making particular components in large numbers. In the past, particularly, a factory worker did the same task over and over again. Today, by contrast, there is a tendency to move away from this and to reduce extreme specialization of activities. Although there may be a variety of tasks, they are often not overcomplicated and mentally taxing. An individual can expect to do a variety of tasks, usually as the member of a team. Be that as it may, when discussing horizontal differentiation as an element of organizational structure, analysts tend to think quite simply—in terms of the numbers of positions allocated to a supervisor or manager. Thus, organizational structures are discussed in terms of the numbers of people working for managers and supervisors. This is what is meant by span of control: the numbers of positions allocated to and controlled by a supervisor or manager. As an accompaniment to the process of reduction in the number of levels in an organization, spans have been widening. With IT the work of more employees can be overseen than was the case in the past, and so there is a tendency for spans to increase.

Taken together, levels of hierarchy and spans of control in an organization are used to describe the basic organizational structure. This branches out from a single position somewhat like the roots of a tree. The structure, therefore, locates the individual uniquely in relation to authority. Each position in the structure has one position directly exercising authority over it. Traditionally there is no ambiguity about this: each person has one manager responsible for them and their work, and only one. Whether this is an accurate account of the way firms work or used to work will be considered again in this chapter and the next; but there are frequent departures from such unambiguous ideas about structure.

It was thought at one time that some universally valid basic principles of organization could be formulated. The idea of the classical management writers, whose work on organizations preceded the contingency/functional approach, was that there were universal principles that could then be applied whenever sound organization was needed. One principle related to spans of control. Some classical management writers suggested that spans should be of a standard width, typically not exceeding thirty or so people. In support of this, it seems to be true that thirty is about the number that is traditionally found in the smallest groups in a wide range of organizations: platoons of soldiers, classes in schools, and 'gangs' of men in workshops. Contingency writers suggested, against this fixed idea, that all dimensions of the organizational structure might vary. There are, they argued, different types of organizations which have different configurations of structure. These different patterns arise because they are necessary if the organization hopes to function efficiently in the very different circumstances in which organizations are found. The idea of contingency writers was that there would be a small number of standard types of organizations, conforming to different external circumstances.

An organizational chart is a handy device for depicting organizational structure in the way that contingency writers suggest. A simple organizational chart for a small firm is given in Figure 3.1. This is a plan of the formal relationships in an organization. Here we see the branching pattern very clearly. Charts of this kind depict the levels of hierarchy and the spans of control found in an organization. This chart depicts an organization with three levels of hierarchy and spans of three to five positions. Because we are introducing a particular way of thinking about structures, there is no attempt here to make the chart in any way fully accurate by including references to the board of directors.

Given the basic dimensions of 'level' and 'span' we can now distinguish differences of organizational structure. Structures can be tall (having many levels of hierarchy) or flat (having few). Structures may be wide (having large spans of control) or narrow (having narrow spans). Logically any combination of these dimensions is possible, but this is not what we see. Instead, there are typical patterns or configurations. As we have noted, classical management theory tended to suggest that spans should be of a uniform size and, hence, that levels of hierarchy should only grow when the increasing scale of activities dictate it. Hence, if the maximum span was set at thirty, and this rule was adhered to, then one supervisor would be required for up to thirty operatives—at any size up to thirty, then, there would be two levels of hierarchy. Once the organization required more than thirty workers however, three levels of hierarchy would be required. If this rule was adhered to thereafter, however, four levels of hierarchy would only be needed when the number of employees exceeded 900 or so (i.e. when there were 30 x 30 on the basic level).

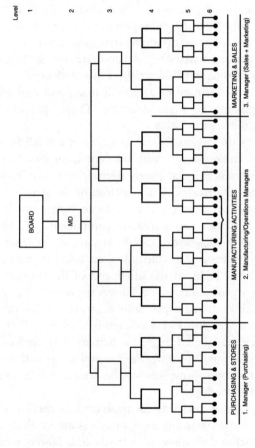

Figure 3.1 Organizational chart of a small manufacturing company. There are 67 positions in total, 2–3 subordinates reporting to each supervisor and six levels of hierarchy.

In practice there is a tendency for more layers in the hierarchy to be introduced well before there are 900 people at the basic level. Spans of control vary a good deal. Because there is usually someone in overall charge, and others who direct more detailed activities, three levels of hierarchy are often present even in very small companies. However, structures do tend to be depicted as if they are uniform. In many books, structures are drawn as equilateral triangles, and this is a convention that is sufficiently realistic for many purposes. If taken literally, however, this implies uniform (and quite narrow) spans of control. But traditional organizational structures were not like this. Spans tend to narrow towards the top of structures. Senior managers typically have only a few subordinates whilst foremen and supervisors have many more. An accurate depiction of almost any organizational structure, therefore, should show it as having a wide base and narrow top. An accurate representation of this has concave sides and a flat base. What mitigates this tendency for organizations to take this form is the creation of intermediate support and administrative functions—to augment the basic structure. These specialized functions increase as organizations grow larger.

Figure 3.1 depicts the organizational structure of a small fictional manufacturing company. In conformity with the functional view of structure, its structure is laid out in a way that clearly relates elements of structure to the activities which are undertaken. At the bottom of the structure, a range of activities are depicted in a series. The sequence begins on the left of the diagram with the purchase and storage of components and raw materials. Next, in the centre of the diagram, under the control of a production manager, are three departments involved in fabrication, manufacture, and assembly of a product, whilst on the right, at the other end of the process, is the sales department of the organization, which delivers the completed product to the customers. Thus, conventional organizational structures like this are usually thought of as being functional in a straightforward way. Each part of the organization contributes something to the activity. Any kind of activity can be considered in this way. Any and every organization will be constructed around some kind of transformation process, which, if it is a private sector organization, must add value.

An elementary way of analysing an organization, then, involves simply considering what kind of transformative processes are involved and how the organization is structured to allow them to occur. It follows that the analyst looks at the ways in which people and other resources allocated to tasks make the processes possible. In the example of Figure 3.1, the value of the manufactured products delivered to the market should exceed the costs of their production (expended on raw materials, components, and human labour) if the business is to remain profitable. A good part of any added-value will come from the activities of the productive employees in the organization—those on the lowest level of the organization, the people actually making products or providing services to the public. But it is also implied that the purpose and role of the management structure erected over the employees also adds value—by making the activities of operatives or the utilization of resources more efficient, for example. By such activities management adds value to the basic transformation process in the firm. Indeed, functionalist writers argue that, unless all the elements of the organizational structure add to the value produced, there would be no need for them, and they would not exist.

Much of this is questionable. It is misleading to think too strictly in terms of benefits as being exclusively economic. The symbolic aspects of organizations are equally as important as the purely economic or rational ones. In some circumstances it is difficult to make economic criteria apply even in principle. Public sector organizations do not make a profit, and, hence, their effectiveness must be measured and thought about in different terms than monetary value added. Yet they tend to adopt very similar structural patterns. There are many examples of organizations continuing to exist even where they are not particularly effective or functional. Also, there are many examples where it is difficult to show that management contributes to efficiency and functionality, and some situations in which it is difficult to imagine how it can (see Box 3.2). Some writers think it has yet to be shown that management generally makes a contribution to efficiency that justifies its existence.

3.2 **Organizational types**

Unlike the classical management writers who took the view that they should try to formulate invariable principles of effective organization—to set out the one best way of managing applicable in all circumstances—contingency and functional writers typically argue that there are some different configurations. For them a given organizational design would not be equally functional in different situations. They argued that organizational structures would vary according to differences in the context of the organization—usually referred to as the organizational environment. The label 'contingency approach' comes from the idea that the differences of the context of organizations can be understood as differences in particular surrounding contingencies. Such environmental contingencies could dictate that a different organizational structure would be appropriate. These writers did not think, however, that the possibilities were unlimited: they usually reduced the number of possible types to four or five.

It has to be said at the outset that the designs are, for the most part, not much different from the basic one, which has already appeared in Figure 3.1.

BOX 3.2 Management as permanent failure

[W]hy [are] the functions of managers . . . so poorly specified in organizational theory, [what explains] why the ranks of management have swollen so rapidly and why conflict is endemic in managerial roles?

A partial resolution of this problem, we argue, requires that our normal presuppositions about organizations be revised and perhaps reversed. As outlined . . . there is a tendency to think of organizations as efficient rather than as inefficient, as performing rather than as non-performing. . . . Our scepticism about efficiency models now takes on an added dimension. Not only are efficiency models incapable of explaining the combination of high persistence yet low performance in organizations, but they also cannot explain parsimoniously the actions of managers, and the growth and contentiousness surrounding many managerial tasks. A different set of state-of-the-world assumptions, departing significantly from the efficiency model, may be needed to account for the salient characteristics of management.

We wish to suggest that the role of management, particularly in established organizations, is best understood within the framework of permanent failure. Organizations tend toward permanent failure . . . because low performance that arises from exogenous conditions causes interests to diverge and contests for power to develop. While all parties may agree that sustained low performance is an unsatisfactory state of affairs, they may disagree strongly as to the desirability of alternative paths from permanent failure. . . . A task of management, perhaps its principal task, is to reclaim control of the organization; often by negotiating among various interest groups in and around the organization so that alternatives to permanent failure are rendered viable. This task is ill-defined. Were disparate interests commensurable, that is, were simple incentives capable of aligning diverse interests, the problem of permanent failure would not arise. This task is also complex. As interests increase, the difficulty of negotiating among them multiplies geometrically. And the task is conflict-ridden. Even when the continuation of an enterprise or portion of an enterprise is not at stake, choices aimed at averting permanent failure carry consequences for people's livelihoods and lives.

M. W. Meyer and L. G. Zucker (1989: 133–4)

If we are indeed in a period of significant change so far as organizations are concerned, it is an open question whether the four or five standard types of organizational structure will cover the range and variety of organizations now existing. However, the conventional account of structure involves the idea that most organizations can be classified as one of a small number of types.

The simple structure/unitary or 'U' form

A. D. Chandler, perhaps the most influential economic historian of organizations, proposed the label 'F' form—short for the functional organizational form—for the basic organization with a few levels of authority (Chandler 1962). O. E. Williamson, the leading organizational economist of his

generation, first coined the term 'unitary organization' for the undifferentiated structure of the small firm (Williamson 1975). This was later shortened
to the 'U' form. Henry Mintzberg, the organizational analyst, uses the label
'simple structure' to describe this form (1973, 1979, 1993). They are all concerned with the same thing. Here the term unitary structure, or 'U' form will
be used. A unitary structure is constructed around a single transformative
process, for which little specialization of tasks is required. As a result the
levels of hierarchy are not elaborate either. There are few layers of hierarchy,
there is a simple, unified chain of command, and there is little horizontal
differentiation.

The basic design of the small company engaged in commercial activities
was developed in more or less its modern form several centuries ago. Braudel
traces the prototypes of the European company to the *ninth* century, though
such enterprises were not firmly established as institutions until the four-
teenth century (Braudel 1983: 433–43). What these structures most obviously
lack by comparison with their contemporary counterparts is a specialized
management and/or administrative structure. It is of course possible for a
small firm to exist without either. As organizations develop from the small
firm to something larger, there are a number of possible routes forward. One
is to develop a more adequate administrative structure; this path is usually
called bureaucratization. Another is to develop a specialized management
structure.

In Britain, both tendencies were apparent, but they were less marked and
took longer to develop than in other countries. Neither development occurred
in any significant way until the end of the nineteenth century, which is more
than a century after the Industrial Revolution, and perhaps 600 years since the
invention of the basic organizational form. It seems clear that if we wish to
understand the periodicity of developments of this sort, we have to look not
only at the properties of organizations themselves and the motivations of the
participants in them, but at the interactions between organizations and their
context. This is not to repeat the catechism of the contingency theorists, that
environment shapes structure, but to notice that there is a complex interaction between organizations and their context. This point will be elaborated
on at many points in this book.

The large unified structure/the machine bureaucracy

Many contingency writers contrast the simple structure or 'U' form with the
bureaucracy. According to them, in the right environmental circumstances,
the simple structure acquires more and more activities—and, especially, a
developed administration. In short, if circumstances permit, the simple structure becomes a bureaucracy.

BOX 3.3 Individual firms: the beginning of a development

To discover the earliest forms taken by such firms in the West, one has to go back if not to ancient Rome, at least to the Mediterranean revival of the ninth and tenth centuries. Amalfi, Venice and other towns—all still very small places at the time—were just embarking on their careers. Money re-appeared. The renewal of trade with Byzantium and the cities of Islam presupposes both the ability to handle freight and the financial reserves needed for long-haul operations—which in turn imply strengthened trading units

One of the first institutions was the societas maris or maritime firm (also known as the societas vera, or 'true' firm, 'which seems to suggest that this kind of organization was originally the only one'). It was also known as collegantia or commenda, with other variants . . .

The compagnia was (originally) . . . a family firm: father, sons, brothers and other relatives—and as its name indicates (cum = with, panis = bread) it was a close associ-ation in which everything was shared—bread and risks, capital and labour. Later such a firm would be known as a joint liability enterprise, since all partners were jointly liable in theory ad infinitum, that is not only to the value of their holding but to the value of all their worldly goods. When we learn that the compagnia was soon admitting foreign partners (who contributed both capital and labour) and money from depositors (which . . . could run to ten times as much as the firm's own capital) we can understand how such firms were potent capitalist instruments. The Bardi, who had established them-selves in the Levant and England, for a while held the whole of Christendom in fee. These powerful firms also lasted a surprisingly long time. On the death of the head of a firm, the maggiore, they would be reconvened and continue much as before. Almost all the agreements that have survived for us to read are contracts not of the foundation but of the renewal of a compagnia.

Fernand Braudel (1983: 433-4)

A very much larger organization developed from the simple structure is not simply the same design on a much larger scale. As organizations get larger they tend to become more complicated, or, to use a more precise notion, they become internally differentiated. Why this happens is not difficult to under-stand. As more and more people work together, there is scope for more spe-cialization of function. Also problems in the coordination of the activities of so many people also emerge. Specialist managers, planners, administrators are not needed in the simple structure; but the need for them quickly becomes apparent as the organization grows. As the organization grows in size, it is possible to specialize the activities of employees. Two kinds of specialist staff are typically retained: technical experts, and managers and administrators whose only task is organization and coordination itself.

Here we have described—in simple form—two processes that accompany the growth of the large organization: increasing technical specialization (requiring professional services) and the need for increasing numbers of managers, administrators, and record keepers. There are different options as to how to utilize staff to coordinate activities. One is generally to increase the amount of management and administration. Increasing the numbers of middle managers is an obvious way to achieve greater coordination and control of an organization. Bureaucracy may be defined as an organizational type with a high proportion of officials whose sole task is coordination and who use authority to secure uniformity of practice. They do this by the formulation of rules and procedures. The bureaucracy can be thought of as a development of the basic functional structure, but one which involves particular kinds of internal structural development and adaptation.

In the bureaucracy, formalization and centralization are key features of the more elaborate structure. These features increase more than proportionately with the scale of operations. We recognize these tendencies in the common-sense understanding of the bureaucratic structure and they are also aspects of the model of the bureaucracy as it is specified in the work of its great theorist, the German sociologist Max Weber. According to Weber, bureaucracy had several features that are distinctive because they occur together. These are summarized, following Huczynski and Buchanan (2000: 489), in Box 3.4. Although these are not an exact rendition of Weber's ideal type, they are close to the essential idea that Weber had in mind. Weber's schematic analysis of modern bureaucracy is part of a long chapter on bureaucracy which he revised several times. It was not published in German until 1921. It was not published in English until 1947. Note that, as they are given here, the first two criteria connect with levels and spans of control, the others relate to the regulatory apparatus of this structure and mostly concern what has been identified here as internal differentiation.

Despite its contemporary image as being inefficient and inflexible, we should recognize that the bureaucracy was a huge step forward when it was first developed. Before this, institutions were often inefficient, not being organized according to consistently applied rational principles. Until rationality was applied to organizations, indeed, it was not usually assumed that there could be any improvement on the institutions that there were. The bureaucracy is a large organization which is distinguished by having a highly developed administrative apparatus; the extent to which large organizations have to have this element is debatable. Indeed, it seems obvious to us now that the bureaucracy is not a final stage of organizational development.

What preoccupied Weber was that the bureaucracy was a significant increase in efficiency over traditional institutions. He regarded the increase in efficiency as comparable to the difference between craft and machine production. He was right about this: bureaucracy was so effective it established the notion that social technology can be as effective as material technology. The bureaucratic machine made possible the first truly mass-scale production of

---

BOX 3.4 **Weber's specification of bureaucracy**

- Authority hierarchy. Offices or positions are organised in a clear chain-of-command hierarchy. Each lower position is controlled and supervised by a higher one, so that workers clearly know to whom they are responsible. (This refers to the existence of many hierarchical levels.)

- Job specialisation. Jobs are broken down into simple, routine and well-defined tasks. People should specialise and thus learn to do one set of activities well. Work is divided so that authority and responsibility are clearly defined. (This refers to the specialisation of activities at each level.)

- Employment and Career. All personnel are selected and promoted on the basis of their technical qualifications and are offered a full-time career.

- Formal rules and regulations. To ensure uniformity and to guide the actions of employees, managers must depend heavily on formal organisational rules. These are set down to monitor employee behaviour.

- Impersonality. Rules and controls are applied uniformly, avoiding involvement of personalities or the personal preferences of employees.

- Career orientation. Managers are professional officials rather than owners of the units they manage. They work for fixed salaries and pursue their careers within the organisation.

Huczynski and Buchanan (2000: 489). (Based on Henderson and Parsons's translation of selections from Weber's book *Economy and Society*, first published in English as *The Theory of Social and Economic Organisations*, Free Press, New York, 1947. The definitive edition of Weber's masterwork in English was published as *Economy and Society* in 1968.)

---

goods and services. Weber was familiar with bureaucracy in this application in the rise of big business in Germany. But all mass production was bureaucratic to some extent; it had to be. The best-known example of the mass-production company is perhaps the Ford Motor Company (which reached its height at the River Rouge complex near Detroit in the 1930s). At the height of its development it had more than 100 000 employees and produced millions of cars a year. It was an impressive technical apparatus, but coordinating it and making it function, was bureaucracy.

It is almost automatic for us today to equate bureaucracy with the offices and services of the state. In organizations of this kind in the twentieth century bureaucracy was abundant. Again, for the provision of mass services efficiently (and without biases) to large numbers of people, bureaucracy was essential. But its application to the functions of the state was only one of its applications, and the extent and the wastefulness of this can easily be exaggerated (Du Gay 2000). One of the general issues to be considered in this book

BOX 3.5 **A need for bureaucracy?**

Few people would fly with an airline that had an organic structure, where the mainten-ance men did whatever struck them as interesting instead of following precise check-lists and the pilots worked out their procedures for landing in foggy weather when the need arose. Likewise, a fire crew cannot arrive at a burning house and then turn to the chief for orders or decide among its members who will connect the hose and who will go up the ladder. The environments of these organizations may seem dynamic, but in fact most of their contingencies are predictable—they have been seen many times before and so procedures for handling them have been formalized.

Mintzberg (1993: 175)

concerns the question of whether the age of bureaucracy has now gone and less rule-bound organizations now predominate. It is true that there is much change in organizations, but whether the move away from bureaucratic struc-tures is extensive and permanent are arguable points.

As far as the contingency writers are concerned, however, the bureaucracy is still viable. The contingency analyst, Henry Mintzberg, for example, argues that what he calls 'the machine bureaucracy' is without equal in the provision of standardized goods and services to large numbers of users or consumers, because it is so reliable (Mintzberg 1993). It is debatable whether the highly bureaucratized mass production organization on the lines of the Ford motor company was ever approximated in this country. Major British com-panies did not develop into the highly centralized bureaucracies that appeared in the USA, though the tendency for centralized administrative structures did emerge strongly in the organizations of the state. However, it is true that contingency researchers who went out looking for fully developed bureaucracies in the UK in the 1970s actually had difficulty finding examples.

The multidivisional structure/divisionalized company/'M' form

Although the internal differentiation of the bureaucracy has been noted, it cannot be said that it is radically different from the simple structure. It amounts to some increase in the complexity of the basic design which allows general increases in the scale of activities. Chandler is usually credited with identifying a somewhat more radical development of internally differentiated organizational design, which he called the 'M' form company (Chandler 1962, 1977). Most commentators follow Chandler's usage, though Mintzberg pre-fers the label 'the divisionalized form'. Most agree that this new organizational development appeared in the USA about the time that the unitary mass pro-duction organization was being brought to its peak of performance. Chandler argued that further development in organizational structuring was necessary to allow companies to serve developing national markets efficiently. In particular, he suggested that firms would be more efficient if they divisionalized themselves, with separate parts of the organization serving different market segments. The market could be split geographically or in terms of differences in the kind of product.

Although in the early decades of the twentieth century in the USA the Ford Motor Company (a unitary structure having developed bureaucratic aspects) was hugely successful, General Motors (GM) emerged as Ford's main competitor. Originally a defensive alliance of the larger (but financially weak) American car companies, GM was anything but unitary. Unlike Ford which, for nearly three decades, concentrated on producing a single type of car, the model T Ford, GM was forced, by reasons of its origins, to produce a wider range of products. It was, at the start, in fact, several different car companies bundled together under the ownership of a holding company. From this rather unsatisfactory position, GM was forged into a single company: one having different divisions producing distinct ranges of car, each aimed to serve a different kind of clientele. With the development of more sophisticated consumer markets for cars in the USA from the 1930s onwards, the differentiated products of GM turned out to be much more saleable than the single product of Ford. In the 1930s, because of its failure to follow a similar strategy marketing a range of products, Ford became less and less profitable.

On the basis of a small number of case studies of large American firms, Chandler (1962) argued that multidivisional companies like GM would allow the development of a more effective mode for manufacture, allowing the delivery of a range of related products. He later consolidated this finding in a more thorough study of American large business (1977). The 'M' form is achieved when the overall control of the firm was in the hands of a centralized managerial group which would decide strategy. Chandler's view was that structure follows strategy, meaning in this instance that the form of organizational divisions should reflect the decisions that corporate management makes about market segmentation.

If we consider how the 'M' form of company would appear as an organizational chart, then what we see as the simple branching structure in Figure 3.1 is changed. In this model, presented in Figure 3.2, there is one unitary structure (the head office) presiding over several other unitary structures (the divisions). Instead of the organization being constructed around a single transformative process, it is constructed around as many processes as there are separate divisions, loosely coordinated by strategic control by head office.

Most commentators agree that companies in the UK were much slower to adopt the multidivisional form of organization than elsewhere, especially the USA. This was despite British managers and owners being told repeatedly that

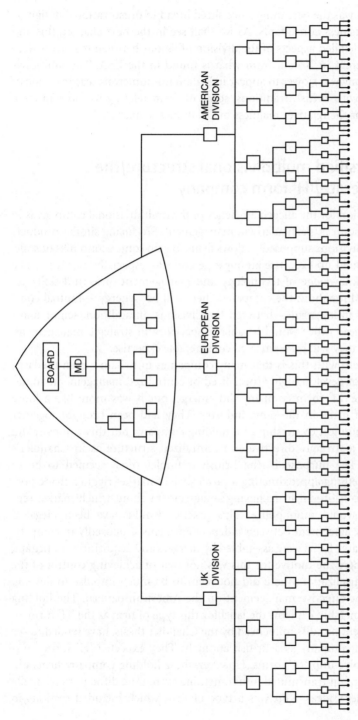

Figure 3.2 Organizational chart for a fictitious multidivisional company, divisionalized by region. Note: This chart is meant to give a general idea of the configuration of this type of company only and it is not drawn to scale with Figure 3.1. The typical multidivisional company will be many times larger than the kind of SME depicted in Figure 3.1, with many more divisions than shown here and perhaps 100 or 200 times the staff of the SME (ie of the order of 10,000 staff as opposed to 67). Often each division is constituted as a legally separate entity with its own board of directors.

the 'M' form was the best thing since sliced bread in organizational design by American business consultants. As we shall see in the next chapter, this and many more detailed aspects of the division of labour between managers were and are different in Britain from what is found in the USA. The multidivisional company was slower to appear in Britain for numerous reasons some of them to do with British traditions, some of them relating to more rational causes such as the relative smallness of UK domestic market.

The diversified multidivisional structure/the conglomerate/'H' form company

The explanation for the alleged efficiency of the multidivisional company is in savings in resources, particularly in management. Producing similar products in different divisions supposedly allows firms to gain some economies of scale, but also to build up expertise amongst personnel—especially managers. The idea is that knowledge of technology and management ideas and skills are transferable throughout the company. There will be 'synergy'—mutual complementarity in lay terms—between the divisions. In addition, senior management at head office would be able to specialize in strategic management, about which they will have amassed considerable expertise.

The problem with this is that many companies in Britain—even the large ones—did not develop highly specialized or centralized management. Something like the 'M' form company did emerge, but it was more like a loose federation of firms in the same industry. They had been brought together under the common ownership of a holding company, but this company did not develop a strongly directive and centralized structure as in Chandler's conception. The purpose in the British examples often seemed to be to develop something approximating a cartel style of market rigging, made possible by the constituent firms having an agreement about which market segments they would monopolize. This practice would have been illegal if developed by agreement between independent firms supposedly in competition. Often, large firms were assembled by mergers and acquisitions in Britain; and, even where the motive for this was not that of achieving control of the market by cartelization, there did not seem to be much impulse to develop centralized or directive management on the American pattern. The holding company ownership explains the label for this type of firm as the 'H' form.

Management pundits influenced by the Chandler thesis, have tended to see the 'H' form company as a British anomaly. They expected 'H' form companies to evolve into 'M' forms. However, these holding company firms did not disappear, but transmuted into something even more difficult to reconcile with Chandler's ideas. This was a type of firm which included sections in diverse lines of trade or business. In Britain, some of the largest and most effective firms to develop themselves in the post-war period have been of this kind, being extremely diverse in the activities they comprise and huge in scale as measured in terms of turnover and employment. Like the original holding companies, however, these firms have always had very small head offices. The lack of possibilities for synergy in their diverse activities suggests that in this case structure was not related to active strategy—at least not a strategy concerned with holding onto total market share. Firms of this type, of which the Hanson Trust is perhaps the best-known example amongst successful post-war British firms, are also called conglomerates. This is because their activities seem to be a mixture or 'conglomeration' of activities without obvious rationale. The headquarters is a holding company in that it serves as a profit centre, and does not otherwise direct activities at the periphery.

In terms of organizational charts, the conglomerate looks not much different from the 'M' form. The divisions have diverse activities, but this would not show up on the standard kinds of organizational chart. The Hanson Trust at one time had constituent companies making bricks, paper flowers, furniture, engineering products and was also heavily involved in retailing. Indeed, some writers see this type of company as being just another type of multidivisional firm, which, considered in terms of its formal structure, it is. Mintzberg sees the conglomerate as a development of the related product divisional form, calling it the 'pure divisional' or conglomerate form. This is markedly different from what some of the supporters of Chandler had in mind, who held that evolution would be towards the 'M' form. Today, both the standard 'M' form of company and the conglomerate are much less in evidence. The conglomerate is particularly unfashionable today, and conglomerates seem to be trying to convert themselves into more focused companies, able to exhibit synergy between their constituent parts. Hanson Trust converted itself into three companies, each specializing in particular lines of business: building products, energy companies, and tobacco activities were 'demerged'.

Other types/the matrix form

Contingency writers usually consider a type of structure which is commonly known as the professional organization or the professional bureaucracy. This will not be considered here because, although it purports to describe some private sector organizations such as accountancy firms, its main application is in the public sector. Accounting for such organizations does not come within the scope of this book.

In addition to the professional bureaucracy there is another type of organization noted by contingency writers. Perhaps because they recognize that the above forms of organization do not account well for the highly variable company forms emerging today, writers usually offer a description of a more flexible and specialized type of structure. A favourite candidate is the so-called matrix structure. Whereas the other forms of organization we have examined are minor variations on the basic 'U' pattern, the matrix is a radical departure.

The matrix recognizes one type of structure might be best for one type of organizational function but another would be best for another. A functional design might be best for the production of products, but not for the optimal use of employee expertise. Thus we could choose to employ individuals with similar skills in different departments (each with its own departmental head)—running the work through the different departments in a linear sequence—as in the conventional organization. Alternatively we could constitute teams of workers with different skills and have each working on distinct projects until they are completed. When products become sufficiently complex that they are best dealt with by groups of workers with different skills cooperating together, this form of matrix becomes appropriate. In this design, employees still have someone to whom they are responsible as a departmental head, but they will also have someone who manages the team of workers engaged on a particular project. Thus, I may be employed as an accountant by a firm of consultants, and, as such, my work may be overseen and costed by a manager responsible for the accountants employed by the firm. On the other hand, I am allocated to a team working on a project, in which the work is coordinated by another manager. Similarly, in a university, a teacher will have a departmental head who is responsible for the administration of his or her department, but also have to work for the organizers of the different degree programmes to which he or she contributes. Thus, as head of my department, I might be nominally in charge of the work of all my departmental colleagues, but, as a member of a teaching team, I will be answerable to the director of a programme.

The matrix is radical because it dispenses with a single path for authority. In the 'U' design and all the other organizational types—which can be considered as variations on it—a position within the structure has one and only one superior. The classical management writers thought this was necessary to avoid confusion, and the proposition was implicitly taken over by the contingency writers. With the matrix, however, this principle is abandoned. It would be going too far to say that the matrix form abandons authority as the main means of producing coordination, but it is a decisive shift from exclusive reliance on a single person embodying organizational authority for every subordinate. This is predominantly the case for the other organizational forms. All the designs so far outlined—from the basic 'U' to the bureaucracy and the 'M' and 'H' forms—rely on each person having a single person with authority over them. In principle they have unity of command as their basis. It is the responsibility of those with authority to ensure the coordination of the activities for which they are responsible. The higher one is in the hierarchy, the more authority one has and the more responsibility one has.

The matrix structure departs from this simple idea of a unique chain of authority. It is built around the idea that it may be necessary to use employees in very different relations with other employees. Employees come together for the discharge of specific tasks, and the expertise and capabilities of team members are obviously important in achieving successful outcomes. The matrix makes undertaking diverse activities at the same time—as well as rapid changes in kinds of tasks undertaken—possible. The matrix has been described in terms of two competing organizational principles. It is of course not necessary to stop there, but to think in terms of multiple organizational priorities. Employees could join very different groups constituted in different ways according to need. In an extreme form of team working like this, people may have no regularity in their work at all, groups being reconstituted for different tasks from time to time as required. Individuals may indeed contribute in different ways to the same organization—and decide for themselves what needs to be done without being told. Thus the matrix form can be thought about as the beginnings of a more flexible type of differentiated structure in which authority is progressively diluted as an organizational principle. Morgan (1988: 65) depicts the matrix as a point in an increasingly radical unbundling of the basic organizational design (a version of this is given in Figure 3.3). Some analysts have a general name for these new structures, describing them as organic—as opposed to mechanical. Contingency writers regularly use such language, arguing that bureaucracy is fine in stable markets, but more organic structures are required in other market conditions (Burns and Stalker 1961).

The advantages of the matrix structure are as follows. It improves communication and integration, it encourages innovation, is flexible, and makes efficient use of specialist expertise. It allows individuals to develop their capacities to some degree and can strike the right balance between flexibility in production and the maintenance of authority. The disadvantages are that it creates dual or multiple sources of authority, and so sets up the conditions for conflict over scarce resources. It can inhibit individuals from displaying their specialist expertise—because their skill may be copied. Being highly adaptive and team based, imposing direction on a matrix structure is difficult; and planning—other than broad indications of direction—is impossible. It gives rise to uncertainty about career paths. According to contingency writers, however, there are some environments in which this kind of organization is likely to flourish more readily, for example, where there is a scarcity of human resources and where tasks are uncertain, complex, and interdependent.

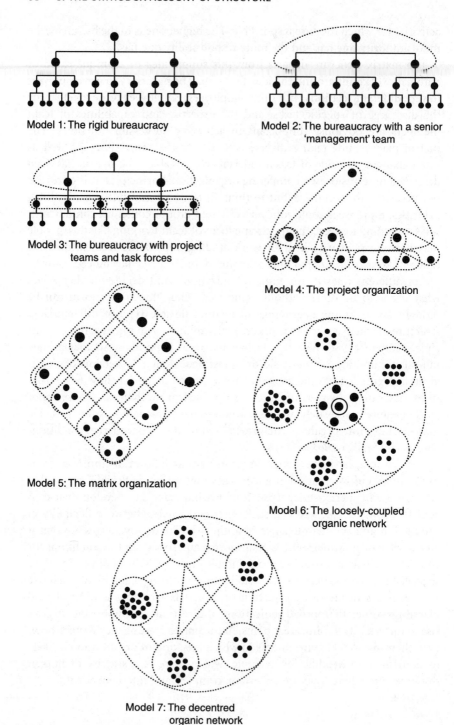

Model 1: The rigid bureaucracy

Model 2: The bureaucracy with a senior 'management' team

Model 3: The bureaucracy with project teams and task forces

Model 4: The project organization

Model 5: The matrix organization

Model 6: The loosely-coupled organic network

Model 7: The decentred organic network

Figure 3.3 Transition from mechanical to organic organizational structure. (After Morgan 1988)

3.3 Explaining the differences in organizational structures

Organizational structures as adaptations to external contingencies

The functional/contingency approach to explaining the existence of different organizational structures lies in what is outside of the organization—in its environment. Writers in this tradition argue that one or another of the small number of possible types of organizational structure will be appropriate to a particular organization depending on its situation. This approach to the theory of organizations is called contingency theory because it suggests that organizations adopt a different structure according to the particular conditions (called contingencies) they happen to face. Some features of the organizational environment are so potent, they argue, that organizations must adapt their structures to accommodate them. Thus it is that the forms of organizational structures we have discussed are functional adaptations to their context. There is a clear parallel with biological thinking here. A more than trivial similarity is postulated between organizations and organisms, which have adapted themselves to their physical environments.

Writers differ over the number and types of contingencies which they see as having formative effects but there are points of agreement. Different kinds of technology is one 'contingency' that is often cited, while different market conditions for the products of the company is another. Contingency theory may be fairly said to have originated with the finding that organizational structures were found to vary according to the kind of technology they use (Woodward 1958; Burns and Stalker 1961). Mass-production technology seems to imply large numbers of unskilled or semi-skilled employees for example (and therefore these structures will have wide spans of control as well as many levels); on the other hand, process technology—as in chemical plants—will imply many highly trained employees (chemical engineers and technicians) and, by comparison with the mass-production factory, they would employ only quite few labourers and unskilled workers. They are thus likely to have many levels but narrow spans. In this way, the prevailing technology in an industry is seen to have an effect on organizational structure. This point was then generalized, other commentators arguing for other external contingencies that also have an impact on the structure.

There are many criticisms of the functional/contingency approach to organizational structures but only some will be discussed here. One general problem is the question of why it is that there are only a few distinctive types of organization. If there are many external contingencies and each of these may seemingly vary a good deal, it would seem that each organization would be the unique product of its particular situation. This would imply as many organizational forms as there are unique sets of contingencies. But only a few contingency theorists draw this kind of conclusion. Most imply that a few distinct types of organizations are produced by the impact of a relatively large number of variable environmental contingencies. This is not what intuition would lead one to expect.

How does technology actually affect structures?

Many contingency writers think about the organizational structure in ways that are very contrived. For example, in practice, is technology readily detachable from the organization of which it is part? Only by thinking of the prevailing technology in an industry is it realistic to think of it as something separate from the structure of an organization and capable of having an impact on it from the outside. To make this sort of claim about technology, contingency theorists reason as follows: for an organization operating in a given industry it is almost obligatory to use the prevailing and currently most efficient technology. This, in turn, determines that particular numbers and types of workers will have to be employed. But this sort of reasoning elides the role of choices surrounding the use of technology. Actually, decisions have to be made to adopt a particular technology and then to utilize it in particular ways. Because these choices seem rational in the circumstances does not remove the fact that decisions have been made. The technology would not have been adopted or utilized in particular ways in the absence of somebody making particular decisions and choices. Technology has to be thought about as embedded in a set of social and economic relationships.

Some interesting social science research into the use of technology has shown that the choices concerning the utilization of technology are often made according to common-sense or traditional ideas. Because machines are used by engineers, it is often left to this group to decide about ways they are put into use or 'manned'. Research has shown, however, that the choices made seem the obvious thing to do, but, on more careful consideration, are not necessarily the best (Trist et al. 1963). There are some different ways in which the same kind of technology can be used, some of them being a great deal more effective and creative than others. Moreover, it has also been found in practice that different cultures adapt to and use technology in different ways (Pacey 1983). Even basic familiarity with technology takes a long time to learn. And there are examples in which less advanced countries have found better uses for technology than the people who invented it (Gerschenkron 1962). The Japanese use Western technology to make cars, but if claims about lean

---

BOX 3.6 Did technology produce factories or vice versa?

One politician (Anthony Wedgwood Benn) has said; 'the development of steam for the factory . . . produced a new economic system: capitalism'. Such opinions cannot be substantiated. The evidence is that the first factories of the industrial revolution, and the system of capitalism that went with them, did not depend on the steam engine at all. By the end of the 1740s there were several textile factories in Britain with power driven machines, and more after 1769, but these used water-wheels or horses as their energy source, and it was not until 1783 that steam was first employed. In any case, most so-called factories were no more than glorified workshops, with machines 'powered by the men and women who worked them' (Landes 1969: 65). Granted, the factory system could not have expanded very far without steam power. But primarily, the factory was *an invention concerning the organization of work*, with an earlier origin than most of the machines it contained.

The machines in early factories were very simple and built mainly of wood. However, they worked just about well enough to demonstrate the potential of the factory, and the demand grew for better machines, made of more durable materials. By 1790, these were increasingly often driven by steam engines, which of course the British had pioneered . . .

Merchants . . . wanted better control over production than they could achieve while spinners and weavers worked in their own homes. They believed that if they brought these people together in supervised workshops, they could stop embezzlement of materials, achieve more consistent quality and enforce longer working hours and a faster pace of work. Early writers on the factory system stress these organizational advantages. In 1835, one admirer of Richard Arkwright wrote that to invent a spinning machine was less remarkable than Arkwright's other achievement, 'To devise and administer a successful code of factory discipline' (Landes 1969: 66). Rather less often, modern writers remind us that the essence of the early factories was discipline, and the opportunity which this subsequently gave entrepreneurs regarding the direction and coordination of labour.

Arnold Pacey (1983: 18–19) emphasis added

---

production are correct (Womack *et al.* 1990) they seem to have found much more economical ways of using it than have developed naturally in America and Europe; and yet it is technology that was invented in the West.

More generally for many purposes, therefore, the technology in use in an organization is not best conceived as something separate and distinct from the organization in which it is used. Technology is always embedded in social relations in complex ways. These make that technology more or less productive or amenable to control. It is necessary to think of the connections between technology and social relations—including any organizational structures—as a set of relationships. Their complexity has to be unravelled and understood. It is simplistic to say that technology straightforwardly determines the organizational structure. In this analysis a new form of technology is implicated in organizational change. But it is much more realistic to see IT as a resource or tool that is used by groups in particular ways. The interaction between structure and technology is variable, and understanding the way it impacts in particular circumstances is clearly crucial if our aim is understanding contemporary organizational change.

Problems in the methodology

There has been a recurrent tendency for contingency writers to try to quantify and to measure very precisely, and to try to prove the causal relations they think are there by demonstrating statistical associations. One of the most influential schools of thought, known as the Aston group (Pugh and Hickson 1976; Pugh and Hinnings 1976), went to considerable lengths to count and to measure aspects of organizational structure and to try to correlate these with other 'variables' relating to the organizational context.

This led to some very contrived ways of thinking about the organization and what was outside of it. The Aston researchers, for example, persuaded themselves that an organization's size (whether measured in terms of the numbers of employees or not) was not an attribute of the organizational structure but an aspect of its context. They arrived at this conclusion by reasoning thus: the organizational structure should be understood as a set of abstract but measurable attributes—the degree of specialization of the structure, its standardization, and so on. Measures of these variables were found to vary according to other measurable attributes of the organization of which organizational size was one. If the organizational size was not an aspect of the structure, it had to be external to it and so it is, presumably, part of the context of the structure. They had a similar view about the age of the organization being part of the context. This reasoning defies the assumptions that most observers would bring to bear. The way of approaching organizational structures that has been adopted by the Aston researchers is called positivism, and it has many defenders.

This is not the place to discuss positivism and its critics (but see Ackroyd and Fleetwood 2000). Suffice it to say that, in this study, although quantitative methods as such are not by any means ruled out, the assumptions that underpin much positivist research quite definitely are. Despite the spirited defence of this positivistic approach to contingency theory by Donaldson (1996), positivist contingency theory has mostly been abandoned in Britain.

The importance of markets

Contingency/functional writing survives in its most defensible form today in the work of writers who attempt to relate organizational types to differences of product markets. Thus it is argued that the machine-like properties of the bureaucracy will continue to work if there is a mass demand for standardized products. In these circumstances, the bureaucracy will be the most efficient form of organization possible. As markets become more turbulent and consumers more discriminating, however, there is a need for firms to be flexible and to produce a differentiated product. According to this reasoning, there is basically a continuum along which firms can be ranged. At one end (stable markets) we shall have bureaucracies, at the other end (turbulent markets) we shall have flexible and much smaller firms using matrix designs. Other possibilities (the 'M' form, the 'H' form, and the professional bureaucracy) are found somewhere between.

Others have argued that types of markets can be further distinguished, and types of organizations related to them. In addition to the highly stable and predictable mass market, and the highly turbulent one, there are different conditions of instability between these. There are *complex markets* in which there is a variety of products available, but which are not really alternatives to each other. The Nissan Micra and the Rolls-Royce Corniche are both cars, but they are not in competition with each other. Similarly, the Dell PC and the Cray Super Computer are both computers, but they are not really alternatives. The Rolls and the Cray are saleable items despite their huge price tags, suggesting that they can do things the cheaper products cannot. (The Micra will not allow a suitable entrance to a film première, or advertise the owner's success; the Dell will not calculate movements in stock market prices in sufficient density to make accurate price predictions.)

By contrast with this, there are *unstable markets*. These are not necessarily complex, they are simply volatile and subject to wildly fluctuating demand. This year people want Nike, next year some other kind of exercise kit may be more popular. The 'M' form of company can be seen to deal effectively with complex markets—each different division can be thought of addressing a distinct market segment. But because the 'M' form company is also very large, it does not respond well to great fluctuations in demand. A conglomerate, on the other hand, can deal with turbulence better because it deals in unrelated products and so is not overreliant on any one market. Conglomerates it will be remembered are prepared to buy into unrelated markets if there is the prospect of good profits being made. If, on the other hand, markets become both complex and unstable, the only way to respond may be a highly flexible organization utilizing a matrix or other more organic design. The contingency formula—context shapes organizational form—can be made to work in the current context where a great deal of organizational change is occurring.

Numerous criticisms have been put forward of the functional/contingency approach, but only a few will be given attention here. The starting point is to note that there now seems to be a general questioning of the appropriateness of all traditional organizational forms. Bureaucracy is under ferocious attack. Few have any good word to say about it (though see Jacques 1990; Du Gay 2000). One way of defending the orthodox approach to structure is to say that this view is not wrong but circumstances have changed very radically. (Morgan's developmental sequence, see Figure 3.3, might be explained in this sort of way.) Bureaucracy is no longer much utilized, but only because there are no stable markets any more. Should these reappear, the model will be valid again. The problem of bureaucracy and other mechanical organizational designs is that all markets are becoming turbulent due to intensifying competition. There is much to point to in support of this thesis: domestic markets certainly are becoming more competitive. Owing to such things as the freeing of global trade, technical improvements in production, developments in IT and other communications, improvements in transportation facilities (such as containerization) and so on, it is now much easier for foreign-based producers to penetrate our markets. It is also much easier for foreign companies to set up in new locations. However, it is difficult to credit that the majority of markets are now so turbulent that all organizations need to radically change their modes of organization towards the matrix type.

Limitations of market-based arguments

This set of propositions does work to some extent. There are connections between the typical form of organization and the markets which they serve. America has some of the largest firms because it has the largest domestic market. Such effects are undeniable. But seeing the organization as the product of its markets is to make another error, which is to see the organization as being too passive in relation to the economy and society of which it is part. US firms—or British or German or Japanese firms—did not grow large simply by adapting to their markets. They grew as much because they actively responded to markets, taking a whole series of actions to enact their circumstances rather than adapt to them. They took (and take) a whole series of actions not only to manipulate their markets but to favourably affect other aspects of their social and political context too. These actions range from the merely inventive (creating products in advance of the demand for them, cleverly differentiating products, and marketing them) to the unethical and clearly illegal (Punch 1996; Slapper and Tombs 1999).

There have been periods when what organizations have done to bend the rules (in order to acquire market share and/or access financial resources and/or government support) have been particularly blatant. During the period of rapid business growth in the USA around the turn of the last century, for example, many growing businesses which subsequently became market leaders and their owners household names adopted some very questionable

---

BOX 3.7 **From robbery to respectability**

The Men who [simply] did in their customers fared far better in the public mind [than those who also robbed investors] and their families achieved high distinction. This was true of Vanderbilt. It was equally so in other fields of endeavour of Rockefeller, Carnegie, Morgan, Guggenheim, Mellon, *all of whom made their money by producing cheap, suppressing competition and selling dear.* All founded dynasties of the greatest respectability. . . . The point is an interesting and perhaps predictable one. To mulct investors—other capitalists—left a nasty taste in the public mouth. Public predation— the mulcting of the people at large—though criticised at the time—eventually acquired an aspect of high respectability and great social distinction. Even within their lifetimes, many of its outstanding practitioners gained the reputation of being impeccably God-fearing men.

J. K. Galbraith (1977: 53–4), emphasis added

---

practices to grab a larger slice of the market. A large group of well-known American businessmen (see Box 3.7) are now widely known as 'robber barons'. Ford grew large by gobbling up its competitors and suppliers. Those inclined to think this kind of behaviour is a thing of the past are invited to look at some of the realistic recent writing on business behaviour (Punch 1996; Slapper and Tombs 1999). Punch argues that criminality, while never publicly acknowledged, is actually endemic to the business activities of large corporations.

Research has shown that although many organizations are adopting organic structures there are many that are not, even though they are in similar kinds of markets. Firms emerging in the business services sector identified in Chapter 1, are, many of them, differently organized from the traditional 'U' form of organization (Ackroyd 1995; Alvesson 1995). On the other hand, there are firms even in rising industries—computer industry suppliers, for example— that are highly orthodox in organizational structure. Again, as with the question of technology, there is no substitute for unravelling the connections between organizations and their contexts if one is to explain differences in organizational forms.

3.4 Conclusions—rejecting the orthodox account of structure

It is argued here that the contingency approach is a deficient understanding of organizational structure, and of the relationship of the organization to its context. This was always true, but the changing times show this up particularly clearly. Against the assumptions of functional/contingency writing, it is proposed: first, that structures are not simply functional and, second, that organizations do not always simply adapt to their environment. Against the first point it will be argued that organizational structures embody and express power relations. Against the second point it will be argued that, far from passively adapting, organizations commonly shape (or enact) their environments. This point will be dealt with in later chapters.

An alternative account of organizational structure is developed in the next chapter and applied to the explanation of structural change in much of the remainder of this book. At this point, however, some general pointers to the approach will be set down. The first point is that the parallel drawn between the structure of a building or of the human body at the start of this chapter is potentially misleading and must be thought about carefully. The structure of an organization must be functional to some extent, but this is not the most important point about it. If it works only in a minimally effective way, then it may not perform sufficiently well to survive. But it is a mistake to assume that any organization is as functional as it can be merely because it survives. Often we are probably right to suspect that firms function suboptimally even when they make healthy profits.

Also, it is implausible that the explanation of organizational structure is *simply* that it contributes to functioning. The writers whose work we have reviewed in this chapter do not deny that organizational structures are meas-ured in terms of power (authority is legitimate power). The basic dimensions of structure in this approach are defined in these terms: levels of *hierarchy*, spans of *control*. The implications are studiously overlooked. The same struc-ture that contributes to function also ensures that the costs and benefits that come from the organization are differentially distributed. For some of the parties, it distributes largesse; for others it is an apparatus of coercion. Struc-tures institutionalize inequalities and therefore any conflicts and tensions that arise from this. The structure is not likely to be optimally functional for this reason.

The functional/contingency writers reviewed here say little about man-agement other than to imply that it coordinates organizational activities. An organization somehow automatically adjusts its structure when it responds to its environment. There is no mention here that, if an organization changes its structure, some person or group will have to make plans and take initiatives, they will have to move people around, change job specifications, and reallocate tasks. There is no mention here that anyone doing this sort of thing will almost certainly encounter resistance and that, consequently, they will have to exert more power to get their way (Ackroyd and Thompson 1999; Buchanan and Badham 1999). When, at a comparatively late stage in the development of the contingency approach, one of their own leading members suggested that senior managers would have to exercise 'strategic choice' if organizational change is to be achieved, it caused considerable controversy (Child 1972; Donaldson 1996). The approach tends to remove recognition that organizations are made up of people with motivations and projects.

In the orthodox approach to structure, there is seldom any glimmering of recognition that people create organizations to gain particular benefits. Overlooking this is a large oversight, analogous to an architect thinking a house needs a structure purely so that it will continue to stand up. Actually, a house requires a structure because people want to live in it, and this is the basic reason for it having the attributes it does.

4

The alternative approach to structure

4.1 The corporation as a set of relationships

In this chapter, organizational structure will be considered in a different way. This time, instead of looking at the structure in terms of its contribution to organizational functioning, we are going to look at the different groups that make up the organization and consider them in relation to each other. On this view, the structure of an organization is what emerges from the ongoing relationships between the people in the organization. The orthodox view assumes that almost everything in the organization is, in some way, required and contributes to its functioning. Some early functional writers suggested that there would be non-contributory aspects of organizations, which they called 'dysfunctional'. Later writers have had far less to say on such matters, and have argued that the great majority of the organization—and certainly the organizational structure—must be functional for the organization to continue to exist.

From the alternative view, an organizational structure will usually have to be functional to some extent. However, it does not follow that any organizational structure that exists functions optimally—or anything like it. It is difficult to show an association between organizational structure and performance anyway, and, even when this can be done, only a fraction of the variance is explained. In addition, it is not clear that a given configuration of structure is the reason for the superior performance (see, for example, Child's discussion of this issue 1984: 207–16). We only know for sure that a given structure is effective enough for the organization to survive in the prevailing economic and social conditions. We do not know whether a given organization is the most efficient utilization of resources possible; in fact, we often, with justification, suspect that it is not.

The alternative view also asserts that structure is enduring relationships. However, here the organization is thought about as a coalition of different groups—all of which have some interest in it and its continued effective performance. However, the main point is that the different categories of employee have different interests and powers and resources, and, as a result, the relationships in the organization reflect compromises between different groups. The organization of a company into a hierarchy, with managers controlling the activities of employees—from relatively highly paid professionals (in, say, accountancy functions) to relatively poorly paid unskilled workers (say on a production line)—reflects the scarcity of different skills and the organizational capacity of occupational groups. However, it should also be noted that the interests of different participating groups are not, in fact, identical. Hence, whilst all of these groups have an interest in the organization, this does not mean that they are entirely willing to subordinate their interests and what they hope to gain by participating in the interests of other groups.

Like the functional approach, this view also regards organizational structures as an emergent property, allowing more benefits for people than if they worked alone. It does not make assumptions about effectiveness. It attributes the power of action to individuals and groups (cf. Child 1984: 230–3). By contrast, the functional/contingency view tends to imply that any action taken that does not contribute to bringing the organization into adjustment with its environment will be a waste of time, or ineffective or damaging for the organization. Here we examine the motivations of groups and their resultant behaviour more realistically. The implication that organizational arrangements are necessarily functional is now set aside, in favour of working out why particular organizational configurations emerge and who benefits from them. The starting point for the consideration of structure therefore is: who are the parties to the typical organization, and what are their involvements?

In the following discussion, we shall distinguish managers from owners, managers from other white-collar employees such as professionals, and managers from ordinary employees. Clearly we must not think of these relationships as fixed or permanent: they are being renegotiated all the time. The position of ordinary employees, for example, has been greatly weakened in recent years because of the collapse in demand for traditionally trained skilled operatives, which has in turn had a huge impact on their capacity to form trade unions. Present organizational structures are just the typical forms of compromise that have come to exist; that is all. What we take as the obvious pattern of a structure of roles for a company is not any such thing; it is just a point that has been arrived at in the relations between groups at a given time. Because the actions adopted by groups are customary as much as instrumental, it is often possible to identify a British pattern of roles making up the structure of a company.

BOX 4.1 **Organization as a source of power**

No collective category, no class, no group of any kind in and of itself wields power or can use it. Another factor must be present: that of organization. Some scholars, among them Charles E. Lindblom, hold that organization, including that manifested in government, is the ultimate source of all power. . . .

Power, especially when its source is in organization, is not a simple . . . thing. We see how much is concealed in the familiar reference to a strong or powerful organization.

For, as individuals and organizations seek to extend their power to win the submission of others to their individual or collective will—so others seek to resist that submission. And as personality, property, and organization and the associated instruments of enforcement are brought to bear in extending power, they are brought to bear in resisting submission.

It is this resistance, not any internal limits on the sources of power or the instruments of its enforcement, that provides the primary restriction on the exercise of power.

J. K. Galbraith (1983: 65 and 79)

4.2 Managers

We take it for granted that managers are key players in any organization and any description of an organization will make the management and its functions and activities central. Many of us find it difficult to imagine an organization actually working without managers to coordinate and control things. This view makes the role of management central to organizations, and suggests that if it were not there, nothing much would happen.

The importance attributed to management can be indicated in many ways. Some discussions of organizational structure, for example, concentrate on the management structure only. Such charts often show the managerial division of labour: they depict the areas of responsibility of different managers, their subordinate managers and so on. The main reason is because the purpose of an organization chart is precisely to map out areas of management responsibility. Who is in control is more important than who is controlled. This emphasizes the importance of management by comparison with other organizational roles. Similarly, many accounts of organizational structure overlook the place of the owners of the organization, a point to which we shall return.

Is management necessary?

It is important to reflect that things were not always like this. There were not always managers. Complex activities requiring extensive coordination and control of large numbers of people have been accomplished throughout history, but there have not always been managers to do them. You might express this idea thus: tasks requiring management skills and abilities have always existed, but managers have not always been there to discharge them. Historically, the peculiarity is what we do now: to specialize coordination and control activities, to make them the sole responsibility of a designated group. The usual thing has been to subordinate such tasks to other roles and not to differentiate them as a specialist activity.

There was not a site manager's office at the foot of the pyramids of Giza when they were being built, nor was there a civil engineering company with a chief executive and a team of specialized managers responsible for the project. It used to be assumed that the labour to build the pyramids must have been slaves, but recent archaeology suggests that every community in ancient Egypt provided some labour on a rotational and voluntary basis. The organizer of the labour to move the blocks of stone for the pyramids was a functionary of the ancient Egyptian state, although the bureaucracy of Ancient Egypt was not at its highest point of development at the time. The Egyptian state was later to develop marked bureaucratic features (Weber 1968: 964). The Egyptian priesthood also gave a religious interpretation to the pyramids (see Box 4.2). To take a more recent example, Napoleon Bonaparte paid little attention to the problems of supplying his armies as they rolled up continental Europe in the early years of the nineteenth century. Indeed, it is thought that Napoleon was a successful general because he firmly concentrated his attention on strategic concerns. For Bonaparte, moving his armies to places where the enemy did not expect them to be was one of his main concerns. He concentrated on generalship, and if this meant making his troops travel light and forage off the land, so be it. In both these examples, management is firmly subordinated to other definitions of the basic task.

In case it is thought that these are historically remote and hence not very good examples, there are many instances from our own day where the tasks of management are subordinated to other activities and priorities. There are many large German companies today in which the top executives are, almost without exception, educated to a high level in the science underpinning the industry in which they are employed; and it is thought necessary and right that they should be so. The chiefs of German chemical companies are chemical engineers usually holding doctorates in chemistry. The same is true for the top executives of German engineering companies. Technical knowledge is held to be the basis of the knowledge required for running a company. *Vorsprung durch Technik* is not just an advertising idea. In Britain and America, there is not seen to be the need for any such connection. In fact, when they join the top management of their company, British managers usually distance themselves from any specialist professional or technical background they may have. This is an interesting contrast which suggests that there are very different traditions in the recruitment practices and activities of managers in different countries.

BOX 4.2 Tasks requiring management skills have always existed ·

During the old kingdom, the cult of Re spread from Heliopolis to the rest of Eqypt until he achieved nationwide recognition, enabling his priesthood to exert great political power. From Dynasty III onwards, the building of pyramids shows that Re had become a powerful influence on funerary beliefs and practices.

In Dynasty III, King Djoser's architect, Imhotep, designed a tomb at Sakarra which consists of six mastaba shapes of ever increasing base measurements, placed on top of each other until the monument reached a height of 60 metres, forming a stepped pyramid.

The ... priests of Re at Heliopolis found a magico-religious explanation for [step pyramids], an explanation which associated the king with their god, Re. It was believed that Re sailed through the sky every day in his Day Barque. What more natural ambition could a dead king have than to join the Sun God on his daily journey and thus spend his Afterlife with him? But how to reach the Barque? Why, by means of a staircase up to heaven. The step pyramids, with the aid of magic spells, provided a stairway to the sky by means which a dead king could join Re in the heavens. . . .

At the end of the Third Dynasty, a straight-sided pyramid was built Meidum, and two more straight-sided pyramids were built at Dahshur for the Fourth-Dynasty king, Sneferu. The earliest geometrically true pyramid is constructed at Giza for Sneferu's son, Khufu, and geometrically true pyramids were built at Giza for Khufu's successors, Khafre and Menkaure. Khafre's tomb is comparable in size with that of his father, whose Great Pyramid is 146 metres high and covers an area of more than 50 000 square metres; Menkaure's pyramid is less than half that size. Together, these three pyramids formed one of the Seven Wonders of the ancient world.

The Giza pyramids were built during one of the most powerful dynasties of Egyptian history, and have been described as an exercise in nationalism.

D. Watterson (1984: 44–6)

Comparatively speaking, it is the British and the Americans who are the oddities. Actually, it is only British and American companies in which it is normal to be a career manager and to make no claim to particular technical competence. However, in some areas traditional thinking survives in this country too: in every single British police authority, the executive head was at one time an ordinary policeman. (He or she is called 'Chief Constable' not Chief Executive.) In almost every university also, the executive head was once upon a time a research fellow or ordinary lecturer. Although some have taken to calling themselves Vice-Chancellor *and* Chief Executive, they usually regard themselves as academics who have turned their hand to management. From the point of view of an employee in such an organization, it is in fact reassuring that this is so. It does matter that the management of the organization has at one time done my job; and not learned how to manage in a baked bean factory.

The notion that the practitioner will also make the best manager is a clear violation of Anglo-American ideas about management. This suggests that management is a generic skill. Management is thought about as a distinct and effective set of practices which can be applied to the coordination of any complex task. According to this view, it does not matter what the task is: a good manager should be able to manage anything from a factory to a public service. This view now tends to be increasingly accepted. In recent history we can see the acceptance of this notion spreading out from its point of invention in the USA in the nineteenth century. Managerialism is a rising—if not already dominant—ideology of our times; it is the leitmotif of our epoch. There is a need to be clear about what changes it supports, justifies, and promotes.

Historically distinct definitions of management

For many years, management tasks were done by people who were not managers in the generic meaning that is now ascendant. Indeed, there has been a noticeable tendency—which will be looked at later when we consider the professions—for technical specialists to take over management. Thus, in American industry at the beginning of the twentieth century, there was an attempt by engineers to take over the activities of management—to define it as an extension of engineering (Weitz and Shenav 2000). Even today there are academics—calling themselves management scientists—who think that the basic expertise of management is (or should be) to apply statistical and mathematical modelling to managerial problems. The origin of management science as it is practised in Britain is in the application of maths and statistics to operational problems encountered in the last war. It is now an academic field called operational research. One of the ways that management continues to be defined, then, is as an appendage to a technical specialism, or as a technical specialism in its own right.

Another way management can be defined and which has endured is as administration. In several European languages, including French and German, there is not a word that translates the meaning of the word management adequately, but there is for the word administration. However, administration is the tendency to turn the tasks of management into a set of routines and procedures which are normally followed. It is a very common response to the realization that there are special problems of coordination and control. It is the tendency of states and the tendency of large organizations wherever they are found. It is a key feature of bureaucracies and what Weber most respected in them. It is because the routines are rational that they are effective. In this definition of management, things are done—decisions are made and resources allocated—by the book. That is, by reference to an established set of procedures and rules. Senior administrators write the book while middle administrators see that the procedures are followed and may advise about amendments to the procedures, whilst junior functionaries simply apply the rules.

There are interesting similarities in the definition of management as a technical specialism and as administration. Both attempt to narrow it down, and make it amenable to being easily communicated and hence being taught. Both take the knotty problems of decision-making and resource allocation and routinize them: they attempt to take the politics out of these things, and often to a considerable degree succeed. These features are attractive, but many think that they both ignore and devalue something essential to the activity of management. For some, management is essentially political. There is much to be said for this view. Try as they do, technical experts and administrators cannot take this element out entirely. In addition, technical definitions of management tend to overlook and downplay the fact that management often takes the lead in innovation, change, and risk-taking. The single word that sums up this aspect of management is entrepreneurship. Entrepreneurship is active—it involves moving things about. It is likely to disturb existing arrangements and give rise to lots of contention. When we look at what managers actually do, we find that it is a mixture of different activities, but negotiation, the active resolution of contentious issues, is at the heart of it. In the memorable phrase of Gowler and Legge (1983), 'The meaning of management is the management of meaning.' This is the view of management that is now ascendant.

Research into management activities

The academics who have tried to analyse management have not fared well in establishing that there is anything but negotiation to be the core activity of the practice (Hales 1986; but see also Tsoukas 1994). It is an almost universal finding—especially from studies in Britain and the USA—that managers spend a great deal of time dealing with people and, in particular, in exchanging information in meetings, on the telephone, and in conversations of all sorts. The findings from recent research by Kotter (1999) are no different in this respect from a string of earlier studies (Carlson 1951; Kotter and Lawrence 1974; Stewart 1976, 1982; and so on). Kotter (1999) suggests that the average manager spends only 25 per cent or his or her time alone, while it is not unusual to find managers with other people for up to 90 per cent of their time. As Stewart (1976) has shown, some of the variation in the activities of managers is explained by the kind of industry the manager is operating in or the kind of manager—whether they are in a general or a technical managerial position for instance. From this research, management involves a wide range of activities. A study that suggests there is a great deal of diversity in what managers do is an early work by Mintzberg (1973). This suggests that management can be analysed as comprising no less than ten different activities or roles. These types of analysis tend to support the view that management is a broad bundle of activities, the common theme of which is communication and negotiation.

Unqualified 'generalist' managers

British management practice as it has emerged does tend to conform to this picture. It is the case that the British management cadre has emerged as a group which does not have—or make any claim to—technical expertise. It draws most strongly on the administrative definition of management, either the technical or the entrepreneurial definition. Recruits to management are typically selected from amongst the recruits to an industry; what they will know about management derives from their experience of the industry, rather than from theoretical knowledge. Surprising though it may be, the attained educational level has always been low for this occupation—and much lower than is found in most other advanced countries.

Surveys of samples of British managers show that the proportion of them with degrees (of any kind) was around 20 per cent in the early 1950s, rising to around 30 per cent by the beginning of the 1980s (Savage *et al.* 1992: 71). Some of the largest surveys have shown the lowest proportions of managers with degrees and other qualifications, though this may be because they have

---

BOX 4.3 **Management education in the 1980s**

Overall the UK has about 2.75 million people exercising managerial roles, 1.1 million of whom are in senior or middle management positions. Yet of these, only 116 000 had first or higher degrees in 1981, and over two-thirds of a million had no formal qualifications at all. And lacking formal qualifications, they often lack formal training as well. The Constable and McCormick study for the BIM/CBI found 90 000 people entering management roles each year in the UK. 'The great majority of them', they reported, 'have no prior formal education and training', and on average, as managers, would receive only one day's off-the-job training a year. . . .

Of course, it is more common in the UK than abroad for managers, once in post, to study part-time for professional qualifications of various sorts. This is particularly the case in the engineering industry, the stronghold in Britain of the part-time qualification, and in accountancy; but still, in general, there is no getting away from the fact that the lack of formal education and training 'runs through the whole supervisory structure, and does not occur only in the director's offices'. As Barsoux and Lawrence observed, 'compared with their counterparts in other advanced nations, British managers are still under-educated and poorly trained.'

David Coates (1994: 141)

included all levels of management in such broad-ranging studies. Given the huge rise in the proportion of the population going to university between 1950 and 1980 the proportion of managers with higher education has declined relative to the general population. The proportion of managers with education from the elite universities is tiny. Writing in the 1980s, Handy reports that 85 per cent of top managers in Japan and the USA have degrees, many of them from the best universities. The comparable figure for Britain was only 24 per cent having a degree of any sort (Handy 1987: 1). Other estimates from about the same time suggest that only about 4 per cent of British managers had degrees, whilst up to a quarter had no qualifications at all! (Nichols 1986: 108; Constable and McCormick 1987: 3).

The lack of an adequate education for managers is a deeply rooted tendency and will take some time to change. But what is more serious is the lack of perceived need for education for this occupation. There is not just a rejection of the idea of the value of technical education, but of the idea that management expertise can be and should be taught. There is a widespread view that management is a practical skill that is best acquired by doing the job rather than as a result of education and training. Correlli Barnett, a perceptive commentator on this issue, argued that British manufacturing has 'lagged badly in advanced industries like chemicals, electrical and machine tools, and even in basics like steel, partly because of a lack of trained personnel at all levels' (Barnett 1985: 681). He pointed to 'the survival of the practical man over vast tracts of British industry' (Barnett 1985: 685). Even today, it is a commonly held view that graduate recruits to management must also learn their trade as managers, on an informal apprenticeship basis. On the other hand, the wholesale reduction of middle management, which is occurring today, may be, at least in part, a recognition of its general lack of competence.

In many respects British business practices are similar to those found in America; so much so that commentators are apt to lump Britain and the USA together and to refer to 'the Anglo-American system' (see for example Scott 1997: 55–92). However, this is not so for management education, where there are important differences. A much higher proportion of American managers are graduates. There have been much more concerted attempts to professionalize management education, and to base general management expertise in formalized education. The MBA has been available to American managers for a century or more, whereas in Britain the provision of such courses is a recent development. Although the provision of MBA courses has expanded greatly in this country in the last twenty years, a disproportionate number of graduates from such courses taught in Britain are from overseas. The number graduating is still a tiny proportion of the output from American Schools. Each year one new MBA graduate per 2000 members of the working population is added in the USA. The comparable figure for Britain is one new MBA per 22000. On this measure, the British higher education system is more than ten times less productive than the American. Management in this country has never become very professionalized, as has been fully exposed in debates about management education (Constable and McCormick 1987; Handy 1987; Reed and Anthony 1992).

Management in the UK, even at the highest level, seems to have remained remarkably generalist despite the emergence of large-scale organization. One reason why the management role is seen as general and not technical is that there is much awareness of the essentially contested and political nature of corporate relationships. Yet British managers, like their American counterparts, have opened out for themselves an area in which they exercise considerable authority. While we have to explain the particular qualities (or lack of them) of the British managers, this occupational group has been successful in developing a sphere of operation for itself.

4.3 Managers and owners

Organization predates management. As we have seen, for much of history there was no such occupation as that of the salaried manager—a group that routinely exercises control over businesses which it does not own. Originally, as can be seen from the quotation from Braudel in the last chapter (see page 54) the first companies were constituted by their members, who owned the assets. Typically this owning group was a family who would employ 'servants' to work for the company in much the same way that servants were used within a household. But the work—especially that of managing—would be done by the owners themselves. The arrival of the salaried manager did not occur in the space of a single generation. Because there was often not any purchasable stock in early companies, it was difficult to expand an owning group beyond the original founders. Nor was there an assumption of unlimited growth: it was assumed that the company would not expand beyond the size an owning family could handle for itself. Companies, like monarchies, might well discontinue if there were not enough family members to succeed to ownership.

Historians usually describe the process by which the owners of companies gradually accepted the need to cede control of their companies to salaried managers: people who would run the company on their behalf. This was an inevitable development once—with the growth of markets and the achievement of limited liability for owners—the growth of companies was established as normal. However, the system of control by salaried managers acting as the agents took time to be established and institutionalized as a workable system. Initially there were considerable problems of trust, with employees regularly stealing the company's assets—'embezzling' as it was called. Only gradually did the managerial group come to acquire its modern attributes as an occupation offering reliability, trustworthiness, and independence.

Today, the manager's role has become so important that observers often overlook the fact that, legally, managers only control companies because they are employed to do so by the owners. Just as organizational charts often do not show the ordinary employees, they also show the structure as culminating in the office of the chief executive. The authority of this office actually comes from a committee representing the owners; that is, from the board of directors. The legal position of the company chief is reflected in the title of his or her position: Chief Executive. Historically at least, what this person did was merely 'execute' the policies of the owners or of the board. Policy for the direction of any company is, or should be, decided by the board: what the executives do is execute policy; that is all. The traditional British title for the position of company head—managing director—is also revealing. He/she is a director who also manages. For this reason organizations should not be depicted as a triangle with a single point at the apex, but, rather, as Henry Mintzberg (1993) draws them, showing a group—the board of directors—at the top.

The persistence of family control

In the absence of devices for broadening the social base of recruitment in the West, and in the face of the rapid growth in the size of businesses, the kinship basis for recruitment caused a serious problem of business organization. If the only eligible recruits to management were restricted to a few sons or male first cousins, then there was likely to be a recurrent problem of sustaining effective management. After the Industrial Revolution as the nineteenth century progressed, firms had a tendency to grow rapidly and could become large in the space of a generation or two (20–40 years). The pattern of company control that is developed in any place will depend on traditional patterns of families and the law in relation to companies as well as economic factors such as the need for capital. In Britain and other Western countries, family control of businesses declined inexorably as businesses became large and the need for capital led to the relaxation of the law relating to the ownership of company assets.

In Eastern societies where capitalism has developed, the direct control of business by families is still important and seems likely to continue to be so. In businesses belonging to Chinese people in Taiwan, for example, firms retain family management because they are often split into smaller units. The family is understood to encompass a wider range of kin in most parts of the East than is typical in the West. An interesting expedient used strategically in Japan to perpetuate family control was adoption. The Japanese have a tradition of adoption by which the able and favoured employees can become adopted members of the owning family (Alletzhauser 1990; Kerbo and McKinstry 1995). Such people are recruits to the family and not merely the management of the family company. Strategic strengthening of the kinship system in this and other ways has contributed strong control of the economy in Japan by the ruling elite (Kerbo and McKinstry 1995). Many cultures—including the Western—have used recruitment through marriage to perpetuate a dynasty.

Family control of business has been retained in other societies for longer than in the West for a variety of reasons. However, in Europe and America, family control has been much more tenacious than is widely believed. In Britain, family owner-managers persisted well into the twentieth century in many large British companies (Payne 1984; Elbaum and Lazonick 1986; Scott 1997). Even today, there are numerous large British companies that are privately owned and where the majority of the stock is still owned by family members. A sizeable proportion of our largest companies continue to have such representation of the original owning family as members of their boards that they are, effectively, controlled by that family. Scott noted, for example, that 'about a third of the top enterprises were family-owned in 1954 and 1966' (Scott 1997: 81). However, Scott notes the decline of the numbers of firms subjected to family control in his most recent research.

The significance of joint-stock ownership

In the West, a key device to expand company ownership, assisting the emergence of the independent salaried manager, was the early adoption of joint-stock ownership. In the first companies all members of the company directly owned a share of the companies' assets. But, in the beginning, these shares were not readily sold or transferred and an owner could not take his investment out unless the company was disbanded. The invention of transferable share certificates—and the development of markets in which they could be traded—substantially solved the problem of companies acquiring capital for growth. The joint-stock company, as those with transferable ownership are called, is often thought of simply as a solution to the problem of capital supply for growing companies.

As companies grow large they require larger and larger pools of capital which can be raised by retained profits, loans (from banks, say), or by raising money by the sale of shares on the stock market. It is true that large companies could and did outgrow the ability and the willingness of an owning family to supply the capital necessary for expansion. Joint-stock financing also solves the problem of family recruitment to management because it admits a larger group to a share of ownership. But it does this in such a way that it potentially

BOX 4.4 **The decline of family ownership in Britain**

Like the United States, Britain has experienced a long-term decline in the number of large family-owned enterprises. The formation of a 'big business' sector, however, was somewhat slower in Britain, and the smaller size of the British national economy meant that the founding entrepreneurs and their heirs came under far less pressure to dilute their controlling shareholdings until relatively late in the present century. Many of the largest enterprises at the turn of the century were the long-established railway, dock, and canal companies in which more dispersed forms of ownership already existed; but a large number of them, especially those in manufacturing industry, were family-owned, and this number increased for the first part of the century. . . .

Florence's data also suggest that the decline in family ownership was associated with a shift from personal shareholding to institutional shareholding and a consequent increase in the number of enterprises that were controlled through constellations of interests.

Although there was an increase in the number of enterprises without a dominant ownership interest, there was also an increase in the number where the top twenty shareholders held between 10 and 20 per cent of the capital. This move towards control through a constellation of interests was strongly confirmed in a study for 1975, which found that 39 per cent of the top 250 British non-financials had no holder with as much as 5 per cent of the capital, and a further 10 per cent of enterprises in which no holder held more than 10 per cent. Almost half the large enterprises were, however, found still to be majority– or minority–controlled by a cohesive group. . . . About a third of the top 250 of 1976 were wholly owned or majority controlled, and a further 20 per cent were minority controlled (Scott 1986). Over a half of the top 250, then, were subject to control by a dominant shareholding interest or a group of closely allied interests. Among the companies with a dominant controlling interest, the largest single category comprised the 46 family-controlled enterprises, this personal ownership being equally divided between the majority and minority forms.

John Scott (1997: 80–4)

transforms the basis of company control. An owning family may easily lose control of their company more fully than they might wish: as the family's ownership is diluted, so will its capacity exclusively to direct policy in the use of company resources.

Even when there is an absence of family control, it is not appropriate to assume that the salaried managers can manage in their own way without hindrance. The boards of companies still control the broad policies and activities of companies. Boards are aptly named boards of directors, for direct is what they traditionally do. Where the boards of companies are not directed by family interests, they are, nonetheless, directed in one way or another. Scott refers to a 'control by a constellation of interests' (Scott 1997) by which he means to draw attention to the fact that identifiable factions on company boards can exert control over companies. However, joint-stock ownership and the wide dispersion of share ownership has fundamentally altered the politics of company control.

Again—although there are some similarities—this is an area in which British and American experience and practice is decisively different from other countries. In these countries the independence of managers is marked.

The interests of salaried managers and owners' representatives are not exactly the same. These groups are likely to disagree over such things as the salaries and benefits coming to the managers and the dividends going to shareholders. They may also differ over policy concerning the development of the company: the extent to which the business should be made to grow, or the precise choice of direction in which it should develop. Where significant managerial independence develops, company policies are likely to pursue the priorities of managers over those of shareholders. Boards are a source of pressure for managers whether or not they are representing the views of shareholders, and who they represent may also be important.

It is a recurrent finding from research, for example, that in Britain institutional investors such as insurance companies, unit trusts, and pension funds, which are interested in obtaining high returns, are strongly represented on the boards of large companies. Such investors are primarily motivated by the need for high profits, and the long-term growth of the value of the company is a secondary consideration. Such groups will withdraw their shareholdings if they do not get the returns they expect on a regular basis, pushing the company share price down, and making it a potential takeover target. However, management is likely to experience little interference from its board only so long as the company concerned remains profitable and sustains a good price for its shares.

Issues in company governance

The matter we are now considering is called company governance. This refers to the arrangements between the groups at the top of companies: who belongs to them and what their respective powers and responsibilities are. Considering the effects of different arrangements of governance is a complicated subject. There are three parties to governance structures, each of which has overlapping membership. Firstly, there are owners (the shareholders) which is a large group (there are millions of shares available in a major company). Some of these will hold many shares and will expect to have their opinions heard and to have representation on the board. In addition, there are significant individual holders of blocs of shares and institutional shareholders. These distinctions can be decisive in deciding the direction of policy that companies may adopt. Secondly, there is the board of directors itself. This will have directors selected because of their ownership, directors selected because of their expertise (non-executive directors), and directors who are managers of the company. Finally, there is the senior management of the company: some of whom will also be directors of the company. This group obviously includes the managing director or CEO. Clearly the outcome of the (essentially political) processes associated with governance will vary a good deal in different companies and in different circumstances.

Given the size and economic influence of major companies it is remarkable how little attention is given to questions of their governance, with some honourable exceptions (Scott 1986, 1991, 1997; Charkham 1994). True, there have been numerous studies by econometricians—typically looking for statistical relationships between executives' pay and company performance—but these are unlikely to cast light on the overall effectiveness and fairness of these arrangements. The constitutions and arrangements for the governance of countries are exhaustively studied, and the effects of their constitution and

---

BOX 4.5 **Problems of governance**

During the last decade I have heard at first hand from countless directors *how poorly the UK governance system often works*. This is in flat contrast to what one hears at any general meeting of the good and great of industry whose companies are on the whole impeccably run; it seems axiomatic on both sides of the Atlantic that any meeting about the reform of corporate governance is attended only by industrialists whose companies do not need it. Even so, there are 2 000 quoted British companies, *and the evidence I have seen has convinced me that nothing less than a major review is now required*, with the government at the end of it being ready to put its own shoulder to the wheel of enforcement instead of leaving it to others. . . .

No one who talks to any of the protagonists in the worlds of commerce, politics, unions, or even in its own way academe, has the slightest doubt that beneath the elegant logic and complex arguments, the basic dynamics are those of power. Everyone speaks their own book. . . .

It is little wonder, therefore, that governments tread gently if they move at all. . . . There must be some doubt, however, about the adequacy of the process of consulting the interested parties. It is no use asking butchers whether to eat meat or a fiddler to be dispassionate about help for the arts. . . . Consultations with powerful 'interests' do nothing to protect those affected but not technically 'interested'. The government has a far more difficult task—to consider those whom the interested parties' actions affect, and that includes society as a whole. It is a fallacy to believe that the common good will be served by leaving it solely to the interested parties, as Adam Smith recognized. . . .

The joint stock company is a legal construct, not a product of nature. It is not interventionist or dirigiste for governments to ensure that the balance of interests between all parties affected by companies is maintained. The Companies Act now creaks in some fundamental ways

Jonathan Charkham (1994: 340–1), emphasis added

associated systems of politics are examined minutely by academics. By contrast, study of the governance of companies, large or small, is only beginning. However, it is widely believed today that the owner interest is often too weakly represented on company boards and that the managers have too much power. The executives of many British companies have recently secured significant independence from control by their boards and secured large rises in their pay.

BOX 4.6 **Who is in the driving seat?**

Cable & Wireless chief executive Graham Wallace remained relaxed yesterday after a shareholder revolt failed to stop a controversial incentive plan that could see him awarded share options worth £4.5m, six times his salary. Mr Wallace said he was 'not concerned', despite 29 per cent of voters rejecting the package at the annual meeting of the telecoms group. The shares, which have plunged more than 75 per cent this year, closed down 6 at 349p, a five-year low. Mr Wallace said Cable and Wireless had consulted large shareholders on the scheme. However, four major institutions, representing 10 per cent of the shareholding, voted against the deal. They included Schroders Investment Management, which holds 3 per cent of the company and Hermes Investment Management, which holds 1.25 per cent. Standard Life Investments, which owns just under 2 per cent, and Barclays Global Investors, which owns around 3 per cent, are believed to be the other two big institutions involved.

Under the Incentive Plan 2001, Mr Wallace would be awarded £4.5m worth of options if the company's total shareholder return is in the top 25 per cent of the FTSE Global Telecoms Sector Index between the third and fifth anniversary of the grant of the option. Under the same scheme, the company's top 100 executives could get options worth up to four times their salary. Most of the revolting shareholders were angered, however, that half of the options would be awarded if the company's performance was only average compared with peers. Michelle Edkins, director of corporate governance at Hermes, said: 'They should only get such awards for strong, clear, exceptional performance. This scheme means the directors can be awarded generously for running and standing still.' Speaking after the meeting, Mr Wallace said: 'The tougher the performance criteria are in share options schemes, the less attractive employees find them and that is a basic fact. This issue is not only about aligning the interests of directors with shareholders, the biggest part is about how do we retain and recruit the best people.'

The disgruntled shareholders called on the company to take notice of the result. Miss Edkins said: 'I think directors should be concerned about such a significant vote against them. Institutions don't vote against the management lightly, but we have to protect our clients. They are pension funds whose members don't earn that much money on the whole.' Earlier this year C&W was forced to make 4 000 redundancies because of pricing pressures for its services in the US and Japan, which sent underlying profits tumbling almost 20 per cent to £871m. The company came under fire yesterday for its decision, announced at the time, to cut its dividend from next year onwards, to reflect the changing shape of the business.

Dominic White, *Daily Telegraph Business* 14 July 2001

Increasingly executive pay is supplemented by share allocations and share 'options' (i.e. shares that they may buy at their discretion often at a fixed price). It is thought that managers pay themselves too much and have too much influence on policy, and that this is a bad thing for company prosperity. Commentators have long argued, not without reason, that executives are acquiring growing independence generally (Berle and Means 1947; Chandler 1977; Fligstein 1990). This process is continuing in Britain today.

4.4 Managers and professionals

The American economic historian Alfred Chandler (1977) argued that the creation of a 'professional' management, by which he means salaried and technically qualified, occurs in a more or less direct ratio to increases in organizational size. In his discussion of the emergence of large-scale industry in the USA, Chandler contended that: 'The careers of the salaried managers who directed these (new) hierarchies became increasingly technical and professional' (Chandler 1977: 8). He argues that, as companies become larger, the number of managers increases in proportion. In Britain, there was a tendency to employ technical specialists from the beginning of the nineteenth century. Such people as engineers, accountants and chemists adopted the traditional form of professional organization, and were largely excluded from the top management of companies. Professions received little sponsorship from the state, as has been the case in continental Europe (Campagnac and Winch 1997) and have remained highly independent. Despite the increased employment of technical specialists, senior management having a non-technical bias has remained dominant in the UK until the present day.

In Britain, professional management did not emerge in the manner suggested by Chandler. Businesses became large before salaried managers were employed in numbers and even then there was a preference for general managers qualified by experience. The view of Savage and his co-authors about the development of the British management cadre tends to support this conclusion. They write: 'A distinct managerial grouping did emerge (by the early decades of the twentieth century) but it remained weak and subordinate. . . . Managers continued to be dependent on their capitalist employers' (Savage *et al.* 1992: 49). This dependence of professional managers was ideological in character. Owing in part to the constitution of company boards (on which institutional investors were strongly represented) and in part to the lack of involvement of bankers in company affairs, the main concern of the management of British companies often seemed to be simply the continued profitability of the concern. Certainly, also, the top management of British companies did not develop a strong identification with technical expertise as a basis for its authority. There seemed to be only a weak tendency for the directors of companies to be drawn in large numbers from the ranks of professionals having relevant expertise, as in Germany.

The subordination of professionals to generalists

Even in industries where, of necessity, such groups were strongly represented, such as engineering, senior managers were usually not a dominant voice on company boards. A study of the vehicle industry in Britain, for example, showed that, between the two world wars and after, and with recurrent cash flow problems, car companies reduced and marginalized the engineering professionals represented on company boards. Even where they were set up by engineers in the first place, such as the Austin car company, directors of British companies often were not able to ensure that product development concerns were given the highest priority when major strategic decisions were made (Ackroyd and Lawrenson 1995). A profit-conscious and generalist management controlling industry has been relatively unreceptive to the qualities of management by technically specialized professionals.

In Britain, there are large numbers of professionally qualified employees. Obviously in production companies, there must be many designers and engineers, chemists and technologists. Clearly also, such groups have the power to organize production. They are, however, excluded from general power within management and so define their competences in narrow rather than broad ways. Professionals themselves occupy distinct enclaves as technical experts within management (Ackroyd 1996). Generally, they recognize that they will have to shed any professional identification they have if and when they become admitted to the senior management of a company. The extent of this specialization in Britain and the effects of the attendant competition between professional groups has seldom been fully appreciated, except by researchers working in a comparative framework. However, the analyst who has done most to expose the extent of the peculiarity of the sharp division of labour amongst professional groups in UK management is Armstrong (Armstrong 1984, 1985, 1986, 1987a, 1987b, 1989). Beginning with papers that have identified the conflicts between groups of 'professionals in management'—which we must distinguish from management professionals—he has passed on to the detailed discussion of particular professions—engineering, accountancy, and personnel management.

BOX 4.7 **The soft control of professionals**

Organisational Control need not be exerted exclusively in a formal way; it can be as effective using softer methods. . . . The desired effect of softer methods is that a balance between professionals' needs and managerial goals results in a commitment to the organisation's mission. It is a people-centred form of control. . . . Since professionals do not see themselves as inferior to management (certainly when it comes to knowledge and expertise), they tend to prefer control systems allowing more discretion. . . .

Professionals desire to work in an atmosphere relatively free from pressure and conducive to personal autonomy and creativity. *Although they may need to be reminded from time to time about the overall objectives of the organization*, direct orders or formal and impersonal controls will be no more effective in inducing commitment to the enterprise than give-and-take conversations. The ultimate aim of control interactions with professionals is to demonstrate how voluntary compliance with basic organizational procedures, accompanied by self-imposed personal and professional controls, serves their self-interest. As the professional gradually adapts to the corporate culture, the manager can rely more and more on professional self-management and peer control rather than having to resort to excessive external operating rules.

Joe Raelin (1986: 232–3) emphasis added

Failed collective mobility projects

Armstrong makes use of Larson's conception of the 'collective mobility project' (Larson 1977; Abbott 1988) in which professional groups organize themselves to enhance their status. According to Armstrong (1985), by offering techniques to solve particular and pressing problems within the capitalist enterprise, professionals prove their value to management. They can use such projects as the basis for bids to acquire more power and authority within organizations. Hence, well-placed and knowledgeable professional groups will take over the control of management, especially if they can promote the importance of particular new kinds of expertise. This does seem to have been achieved by professional groups in some countries, Germany and Japan being obvious examples, where engineers are in control of whole tracts of manufacturing industry. This sort of analysis is, then, more than plausible, but it does not explain the extent to which, although they have not been successful in taking over the management of British firms, professional groups nonetheless preserve their distinct identities in the UK and there is sometimes intense competition between them. In this country there is little to break down the separate identities of different professional groups. There is little unifying ideology, either emanating from elite professionals, as in France (Burrage and Torstendhal 1990; Lane 1995) or from general management education.

Armstrong argues that engineers in the UK might well have acted as they have evidently done in Germany and Japan. However, the extent of such tendencies and their likelihood of success are both exaggerated in his account. On the other hand, as Armstrong also argues, a professional group that does seem to have been influential in British management is accountants. Chartered accountants are the most numerous professional group on company boards, and organizations whose main policy considerations are formed by accountancy considerations have been identified (BTR, the Hanson Trust, and other conglomerates). It has been argued convincingly by the American institutionalist author Fligstein that accountants became increasingly represented and influential on American company boards during the twentieth century (Fligstein 1990). This is despite the huge growth of the engineering profession in the early decades of the twentieth century. The rise to influence of the accountancy profession is a plausible argument for the UK as well, but the detailed research to back this conclusion has not yet been undertaken. It would certainly fit with the emphasis of British management on profit-making: how else do you decide if you can declare a profit other than by asking your accountant? A comment by a leading commentator on British industrial performance, David Coates, is suggestive. Coates writes: 'What the UK is good at producing is accountants. There are now over 120 000 qualified accountants in Britain, but only 4000 in Germany and 6000 in Japan; and UK boards of directors are disproportionately prone to be full of them' (Coates 1994: 140). Roughly speaking, then, one in every 230 working people in Britain is an accountant whilst the comparable figure for Germany is one per 8000 and for Japan one per 21000 of the active population.

In summary, there is a distinctive tendency in Britain for professional groups employed in industry to retain their own distinct professional identity and ideals. In addition, professional groups—other than accountants—have tended to be excluded from the higher levels of management. If people with professional qualifications are recruited to senior management, it is because of their general ability and not because they are seen to have relevant expertise. As collectivities, professional groups in this country are perhaps too imbued with anti-entrepreneurial values either to seek, or be allowed to occupy, the commanding heights of industry.

4.5 Management and labour

Eventually, in the late nineteenth and early twentieth centuries, large organizations did emerge in Britain. This is usually dated as beginning in a serious way in a period of economic consolidation following a deep and long lasting economic depression at the end of the nineteenth century (1883–96). Thus, the sustained development of large businesses occurred some 150 years after the Industrial Revolution began in this country; and must be seen as a new phase of development in economic organization. In that period, Britain was feeling for the first time the acute pressure of competition from rapidly developing economies in other parts of the world. The second wave of industrial powers—in the shape of the huge economies of the USA and Germany—were having an impact on British markets and the profitability of British firms. The response was a wave of mergers and industrial consolidations allowing British firms to develop economies of scale and become larger.

Before this, small business had predominated, and the success of the British economy as the 'workshop of the world' and the only supplier of manufactured products was built on dense concentrations of small firms in specialized industrial areas. It was, in fact, small firms working in concert which together produced the quantity and variety of manufactured goods on which Britain's initial industrial prosperity was based. In this small business capitalism, skilled labour had flourished and had been extensively utilized. The most powerful and effective trade unions, which began to emerge around the middle of the nineteenth century, were those of the skilled workers, and the work of large numbers of skilled artisans was indispensable to the early British industrial capitalism. When industry began to consolidate to meet foreign competition, it did not do so by dispensing with skilled labour. Around the turn of the twentieth century, the working class in general was developing its power bases and extending its industrial organization (in the form of unions) to political representation by acquiring the vote and forming political alliances (in the form of the TUC and the Labour Party). Despite some intense confrontations between capital and labour before the First World War, management was not able to remove skilled labour.

The persistence of skilled labour

British managers found that they could not deal with labour in the manner that was undertaken in the USA, where the ideas of management consultants like Frederick Taylor (1911) were influential. Taylor, who is usually identified as the originator of the system of scientific management, proposed the introduction of what is now known as job design. In this, tasks are made as simple as possible so that they can be undertaken by unskilled labour. Although variants of 'Taylorism' did become extensively utilized in this country, their adoption was resisted by both skilled labour and groups of managers until the 1930s if not later (Littler 1982). Even then, the uptake of scientific management was initially sparse. The extent to which these techniques were used, and the nature of their impact on people's work and lives, are issues which have generated much research and discussion. Much of this has centred on the ideas of Braverman, an American scholar who argued that the thrust of most modern management as it developed in the USA was to take skill away from labour—to deskill it—and so to reduce the wages paid for labour (Braverman 1974).

It is now generally agreed that deskilling, which has the aim of breaking the power of organized labour and also of reducing the wages paid to production workers, is a recurrent goal of management (Thompson 1984). However, subsequent research has sought to modify Braverman's basic thesis. Littler (1982), for example, showed how scientific management developed in different ways in different countries. It was not until the 1930s—during a period of sustained depression when labour was generally weak—that scientific management was introduced into British industry in a concerted way. Even then it was not introduced in the full-blown form of Taylorism with any success. Partly for this reason, mass production techniques were also not introduced in the form that was possible in the USA. Friedman (1977) has drawn a useful distinction between the managerial policy towards labour of 'direct control' (of which scientific management is a developed version) and the policy of extending 'responsible autonomy' (which leaves workers to organize themselves in return for self-discipline). Where workers were skilled and work relatively complex, it is often less costly to acknowledge this and to achieve control of labour indirectly. For this reason, the initial rise of big business in Britain largely left skilled labour alone.

By the 1930s, British factory owners had worked out their own variants of labour control which featured piecework incentives combined with the use of skilled labour. It can be argued with some plausibility that British managers never undertook thorough programmes of scientific management on the American pattern. Certainly, American mass production techniques (often called 'Fordism') were found difficult to reproduce or approximate in this country, even in industries where they were thought most appropriate. Mass production facilities, based on the use of formally unskilled labour, were only introduced into British industry at a very late stage, in the 1950s and 1960s, provoking mass confrontations between management and labour in the car industry. The irony of this was that mass production was pushed through at huge cost at a time when the mass markets (which made these techniques appropriate) were already breaking down and disappearing.

The significance of recent developments

Much of this has now changed because many British firms have changed their patterns of activity. There has been change in most sectors of the economy including, among other things, that manufacturing firms have substantially withdrawn from attempting the mass production of complex products. The indicators of the extent of the changes are numerous: there is the reduction in the numbers of people employed in individual organizations, there is the stripping out of middle management, and there is the collapse of the demand for traditionally trained skilled labour (Gospel 1995). The power of organized labour has been reduced, but the capacity for autonomous working remains.

The mechanisms behind this have been revealed to some extent through the above discussion. Changes in the resources available have allowed senior managers to reconfigure their businesses and initiate waves of change that have affected social life as well as economic organization. Taking advantage of the availability of new and powerful IT systems and the liberalization of access to finance, new ways of producing profitably have been sought by senior managers. This shift in the balance of power within organizations has led to yet more activity in reconfiguring their companies by managers, and to the emergence of an international elite of senior managers.

4.6 Management as mediation between stakeholders

The realization that management is a group that stands between a range of other groups with divergent interests has led to the view that the fundamental role of management is that of mediation. This is sometimes linked to the idea that there are numerous parties that have a 'stake' in companies, and hence it is the role (and even the duty) of management to balance the interests of these parties. An account of management, which defines the central task as mediating the interests of different groups with an interest in the firm, has been accepted for some time (Newman and Rowbottom 1968). Twiss and Weinshall (1980) first developed this view of management. A version of this is now in textbooks (Wilson and Rosenfeld 1990; Huczynski and Buchanan 2000). What we might call the mediation approach to management suggests that managers stand at the interface of many competing and to some extent opposing interests, which nonetheless in some way have to be mediated in the interests of the corporation.

In addition to shareholders, who want higher dividends and perhaps longer-term growth, professional employees want more resources and to have their expertise to be taken more seriously, employees would like more wages and more interesting things to do—there are other groups with interests in the company. These are: bankers and other lenders, who want higher interest and short-term loans; government departments, which want higher taxes and fewer subsidies; customers, who want quality goods at lower prices; suppliers, who want higher prices for their products, longer credits, and longer delivery times, and so on. The manager stands between all these competing claimants or stakeholders, and has to reconcile their demands whilst still making gains.

As we have seen, research into management activities suggests that managers are highly interactive and communicative. This is consistent with the idea that they are constantly negotiating between stakeholders. But it would be an error to think that management is purely a neutral means of reconciling the interests of different parties. Business generates surpluses that could not be created without the cooperative activity of employees. This does not mean that such surpluses are fairly distributed. Management of a firm is the dominant group in a field of other groups all holding some power.

Supervisory and middle management as negotiation

The mediation view of management does apply to middle and supervisory management. They do not exercise significant power by comparison with senior managers. They are excluded from strategic decisions with long-term consequences. At the lower levels of management particularly, it is often inappropriate to think that management does anything other than broker cooperation and so ensure that work continues smoothly. Job specifications do not allow time to spare for planning: it is not an expected part of the role, and solving immediate problems is a central concern; for example, shifting bottlenecks and moving things around to prevent one potential crisis after another. Managers call this 'fire fighting' and bemoan that they have to do it (whilst, secretly, many of them love every minute). Because of corporate change supervisory and middle management is becoming more and more interactive.

At middle management level, politics can be intense, because managers do see it as part of their job to push for change and their projects can conflict with the ideas of other factions (see Box 4.8). In practice, because it is so centrally involved with mediation between different and partly opposed interests, the role of management is riven with contradictions, cross-pressure, and conflict. Time has to be spent by managers coping with and reconciling the conflicts as best they can. But before we decide that the role of management is impossibly difficult and the wise person would have nothing to do with it, it is well to bear in mind that managers do, often, achieve some practical reconciliation of the demands of the contending parties whilst still leaving a surplus. Business organization is a money-making machine; and it generates surpluses effectively. These surpluses may belong to the owners, but what happens to them is in the power of management to decide. The process by which management has acquired more importance and more independence is best thought of as a process by which this group has acquired the power and resources with which to act more autonomously.

BOX 4.8 **The politics of middle management**

I have a long-term strategy here. I know that in order to either get him to change, or to get rid of him, my department has to take a controlling hand in his account. That is where all of his power comes from. It's not his personality, it's not his background, he doesn't have friends in high places. It comes purely from that account. So, I have to take control of that. And I do that through selecting and motivating and encouraging my team to go in there with a certain agenda. . . .

[J]ust make yourself very important in there. Make it so that the business is coming through you. Keep Simon in copy of everything you do. But if you are developing the order yourself, if you're bringing that order out, and then you inform Simon what's Simon's purpose in there any more? He's no longer required. His power is getting less, to the point where I think he'll know that he no longer has any influence and on he'll move from that. So the politics, my fighting against him, is working on behalf of the organization.

So, bit by bit, I squeeze him tighter and tighter. I think another six months to a year and I'll have him out. Which is nasty, I know. I consider that to be a professional approach. I consider that because I don't believe that his attitude and his motivations are for the good of the organization. Whereas I consider mine to be. . . .

Yes it can be damaging and time-consuming. We've had a number of situations recently where Simon has threatened to resign. I very nearly had enough of it. Just couldn't be bothered with the fighting anymore. So there are times when it becomes a very negative thing. But I believe the outcome will be positive for the organization. I've not sat and worked it out on paper but there is a cost-benefit there. . . .

The fact [is] that Simon might be thrown on the streets at the end of this. The fact [is] that he's 37 years old and possibly is going to struggle to get another job. [That he is] Recently married, hoping for children . . . actually doesn't come into it at all. In my perception, he is damaging to the company, and he is certainly damaging to me. So he's got to go. Or change. I'll give him the choice. He can do one or the other. . . .

Incident Report 2: from Buchanan and Badham (1999: 83–4)

Senior management and strategy

The power and independence of management is most clearly seen when we consider the activity of senior managers. It is this group that decides on strategic developments. This function has fallen to the managers because they have increasingly taken over the functions of determining the strategic policies of their companies. When it comes to important decisions, senior managers are still dependent on their boards of directors, particularly to finance the activities they decide to undertake. Hence, concerning key decisions about such matters as deciding on changes of direction, and major changes in organization, managers make decisions with the agreement of their boards. But let us not make any mistake, the widespread changes in the forms of organizations to be seen today have their origin in the decisions of these

---

BOX 4.9 **One of a new breed: the chief executive of Spirent Plc**

Nicholas Brookes is the Spirent chief executive. Brookes was recruited to the board of what was then Bowthorpe Ltd in 1995. Before his appointment, Bowthorpe was a well-established firm designing and fabricating a wide range of electrical and electronic products and components. In 1994 the Company had a strong engineering emphasis, and had grown organically from modest beginnings. The executive head was an engineer, Dr John Westhead (appointed, 1980). Prof W. A. Penny, an engineering academic, was an influential non-executive director (appointed 1992). Bowthorpe had multi-divisional organisation with 12 divisions and 97 operating companies. The company had a market capitalisation of £540m, a turnover of £417m and 6 324 employees.

Brookes joined Bowthorpe after 20 years at Texas Instruments, working mostly in America. He had risen through the ranks to become one of the company's four vice-presidents and the only non-American on the board. Describing it as 'a very Texan company' it became clear to him that the board would never appoint a British expatriate as chief executive. So when Bowthorpe's headhunters gave him a call in 1995, he was ready to move back to Britain. What he found came as a terrible shock. 'I didn't find it different at all and that was the problem.' Things hadn't changed. Brookes was appointed chief executive at Bowthorpe at the start of 1996 when he was 49 years old.

'At Bowthorpe, I discovered directors' dining rooms', he says, screwing up his face in disgust. The dining rooms went, along with all of the divisional structure and the majority of the operating companies. There was allegedly some duplication of activity, but the main thrust of the new business strategy was to divest businesses that were not earning high profits and/or were not seen as central to the main area of activity. Brookes decided to concentrate the Company's activities on telecommunications. 'There were so many opportunities', he said.

Brookes also rid the company of what he regarded as its corporate bureaucracy. The company slimmed down its headquarters staff and, among other things, removed the human resources department. It is no accident that this reflects Brookes' experience too. He was HR director at Texas Instruments for a short period. 'It was a waste of time', he says. 'You're there to solve problems that managers created in the first place. Well, managers should manage.'

These days the renamed and reorientated company, now called Spirent Plc., is a FTSE 100 company which derives three-quarters of its revenues from America.

Compiled from different sources including especially 'The Kate Rankine Interview',
Daily Telegraph, 17 March 2001

---

key groups. What has happened in the reorganization of businesses must be attributable to decisions by boards and senior managers to act in particular ways to defend and develop their interests. Indeed, in large companies today the senior managers have awesome powers. They decide on the expenditure of billions of pounds of cash, buying and selling businesses, and putting in place massive investments in technology. Among other things, while they are doing this, they decide whether thousands of people will lose their jobs and the conditions under which thousands of people will work. To use a Weberian term, the elite decides the 'life chances' of many people.

The way that boards of companies and senior managers choose to exercise their power depends on their situation. They are not so limitless in power that there are no constraints on their activities. As we shall see in the next two chapters, both large and small businesses have been hedged about by the pressing demands of other institutions, and their activities have been shaped by these constraints. Today however, business people, especially those in control of our largest companies, have the power to decide the forms of their businesses and are making major changes to put themselves in a position to become even more profitable in the future. Any changes they engineer may not be entirely determined by what these groups expect or desire. They are constrained because they have to deal with other groups to realize their objectives, but the actual outcome of decision-making processes will bear some relation to initial expectations and plans.

Now the bureaucracy is being abandoned in favour of some new organizational structures, it is because of the decisions of identifiable groups of people. It is strategic managers who redesign their corporations, who ensure that the necessary resources are available, and who compel many junior managers and employees to make the necessary changes in their working habits, and so on. Other groups must, at some level, go along with, conform to, and/or act to support the consequences of such decisions. From the compromises made with the exercise of executive power, new organizational structures emerge.

The outcome of such processes is shaped by the social and institutional situations in which they are embedded. There is no suggestion, for example, that powerful groups achieve the results they want, in the ways that they want; they too have to compromise, and the outcome may well be less than perfect from their point of view. For example, small businesses have often been placed in difficult situations because the institutional circumstances are not conducive to their continued prosperity. Again, the pursuit of profitability in the short term by many British companies compromises the need for long-term planning, so that the development of new products is not contemplated often enough or the resources set aside for adequate research and development. It also makes the level of investment required for the production of complex products extremely problematic. However, such things as the strategy of closing down large factories in established industrial areas in this country, and opening up new, much smaller, production facilities in non-unionized greenfield sites in East Anglia and/or East Asia, as many British companies have been doing, are not events that happen by accident. For all these examples, to understand what is happening the procedure is the same: to identify key groups of actors and then to identify the opportunities and limitations on their courses of action.

4.7 A theoretical conclusion

This argument about the origin and nature of changes in the structures of British business can be contrasted with the one presented and discussed in the last chapter. In contrast to the account offered in this chapter, people in organizations actively pursue their own interests. The organizational structure is one of the emergent properties of this interaction. Similarly, organizations do not simply adapt to their circumstances, but they actively engage with or 'enact' them (Weick 1969; Morgan 1988) with various degrees of success. In this view, instead of organizations adopting one of a number of standard possibilities which are functional for them, interorganizational arrangements also with distinctive properties emerge at this level too. In this account, the patterns of enduring relationships which define structures at every level are not explained mainly in terms of their functionality but in terms of the differential powers, resources, and opportunities of groups. Senior managers have been exercising their ability to control the resources of major companies. The result has been the production of new forms of business organization and the emergence of new forms of interfirms relations.

An alternative view of structures, then, emerges as the outcome of continuous negotiations between different groups in the organization. However, in this view, the salient aspect of these relationships is that they describe the relative powers of the different individuals and groups: overwhelmingly, authority defines the lineaments of organizational structures. In this perspective, a basic idea accounting for organizational structure is the capacity for action of individuals and groups. Hence, this account is in agreement with what is often labelled the action approach to organizations (Silverman 1970; Brown 1992: ch. 4). This takes the identification of different groups and their characteristic motivations as basic to any adequate analysis of organizations. However, willingness to identify different groups with different motivations is not enough for our purposes in explaining structures. How are we to account for the emergent properties of organizations, which give them identity and coherency?

The capacity for action alone does not explain why organizations have these features or why there are characteristic outcomes to the negotiations between the groups resulting in particular patterns of organizational structures. That the parties to an organization have different powers and interests might lead us to think that organizations from time to time simply disintegrate. But such events are in fact remarkably infrequent if not unknown. Organizations can be disbanded, and, indeed, frequently are, as when, for example, businesses are liquidated. But they do not spontaneously disintegrate, as marriages and families may do. To consider why not is instructive. Also, there is not an infinite variety of organizational forms, but some typical structures. There is a reality to the organizational types that were examined in the last chapter that cannot be ignored. The description of the traditional forms of organizations adduced by functionalist/contingency writers does have to be explained.

The major reason why organizations do not disintegrate is the existence of power and authority (Pfeffer 1981, 1992; Clegg 1989). The ability of managers to decide who is employed and then who gets what in terms of wages and conditions, is the most obvious source of power held by this group. In some aspects then, organizations are obviously coercive and indeed this is an important point about them. For some commentators, it is the fact that organizations are structures through which control is exercised that is salient (Clegg and Dunkerley 1980: ch. 12; Clegg 1989). Many of the organizational analysts in this tradition have concentrated their attention on explaining the process through which labour is controlled. They have been labelled labour process analysts (See, for example Thompson 1984; Littler 1982; Smith and Thompson, 1992). Whatever the label used, there are many organizational analysts who have drawn attention to the basic character of organizational structure as a device which embodies the exercise of power used in the pursuit of particular interests.

It is true that those who have more authority do not always impose their will in any straightforward way. Differences of interest give rise to power struggles that may not be easily resolved. During the 1930s managers introduced forms of Taylorism involving piecework incentives. This gave rise to resistance from labour which, very gradually, undermined the system. It was only abandoned thirty or more years later. Another example has already been discussed in this chapter, in which managers have, from a position of sub-ordination, achieved considerable independence. Formally considered, the powers of owners are much greater than those of managers. Legally speaking, the assets of the company belong to the shareholders. However, the difficulty for company directors (as the representatives of the owners and perhaps as owners themselves) is that it is difficult to translate their legal power into actual power. The point is that managers have actual day-to-day control of company resources—which they have to have to run the business. Exercising the rights of owners, as directors are legally empowered to do, is not easy. If they are not satisfied with what the managers are doing, they have to act concertedly and it may take a long time to organize effectively.

As well as power and authority, tradition and habit play their part in dictating that organizations adopt standard forms. Another group of organizational writers, usually called institutional theorists, have emphasized the importance of factors of this sort in explaining why organizations take standard forms (Powell and DiMaggio 1991; Scott 1995). According to these writers, organizations take standard forms because they are customary, and are copied and reproduced for this sort of reason. DiMaggio and Powell call this sort of effect isomorphism (*iso* meaning same + *morph* meaning form) (Powell and DiMaggio 1991: 63–82). The tendency of organizations to mimic each other is also important in the explanation of the adoption of standard organizational forms. This process is sometimes called 'mimetic isomorphism'. A concept drawn for the sociological theory of Giddens—proximate structuration—is also used (Giddens 1979). This suggests that organizations come to adopt the forms of other structures around them. These ideas are really important for explaining why it is that we see particular types of organization and not an infinite variety.

The idea that the environment has an effect on organizations is not completely abandoned; however, it is thought about here in ways that are somewhat different from the conceptions of the functional/contingency writers. Most importantly, in this account, what is outside an organizations has the capacity to affect it if, for example, it has, or controls access to, the things that the organization needs in order to function. Organizations need raw materials, components, machinery, labour, and capital for investment; these they have to secure from the outside. To the extent that they are dependent on these resources they are susceptible to influence (Pfeffer and Salancik 1978). Hence, there are undoubtedly institutions surrounding organizations that induce conformity in them. For example, the dependency of small businesses on banks has affected them greatly. Similarly, it makes a great deal of difference what a manager can do if he/she is the proprietor of an independent company or, alternatively, managing a business unit belonging to a major company. These external features are significant because they constrain managers to act in particular ways.

Finally, of course, there are situations in which organizations are not so much affected by their environment as affect it in their turn. Traditional forms of organization are being changed because the balance of power has shifted in fundamental ways. Technical innovation has placed a new resource in the hands of the managers. New technology has made it possible for new forms of organization to emerge which are very large and dispersed and yet need few people to function effectively. The technology has made it possible for organizations to begin to operate effectively on a much larger scale, and this has opened the possibility of big businesses escaping the confines of their place of origin. Among other things this has produced an intensification of competition in the home markets of large firms in the developed world, which, in turn, has redoubled the impulse of large businesses to seek to become significant players on a larger terrain. There has been a surprising level of complicity by national governments, especially the British government, in this kind of development; and the consequence has been that it has been relatively easy for businesses to move into multinational if not global activities.

In the rest of this book this thesis will be illustrated by considering organizational change. The discussion begins by considering some typical processes within small and large British businesses analysed in terms of the relations between different groups within them. This analysis will then be used as the basis for a critique of alternative arguments about the patterns of institutional change and their causes. Whilst we must be careful about the conclusions we come to, and disciplined about the evidence from which we draw our conclusions, the basic approach is promising. It is much more promising indeed than the structural-functional mode of analysis discussed in the last chapter, which largely fails to recognize the momentous changes with which we are now faced.

5

SMEs and business units

5.1 What are small firms?

SMEs are small and medium-sized enterprises (i.e. firms). Size is usually measured in terms of numbers of employees. In Britain, the government defines small businesses as those having fewer than 200 employees and the medium-sized as those having between 200 and 500. With the general reduction in the size of organizations, however, a business with 200 employees is now comparatively large, and it would be better if the definition of the small business could be revised downwards. In France and Germany the small business is defined as having up to fifty employees only (Lane 1995). Certainly, for policies aiming to support small business, a low cut-off point of around fifty employees would be relevant. It is now possible for quite small firms to be very effective. An example would be an investment house with assets in the billions, but with only a few dozen staff.

In much of this chapter, however, little attention will be given to the very smallest organizations—the small partnerships and sole trader organizations—of which there are many in the British economy. The number of these small organizations is fewer in Britain than almost any other advanced nation, but this is not the reason for overlooking them. Small organizations do make a significant contribution to the economy, especially in these days of new technology. One highly efficient organization which was found in the course of a research project into small IT firms consisted of five employees compiling and using a data base, access to which they were selling to clients world wide. The entire organization—including all personnel and its computer hardware—occupied the downstairs floor of a small suburban house in the north-west of England. But it had a huge turnover for such a small organization. The reason for not including very small organizations is in fact somewhat arbitrary. There is a great deal of diversity amongst very small organizations, and the area is underresearched. It would be difficult to give a good account of their structures.

Hence, attention will be restricted to the consideration of the organizational structures that are being developed by small but not very small businesses. For those who think quantitatively, the discussion will be concerned with firms and business units having more than fifty employees up to 300 or so. Even by restricting our attention in this sort of way, however, there can be no claim to complete coverage of all sectors of the economy even in recent decades. The discussion will, in fact, be largely conducted by considering the models that have been proposed as descriptions of new small organizational structures in recent years. It is evident from this admission that, as a discipline that claims to make sense of contemporary developments in organizations, organization studies has far to go. There is a great deal of research that needs to be done to establish what kinds of organizations actually exist, never mind explaining why they have come about. Nevertheless, there are some interesting proposals to be reviewed as a starting point for discussion.

5.2 The traditional small firm

The way to start is by looking at the structure of the traditional small firm and its situation. Although there has been much innovation, and it is widely believed that there are many new and distinctive organizational designs to consider these days, it is useful to consider what we are moving from.

The traditional small firm had a structure that is fairly well represented by the simple structure or 'U' organizational form as discussed in Chapter 3. There is marked formal hierarchy in the form of different levels of management and specialized division of labour. Moreover, all the groups that were identified in Chapter 4 are represented. Consider an SME that is an independent firm—i.e. one that is not owned or controlled by another company—of 200 or so employees. Such a firm has a developed managerial hierarchy and much specialization in the kind of work employees would be expected to do. It would be usual for such a firm to be a private limited company. 'Private' in this context means only that the shares in the company are not publicly traded. In terms of the groups making up the organization it will have shareholders or members, directors, managers, and employees. There may be some technically qualified employees such as systems analysts, there may even be some professional employees such as accountants or engineers. However, the informal dynamics of such a firm are likely to be very different from a large manufacturing firm, with its high degree of specialization and extensive division of labour.

Thus the groups discussed in the last chapter are all present in the small firm. There have to be shareholders: there are legal requirements that prevent firms buying out all the shares and so ceasing to have any members at all.

There has to be a minimum of two shareholders to have a legally registered company. This is true for both public and private firms these days. Of course, there is nothing to prevent owners also being directors; indeed, this would be the normal course. In private companies all significant shareholders can expect to be directors of their company. In addition, it is quite normal for directors to be managers as well. In such cases, the problems of governance that were described in the last chapter—where there are conflicts of interest arising between owners, directors, and managers—obviously do not arise. They can hardly do so if it is the same people occupying these positions. However, this does not rule out the possibility of differences between directors and managers. But, as with all companies, they are bound by legal rules which, among other things, are designed to prevent them abusing the benefits of being a company. If an organization does not take this legal form, there is a high probability it will be a partnership—which is the other popular legal form for small organizations in this country.

At other levels within the traditional small company, there will be organizational effects arising from the small number of employees. The specialization of employee jobs cannot be as extensive as is possible in large and bureaucratic types of organizations. In small companies the rigid demarcation between activities cannot occur. This is obvious when we consider managerial roles: a small company will not be able to employ specialists for every activity, so the managing director may have to organize a marketing campaign, or the manufacturing manager procure materials. If a new need arises, it will not be possible, unless trading conditions are extraordinarily favourable, simply to hire more people. There must be more flexibility in such companies. This is not the same thing as saying that such companies are basically more cooperative and there is no room for combative politics in them. If this were so, it would go a good way to invalidating the theoretical ideas proposed in this book about the importance of conflict and negotiation in shaping organizational structure. Politics is not absent from small organizations, it just becomes more subtle and personal.

In their account of what happens in firms, Goffee and Scase (1995) argue that because of the lack of staff in small companies the capacity for mutual adjustment between individuals is very important (see Box 5.1). But this must not be taken as implying that mutual adjustment and cooperation invariably occur, or that when they occur there is not a residual tendency for conflict. On the contrary, in the traditional small firm, pressures arising from the need for flexibility from the workforce often led to industrial relations problems. However, that there is mutual adjustment with small firms suggests that they are not rigid as the typical organizational chart implies. In practice there is familiarity with the need for adaptiveness in the British workforce.

BOX 5.1 **The importance of mutual adjustment in small firms**

If in large organisations some type of division of labour is more-or-less taken for granted, and is embedded within structures of authority and responsibility, this is less so in small businesses, with the result that the allocation of duties is always more *uncertain, variable and problematic.* Accordingly, the division of tasks and the specification of jobs is the outcome of a process of mutual adjustment. The division and integration of the work process is based upon the interdependence of employees undertaking duties in a flexible and broadly defined manner. This can be a source of employee work satisfaction because the delineation of job duties through mutual adjustment offers task variety, which may not be available within the more bureaucratised structures of many large organisations. Mutual adjustment also binds individuals into teams, with the result that a high premium is attached to personal compatibilities between employer and employees as well as among employees themselves. Equally there is the need for high-trust relations since, *without these, mutual adjustment as an organising process is unlikely to generate productive and profitable business performance.*

R. Goffee and R. Scase (1995: 11) emphases added

The historical situation of small British firms

In recent history the British economy has had relatively few small businesses compared with other countries in Europe (Lane 1995). For a long period after the Second World War, the prospects for the small firm were, in many accounts, not bright. The institutional context has not been supportive of small firms. The banking system in Britain, for example, was never highly adapted to the needs of businesses. This is still the case. The lack of support for small business from banks has been a considerable problem. Banks have traditionally been willing to lend only in the short term, and they insist on loan agreements that allow them to recall their money at short notice if they feel need to do so or if there is a problem about the financial viability of a client. In Germany there are banks which specialize in lending to industry and which can provide long-term and low-interest loans. In Japan, not only is there likely to be a long-term relationship between banker and client firm, but the bank will tailor a loan to the needs of the business. Moreover, the interest rate charged is lower than in Britain. The problem is that British banks are not closely involved in the businesses to which they lend. In addition, in this country there was for many years little government support for SMEs and businesses were generally left very much to fend for themselves. There was a relatively high incidence of small business failure by comparison with other countries.

For small firms that survived, there was another danger: they might be taken over by larger firms. Large British firms often had a predatory attitude

---

BOX 5.2 **Bank robberies**

Like many people, Chris Hall does not like banks. But the 50-year-old owner of Simpson-Hall, a construction business based in Cambridge, has more reason than most to feel aggrieved. Hall reckons his bank overcharged him by £60 000 in interest on his business overdraft and he is now fighting for compensation. The dispute, which is still going on five years after he left the bank, nearly crippled his business, almost wrecking his chances of ever getting another bank to back him. He is reported to have said of his bank: 'It overcharged me a lot of money and the effect on my business has been insurmountable. I have effectively lost £1 000 000 when you add up all the knock-on costs.' At one stage, Hall was fined £14 000 for failing to pay his Vat bill on time as he struggled to find cash, ignorant of the money haemorrhaging from his account because of the overcharging. Not surprisingly, perhaps, Chris Hall is reported to be angry: 'There is nobody to control the banks, yet they are controlling the country.' As he said to a *Sunday Times* reporter recently: 'It is a monopoly of the four big banks—if you fall out with one, you fall out with all.'

In early 2001, the British Competition Commission produced an interim report on banking for small and medium-sized firms. The report suggested that there is a 'complex monopoly' in the sector, dominated by the Royal Bank of Scotland Group, Lloyds TSB, Barclays and HSBC. This conclusion surprised few in the small business community. Concentrating market control in a handful of banks means more than just bad customer service. Not content with abusing existing customers, many institutions throw obstacles in the way of owner-managers who try to leave them for a competitor. The Competition Commission has identified two ways that banks prevent small businesses from switching accounts. It says the son-code system, under which cheques are cleared, is run inefficiently by the banks, which makes it difficult for owner-managers to move accounts. It also criticises the banks for disguising their true charges, making it impossible for small companies to compare the offerings of different institutions accurately.

Extracted from an extended report by John O'Donnell in the *Sunday Times*, 11 March 2001

---

to small firms. This was for a number of reasons: takeovers of publicly quoted companies are relatively easy to achieve in Britain and large firms have grown by acquisition of other firms, as much, if not more than, by growing organically. It has also been argued that small business proprietors themselves were often not adverse to selling their businesses. It has been suggested that because of the importance of the gentlemanly ideal in British culture, to live as a gentleman with a private income (drawn exclusively from landed property and other investments) was the goal of many members of the business class (Wiener 1981; for an extended critique of Wiener's thesis, see Rubenstein 1993). Such people saw involvement in business as simply a temporary means to the goal of social success, and would sell their businesses given the right opportunity. Whatever the reasons, there is evidence that large firms would often seek to buy out small firms.

Taken together, such factors as the high costs of capital, little government support, and predatory large businesses often added up to a generally hostile set of circumstances for the survival of small firms. The consequences of this can be traced through to a characteristic set of outlooks and policy emphases on the part of the management of British SMEs. Figure 5.1 sets out the general argument being put forward here in a summary form. As with many of the attempts to sum up the processes within firms Figure 5.1 is an ideal type or model.

Pressure for profit

In the traditional British small firm, managers were likely to be under pressure to produce profits from their business in a relatively short period. This is because, traditionally, ploughed-back profits are a major source of capital for investment. Unable to rely on banks or other sources of capital over much, small businesses have traditionally generated a high proportion of their investment capital from their own profits. This was a workable strategy when markets were stable and growth could take place over a relatively long period. However, if loans were taken from banks to finance expansion or to tide over cash flow problems, then this strengthened the demand for profitability to service loans. Such considerations tended to make managers both profit-conscious and averse to making any investment that might be considered risky. This is a debilitating combination, as high profits are likely to come mainly from putting capital at risk as investment. Only capital investment will greatly increase the productivity of labour and dramatically drive down the costs of production, making a business profitable. By contrast, small British businesses would have to look hard at the likely return on an investment (ROI) before making any investment decision.

Investment by British companies, particularly that by SMEs, tended to be low by international standards, with low research and development budgets and inadequate product planning and market research. On the production engineering side this meant, too often, making do with old equipment and with poorly planned and late introductions of new technology. In turn, inadequate investment had a series of effects on the attitude of management to labour and on its typical pattern of labour utilization. Making do with old equipment meant a high reliance on labour to respond flexibly; and to follow the management lead of making do. The low capital per person employed tended to produce low productivity and for relatively low wages to be normal even for skilled men. At the same time, managers were forced to substitute labour for capital much of the time in order to produce; and hence firms did employ a high proportion of skilled workers with a depth of industrial experience and capacity for adaptation.

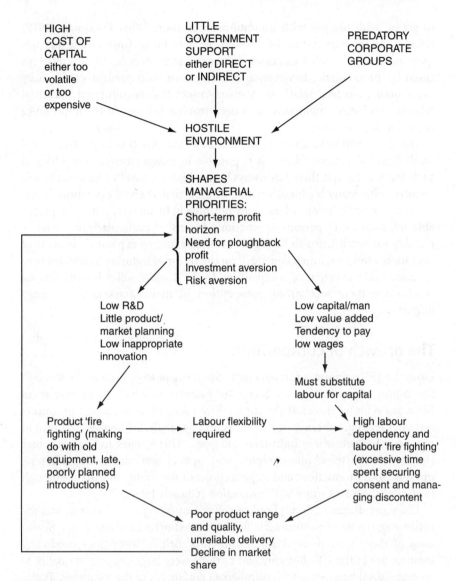

Figure 5.1 External pressures on a traditional small firm and associated internal dynamics

A high level of responsibility was often demanded from labour and, in many British firms, a good deal of autonomy was extended to them. As was also noted in the last chapter, the tendency to import and apply scientific management in the form of Taylorism, involving direct supervision of unskilled labour, was limited. Piecework payment was developed and widely used, often in conjunction with skilled labour. Employees were often required to get on with the job with minimum supervision. What Friedman (1977) refers to as the expectation of 'responsible autonomy' from employees was quite normal in small businesses. In these circumstances, labour relations could be problematic, however, and overzealous management could easily cause poor industrial relations. A management that encountered industrial relations problems might well be in deep trouble, because of the importance of labour to production.

This may seem to be a pessimistic picture of the situation of the traditional small British business. Clearly it is possible to exaggerate the difficulties of such firms. Although there has always been a high turnover of business in this country, with many businesses failing in their first years of operation, it was possible for small independent firms not merely to survive, but to be profitable and to grow. In periods of economic expansion particularly, it would be possible for small firms to be highly profitable and to expand their areas of operation. However, much depended on the sector of industry in which a firm operated and the extent of competition. In the decades following the Second World War there was strong competition in many markets from cheap imports.

The growth of competition

From the 1950s onwards foreign competition began to grow, initially through the import of finished goods. Sectors of industry in which there were small firms came under threat. If the competitive pressure from foreign producers was intense, in the absence of any protection by tariffs, businesses could fail in numbers. Indeed, whole industries collapsed. This applies to the consumer electronic industries, photographic and optical instrument manufacture, machine tool production, and large sections of the motor industry, although the last of these had some tariff protection (Church 1994).

The most dramatic example of the effects of foreign competition was the collapse of the British motorcycle industry. As short a time ago as the beginning of the 1960s, there were around forty British companies producing motorcycles in the UK. Roughly half of these were large enough to qualify as medium-sized businesses with numbers of employees in the hundreds. Typically the larger firms designed and produced the engines for their machines and many other component parts. In addition to these firms there were many smaller firms producing small batches of specialist bikes of their own design to which they would fit proprietary engines and other components they did not produce themselves. Supplying these assemblers were many small firms producing parts and accessories for motorcycle and car firms in small batches. All these companies, including the larger assemblers, were small batch producers, utilizing a high proportion of skilled labour and relatively little capital

---

BOX 5.3 **The best in the world?**

Pick up a yellowing copy of either of the two weekly motor cycle journals that flourished in Britain in the decade immediately following World War II, and somewhere or other there is sure to be a BSA advertisement proclaiming this to be 'The Most Popular Motor Cycle in the World'. Publicity man's licence? No, just a bald statement of fact: in those heady days of peace the BSA was indeed the world's most popular motor cycle.

Nor was BSA alone, for Triumph at this period were supplying (or so it seemed) half the police forces of the globe with their excellent vertical-twin patrol machines, while Norton—and to a lesser extent Velocette (world 350cc road-racing champions in 1949) and AJS—still dominated the Grand Prix circuits.

It must be said, however, that the motor cycle world at that time was a much smaller place than it is today, and even at the very height of its fame the British industry—taken as a whole—enjoyed an output only a fraction of that of *just one* of Japan's present-day giants. . . .

Bob Currie in Ian Ward and Laurie Caddell (eds) (1987: 6), emphasis added

---

equipment. By the middle of the 1970s there was only one significant British group (Norton–Villiers–Triumph) still involved in the production of motor-cycles, and this was hanging on by its fingertips. Both Conservative and Labour Governments of the early 1970s tried to intervene, but ineffectively and much too late.

The Japanese with their cheap and relatively high-quality mass-produced products finished off the British motorcycle industry in the space of little more than a decade. Although it took longer to accomplish—because it was larger and, for a long period, protected by the state—a similar process of demolition took place of the British car industry.

What happened?

The collapse of the motorcycle industry was an extreme case, of course. In many areas of economic activity, competition did not drive companies to the wall. However, foreign competition has had a big impact on the economy—which has been more open to the penetration of foreign suppliers than most other advanced countries. This competition has helped to initiate processes of change including much corporate reorganization. Through the 1970s, many sectors of British industry continued to contract, especially in the numbers of independent small firms; and the process continued in many sectors into the 1980s. Yet, in the 1980s, while the loss of capacity in terms of the numbers employed continued, especially in manufacture, the number of organizations stabilized and then moved sharply upwards. As we saw in Chapter 2, there was a 20 per cent increase in their numbers between 1980 and 1999.

This growth was not a result of the revival of independent small firms, still

less the re-establishment of the viability of the traditional organization of the
small business. It cannot be shown that what happened was the discovery of
new and more effective patterns of organization for the small firm which then
led to the revival of the economy from the bottom up. On the contrary, the
obstacles to the growth and transformation of small firms has been shown to
be considerable, and it would be surprising if, in the circumstances in which
they found themselves, they had managed to reorganize to such good effect
that they could revitalize the economy. But many British businesses obviously
did survive. How they did will be argued in the course of this chapter and the
next.

Before passing on let us consider how strong the overseas challenge was and
why foreign competition had such an effect on British industry. In the 1960s
when the first significant effects were felt in Europe and America, there was
almost no manufacturing by Japanese companies in the West. (It is still true,
despite the attention paid to Japanese and other foreign firms operating in this
country, that the amount of manufacturing actually undertaken here by such
companies is very small (Procter and Ackroyd 1998).) To compete with British
firms, the Japanese were manufacturing products such as motorcycles and
televisions, putting them in boats, bringing them halfway around the world
before selling them in our markets more cheaply than our own companies
could manage. These aspects of Japanese activity suggest that—whatever
other advantages they had—they were producing on a much larger scale than
British firms and able to make more units than were needed in their own
market. Also, there is a point about long-term finance. All the time before
their exported products were actually sold, they would represent a cost to the
company that made them. Somehow, these costs were being borne without
too much difficulty. These facts suggest that Japanese industry was competing
through traditional means as well as adopting the new patterns of production
for which they are famous. In addition to new production methods it would
seem that the Japanese undertook large-scale production—from which economies of scale ensued. Also, they had the availability of cheap long-term
credit—which allowed them to export.

There was almost no recognition of the situation of the British motorcycle
industry at the time of its demise during the late 1960s. To the credit of the
consultants commissioned by the British government to diagnose the
problems—which occurred much too late—the root problems were identified
(Boston Consulting Group, 1975). Among other things, they did point to
the need for much higher levels of investment than the short-termism of the
British firms' pursuit of high profits promoted.

Nor was it very high on any agenda to reform financial institutions in order
to provide the capital that industry clearly needed (Coates 1996; Ingham
1984). There was a brief episode, in the Labour government of 1964–70,

---

BOX 5.4 **What happened?**

By this time (1960) the Japanese had developed huge production volumes in their domestic markets and volume related cost reductions had followed. This resulted in a highly competitive cost position which the Japanese used as a springboard for the penetration of world markets with small motor cycles in the early 1960s. Meanwhile, the primary focus of the British industry was on maintaining short-term profitability. The British found it impossible to match low Japanese price levels on small bikes and remain profitable. They therefore responded by . . . withdrawing from the smaller bike segments which were being contested. This was a fundamental strategic error.

Report of the Boston Consulting Group, (1975: p. xiv)

---

attempted to promote change in industrial organization by encouraging mergers, but financial institutions were not targeted for reform. At this time, it was briefly a key part of industrial policy to create 'national champions' by putting together large businesses from the largest of the remaining companies in manufacturing sectors of the economy. But such policies were ill-conceived and were too late. By and large, any response was left to private industry to arrange, especially after 1979. In the 1980s, a lot of industrial capacity was lost, but some kind of response that has allowed our remaining business to remain viable was worked out. This will be a matter given consideration in this chapter and the next. It will be argued that the response worked out involves changes by both large and small firms. However, this is not the view of many writers who have concentrated much of their energy on producing ideas about possible ways in which British firms might be changed.

5.3 Reorganizing the firm

In the 1980s it appeared to be obvious to many people that the traditional ways of organizing would have to change. There was much evidence from the lack of profitability of firms and their bankruptcy and closure—especially in manufacturing—that pointed to the need to reorganize. The main point most people agreed on was that businesses needed to become more efficient. The term 'lean production' was not coined until 1990 or so, but the need to reduce overheads and make companies more productive was the predominant view in the business community. If they could not do this, they would be allowed to fail. Undoubtedly the most widely considered proposal for changing the structure and organization of British firms in order to make them more productive was the model proposed by Atkinson and his co-workers (Atkinson 1984; Atkinson and Meager 1986; NEDO 1986).

The Atkinson model of the flexible firm

According to this account, lack of flexibility was at the heart of the problems of the traditional British firm. What was needed instead was a much more flexible design. The solution was a design for the firm or business unit that supposedly maximized flexibility. Atkinson in fact proposed a simplified model of the flexible firm. But so popular has this package of proposals proved to be amongst proponents and critics alike, that it has became widely referred to as the 'the flexible firm'. Implicit in this was the idea that, if the average British firm could be reorganized along these lines, British industry could be rebuilt. As can be seen from Figure 5.2, the Atkinson model of the flexible firm is nothing like the traditional 'U' form of structure.

Atkinson's model of the flexible firm focuses on the utilization of labour. It embodies the suggestion that increased flexibility may be achieved from different and new ways of employing and using labour. The implication is that, by a number of innovations in the areas of training and employing labour, a great increase in productivity, as well as in the variety and quality of goods and services produced, would result. Amongst other things, the model proposed dispensing with traditional kinds of skilled labour, and having a multi-skilled core workforce instead. By such a change it was implied that barriers in production could be broken down and more adaptability in activities secured. Atkinson claimed that firms were increasingly seeking and achieving greater flexibility from their workforces by such procedures. The flexibility that Atkinson suggested could be secured was of two main kinds: what he called numerical (NEDO 1986: 3–4) and functional flexibility (NEDO 1986: 4). Atkinson's model of the flexible firm is usually summarized by reference to the diagram he used to illustrate the model, reproduced in Figure 5.2.

Here we can see more graphically how the flexible firm combines functional and numerical flexibility. The workforce is divided into two basic groups. On the one hand (in the centre of the diagram) there are core workers, and on the other hand (surrounding the core) there are groups of peripheral workers. Core workers would mainly contribute to functional flexibility for the company through having diverse skills and hence the ability to turn their hand to any task. By implication too, core workers provide functional flexibility in return for greater security of employment. Peripheral workers are mainly expected to provide the firm with additional capacity for work, though they also contribute to functional flexibility where possible. As the level of activity increases, so a firm can draw increasingly on the groups in the periphery. The periphery would be made up of groups of workers not in a permanent employment relationship with the firm.

There are several kinds of peripheral workers: those who are on short-term

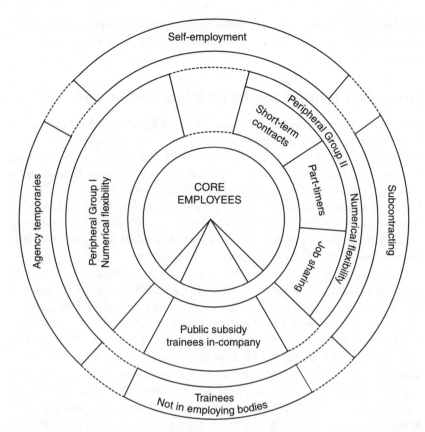

Figure 5.2 Atkinson's model of the flexible firm. (From Atkinson, J. (1984), *Institute for Employment Studies, Report No 89*)

contracts and those having work training through public subsidy; then there are possibilities of job-sharing, part-time contracts, etc. Some of these may be expected to join the core in due course. A further area of numerical flexibility is achieved through outsourcing, agency staff and subcontracting. Peripheral workers are less central and disposable and disciplined by the precariousness of their position and the possibility of gaining access to the core workforce. Indeed, the disciplinary implications of the model have led some writers, not without reason, to associate flexibility with the degradation of work (NACAB 1997; Legge 1998). This is a point further developed by the notion of financial flexibility, which is also proposed by Atkinson. Financial flexibility, as Atkinson handles it, is not a proposed solution to the problem of the high cost of borrowed capital or the inflexibility of British banks, which was mentioned earlier, so much as an expedient to limit the wage bill. All this means is that firms should take steps to strictly limit their outgoings, especially the costs of employing labour. Atkinson sees financial flexibility as coming from the strict control of labour costs, and that means employing a higher proportion of peripheral labour.

Does the Atkinson model look like a solution?

There have been numerous criticisms of the Atkinson model. Since it was proposed it has been at a focus of heated debate. For this discussion, however, the central question is: does the Atkinson model deal with the problems of the traditional British small firm? The account does not mention technology or investment except indirectly. By implication, it suggests that labour costs and the recalcitrance of labour are key problems that have to be addressed. It has not been denied that there was a problem of labour in the traditional small firm, in that firms have been heavily dependent on it. But this is to misunderstand the origin and nature of this problem.

As has been argued, management of small firms in Britain has habitually invested too little in technology and been forced to rely on the contribution of labour as an alternative source of production efficiency. As a consequence, if the workforce was disposed to be argumentative, they often had reason to be. In the circumstances they were in, their action could be highly effective. However, the problems of the British firm have more to do with the lack of an adequate supply of capital on appropriate terms than any labour problem. In support of this, it is surely implausible to contend that a highly effective, modern, and competitive industry can be secured simply by altering the way labour is utilized. Securing and using appropriate technology is the main way of securing efficient production. Atkinson says little or nothing about the possible role of technology.

Ironically, a realistic understanding of the history of British small business reveals that the way labour was actually employed was remarkably similar to what Atkinson proposes. As Pollert (1988, 1991) has pointed out, much of British industry has always had a periphery of workers whose contracts of employment are temporary or part-time. Subcontracting and self-employment have also been traditional and extensively used in many parts of British industry. As has been suggested in the early part of this chapter, core British workers were often allowed considerable autonomy, and were in fact highly cooperative in practice. These pointers indicate that, in terms of the variety of goods that were produced, British industry was highly flexible too. British industry was probably without equal in the number of options that could be provided for its manufactured products. The motorcycle industry is a good example of this. Flexibility of output—supposedly one of the central benefits of the Atkinson model—was simply not a problem.

The problem of British firms was that even the largest firms in almost every

---

BOX 5.5 The pursuit of flexibility is nothing new

[There] has been an assumption of a radical break in employers' policies and practices, and a tolerance for a-historical analysis. For instance, much of the flexibility preoccupation has presented legally unprotected forms of work and labour market segmentation as something new, as though casualisation were a direct and recent employers' implementation of state deregulation policies. . . . Dual and segmented labour market theorists have long pointed to the link between competitive labour market conditions and employers' strategies to exploit a cheap and variable labour force. . . . Similarly, 'flexibility' in work—removing occupational and skill boundaries, altering work arrangements and shift patterns, rationalising and intensifying labour—was a keynote of the productivity bargaining of the 1960's and 1970's. . . .

Anna Pollert (1988: 282)

---

sector were too small and undercapitalized to meet the competition from foreign firms. But had these problems been solved, there would have been great flexibility forthcoming from the economic system—because of the traditions of securing this from employees and because of the history of sub-contracting between firms. Of course it was and is possible to squeeze more productivity from labour, but there is a more likely source of greatly increased productivity. In short, the Atkinson model does not seem to be looking in the right direction.

5.4 How to achieve flexible output

Distinctions between types of flexibility made in the literature are numerous. Sayer and Walker (1992: 199), for example, offer a list of seven types of flexibility, and even this is far from being complete. However, the discussion of different kinds or dimensions of flexibility cannot take us very far. Clearly, flexibility in the variety of output (at high quality and, if necessary, in large volume) is what is needed. This means, in effect, to be able to introduce variations to the product or service produced as a matter of routine and even to change the kind of product entirely. These changes in direction must be associated with the ability to increase output volume. Because output flexibility is desired, flexibility in production arrangements and systems is sought.

Hence it is not disputed that flexibility is needed: the ability to produce differentiated and high-quality goods and services is essential in today's market conditions. Since the Atkinson model was proposed, the subject of flexibility has been extensively analysed and debated, and the conclusion has been drawn that there are different ways of achieving the desired end of a wider range of higher-quality goods and services. It can be realized by placing emphasis on the contribution of labour—as in the Atkinson model—or by seeking a sophisticated technical solution by investing heavily in the technology. Then there is the possibility of engineering some kind of judicious mixture of improved technology and use of people. We now consider the possibility of producing a technical way of realizing flexibility.

The high-technology solution

For some writers, the problem of the flexibility of British industry is not centrally to do with labour as Atkinson implies, but arises from insufficient attention being paid to technology (Gerwin 1987; Boer 1994). There is now the possibility of taking much of the labour out of production processes and substituting it by machinery (Dorf 1983; Hartley 1983). It is not only that there is new technology available, but there is possibility of new configurations of technology to consider. In particular, information technology can be applied to a range of different production sequences and whole manufacturing processes can be also coordinated and controlled using computers (Slack 1983). Clearly there are ways of organizing production that make such extensive use of technology and it is now thought that technology can solve all the problems in this area.

A firm using high-technology solutions to the problem of production will require a different range of inputs to those specified by the Atkinson model. This kind of solution to the production problem involves not only advanced production technology—programmable machine tools and advanced robotics—but also information and material handling machinery to coordinate the productive output of such machines. What engineers have in mind is what used to be called 'automation' and is now called computer-integrated manufacture; that is, the development of connected sets of activities which become a single, complex but integrated process. Automation is, arguably, a better name: because the objective for such processes is for them to be almost totally automatic. There is no need of labour—flexible or other—in the interstices between the machines, as in Fordist mass production, because there are no gaps. What this model does imply is that the few remaining employees are extremely highly skilled. Their expertise must not only bridge across some manual skills but also include machine modification, machine programming, and integration of productive sequences using general computer programming. On this model, labour costs are secondary to technology, but the labour costs will remain relatively high because of the levels of training and the scarcity of skills required by the few employees who remain.

There is evidence that this approach to flexible production is being taken seriously and developed in some countries (Jones 1991). However, there is little evidence pointing in this direction for the UK (Jones 1988, 1989). UK firms have not, on the whole, pursued a strategy of technology-centred flexibility. An examination of the adoption and operation of advanced manufacturing technology (AMT) shows that even in its more primitive forms it remains rare in British industry (Pike *et al.* 1989). Research has been undertaken into the extent of the introduction of high technology into British industry and it has been found that there is rather little progress being made on these fronts. With regard to numerically controlled (NC) and computer numerically controlled (CNC) machine tools, Tidd (1991) found that the proportion of pre-programmed tools was half in the UK what it was in Japan. On robotics Tidd (1991) paints a similar picture: proportionate to the number of employees, the use of robotics was ten times greater in Japan than in the UK. Their use in Britain, moreover, was often confined to the performance of a single task. As to higher levels of automatic system integration, these were also rare in the UK. The component parts of computer-integrated manufacturing (CIM)—such as computer-aided design—are difficult to detect (Edquist and Jacobsson 1988); while McLoughlin (1990) demonstrates the difficulties firms have encountered in the use of CAD. Finally, Rush and Bessant (1992) estimate that there were no more than 100 flexible manufacturing systems (FMS) in the UK by 1990; while Jones (1988, 1989) reports on the difficulties firms had in using them to achieve greater flexibility.

The high-technology flexible firm is very different from the Atkinson idea of reliance on labour to produce flexibility. It goes to the opposite extreme to the Atkinson model in suggesting that technology alone can solve the problem of flexible manufacturing. Clearly, if we take the Atkinson model seriously we do need reminding that technology can make significant contributions to the problem of production. It is interesting to speculate why a model so conspicuously lacking was taken so seriously. It seems clear that the appeal of the Atkinson model was partly ideological in featuring labour so centrally. A key point is that the model proposes that there is a future for skilled manual labour in Britain, which is something that many liberals would like to believe. However, as a counterpoint to this, Atkinson also proposes that it is appropriate to continue with the old ways of wringing productivity from labour. So, the model completely fails to recognize (never mind to address) the much more fundamental problem of securing adequate levels of investment to make production effective. The Atkinson model may well lead readers to infer that the problems of British firms are mostly to do with labour and its poor contribution, and nothing at all to do with management's failure to solve the problem of chronic underinvestment.

However, there is an obvious problem with proposing the high-technology firm as the solution to the problems of the small British firm. This is also implausible as a solution to the traditional problems of the British small firm

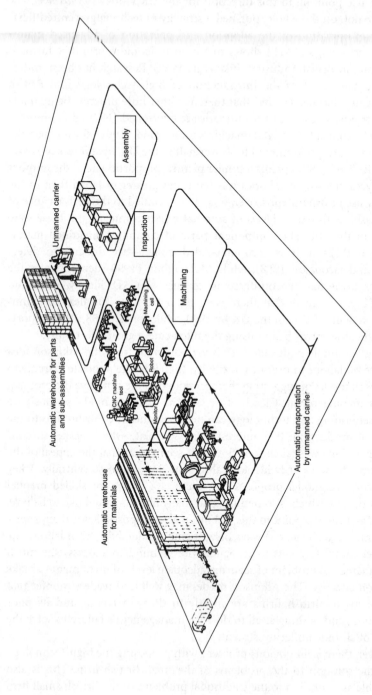

Figure 5.3 A stylized flexible manufacturing system. (From Hartley 1983)

Unmanned carrier

Assembly

Inspection

Machining

Machining cell

Robot

CNC machine tool

Monitor

Automatic warehouse for parts and sub-assemblies

Automatic warehouse for materials

Automatic transportation by unmanned carrier

as we have described them. The high-technology firm model obviously requires high levels of investment and high levels of employee education and training, neither of which fits with the established pattern of British business organization. To be attempted, the high-technology firm model would probably have to be the subsidiary of a well-resourced business group willing to commit a high level of investment to a business unit which would be experimental, and unlikely to show a high return until all the necessary development work had been completed. In short, the high-technology route will not be taken by the British small firm because it will pose the problem of capital supply that was cited at the start of this chapter. It is not difficult to see, therefore, why it will not appeal to British managers and owners and why it is not widely adopted by them as a solution to their problems. For Britain, by contrast, such evidence as there is of this combination is restricted to a few very large companies (Jones 1991).

5.5 A middle way?

If the Atkinson model is ruled out on the grounds that it does not say enough about technology and the high-technology model because it demands too much investment, are there any alternatives? Although there are some enclaves in the economy where little change has been demanded of small firms, and they have recognizably remained in their traditional forms, in many areas considerable structural changes have been undertaken by companies. It will be argued here that there are at least two plausible but competing models of the organization of the small firm or business unit. These purport to be descriptive of what actually happens, and are not so obviously prescriptive as the Atkinson and high-technology models. Both also recognize that a model of the effective business unit must say something about improvements in the use of both labour and technology.

The high-surveillance firm

In the model of organization and management that will be labelled the high-surveillance firm is a judicious mixture of technical innovation and labour control. It does not envisage exceptionally high levels of investment as in the high-technology firm, but does undertake investment as required to keep pace with industry standards. However, in this model, thought is also given to how to use labour to obtain high levels of productivity from the available technology. Technology and labour are both thought of as adjustable to meet the markets a firm is facing, and continuous thought is given to how to improve the yield from the resources available. With standard products, such as electronic circuit boards, there is a tendency to raise the level of technical input so that the whole task can be done by machine; but since, on balance, people are still more adaptable than machines, there is no tendency to try to eliminate them entirely from production processes. In the production of many consumer goods, novelty in product design and appearance is now important. Although volume production is indicated, there need to be relatively short production runs of marginally different products and the contribution of workers is to customize products.

Where higher-volume production is indicated, and yet some variety is required, modification to standard production technology is introduced. Thus, instead of having the standard assembly-line format, laid out in a straight line, which is appropriate for large volumes, the horseshoe shaped design has been devised. Here, the line turns round and comes back parallel to the start. Workers manning the process can move from work-stations at the start of the process to work-stations at the end without moving very far. The whole process can be overseen by those participating in production, and workers can see where contributions need to be made. This is a relatively high-technology solution to production which nonetheless involves flexible use of labour. Despite the relatively high input of technology, labour does not have to be highly trained (O'Reilly 1992; Keep and Rainbird 1995). In this sort of regime, training is usually done on the job; with considerable attention being paid to the importance of self-surveillance as well as close supervision.

Whatever the mix of people and technology in a particular production set-up, there is always strong emphasis placed on procedures and techniques to monitor and oversee the quality and variety of production (Delbridge *et al.* 1992; Sewell and Wilkinson 1992; Conti and Warner 1993). Control is exercised over individuals and groups by constantly monitoring, measuring, and reporting their performance. In this view, contemporary managerial regimes are distinctive and effective because of systematic gathering and appraisal of data relating to production. At the heart of the new management is the routine surveillance of technology and manpower. This facilitates the identification and reduction of waste. When waste is identified, technology is configured and labour productivity monitored so as to remove it. Procedures originating in Japanese industry such as Just In Time (JIT) and Total Quality Management (TQM) are seen as being techniques requiring new procedures for data collection and vigilant surveillance. Such systems are sometimes held to exercise an absolute control over employees, thus providing the modern-day equivalent of the panopticon, through which such control was achieved in nineteenth-century prisons (Sewell and Wilkinson 1992).

High-surveillance management techniques were discovered in Britain in studies of Japanese firms or their affiliates (Delbridge *et al.* 1992; Sewell and

---

BOX 5.6 **Management control at Nippon CTV**

The numbers of mistakes per day are totalled, and displayed on a monthly basis. The display includes a colour-coded chart above each individual operator's head. There are red, yellow, and green charts with the words 'danger', 'warning' and 'good' respectively marked on them. The allowed number is 20 errors for a month [from a monthly average of over 200 000 insertions], if this is exceeded then the operator is 'taken into the coffee lounge' and 'counselled'. In other words, they are asked about why they have made so many mistakes and told that an improvement will be expected or else they may receive a written warning. Apparently, this counselling will include an intrusion into the personal details of a worker's home life to find out if there are any worries there that are causing problems . . . this was anticipated by the workforce and is regular practice regardless of the relationship of the two. . . .

Janie, the girl I sat next to today, had had 40 plus rejects in April and had been counselled, 'I just got told that that wasn't good enough and I would have to improve'. . . . Janie had to improve or else face disciplinary action and ultimately the sack. She had reduced the number of recorded rejects to 21 in May and did not receive a second counselling session. Instead, Angie, the team leader, leaned over her shoulder today while I was in easy earshot and said, 'That was better last month Janie, let's make sure you keep up the improvement. Try and get below 20 this month, alright', and then Angie was off as Janie nodded and then turned and said to no one in particular: 'Silly cow, I hate her!'

Rick Delbridge (1998: 52–3)

Wilkinson 1992). However, it has also been argued that they are used by British firms. Some authors suggest there is a general process—called the 'Japanization of British industry'—in which all firms operating in this country are adopting these techniques (Oliver and Wilkinson 1992). In principle, if these production methods are effective, we might expect them to be used by British firms. The problem with this argument is that the managerial regime is still relatively costly in two ways. Firstly, it is technologically quite advanced and it calls for considerable investment. This comes up against the problem of investment from which, as we have seen, many British firms suffer. Secondly, this production regime is relatively costly in terms of its requirements for supervision and management. Engineers have to be constantly thinking about redesigning the production process, and supervisors have to be constantly appraising the work and output of individuals and teams. True, the direct costs per unit of production are the lowest possible, and these may, to a degree, be further defrayed by inducing employees to monitor their own work; but the system is inevitably management-intensive.

There is debate about the extent to which these production methods are adopted by British firms. Oliver and Wilkinson have argued that something like them have been widely adopted by British industry. Others have argued that they have not and actually the adoption of new production methods by British companies is much more selective (Scarborough and Terry 1998; Procter and Ackroyd 1998). Ackroyd and Procter argue that there is a version of the flexible firm—having some vestigial resemblance to the Atkinson model—which British firms have adopted as an alternative to the high surveillance model. This they labelled the new flexible firm.

The new flexible firm

There is an alternative to the high-surveillance type of regime for a firm or business unit, which there is reason to think is being widely adopted by British firms. Like the Atkinson model, the model of the new flexible firm proposes that there will be continued reliance on the contribution of labour to production, although the proportion of skilled labour employed is also drastically cut. There is no core of highly skilled labour in the new flexible firm. The amount of management and supervision available in the new flexible firm is also greatly reduced, and here there is a strong contrast with the high-surveillance regime. Unlike the Atkinson model, however, there is recognition in this model that technology cannot be ignored; and some use of advanced technology is inevitable.

On the technical side the new flexible firm is simple. At the heart of it is the adoption of what is called cellular manufacture. This involves nothing more than the regrouping of existing machine tools and/or other equipment into cells, or small groups of machines that allow related 'families' of products or sub-assemblies to be manufactured in batches (Alford 1994; Procter *et al.* 1995). Existing capital might be supplemented by limited new investment—such as small numbers of CNC machines—which are added to cells or constituted as cells. Cellular manufacturing can also be applied to complex production processes (Alford 1994). Here a production process is treated as if it were discontinuous, and segmented into cells which are treated in the same way as product cells. The workforce can be considered as a series of separate groups or teams. Ingersoll Engineers conducted extended studies of cellular manufacture in the early 1990s (1990, 1994) and found it to be adopted in some form by the large majority (73 per cent) of firms they contacted. Its application to complex processes was rarer: a smaller proportion of their companies (58 per cent) were using it in this way.

Cellular manufacturing is a relatively low-technology system of production requiring some task flexibility from labour to provide varied output. The allocation of groups of employees to groups of machines limits the need for all employees to have a broad spectrum of skills. Hence, any emphasis on team-working follows from contributions to task coordination and wage cost reduction within cells, rather than a general attachment to the value of team-working as such (Benders and van Hootegem 1999; Procter and Mueller 2000). Certainly, for both production and process cells, provided there is sufficient experience with the technology amongst the members of the group designated as a cell, the skill required to produce is not high; and productivity increases may be, fairly readily, achieved by specific on-the-job training (O'Reilly 1992). Systematic enskilling is not required so much as a willingness and ability on the part of the cell members to keep the existing machinery functioning.

In sum, the contribution of labour to flexibility in contemporary manufacturing in the new flexible firm is considerable. It contributes basic functional flexibility in production tasks (Elger 1991). In systems of cellular manufacture, workers move between tasks, and acquire competences that were formerly the preserve of skilled workers. In the case of product cells, they provide for flexibility through the coordination of elements of the production process. These tendencies may be summed up as employee contributions to the coordination of production. Skilled labour is not always eliminated, but is generally not as privileged as it was. Skilled workers are often found working in cells with multiple tasks and with other grades of labour and there are expectations of elements of skill being passed on. Finally, there is the flexibility which labour contributes in terms of dispensability. Hence, Atkinson and his co-workers were correct to identify labour as a significant source of the flexibility that is achieved by British manufacturing firms. However, they exaggerate the opportunity offered by this for significant enskilling of workers. In almost every other respect, however, there are significant differences between the Atkinson model and the way that flexibility is actually being realized in manufacturing operations.

The above changes in emphasis in the utilization of labour have to be seen in conjunction with broader changes in management and organization. There are many indications that contemporary British factories do not involve the introduction of new surveillance procedures and techniques by management. The continued decline of payment by results and the long-term rise of group incentive payments, indicates only the removal of traditional, direct control of individual work activity. There is also evidence of departure from the traditional approach to job design and the attempted elimination of unproductive activities from job specifications. A survey by Poole and Jenkins (1998), for example, records that more than 80 per cent of manufacturing managers in their sample reported at least some involvement of employees in their own job design activities, whilst 75 per cent, 70 per cent, and 59 per cent had at least some involvement in their own work-scheduling, inventory control, and budgeting respectively. This suggests a broadening of roles and responsibilities, and much movement between tasks, but not increased surveillance and control. Widespread evidence for the inclusion of responsibility for quality in job specifications also points in a similar direction.

By treating groups of workers as discrete modules or cells, cellular manufacturing focuses the attention of the production engineers and managers on the performance of each part of a production facility. The system recommends itself because of the ease with which calculations of marginal costs and benefits flowing from the contribution of different groups can be made (Ezzamel and Willmott 1998). Knowing which segments of their operations are not performing provides management with the capacity to identify and to dispense with whole areas of production if they are unprofitable. Marginson *et al.* (1993) show how large companies tend to deal with underperforming business units by dispensing with them rather than taking corrective action. The knowledge that whole areas of activity may be cut out if a component cannot be made profitably can be the basis of potent forms of indirect managerial control. Moreover, if the range of activities, and, through this, the scale of operations, is constantly adjusted, the organization must also constantly adjust its external relations as well. Such developments help to make sense of the growth in the importance of interfirm networks and cooperative relationships. In these emphases on identifying profitable and non-profitable areas, there are distinct continuities with the historical concerns of the managements of small British firms.

Figure 5.4 lists the attributes of the new flexible firm in a summary form and Figure 5.5 offers a more graphic representation of its segmented character. From this it can be clearly seen that there is in this model almost no core. This implies that the performance of the organization is monitored remotely using key variables. In some ways, provided the activities of the work

---

- Production is organized through the arrangement of machines and workers as cells capable of producing 'families' of components or products.
- Advanced manufacturing technology is little used, except as additions to existing configurations of equipment.
- Employed labour contributes to flexibility as teams of semi-skilled workers performing a range of specific tasks and given on-the-job training.
- Employees do not enjoy privileged status or high employment security, but compete with subcontracted labour and alternative suppliers.
- Production operations are considered as dispensable separate 'segments', about which calculations of cost are regularly made.
- Management takes the form of intensified indirect control based on the allocation of costs.

© Blackwell Publishers Ltd/London School of Economics 1998.

Figure 5.4 The new flexible manufacturing firm—summary of features

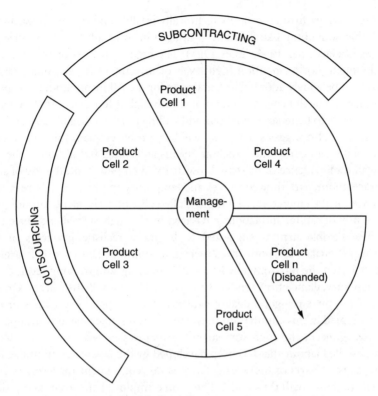

Figure 5.5 The new British flexible firm: diagrammatic representation

cells are judged to be cost effective, there is scope for a good deal of self-regulation in such a regime, a point which again shows great continuity with traditional practices in many small British firms. However, it ought to be clear that such a regime of production cannot compete effectively with more adequately designed and technically more advanced combinations of factors of production. It depends for its continued profitability on market distortions and temporary inadequacies in supply.

5.6 **Beginning to sum up**

Of the four kinds of organization considered in this chapter, two are unlikely patterns for the type of organization that has replaced the traditional firm. These are the Atkinson model of the flexible firm and the high-technology firm. Both are more prescriptive than descriptive. The one places too much reliance on labour and the other too much on technology. The high-technology firm is certainly technically feasible and there are reasons to think that something like it has been utilized in some advanced countries of the world (Jaikumar 1986; Jones 1991). The high demands for research and development, not to mention high levels of investment it demands, make it unlikely to be widely adopted in Britain. As for the Atkinson model, it expects too much can be done with labour alone. Although it recognizes that management is likely to be reliant on labour and willing to take a disciplinary attitude towards it, it also suggests that there will be a protected place for some highly skilled labour in companies. Such an idea is appealing. But although there is quite a lot of evidence of increased insecurity in employment, the use of subcontract labour, part-time contracts, and temporary employment, there is little evidence for the emergence of a multi-skilled elite of 'polyvalent' employees.

The mix of capital and labour envisaged by the high-surveillance firm and the new flexible firm is suggested to be more realistic in terms of the demands it makes for both investment and training. However, it is argued here that even the relatively low levels of technology and training required by the high-surveillance firm render it too costly for many British firms. On the other hand, there is a good deal of evidence that the high-surveillance firm is being adopted in this country amongst Japanese and other Asian firms operating here. Indeed, the high-surveillance firm involves well-tried technology with unskilled labour that has been developed by the Japanese and utilized by them in many parts of the world. There is no requirement for workers with special attributes with this model. The people employed are given instruction, and their performance is carefully supervised and monitored. This recipe for the organization of production is in some ways in sharp contrast with the regime of indirect discipline found in the new flexible firm. Here groups of workers are substantially left to regulate their own activity. In this sort of regime, relative freedom from close control is extended along with an implied threat that if the work completed does not come up to expectation, employment is not guaranteed.

Not firms but business units

The high-surveillance firm and the new flexible firm are workable models for the organization of production, and there is considerable evidence that they are widely employed. However, they both have another feature worth noting. In the discussion of the high-surveillance firm it has been stated that the organizations being described are actually the subsidiaries or affiliates of Japanese companies. Strictly speaking, because they are not independent companies, we ought to use the term business units to describe them, following the suggestions made in Chapter 2. In fact, the same point can be made about the new flexible firm. In their discussion, Ackroyd and Procter suggest that these firms are often owned by the very largest companies still involved in manufacturing in the UK (Ackroyd and Procter 1998). New flexible firms are not always subsidiaries, but often they are. Here we arrive at an interesting suggestion: that the companies surviving to replace the independent small firm (with which the discussion of this chapter began) are themselves not independent firms.

It seems that not only has there been significant reorganization in the firms and business units that produce good and services, but there has also been considerable development in the relations between firms. It is now common for what appear to be independent small firms actually to be business units belonging to large firms. If they do not actually belong to large firms, it is quite likely that they are in some way affiliated to a large firm. They may not be owned or partly owned, but they do have continuing contractual relations with large firms. There has been a marked development in recent years of 'supply chains', in which large numbers of firms cooperate in the production of the components for complex products. Hence, the response of firms to intensifying competition, as described at the beginning of this chapter, has not only resulted in firms reorganizing themselves internally: there has been significant development of interfirm relationships as well.

Because of the low commitment to technical improvement, and the considerable reliance on the continued contribution of labour, it is more difficult to see the new flexible firm as viable in the medium to long term. However, it is a pattern showing some obvious continuity with the traditional kind of organization discussed at the beginning of this chapter. It might be thought surprising that this pattern of organization is being applied to the management of firms belonging to large business groups in this country. A higher level of investment might be expected to yield a higher level of return. However, the policy explaining the use of the new flexible firm is that it does not cost very much, and yet can make useful profits in the right markets. In short, what is involved here is a continuation of the goal of realizing high profit in the short term. There is no long-term commitment to any particular sphere of activity.

But before passing on, there is a last candidate for new type of firm. This is called the knowledge-intensive firm (or KIF), and is regarded by many as a prototype organization for the emerging new economy. The models we have considered have their most obvious application to production. Although we have suggested that these firms may also produce services, much of the discussion has had productive activities centrally in mind. However, if the knowledge economy is the shape of things to come, none of these models will really do. We saw in Chapter 2 that the main area of growth in the numbers of British organizations in recent decades has been amongst business services companies. It is therefore a good question to ask what such companies are like.

5.7 The knowledge-intensive Firm

The knowledge-intensive Firm (KIF) has been considered by many as a highly significant new type of organization (Starbuck 1993; Blackler *et al.* 1993; Alvesson 1995; Blackler 1995; Reed 1996; cf. Ackroyd and Lawrenson 1996). Some firms in the information technology industry have been identified as KIFs as have many firms which define themselves as management consultancies. There are numerous other types of organization that might also be considered as KIFs such as organizations which offer such services as customer relations, marketing, and advertising. Starbuck has specifically suggested that certain manufacturing firms can be KIFs. Mats Alvesson, a highly perceptive analyst, identifies KIFs as 'human-capital intensive structures' (1995: 6) and asserts that their typical area of activity is management consultancy. Alvesson argues that KIFs are in the business of tailoring their products—business and management services of various kinds—to what are conceived to be the unique needs of their clients. Hence it has been argued that this type of organization is found in a number of sectors and is becoming increasingly important.

The main organizational features of the firms we are concerned with here are not in dispute. In the view of most exponents, KIFs are firms displaying the following properties. The contribution of knowledge to value added is large and indispensable whatever the importance of other factors of production. In the utilization of knowledgeable employees, many being professionals with high levels of education, there is extensive use of team-working and project groups. At the level of organizational structure, there is decentring of authority and the use of highly developed matrix designs. To offset the loss of centralized authority there are distinctive forms of management and new devices for the incorporation and control of personnel. Here we have informality and friendliness in personal relations, employee-centred personnel policies, and distinctive cultural values. The last of these is specially featured by radical analysts of KIFs, who see in this 'new human relations' the devious working of extremely controlling systems (Kunda 1992; Willmott 1993; Alvesson 1995).

KIFs are firms which are organized around flexible teams. They are departures from the orthodox organizational designs discussed in Chapter 3, with the possible exception of the matrix pattern. However, the membership of teams is not fixed. Services are put together by teams with different mixes of expertise and training, according to need. Teams vary in size but typically are quite small, having about seven members. Small firms contain a small number of teams—perhaps as few as one. Larger firms will be, at any one time, configured as a large number of discrete project teams. Individuals and groups may make contributions by subcontracting work outside the firm itself. Consultants, for example, use other consultants as ancillary staff. This is facilitated by the widespread use of the associate structure; where small firms are sometimes constituted by a network of self-employed, affiliated staff (Ackroyd 1995). Software designers and information systems teams come to similar arrangements with people outside their employment. These arrangements can be thought of as firms developing permeable boundaries and help to explain the appeal of the network metaphor to describe some of these organizational arrangements. In all these respects these firms are quite different from the organizations considered earlier.

Functions of the KIF

The way that knowledge and skills are packaged and deployed is undoubtedly new, but the idea that this in some way involves new kinds of knowledge as is sometimes the case (Blackler 1995) is more difficult to defend. Even the idea that KIFs possess and deploy very high levels of expertise is questionable. Alvesson describes one of their main activities as being 'ambiguity suppression'. If this is true, a good deal of the activity of KIFs is far from being esoteric or innovative, it is mostly aimed at helping client companies through periods when their own staff are overloaded, or to initiate facilities that then can be run by the client organization's own staff in the medium term after the initial labour-intensive phases of design and installation. In these circumstances, it is hard to judge the value of the inputs of project teams or to estimate their level of technical competence. Even if KIFs are outstanding contributors to wealth creation, all KIFs operate in environments of considerable ambiguity and, for this reason, their contribution is also steeped in rhetoric. None of this is to deny that KIFs are often genuinely 'knowledge-intensive' or that knowledge is their main resource.

However, Alvesson (1995) also argues perceptively that it is their distinctive relationship with their clients that makes KIFs really interesting and important. The relationship of KIFs to their clients—and the demands that clients make on them—is the key to understanding the novel internal structuring that KIFs adopt. They are in the business of tailoring their products—business and management services of various kinds—to what are conceived to be the unique needs of clients. To do this they have to be highly flexible and adaptive. While KIFs are often internally open and participative, and their employees are necessarily self-directed, they are often engaged in constructing technical and managerial systems of control for client organizations. Where they are not directly engaged in augmenting the wealth-creating capacities of the major companies that are their clientele, KIFs draw their earnings from augmenting and contributing to the functioning of larger business units. KIFs are organizations dedicated to serving the needs of client organizations in particular situations. However, whether they are management consultancies or not, a recurring feature of these firms is that their clients are relatively few and usually much bigger than they are.

Commentators too often rely on the implication that KIFs create value independently of their client organizations. However, it is clear that KIFs develop and succeed, not because of their human coordination and supposedly specially intensive use of human talents, but because of some extremely fortuitous market conditions in which they find themselves, in which large corporate clients have an acute need for external services. The market niches in which KIFs operate arise because of the needs of large corporations. Such clients require services which will protect their investments, and will pay well in order to secure this. It is in fact difficult to imagine there being a need for KIFs if there were no large corporations with needs that the KIFs supply. In trying to work out why there are KIFs in large numbers, it is well to think in terms of their clientele and the needs they supply, rather than imagine that they are an independent source of wealth creation.

5.8 Conclusions

Finally, we return to the question raised in the introduction to this chapter. This concerns the contribution of the small firm to economic regeneration and growth. It does depend somewhat on where one looks, what conclusion is drawn. However, there is not a lot to support the idea that the fortunes of the manufacturing economy are being reversed through the spontaneous development of new and more effective small businesses. The factors that made the environment hostile to the independent firm are still there. Despite an unprecedented loss of capacity in the last two decades, and the drastic reorganization of the British manufacturing firm along the lines of the new flexible firm, it is still not clear that a viable (not to mention a regenerating) manufacturing sector has developed. What is clear is that large firms and business groups are now deeply involved with small firms in the manufacturing sector, and much of the alleged growth of small firms is attributable to their ownership of large numbers of specialized business units which are indistinguishable from SMEs. The penetration of the economy by foreign firms has not put British businesses back on a competitive footing, but simply made them finally withdraw from a range of activities and pushed them into new modes of operation.

Evidence for the importance of the small firm is strong in the sector of business services and consultancies. The KIF does look like a kind of small company that is growing in importance. Discussion of the KIF and the knowledge economy generally is often accompanied by strongly drawn diffusionist arguments, in which new types of effective organizations are seen as spreading out from the sectors in which KIFs were first created to increasingly take over the economy. According to this they offer a new and powerful basis for wealth creation. This is another version of the argument that economic renewal will occur from the bottom up. This time the hoped for creativity and growth is seen as springing from KIFs rather than manufacturing firms, but the basic argument is the same. However, when we examine the evidence for the idea that the KIF is a new form of organization able to revitalize the economy from the inside, any convincing explanation of how this is possible is not provided.

Here again it can be shown that the wealth creation of this type of firm is at best synergistic with and at worst parasitic on the earnings of large businesses to which they sell services. It is difficult to see what such firms do as a source of wealth creation independent of the large corporate sector. Wherever we look, then, it seems that there is little to support the argument that the British economy is being reconstructed from the bottom up, as it were, by spontaneous growth from the grass roots. If it is being reconstructed, there is much more to point in the other direction: small businesses are changing because large businesses are changing. It would be nice to think that with just a little thought and some readjustment here and there British industry could have been revived; but this is not what has happened.

Many commentators accept that the revival of the small firm is connected with the revitalization and redirection of large businesses which began at the same time. Owen (1999) has recently argued that the chance conjuncture of reviving economic prosperity in the world (especially the increasing opportunities for world trade), and a government with a highly supportive attitude to big business (in the shape of Mrs Thatcher's right-wing governments) allowed British businesses to prosper once again. Small business, as the junior partner of large business in many industries, shared in the general prosperity. A more extreme account, which lays even more emphasis on the role of large firms in the revival, advances what is called the fragmentation thesis (Shutt and Whittington 1987). In this it is argued that the growth of the revival of the small firm is due to the tendency of large businesses deliberately to deconstruct their domestic operations and to move their assets around by buying into existing small businesses or setting up their own small firms outside traditional industrial districts. This was done for reasons of their own: to defray and reduce the costs of continuing in production in the UK and to release capital for expansion overseas are among their main motives.

This trend has continued apace: large organizations are fragmenting themselves into a large number of small businesses and operating units. It is now the case that the population of organizations seems to be made up of large numbers of small organizations in different degrees of cooperation with each other. Large firms engage in outsourcing, subcontracting, and 'unbundling' as a business strategy to spread their risks and in the process small firms emerge and develop. What appear to be small businesses often are not. Many of them are owned or otherwise affiliated to very large businesses. To the direct consideration of these we now turn.

6

Large corporations

6.1 The importance of large corporations

Large firms play a significant role in the developed economies, and have done so for much of recent history. This is certainly true of Britain. During the last century, the tendency towards the concentration of capital and the domination of large firms greatly increased. During that period, large firms contributed disproportionately to both employment and earnings. Firms grew particularly in the post-Second World War period as much by takeover and merger as organic growth (Hart *et al.* 1973; Meeks 1977). During the 1960s and 1970s there was contraction in the numbers of small firms and a huge surge of take-overs during which large companies grew greatly in size. In the manufacturing sector alone, the annual number of firms disappearing as a result of merger was more than 500 in most years between 1961 and 1975 (Hannah 1983).

As a result, in recent decades, Britain exhibited the highest capital concentration of any advanced society, more so than the USA, and any of the major European economies (Chandler and Deams 1980). According to Hannah (1976: 216), the share of net output produced by the 200 largest British firms rose to more than 40 per cent by the end of the 1960s. Williams *et al.* (1983: 32) suggest that the percentage was higher, with around 50 per cent of UK manufacturing output and employment being contributed by the 100 largest companies. The increase in industrial concentration levelled off in the 1980s, through a combination of firms reducing the scale of their operations in this country and the tendency for them to export their capacity overseas. There is now consolidation—firms are adjusting their portfolios of subsidiaries and affiliates by buying and selling them. Divestment activity became prevalent during the 1980s (Shutt and Whittington 1987; Wright *et al.* 1989: 116). However, the volume of buy-outs in Britain in the second half of the 1980s was still double that of the rest of Europe (Prowse 1994: 49). Hence, the practice of merger and acquisition has not disappeared. In very recent years there has been a spate of huge mergers and takeovers, many of which involve cross-national alliances being formed. The effects of this are not fully known.

The largest British firms are now very large indeed. To get some idea of their scale, we can consider them by comparison with whole nations. Anderson and Cavanagh (2000: 67–8), claim that half the 100 largest economic agglomerations in the world are now organizations. To make such comparisons it has to be assumed that the sales turnover of a company is roughly comparable with the gross national product (GNP) of a country (see also Gwynne 1990: ch. 9). On this assumption large companies are larger than many countries. For example, in 2000, General Motors (GM), Anderson and Cavanagh suggest, was larger than Denmark and Norway and Poland and almost as big as Indonesia, the fourth most populous country on earth. The British oil company, BP (since merged with the American company, Amoco), and its Anglo-Dutch counterpart, Shell, are in the same league as General Motors and Ford. In 1998, Shell was rated by *The Times* as the sixth and BP (even before merger) as the thirtieth largest companies in the world as measured by the value of the capital they employ, (*The Times* 1000, 1998). In Anderson and Cavanagh's terms, Shell is economically larger than Greece, Finland, and Malaysia.

Large British firms and those of other countries compared

Until recently, Britain stood comparison with any European economy in terms of numbers of large firms. Lane (1995: 66) reports that, of the 100 largest firms in Europe at the end of the 1980s (as measured by turnover), 28 were British, 24 German, and 17 French. At the end of the 1990s, a similar calculation for European companies measured by capitalization (perhaps a more appropriate measure as British firms tend to have high turnover in proportion to the capital they employ), shows that 17 were British, 28 French, and 20 German (calculated from *The Times* 1000, 1998). The most telling comparison, however, is the size of British industrial companies by comparison with the rest of the world. The designation 'industrial' here is roughly equivalent to the category of production used in the British statistics although it also includes telecommunications and media companies (see tables on pages 20 and 23).

Table 6.1 compares the fifty largest industrial companies in the world (as designated above). Although British companies are represented, there are fewer than one might expect for the size of the British economy, with average capitalization lower than for any other country in the table. This suggests that Britain has a disproportionately small share of the world's largest companies, and it is holding on only in a few sectors.

Table 6.2 offers a classification of the 200 largest British firms in 1997, and shows that Britain's largest firms are concentrated in a few sectors. Only

Table 6.1 Nationality of the 100 largest companies in the world, by capital employed 1998.

Country	Number	%	Capital employed (£m.)	%	Average capitalization
JAPAN	16	32	494	37	30.88
USA	11	22	273	20	24.82
EUROPE					
Germany	8	16	226	17	28.25
UK	2	4	38	3	19.00
Other	11	22	275	20	25.00
EUROPE TOTAL	21	42	539	40	25.67
OTHER	2	4	37	3	18.50
TOTAL	50	100	1 343	100	26.86

Source: Calculated from *The Times* 1000, 1998 (1999)

British oil, pharmaceutical, and telecommunications companies are comparable to the largest firms of other countries. Indeed, since the compilation of this table, with the collapse in the value of major British telecommunications stocks, whether British companies will retain their importance in this sector has become questionable. For many, the only conclusion to draw is that major British firms are struggling. In several areas, particularly manufacturing, British large businesses are judged to be growing slowly, and their long-term future is questionable.

As Table 6.2 suggests, manufacturing companies have been overtaken in average size by media, commercial, and retailing companies as measured by their stock-market capitalization. Certainly, if the main advantage of large production units lies in economies of scale and the ability to operate a large distribution and/or service network, then it is clear that the size of German and Japanese corporations renders them able to reap benefits by their adoption of large-scale production. Although Britain has many large manufacturing companies, they tend to be smaller than the largest comparable companies in the USA, Germany, and Japan. This is shown in a graphic way by Table 6.2 which indicates that the largest British manufacturers of products are, for all their size, much smaller than comparable companies based in Germany and Japan.

In the 1980s, it was commonly suggested that British manufacturing was doomed, so much capacity had been lost (Hirst and Zeitlin 1988; Williams *et al.* 1990*b*). The extrapolation of trends suggested that there would be no

Table 6.2 Market capitalization (£bn.) of selected foreign and British manufacturing firms in early 2001 as quoted on the London stock market

Toyota (Japan)	90.4
Mitsubishi (Japan)	70.0
Siemens (Germany)	38.3
Honda (Japan)	30.7
Volkswagen (Germany)	10.2
B.Ae Systems (Britain)	10.5
Marconi (Britain)	7.0
GKN (Britain)	4.9
Invensys (Britain)	4.8
Rolls-Royce (Britain)	3.6

Source: Compiled from the *Financial Times*, March 2001

NB. Not long after this table was compiled the Marconi share price fell and the market capitalization of this company was drastically reduced. Later in the year also, world markets entered a period of 'correction' and fell significantly. These values may not therefore be reflected in the current capitalization of these firms.

manufacturing industry left. It has not proved to be the case even in manufacturing. Major British businesses in most sectors have found new modes of organizing including the development of distinctive kinds of interfirm relationships (Dunning 1997). However, few would contend that all is well and British capitalism is set to compete effectively with the rest of the world (cf. Owen 1999).

6.2 The explanatory task

Setting out the special features of large British companies, and explaining why even the largest of them have not performed very well, is the main concern of this chapter. The discussion concludes with a consideration of some of the new organizational structures and the associated strategies of large British companies. While there are distinctive patterns to be observed, there are also interesting contemporary developments. The argument will be that British companies have, with the aid of distinctive managerial strategies, begun to transform themselves into distinctive new structures which have not been identified until now. Once powerful technologies and other resources became available to executives—who have themselves acquired new levels of freedom with which to act—corporate structures have been transformed in distinctive ways.

In the literature on large British firms it has often been argued that they have distinctive features, which can be traced to their trajectory of historical development. This conclusion is hardly unexpected. It was argued in Chapter 4 that the groups in British companies have distinctive patterns of relationships. If the proposition that structures are a product of the relations between groups has any validity, it follows that the patterns of relationships have an impact on the resulting structure and the characteristic dynamics of British firms. One interesting task, therefore, is to look for correspondences between what we know of the constitution of groups and the identifiable features of organizational structures as discussed by economic historians and other commentators. From these discussions, it is easy to conclude that the characteristic organizational forms adopted by British businesses were, for a long period, in many respects simply responses to the institutional context in Britain. These include market conditions and conditions of the supply of finance. This argument was supported in the last chapter for small firms and similar arguments apply to large firms. However, institutional factors impact with less force on large companies. Large companies are, so much more often than small companies, able to shape their environment rather than being shaped by it; and this has become more obviously so in recent years.

Large firms are not so dependent on banks, for example. This is not because they do not need short-term finance, but because they have alternative sources of capital open to them and are able to switch from short-term to longer-term borrowing. There is also a point about the kind of dependency that exists between a bank and a large debtor. The following adage expresses this point. If you owe the bank £10 000 and cannot pay, you have a problem: if you owe the bank £10 000 000, and cannot pay, the bank also has a problem. In the case of Marconi (see Box 6.1), the consortium of banks providing finance for the company is keeping it afloat because, prior to the recent collapse in the share value, they had agreed a new line of credit for the company until the end of 2003. Even if they could demand their money back, no doubt the banks would consider carefully how much of their loan they are likely to recoup if the company were to be sold or otherwise wound up. With large debts it is often more rational for banks to calculate whether they will get their loans back with full interest in the medium term. Often British banks are not willing to do this for small companies.

Of course, there are circumstances which the largest firms cannot ignore. Of the most important here are the conditions attached to the supply of capital from the stock market. In the past and still today, stock-market

---

BOX 6.1 The collapse in Marconi's share price casts doubt on the company's ability to survive

A ghastly profits warning, Marconi's second in two months, and a further collapse in the share price has brought doubt on the company's ability to survive. Lord Simpson [the company's CEO] is now on what might turn out to be an extended holiday. . . . Even the institutional shareholders, not normally bothered by such details as compensation for failure, are demanding that he leaves without a payoff. The peer has destroyed shareholder value on an awesome scale, turning the dull but rich GEC (which was soon to become GEC-Marconi) into a debt-laden company which is now afloat only because its bankers cannot demand their money back.

Lord Simpson inherited a company in GEC that had made a profit of £981m, with £1.4 billion in cash in the bank and a market value of around £11 billion in 1997. In the early days, the emphasis was on selling: in all, £3 billion was raised this way, including the £1 billion flotation of Alstom, the heavy engineering business, in 1998 . . . In 1999 GEC's strongest businesses—its defence related division—was merged with B.AE. The shrunken GEC was left with £2.7 billion in cash, and plenty of ambition.

How did Lord Simpson bring such a well-founded business to its knees? Aided by John Mayo, an aggressive former Warburg banker, who joined in October 1997, the two tested the fashion of focus to its limit. They stripped out many of the company's traditional businesses to create a telecoms equipment manufacturer. Simpson told shareholders he would not be left with an 'inefficient' cash mountain. The natural target was the telecoms equipment market, since the old GEC had been almost a monopoly supplier to British Telecom. [The Company] needed to get into the world's home of telecoms, America. Prices for such businesses were rising fast, and ratings lost all touch with reality. Fatefully, Marconi paid in cash not shares. . . . In April 1999, $2.1 billion went on Ohio-based Reltec, followed by $4.5 billion for Fore Systems

The profits are gone, replaced by an operating loss of perhaps £100m, and so has the cash. Debts now total £4.4 billion, and at yesterday's price of 29.5 p Marconi is valued at £822m. The company has had to make 9000 redundancies this year and is being kept afloat by a syndicate of banks which, just before the storm broke, provided unconditional debt facilities stretching ahead to March 2003. Perhaps the most depressing aspect of the tale is that Marconi is still a weak player in a global market. It ranked fifth behind Cisco, Lucent, Nortel and Alcatel, and remains heavily dependent on BT.

Abstracted from an article by Dan Sabbagh in the *Daily Telegraph*, 8 September 2001

---

financing has been a considerable limitation on British companies. But to say that large companies have had their characteristic policies and strategies determined for them by these circumstances would be misleading. Corporate managers are—in a meaningful sense of the words—*in control* of their firms. In companies of all sizes, firms are controllable bundles of resources, and their executives can choose their direction. Indeed, there is much evidence that business leaders have been active in shaping the organizational structures they control. The process of adjusting the structure of companies by buying and selling constituent parts will be referred to several times in the course of this chapter. The active shaping of companies in this way is obvious to anyone who reads the financial press. A topical example at the time of writing this passage is the dramatic reshaping of the Marconi PLC.

Symptoms of economic decline?

It may be that the distinctive policies of large British businesses are connected with the long-term relative decline in the British economy as a whole which is widely argued to be occurring. It might be thought that the policies of companies are in some ways connected with economic decline: either they are attempts to remain profitable in a situation of decline, or they themselves contribute to the process of decline or some combination of these.

There has been an extended debate about the causes of the relative decline of the British economy, and the debate is not one of recent origin (Coates 1994). It does seem to be the case that the British economy has not grown as fast as other economies of comparable size in recent decades. It is especially noticeable that, in the decades after the Second World War, when much damage had been done to the infrastructure of Germany, France, and Japan, the British economy failed to grow strongly. Despite having many advantages, the British economy has been overtaken by all these rivals. Debate as to causes has covered a lot of ground. Blame for Britain's decline has implicated factors including the capacity of British managers, the problems of capital supply, the role of the City of London in financing major companies, and the lack of concern by the state as well as the alleged recalcitrance of labour.

Large organizations are so important to the economy that it is more than plausible to think that their role could be pivotal in determining the overall direction of economic change. Industrialization, which has been the basis of the prosperity of the advanced economies, is underpinned by particular patterns of organizational development. Large businesses are the key to economic development and may also drive other secular processes of economic change. Clearly also, large businesses may lead to relative decline, depending on how they are configured and how they relate to other institutions. If this is so, it may not be that we have to indict one of the usual suspects—capital, state, or labour—as causes of British decline. It may be that the inefficiency of major companies arises as part of a characteristic pattern of institutionalization found in this country. In this view, questions must concern the way in which institutions have adapted to each other and constrained as much as enabled each other.

This is the kind of argument that is developed in this chapter. Although the institutional context of British firms has been constraining historically, leading to poor adaptation and relative decline in the economy, these same pressures have led major firms to develop distinctive organizational

---

BOX 6.2 Summarizing Britain's relative decline

• There has been a steady slippage in the UK's share of world output and trade in manufactured goods, and since 1966 a fall in the number of people employed in the UK manufacturing sector;

• Except for a brief period in the mid 1980s, rates of growth in GDP have been consistently lower in the UK than those achieved in key competitor economies abroad;

• Throughout the postwar period, levels of labour productivity have consistently fallen below those achieved in more successful economies, with that gap narrowing only in the second half of the 1985;

• Since 1973, both inflation and unemployment rates in the UK have been higher than those found in the majority of advanced capitalist societies;

• And finally, since 1960 wage levels in the UK have fallen to the second lowest in Western Europe, as the country's position in the league table of income per head has steadily slipped.

David Coates (1994: 5)

---

structures. Today these are certainly enabling major organizations to survive and, indeed, allowing many of them to prosper. However, in the context of greater freedom for corporate managers, and with the availability of new resources in the shape of information technology, large firms have embarked on processes of development in the last twenty years that are almost without precedent. Major firms are developing forms of industrial structure that will allow them to expand in the twenty-first century. Because of the particular path of development they have chosen, however, this is not the same thing as claiming that the growth of large firms will reverse the trend of relative decline in the British economy.

6.3 Misleading ideas about the development of major companies

In the main accounts of the development of large companies, there is a tendency for analysts to distinguish a set sequence of development, and to see any deviations from this pattern in different societies as abnormalities. One such pattern is that as firms become larger they become more bureaucratic and, beyond a certain point of development, this centralization and formalization becomes a problem rather than an asset. This is the idea some historians of business have when they suggest that there is development from the large 'U' form of bureaucracy to the multidivisional structure. On this account, the development of the huge, centralized, and integrated manufacturing plant, on the lines of American Ford, is seen to be a necessary stage of development.

Some American historians argued that a particular form of organization is the best and most efficient one for the largest companies and should be adopted by all large firms. These historians have been merciless in their indictment of British businesses for their 'failure' to follow what they see as the expected pattern of development (Chandler and Deams 1980; Lazonick 1991). To these writers, British companies have been slow to adopt the 'M' form, and to forsake their traditional patterns. This, for these writers, is a major key to understanding the failure of British economic development. British companies have not adopted the most efficient organizations and, because they have been less efficient, the economy as a whole has failed to grow. The fact that British organizations have usually been profitable—and yet have not passed through the large-scale and highly bureaucratized stage—does not deflect the critical thrust.

Chandler has written at length of the inherent weaknesses of the British pattern of 'personal capitalism' (Chandler 1977, 1990). By this he denotes a number of things: the lack of specialization of the management cadre and its amateurish outlook is linked with other factors such as the alleged persistence of family ownership and control. This Chandler compares with American 'competitive managerial capitalism'. The pejorative label attached to the British system, and the more upbeat designation for the American system suggest there may be more than a little cultural bias in Chandler's approach. In support of this, the factual basis for the allegation that British firms are more family-based than the American has been challenged (Church 1986). A positive gloss on typical British business management is to say that it is neither bureaucratic nor technically based, and, as such, was capable of a fairly rapid response to different market opportunities.

It is true that very large-scale mass production was achieved by the so-called 'second wave' industrial powers; that is, the USA and Germany in the early decades of the last century. British capitalism led the world in the early nineteenth century, but it was superseded by more efficient forms in the USA and Germany by its end. The British pattern of production, based on large numbers of quite small firms in close proximity in distinct industrial districts—has been identified as an alternative to mass production using large-scale organizations (Sabel and Zeitlin 1985). However, the route to the development of large firms from decentralized patterns of production was not to large firms with centralized bureaucracies, or to the 'M' form of company, but quite often to the ownership of numerous firms within holding company structures. By this route it took longer to develop reasonably efficient major industries.

In sum, British institutions cannot be seen to be replicating a path of development pioneered by the USA. There are some similarities in the development of corporations in different countries, but, realistically considered, these are limited. The key question concerns the actual pattern for the development of major British companies. In this the leading models, including the 'M' form, are unreliable guides.

6.4 The British response to international competition

The challenge to British industry by mass production—as developed by the USA and Germany in the early twentieth century—was severe. This was felt first in some overseas markets where British dominance was under threat as early as the end of the nineteenth century. Competition was felt acutely and proved difficult to respond to in those industries with deep industrial experience. In the newer industries of chemicals and oil, by contrast, British companies did make the necessary investments and became world leaders. As has been shown, in pharmaceuticals and oil, British companies are still amongst the largest in the world. Paradoxically it was in areas of former industrial strength, where production had traditionally been organized on different lines to new (and more effective) patterns overseas that the ability to change was tested. The reduction of overseas markets could seem a relatively remote threat to a British company with a secure domestic and Commonwealth market on which to fall back.

The American historian, Lazonick (1991), attributed the failure of British companies to 'institutional rigidities' (Kirby 1992). These 'rigidities', such as backwardness and family control, help to explain Britain's relative failure in meeting the challenge of mass production. There is an important truth in this, in that, to compete on the same basis as newly industrialized countries in the early decades of the last century, British firms would have needed to make massive investments in integrated plants and to discard working (if obsolete) technology as well as changing traditional practices. This brings us to the conclusion that the circumstances in which British managers found themselves were not conducive to sustained growth and development. British managers were forced to a number of tactical manoeuvres to stay in business. Elbaum and Lazonick (1986: 7) write that the response of British manufacturers to their situation in the early and middle twentieth century was that they

---

BOX 6.3 **An historical perspective on British decline**

Forced to retreat from competition with mass production methods, British firms sought refuge in higher quality and more specialised product lines, where traditional craftsmanship and organisation could still command a competitive edge—in spinning, higher counts of yarn and weaving finer cloth, making sheets and plates of open hearth steel, and building unique one off ships. Unfortunately for the British, in a world of expanding markets, the specialised product of today all too often turned out to be the mass production item of tomorrow. The arrival of mass production methods and the pace and timing of decline varied . . . But all eventually met a similar fate.

Bernard Elbaum and William Lazonick (1986: 7)

---

were unable to invest on the scale required and took refuge in niche markets for high quality goods (see Box 6.3).

In explaining why investments were not forthcoming and other reforms not made, this account lays insufficient emphasis on the situation of the British firms and their stakeholders. It assumes one path to development and neglects the possibility that other countries may find new ways of organizing that may have unexpected advantages (Japan and Korea are examples). The problems for the British in following the American path were several. Markets for the output of British firms were smaller than those of American companies. Because of this, the possibilities for high profits and rapid expansion were less in Britain than America. Some British companies had access to captive colonial markets which were reliable sources of earnings (Hobsbawm 1968, 1975) but, for many, the outlets for goods and services were restricted.

True, British firms failed to invest at the requisite levels to catch up with the productivity of foreign competitors. Moreover, when these competitors began to penetrate domestic markets, British firms were forced to retreat further from capital-intensive areas of activity. Because they were able to serve their own domestic markets reasonably well without high concentrations of new investment, technically advanced mass production was often not seriously considered. The British car industry in early post-Second World War Britain, for example, though producing high volumes by British standards, did not remotely achieve the high-volume mass production of the USA. It has been estimated that, in the 1930s, the Ford Motor Company produced at its main plant five times more units as the entire British industry put together. Output of cars by individual British firms was tiny by US standards until well after the Second World War. British companies did not achieve enough horizontal and vertical integration. Component producers—serving a large number of car-producing customers—became much bigger than the largest car companies. Lucas (electrical components and instrumentation) and Dunlop (tyres and composites) were larger companies than either Austin or Morris, the largest British car producers at the time. This situation did not improve despite investment and modernization policies by British companies in the post-war situation (Ackroyd and Lawrenson 1995).

The development of something approximating American Fordism in Britain came late or not at all. It is interesting that even the Ford Motor Company—which undertook massive investment in Britain in the 1940s and 1950s, trying to establish a version of Fordism in this country—did not find it easy to achieve mass production in Britain. It can be argued that true mass production was only partially achieved, in only very few sectors, at great cost, in the 1950s and 1960s. Ironically, by this time, mass production had been rendered obsolescent as a productive system by the maturation of consumer markets and the associated decline of demand for highly standardized products. The main examples of the attempt to achieve concentrations of capital and large-scale production were the efforts to put together a national shipbuilding and a national car company under the auspices of the Labour government 1970s. The demise of the shipbuilding operation was rapid, while the final abandonment of the national car company took much longer, due to greater commitment of the government to subsidizing it. The formation of British Leyland in the 1970s, and its reprivatization, its sale to British Aerospace and then to BMW, turned out to be an expensive failure.

6.5 The importance of capital supply

This points to the problem of capital supply for British industry. In this case it seems that an inadequate supply of capital, or, to be more accurate, an adequate supply of capital on unhelpful terms, is a key to understanding the limited investment in British industry. More generally the conditions of capital supply are key to explaining the development of industrialism in different contexts. Zysman has studied relationships between banks and manufacturing companies in various countries (Zysman 1983), whilst Stearns has examined the relationship between capital markets and the extent of external control in the USA (Stearns 1990). The most impressive examples of successful industrialization—in Germany, Japan, and Korea—are associated with considerable development in the banking systems of these countries. In Germany, commentators realized that industrialization in that country was associated with considerable development of banking and finance capital, a fact that was spotted by contemporary analysts (Renner 1904; Hilferding 1910). By comparison with Britain stock markets were underdeveloped. Banks which specialized in the supply of capital for industry emerged and there have been typically close ties between banks and their industrial clients. Banks would commonly have directors on the boards of companies which were important clients. In Japan banks were and are constituent parts of established business groups. A bank that is closely tied to a client and has a large stake in a company will be reluctant to withdraw its loans.

British reliance on the stock market

By contrast, in Britain banks play a less significant role in supplying capital to large businesses than elsewhere. As an alternative, Britain had (and still has) some of the most developed financial markets in the world. As we have seen, the original function of a stock market was precisely that of providing large amounts of capital to expanding businesses, and, despite the speculative trading in shares now developed around them, this remains their main function. British companies could draw on these markets for funds rather than rely heavily on banks. In practice, the major companies of all countries draw on all the sources of finance: retained profits, bank loans, and capital from the sale of shares. Often there are other significant sources of finance as well, such as private loans. But the proportion of funds provided by one of these sources and other conditions on which funds are made available will profoundly affect the plans and policies of firms. The British stock market can and does make funds available to British firms, but it is a competitive market, having the highest volumes of trading of any market in the world. The share price responds quickly to perceived changes in company fortunes. If a firm is thought not to be doing well, its share price will be depressed and the company could become a target for takeover.

When judging the effects of stock-market finance on organizations and strategic policies of companies, there is more to think about than the extent to which such finance is or is not available. It matters who owns the stock as this is likely to have an effect on the stability or volatility of equity values. If we compare the ownership structure of Japanese and British firms, there is little difference in the proportion of stock owned by individuals. The big difference is in institutional ownership of stock between the two countries, the kinds of institution they are, and their relation to the company. In Britain, a high proportion of stock is owned by financial institutions such as pension funds, insurance companies, and investments trusts. Dore (1985) estimated this kind of ownership to be nearly 60 per cent of all British shareholding in the early 1980s. Such institutions aim to obtain good returns for their investors, and are likely to shift money about if they do not see a firm in which they have invested declaring good profits and/or its stock price improving. In Japan, by contrast, the largest institutional shareholders are banks and other industrial and commercial companies. Dore (1985) estimated the share of Japanese quoted stocks that such institutions hold was 45

BOX 6.4 Financial structures and the short-term view

In Britain, the stock exchange is not the appendix or the gall bladder of the body economic, but its very heart. It is not too much to strain after epigram to say that Britain's is a financier-dominated, Japan's a producer-dominated form of capitalism.

   The difference manifests itself in various ways: the ease with which 'merchant' banks and stockbroking companies with their high salaries can attract the brightest talent—latterly, also, the brightest engineering talent—away from industry and the public service; the predominance, as measured by column inches of the business press, of news about takeovers, intended, thwarted and accomplished—presumably reflecting the dominance of such concerns among managers; the fact that you make your name as a captain of industry more easily by a bold, if not swashbuckling, acquisitions policy, than by howsoever spectacular a plan for long range research and development. The fact that 'the judgement of the Stock Exchange' does command a considerable degree of respect, combines with the very real threat of takeover for companies with low share values to make the daily share price and the immediate dividend prospects which largely affect its short-term fluctuations—a central concern for corporation managers. Certainly, if they read what the press has to say about their company, they are likely to find half a dozen forecasts of their next term's results for every report—of their long-term development plans. Strong-minded managers, of course, do not let these messages about how the world is judging their performance affect their own judgements of themselves and the way they set their objectives. . . . For most managers of most manufacturing plants in Britain today, the pressures to concentrate on the short-term bottom line come, not directly from the stock market, but transmitted from the main board by the internal accounting procedures of the large and often conglomerate firm which owns their plant—commonly a regime of independently accounted profit centres, tight control through monthly performance indicators, and often managerial bonuses tied to the movement of those indicators.

R. P. Dore (1985: 21)

---

per cent. The banks and companies which hold Japanese company stocks, however, do so to consolidate other business connections they have with the firm. Often there are reciprocal shareholding arrangements. Thus the firms which own a company's stock are those with which there are ongoing business relationships and the fates of the companies involved are interconnected. Often, also, the banks are those lending money and/or affiliated to the same business groups. Such relationships are stable and the business partners are unlikely to risk the long-term viability of a firm to secure short-term advantages.

   There has been much debate about the impact of City of London-based financial institutions on industry (Ingham 1984; Kennedy 1987; Coates 1994: ch. 5; Hutton 1996: chs 5 and 6). It has been repeatedly denied that the City has any culpability for the long-term decline of British industry and the economy. However, the processes involved are subtle. Strategic investment on

---

BOX 6.5 **The stock market and clearing bank system**

The stock market and clearing bank system are the poles around which a very particular financial culture turns. The capital markets have earned a deserved reputation for innovation in clever financial instruments and a willingness to trade in them—but by the same token the system fails the corporate sector, affecting companies negatively at all stages of their life cycle. The system is deeply inhibiting to anything but short-term risk.

Its effects can be seen from the lowest level of capitalist endeavour to the highest and most complex. It could be the proprietors of a small firm having to surrender their house as collateral to the bank. . . .

The system forces larger companies to pay high and steadily growing dividends to a shifting cast of large shareholders, mindful of securing their loyalty against the approach of a predator—whose aim will be to repay the borrowings needed for the takeover by again raising prices and forgoing market share. There is a strong incentive to be 'risk averse' in drawing up investment strategies, because at moments of crisis shareholders retain the right to sell their equity rather than put up fresh risk capital—and are more likely to exercise that right than support the beleaguered company. As a result companies themselves place a premium on stable cash flow, high security and high returns. Technical innovation and building market share take second place to financial imperatives.

The disengagement of the banks, their obsession with short term lending and their unwillingness to support companies in trouble, puts an additional pressure on companies to rely on retained profits as a source of finance—and obliges them to sanction only investment projects with a high rate of return.

Will Hutton (1996: 134–5)

---

the scale required to build industries takes a relatively long time to bear fruit: it may be years, and, in extreme cases, decades, before the full benefits are realized. By contrast, independent pension fund and investment trust managers are looking for returns from dividend and share price performance over a short period. Knowing that if they are to retain shareholder confidence they must regularly show healthy profits is likely to constrain company managers and force them to consider how they are going to declare profits in the next two accounting periods. This detracts from their willingness to undertake investment for the longer term. Such considerations put large businesses in a similar situation to the small firm that is highly dependent on banking finance. Again the problem is the lack of other kinds of involvement (than strictly financial) by institutions in the companies in which they invest. Noting this problem in 1936, Keynes wrote that the remedy for the effects of speculative short-term investment would be to 'make the purchase of an investment permanent and indissoluble, like marriage, except by reason of death or other grave cause' (Keynes 1936; quoted by Congdon 1991). Such a remedy for the British problem of short-termism would be drastic, and had little prospect of being taken seriously, but illustrates that the problem is one of long standing.

Some consequences of reliance on the stock market

Any claim that the outlook and behaviour of City institutions has been fatal for British industry is difficult to sustain. However, City institutions have exported capital throughout the world, redirecting domestic surpluses away from domestic industry. Competitive capital markets do not offer British industry preferential rates. The result is a form of capitalism in Britain that is divided between its financial and industrial spheres, in which these two sides of the economy are not mutually reinforcing or even particularly supportive (Longstreth 1979; Ingham 1984) as in Germany and Japan. The value of flows of money between City and industry have been more or less balanced in recent decades. Mayer (1987) has argued that the financial sector makes little or no net contribution to the finance of physical investment in industry. As Williams *et al.* (1990*a*: 457) also argue: 'The inflow of funds from the financial sector into the real economy is usually balanced by a reverse flow of funds into the financial sector as industrial and commercial companies buy financial assets.' As we have argued, however, when they are used, stock market funds come with the condition that the firm obtaining them must remain profitable in the short term.

If there is validity in this analysis, the question arises: how is it that there are any major British companies at all, never mind many that simply fail to rival the largest in the world? The answers are several. Companies have become adept at identifying and moving into new markets for existing products, at identifying and moving out of activities that are unprofitable, and of moving into new lines of activity that are profitable. Strategies to achieve profitability have included: moving up market to produce luxury items, identifying and monopolizing small, relatively high-tech niches, moving down market into the production of low value-added goods for retail, diversifying activities so as to minimize reliance on one economic sector, diversifying into services (which minimizes the requirement for plant and machinery), and, finally, moving productive capacity abroad. British companies have been adaptable and capable of restructuring. However, before generalizing about patterns of restructuring and clarifying types of British major businesses, there will be a discussion of the general ways in which the institutional circumstances of major British companies have affected the policy and practices of strategic managements.

Consequences for strategic management

Some time ago, Channon (1982) suggested a continuum of possibilities from 'single' through 'dominant' through 'contingently related' businesses to 'conglomerates'. This is similar to Mintzberg's proposition that 'related product' companies and unrelated product companies or 'conglomerates' are part of the range of possibilities for divisionalized companies. Channon, however, brings forward data showing the number of firms classified in each category over a period of years. His data show clear trends: reduction of the numbers of single and dominant businesses in the period 1950 to 1980 and increase in the proportion of related businesses and conglomerates over the same period. Consideration of British companies using Channon's criteria in the 1990s revealed that the trends he identified in 1982 were continuing (Ackroyd and Procter 1998). In the middle of the 1990s, it was difficult to identify a single large British company that was a single product firm. For some time at least diversification has been distinctive strategy of British business.

Goold and Campbell (1987) distinguish 'financial control' management, in which control is exerted almost exclusively in response to performance in respect to profit targets, and contrast this with 'strategic planning' management in which development is orchestrated within a general overview of planned development. Strategic planning firms—operating with a long time horizon—may well shelter constituent parts of a business from the need to show profitability in the short term in order to maximize advantages in the medium to long term. The strategic planning strategy is difficult to sustain in the face of continuous pressure to meet capital market expectations. The importance of basic profitability means that many companies seek out activities with low investment requirements but steadily profitability (which the Boston Consulting Group (1970) have called 'cash cows'); that is, businesses which produce standard products for mature markets. If large firms do not have businesses of this kind in their portfolio, they cannot afford the sheltering and R&D expenditures required by innovation and longer-term development. Firms characterized by financial control strategies are also increasing in number.

Concern about profitability makes British managers conscious of the costs of running their businesses, and, in turn, performance requirements are likely to be set as financial targets. By such measures, failure to hit targets is visible and clear. Affiliated firms, subsidiaries, and units within such firms are likely to be assessed in terms of their own specific financial performance and not in terms of their contribution to the overall pattern of activities. This is one important reason why so many accountants are employed in Britain. Without accountants it is difficult to monitor costs and have a clear idea about the returns on capital invested. Higgins and Clegg (1988) argue that the forms of profit-orientated thinking which have arisen in British and Australian publicly quoted companies have affinities with the logic of accountancy. They further argue that priorities built into this way of thinking contradict and submerge considerations contained in such practices as research and development and investment planning, which are based on longer-term cycles.

In conformity with these financial expectations it is characteristic of large British firms that they are thought about by their managers as aggregates of separate cost centres for which individual performance targets can be set. Underperforming firms or units are likely to be closed, and new profitable businesses acquired, so contributing to continuous organizational restructuring (Ackroyd and Procter 1998). The key role for management within cost centres is to meet targets for profitable operation. Because of the importance of profit, a firm will tend to be interested in acquiring companies that can contribute to profitability and disposing of those that do not. The firms acquired do not need to be similar in their area of activity to that of the purchaser—only more profitable. Thus, how a company is divided up for monitoring and accounting purposes may allow or even encourage particular management strategies.

There is a tendency for corporate managers to move into and out of the ownership of firms, and, if it is expedient, to hold substantial assets as cash. This strategy leads to high levels of expertise in headquarters about how to manage a firm's position within these financial markets but it may also prompt subsidiaries to develop strategic survival skills, potentially resulting in centripetal tendencies. The experience of British firms allows them to be tolerant of wide variations in local practices: there is no commitment to a particular system of work regulation. British firms are not entirely unused to operating with a wide variety of work systems under the one corporate governance umbrella. When such companies become multinationals they can continue to allow the diversity of forms precisely because particular forms of organization for business units are not taken to be obligatory. It is the output of the firm in terms of profitability that is crucial. Firms can exhibit wide ranges of variation without generating severe conflict.

6.6 Some features of large British firms

British companies are smaller, considered as aggregates, than comparable companies in other parts of the world, and display other distinctive features. They are more diverse in their activities, and they have smaller, more dispersed plants and facilities. One way of responding to this is to say that British large businesses are simply ill-organized, with a legacy of past disorganization that has not been rationalized. If we take the evidence of the existence of smaller business units in British companies, for example, it is quite consistent. Prais suggests a rise from twenty-seven to seventy-two constituent parts of large businesses in the 1958–72 period (Prais 1976: 62). A comparison of the British pattern with the German showed that, during the 1970s, the top quartile of British plants was significantly smaller than the top quartile in Germany. Another comparison of British-owned companies with foreign-owned ones of similar size (this time within Britain) showed that, by 1985, British-owned companies still had more and smaller establishments (Marginson 1991; Marginson *et al.* 1988). Writing at the end of the 1980s, Lash and Urry (1987) show that the size of manufacturing plants was continuing to decline. On the other hand, there is evidence that it is dispersion and/or reduction that are being sought by corporate managers. Indeed, there are indications that, in many countries, there are now also deliberate policies of decentralization and disaggregation being undertaken by major companies (Lane 1995: 72–80). If this is so, it might be that the British firms are in the forefront of some new developments.

Focus, diversification, and predation as recurrent strategies

There are features of corporate strategy which make British large companies distinctive in addition to their relative smallness and small constituent parts. They also follow some distinctive strategies. As we have seen they have some-times followed strategies of diversification. However, they have sometimes pursued the opposite strategy, that of focusing, (i.e. to concentrate on the activities they consider to be their main business). If enough time elapses, large firms may return to diversification again—though it may not be the same pattern of activities they had before. These recurrent strategies are made possible by the ease with which companies can be bought and sold: most often large firms take over smaller ones and reorganize them. Of course, when policies of diversification are being pursued, acquisitions are not driven by any recognizable complementarity in activities, but are simply the acquisition of new (profitable or potentially profitable) businesses. There have been com-panies which have grown to power and eminence by the process of predation itself, where profits are made by rationalizing ailing businesses.

Usually, smaller businesses are taken over by larger ones, but not invariably. It has been common for small firms to take over larger ones—the so-called 'reverse takeover'. Indeed, there have been spectacular examples of the growth of large business empires by takeover strategies of these kinds. Anyone inter-ested in this should read the biographies of some of the businessmen who

---

BOX 6.6 **The bagging of Bovril**

In the spring of 1971, Goldsmith was stalking Bovril. . . . The economy was in boom and Cavenham was going with it. The recent rise in the Cavenham share price meant that the company was actually bigger than the much more establishment Bovril in terms of stock-market value, but not in terms of assets. Bovril's profits had not risen since 1961.

On 27 June Goldsmith made his move and immediately became embroiled in his first seriously contested takeover bid. . . .

[By August] . . . Goldsmith was now charging ahead. . . . As the markets opened for business on Monday morning, he went straight in and at the close had bought another 12 per cent of Bovril's shares to take his holding to 36 per cent. The next day his stockbrokers went into the market again and added another 7 per cent. By Wednesday, 18 August he was up to 47 per cent and announced that the Prudential Assurance Company and another group had promised him their holdings, which 'will put us over the top'.

He had scraped up the money from wherever he could. . . . 'We were buying stock without funds, to tell the truth' says Tigret. . . . Goldsmith did not disagree: 'Every penny we had and every penny of credit we could raise was used to buy Bovril.'. . .

By the time Goldsmith had finished selling off the bits of Bovril he did not want, he had recouped almost all his original purchase price, leaving him with the main brands. He cut overheads by £500 000, revamped the marketing and doubled the profits to £2 million a year. Some years later, when he decided to get out of food, he sold the brand names to Beecham for £36 million.

'Bovril was the turning point of Jimmy Goldsmith's career', says John Tigret, and Goldsmith himself does not disagree. 'It was the most important deal of deal of my life.'

Extracted from Ian Fallon (1991: 215–25)

---

undertook these activities—James Goldsmith (Fallon 1991), James Hanson (Brummer and Cowe 1994), or 'Tiny' Roland (Bower 1993). The reorganization of business by these means may seem a haphazard process, and to a considerable extent it is, but they are the main means by which business in Britain is restructured. Major businesses have been assembled and many firms reconstructed by takeover and merger followed by rationalization and resale.

The activities of predatory conglomerates have been spectacular, but it is also common for large British businesses to buy and sell smaller companies and to change their patterns of activity and degree of diversification. The firm, British and American Tobacco, for example, had a stock-market capitalization of more than £11 billion in early 2001 and is therefore one of Britain's largest companies. Its main business is to manufacture and sell tobacco products worldwide. However, for a long period this focus on tobacco was not so exclusive. In the 1970s, the firm changed its name to BAT Industries and diversified first into retailing and then into insurance. In the late 1980s, BAT bought up a number of well-known insurance companies both here and abroad and became a major force in the world of insurance. During the 1990s BAT floated off some of its assets as separate companies (setting up the new retailing business Argos in the process) and sold others. In the early twenty-first century it does not have insurance interests. And it has renamed itself British and American Tobacco once more. Another example is BICC, by the 1970s Britain's only significant maker of cables and wires. In the 1970s it diversified into civil engineering with the acquisition of Balfour Beatty, which was itself a large firm. The civil engineering arm became more important, ending with the sale of the cables division in the late 1990s.

The following section aims to produce some ideal type accounts of major British companies, analogous to the models of types of small firms and business units—the high surveillance firm and the new flexible firm—as outlined in the previous chapter. It would be more precise to say that what we are discussing here are characteristic strategies which companies have made central to their policy and practice and which in turn shape their structures.

6.7 Some types of large British company

The retail-related manufacturer-trader

This type of company may be regarded as a focused corporation. The area of specialization is low value-added activities involved in food processing and other activities related to bringing products to the retail market. The original emphasis in these companies is on producing cheaply and in bulk for domestic markets. The strategy is relatively immune to competition from overseas because of the low value of the products produced or supplied and their relatively high costs of transportation. Even so such firms can be very large, and are larger than comparable companies in other countries with the exception of the USA. In this category, the obvious candidates are food producing and domestic product groups such as Associated British Foods, Cadbury-Schweppes, the Anglo-Dutch group Unilever, and Tate and Lyle. Also to be considered in this category are building materials groups such as Wolseley, RMC group, and Blue Circle Industries. There are also several large drinks, entertainment, and leisure groups companies—such as Allied Domecq, Diageo, and Six Continents (formerly Bass) that have to be considered in this category of large firm. Then there are large retailers which own or control maufacturing firms, and other suppliers of products, such as Marks & Spencer, Boots, Kingfisher, Sainsbury's, and Tesco. The largest of these firms have a global presence owning distinctive and valuable world brands.

Most of these firms have been highly diversified historically. Many of the drinks companies are or have been at some time diversified into entertainment and leisure companies: they own the pubs, restaurants, hotels, and casinos in which their products are consumed. Allied Domecq and Six Continents are both firms that originated as brewers, and which continue to make and sell these beverages, but they are now often listed as leisure groups and represent their main business as the owners and managers of pubs, clubs, and other leisure facilities. These businesses, especially those associated with food and leisure, have been innovative in internal organization, flattening their structures and developing franchising and innovative management arrangements. Again there is a tendency to buy into firms on a speculative basis and to shuffle the pack of subsidiaries to find new lines of business to enhance profitability. These days there is a tendency to seek more focus, as in the example of Kingfisher (see Box 6.7), but in such cases it often does not mean the reduction in the scale of the enterprise as a whole, because the company simply extends its global spread. All large British businesses are capable of being predatory on smaller businesses.

The focused corporation

In this distinctive type of company the dominant strategy is for the corporation to clarify its central or core activity and concentrate on it. Some of the most successful of British companies have exemplified this form and have remained focused for long periods. One thinks of the major oil companies such as the Anglo-Dutch group Shell Transport/Royal Dutch and BP (now BP-Amoco) and some of the pharmaceutical firms such as Glaxo Smith Kline. These companies have survived by consolidating and merging with comparable companies from overseas. Other than companies operating in these sectors, however, it is more questionable whether there are examples of successful companies with substantially British ownership. Vodafone (recently merged with the German company Mannesmann), BT, Cable and Wireless, and Marconi are all large companies, but, at the present time, there is doubt about their future profitability and survival as independent companies.

Of focused companies in traditional areas of British involvement, such as heavy and consumer durable manufacturing, it is more difficult to find examples of successful companies. There are several companies that might qualify and B.Ae Systems, Rolls-Royce, GKN, and Vickers, all of which manufacture significant engineering products—namely, aeroplanes, aero engines, helicopters, submarines, and tanks—as part of their portfolio, are among them. Two points are worth making about these companies—they are not solely engaged on the production of complex products, and also they are highly dependent on defence products and contracts. Almost all other broad-spectrum engineers are struggling or have already passed into foreign ownership (see Box 2.4: Changes in the engineering sector, page 32).

BOX 6.7 **What is Kingfisher fishing for?**

Sir Geoffrey Mulcahy is looking ahead. Having built up the Kingfisher Group to its current impressive size, Sir Geoffrey now has plans to dismantle and reshape the British retailing company he assembled during the last decade. He now plans to fashion a focused retailing company from the group of which he is chief executive.

In early 2001, Kingfisher hit the financial press with the unveiling of Mulcahy's plan to split the retail giant in two. Central to this plan is shedding Woolworth and Superdrug, the general-merchandise chains within the group—either by way of a demerger or, as appears increasingly likely, a sale. This will leave Mulcahy with a group focused on DIY and electrical retailing, which, it is hoped, will have a secure future. He says the new strategy developing 'Big W' superstores at one end and the general convenience store format at the other—is the right way forward. On the decision to part with Woolworth, the business from which he built Kingfisher, Sir Geoffrey is phlegmatic. He hopes to make a final decision—on demerging or selling—very soon. With three firm offers for Superdrug in his pocket, and some potential interest in Woolworth, Sir Geoffrey is confident. 'Woolworth's is a fantastic business that has actually got a huge amount of potential', he has been reported as saying to a *Financial Times* reporter recently.

As Sir Geoffrey also has acknowledged: 'Woolworth certainly has plenty of loyal customers—it is just that not many of them are from the City of London'. The reshaping of Kingfisher is motivated by the need to divest parts of the group that are seen to be a drag on group performance. Sir Geoffrey hopes that sale—or demerger, if he can pull it off—will save the day. When the business is made up of DIY and electrical retailers on their own, it is likely to receive a higher rating on the stock market than the present group. As Sir Geoffrey has explicitly suggested: 'One of the benefits of the demerger, is that we would hope to get a higher rating attached to "New Kingfisher" once general merchandise, which acts as a bit of a drag, is gone'.

Sir Geoffrey also plays down the need to do deals himself once the split is achieved and his group is slimmed down and focused. 'There is a lot of growth to come out of the existing businesses as well as from the foothold we have in emerging markets, such as Poland, Taiwan, China and Brazil', he is reported as saying.

Extracted from an interview with Sir Geoffrey Mulcahy, in the *Financial Times*, 13 March 2001

There are few focused companies in other sectors. Many have been taken into foreign ownership. Pilkington the glassmaker remains, but TI, the maker of precision tubes, and BICC, the manufacturer of cables, have been taken over. The aim of focusing is usually to be the market leader in the chosen area of specialization, to gain economies of scale and, if possible, to dominate the competition in that area. Clearly, what such firms are not doing is defining their area of activity broadly. There is no impulse to be present in and to dominate a whole industrial sector, as it seems clear many Japanese and Korean business groups aim to do. Firms aim to be the leader in relatively high-tech segments of their sector rather than to try to provide the whole spectrum of products and services. The aim is usually to dominate—indeed to monopolize—selected lucrative market niches. Sir Owen Green, at the time Chairman of BTR, the one-time conglomerate, suggested that the policy of his company after a period of focusing was 'to seek niche positions in major markets and major positions in niche markets' (quoted by Cowe 1993).

The rationale for this strategy is to maximize the economies from concentration on a narrow range of related technologies. There is a tendency for focused groups to seek more focus through selling off parts of themselves or demerging. In so doing business groups can become dramatically smaller. In 1993, one of the world's then largest companies, Britain's ICI (Pettigrew 1985), a firm which appeared in every listing of the largest companies, demerged itself into a chemical company (which continued as ICI) and a separate pharmaceuticals group (called Zeneca—subsequently Astra-Zeneca). Other examples are P&O the shipping company demerging its cruising and commercial shipping operations and Kingfisher demerging DIY from other forms of retailing (see Box 6.7). Among British firms of this focused type, however, there is a willingness to invest and to invest heavily to defend a position of domination in chosen markets. Such firms may also engage in more questionable activities such as buying up the patents of competitors and buying out competitor businesses to consolidate control of the selected niche.

Even prime examples of focused businesses amongst British large companies are willing to acquire unrelated businesses, and use them to shuffle the pack and to find new areas of profitable activity. However, it is amongst firms of this focused type that we find the high investors amongst British companies.

The predatory corporation

The predatory corporation is a kind of company no longer active in the British economy but it is discussed here because it constitutes an extreme form of strategy that has been used by large companies to reconstitute themselves and to remain profitable. This is a strategy involving diversification and almost all significant predatory companies were conglomerates. A conglomerate is understood as being a company undertaking diverse activities, usually managed as separate businesses. These companies form a centrally connected but otherwise diverse group of semi-autonomous companies. Hence, they are indeed a conglomeration; that is, a mixture of things. Such firms usually adopt a holding company or 'H' form of structure which has a small head office, and which simply holds a majority interest in a range of subsidiary companies. This type of structure has been referred to already earlier in this book, and illustrates the traditional preference amongst British managements for something that is segmented but not the classic 'M' form of company discussed in Chapter 3. However, although they share a similar structure, the traditional

'H' form of company in Britain and the contemporary conglomerate are in many ways different types of company.

It is characteristic of 'H' form companies that the owners are not closely involved in the management of their businesses. Lord White, sometime joint chief executive of the Hanson Trust, a predatory corporation, used to boast that he never went to any of the companies which he bought (Cowe 1993: 297). Predatory companies proceed by buying up—usually by takeover—an ailing group. Although, invariably, such takeover will be contested by a firm's incumbent managers, the aim is to appeal to the shareholders of the target company. Shareholders, of course, stand to benefit from any bid either directly, because the bidder offers cash for the shares substantially above the current market price, or, alternatively, because the bidder offers shares in the bidding company. (Takeovers are often partly financed not by the offer of cash but with the offer of shares in the bidding company—called 'paper'.) This procedure makes good sense for them because the bidding company calculates that the value of the underlying assets in the target company are worth more than the total value of the shares. Thus it is paying paper for prime assets which may be sold (or 'stripped out') for cash.

There is much to be gained by thinking about a business differently from the way the incumbent management habitually thinks about it. A new owner has the advantage of not being hidebound by what has happened in the past with regard to the utilization of assets. Often things can be rationalized and sold off with no loss of efficiency. An incumbent management is unlikely to think of the head office building as a potentially valuable piece of real estate that could produce cash, but a new owner can value everything there is in a company in new ways. Selling off the parts as separate entities, because there are many more buyers who can afford a lower outlay, may itself bring substantial benefits. Benefits to be gained by this procedure are truly astonishing (see Box 6.8).

The predatory strategy has now become less prevalent. The Hanson Company itself, after becoming a multibillion pound concern, demerged into three separate companies. Hanson Trust is still listed on the London exchange—as a building supply group—and today would be categorized as a retail-related manufacturer. Imperial Tobacco, which had been bought by Hanson, was refloated as a separate company and the large electricity subsidiary Eastern Electricity was sold into American ownership. But what Hanson and similar companies made central to their strategy is a tendency endemic to large firms in Britain. Writing in 1993 Cowe suggested, 'The case of Hanson is the supreme example of the overweening role of financial markets in the Anglo-American economies' (Cowe 1993: 297).

Focused corporations—such as BAe Systems—have gone in for a good deal of buying and selling of companies from time to time (Williams *et al.* 1990a).

BOX 6.8 Handsome profits by Hanson

By any standard, Hanson is now a very large company: it employs 90 000 people (in Britain and the USA) and has a market capitalisation of £23 billion, more than twice as large as B.Ae and GEC. Hanson grew very rapidly during the 1980s; on our calculations, Hanson's real turnover increased more than five times between 1979 and 1989. This was achieved mainly by acquisition than by organic growth. Major purchases in the 1980s include Imperial Tobacco, SCM and Consolidated Goldfields. A substantial proportion of what it acquired is subsequently divested and the company's success in 'increasing shareholder value' rests on the formula of buying companies cheaply and selling dear. After analysing 100 Hanson deals, Dickers concludes that the average buying and selling sequence involves selling assets for roughly one third more than was paid for them (Report for the Credit Suisse—First Boston Bank 1990). The takeover and break up of SCM shows just how lucrative this dealing can be. In January, 1986, SCM cost Hanson £930m. Disposals have since recovered 166 per cent of the price (i.e. £1545 million). The remaining retained businesses, which include SCM chemicals and a 48 per cent share of Smith Corona Typewriters, are currently generating annual profits equivalent to 30 per cent of the original purchase price (i.e. £280 million per year). Everything is for sale if the price is right. When consolidated Goldfields was taken over in 1989, it was generally assumed that Hanson would sell the South African Mines, but retain the aggregates businesses which fitted in well with existing Hanson interests in construction materials; the latest annual report however, discloses that all of Cons Gold is being sold.

Williams *et al.* (1990a: 470)

For many years, GEC had a £1bn plus cash mountain for use in the buying of likely companies and to buffer itself against the possibility of the lack of sufficient profitability from production (Williams *et al.* 1983; see also Box 6.1). Indeed, when the conditions are seen to be right by corporate managers, large firms can dismember themselves in the name of greater shareholder value. Some firms, such as BTR and the Hanson Trust, have moved from predation to focusing, the latter a lot more successful than the former. Because large companies have become used to reorganizing and refocusing the institutional circumstances surrounding British firms have produced a capacity for considerable structural flexibility (Lazonick 1991).

6.8 Conclusion

Understanding the reorganization of large firms

Two important changes taking place in the advanced economies of the world must now be identified and discussed. These are: the increased international involvement of the largest firms, and increasing cooperation and interdependence between firms, their business units, subsidiaries, and affiliates. This phenomenon is sometimes referred to as the network form of organization or, more simply, the network. These two developments are, of course, connected. As large companies move increasingly into international operations, they have limited assets to concentrate in any one place. Even £40 billions of assets spread across five continents and forty or fifty countries will be spread somewhat thinly. The label given to these large but highly extended firms by the present author in other writing is the capital extensive firm (CEF) suggesting that their key feature is not so much their size as their extensiveness (Ackroyd and Lawrenson 1996; cf. Hedlund 1986). When they opt for this spread out mode of organization, even large firms are forced to outsource many of their activities and so to enter alliances with local companies and organizations (Dunning 1997). The question is: how do British firms of this type compare with those originating in other countries?

The capital extensive firm

The CEF is a new and highly distinctive form of organization. It involves many small units, but beyond this necessarily entails many new relationships with firms it does not own. The CEF is a form of large firm with a dispersed structure that defies classification as one of the standard textbook models reviewed in Chapter 2.

It is clear, however, that large companies now are made up of a large number of small units, whose activities are coordinated from a relatively small head office. A large manufacturing company may have scores of constituent plants and depots, many subsidiaries (and perhaps thousands of associated companies) involved in different kinds of activities. Such a company will also operate in many localities in many countries. Such organizations are possible given highly advanced information technology, but changes in form of organization are being driven by complex realignments of international capitalist firms and the change of pattern begins with the activities of large firms. The small firms we examined in the last chapter are themselves aligned with and have to work within the spheres of influence of CEFs. While it is difficult to see British companies, especially those still heavily involved in manufacture, as extensive firms or fully developed CEFs, they enter into cooperative relationships with many other firms. Because they are likely to outsource key elements of their activities, the local coupling of CEFs and other kinds of firms—especially KIFs—is a characteristic emergent structure.

If we broaden our perspective to include foreign firms, it seems that British firms are rather underdeveloped as CEFs go. Two different forms of extensive firms may be identified, the manufacturing-trading CEF, or M-TCEF which produces goods and trades them worldwide (Mitsubishi or Ford).

Alternatively there are commercial services capital extensive firms or C-SCEFs such as Nomura in finance, Time-Life in entertainment, as well as hybrid types (Sony). By the side of giants like these, British CEFs, for all their size, are fairly puny. But there is no denying that British businesses are developing in a way that is recognizably new and innovative, even if they are increasingly leaving behind the economy that nurtured them. British manufacturing companies in the retail-related areas of activity are proving effective as global firms, for example. Their ability to tolerate diversity and to adapt to many different local conditions has also been an asset as firms have extended themselves into more locations.

The British CEF

It is has been argued that there are significant patterns of organization emerging in the manufacturing companies based in this country, patterns which have so far passed unrecognized. The largest British firms have distinctive characteristics and are quite different from comparable firms based in other countries, but some of the emerging structures are similar to CEFs. British firms have certainly reorganized themselves rapidly, and have evidently been able to do so because of their weak embedding in the British social structure. They show the capacity for structural transformation that they have acquired as a result of their history. They have slimmed down their already quite unbureaucratic structures even further at all levels. Information technology has been introduced from an early point, and although it is a necessary condition for transformation, it cannot be seen as the driver of change: it is not a sufficient condition. Nonetheless, the availability of IT has enabled firms to cut out layers of management hierarchy from their organizational structures, and it has also enabled them to continue to monitor the performance of their many business units, subsidiaries, and affiliates. This technology also makes possible the coordination of business units that are widely separated in the world.

British firms, although small by comparison with their foreign counterparts, have proved to be surprisingly adept at adopting CEF-type patterns of organization. Caught in fierce competition from overseas on the one side and recession combined with the need to make profit on the other, many British firms had to cut back radically to remain profitable. They did this so radically that many commentators felt that there would be no industry left in a few years: some referred to rapid industrial or manufacturing decline (Hirst and Zeitlin 1988; Ackroyd and Whitaker 1990) whilst others went further, referring to outright 'manufacturing failure' (Williams *et al.* 1990*b*). However, manufacturing firms have proved themselves able to meet their challenges by cutting out areas of activity and switching others. The traditional sensitivity to financial consideration has made businesses more able to respond to threatening circumstances than has been found in other countries. British firms are now choosy about what they produce. The downside of this is that firms have more or less completely withdrawn from the production of complete and complex products. On the other hand, they have become adept about locating and moving into and exploiting areas where profitable manufacture and other kinds of business can continue. Typically firms have diversified their production and business activities, but continue to manage their diversity through centralized financial controls. Hence, large British firms have become flexible at the fundamental structural level.

These profound changes are not obvious to the outside observer, but have left the British economy more vulnerable to foreign penetration. The network of firms found in Britain is arguably less strongly integrated than those found elsewhere, and more likely to be coordinated by the coercive powers of large firms (Whitley 1999). Many large companies have exported a high proportion of their productive capacity and assets overseas. The British economy has been amongst the largest exporters of capital of any advanced country. Expressed as a proportion of the population, the export of capital is without equal by any other country including the USA and Japan (Hirst and Thompson 1999). Thus, the bottom line is that many of our large firms have survived, but their survival is not likely to change the pattern of decline in the economy as whole.

7

New corporate forms and the network

7.1 Overview

In this chapter some of the abundant recent writing on new corporate forms and other emerging economic structures will be considered. This writing describes new corporate forms and other patterns of economic relations that are supposedly developing. If what we have considered so far is a reliable guide, then there has been extensive change in both small and large organizations in this country. Though the extent of change may vary in different sectors of the economy change is apparent everywhere and distinctive types of both large and small organizations can be identified. To recapitulate briefly: among small organizations and business units in the manufacturing sector and production more generally, organizational structures along the lines of the new flexible firm and the high-surveillance firm are emerging. In the service sector, amongst the new organizations offering business services, there is the knowledge-intensive firm. Similarly, for large firms, there are distinctive new forms of large corporation. The capital-extensive firm as a new form of multinational corporation has been identified and a distinctive British variant of this delineated.

Three kinds of writing will be considered in this chapter. Firstly, there is work which attempts to develop general models of new organizational structures which are alleged to apply to all organizations. Here we shall examine a sample of work including that of Heckscher and others on the post-bureaucratic organization (Heckscher and Donnellon 1994; Donnellon and Scully 1994). Such arguments often make central to the new model organization either that it utilizes employees (Drucker 1988) or new technology (Davidow and Malone 1992) or both in radically new ways. We will pay particular attention to the virtual corporation (Davidow and Malone 1992). These authors identify important features of contemporary change, but misunderstand their causes. Their analysis is too general to be of value applied to organizational change in Britain.

Secondly, we will look at the work of writers who have specifically identified new types of large corporation and have noted that such firms are increasingly made up of large numbers of constituent elements. Some writers have theorized about the connections between organizations in a large business and how these large complex groups differ from the standard forms of large organization, such as the 'M' and the 'H' forms. Here we shall consider what is claimed to be an entirely new type of organization by its exponents. The new form is attributed with different properties and given different labels. There is the 'N' form organization (Hedlund 1994; Solvell and Zander 1995); the Moebius strip organization (Sabel 1991); the network enterprise (Castells 1996); and the boundaryless organization (Ashkenas *et al.* 1995). This writing offers valuable insights into the way large corporations are changing their position in the economy. Among other things, it offers some explanation of why large companies are growing larger but their constituent organizations are becoming smaller.

Finally, we shall consider writing which abandons a focus on the corporation in favour of considering the relationships between firms. Here the focus shifts from the organization as such to the network of organizations, sometimes referred to simply as 'the network' (Thompson *et al.* 1991; Ernst 1994; Cravens *et al.* 1994, 1996). The idea of the network implies that the area for development is not the corporation at all, but is located in an emergent set of relations between organizations. Studying this phenomenon is one of the most important areas for organizational analysis at the present time. For some writers who champion this idea, change in the economy involves a movement from economic organization based on the major corporation to a quite different mode based around the activities of groups of independent organizations that cooperate with each other. These writers sometime argue for or imply the dissipation of hitherto concentrated corporate power.

The first group of writing has limited value. The second and third groups by contrast do help to illustrate some features of change today. Although relationships within firms are changing a good deal, it is in many ways more important to recognize that relationships between firms are changing. Large corporations are being split into many constituent parts to find niche markets at home and abroad. This change gives rise to new patterns of engagement between the business units of large firms and SMEs in many industries. It is, however, Utopian to think that these new patterns of organization have somehow abolished the large organization or rendered its superior power obsolete. The changes that are occurring are quite complex, and their full implications are still difficult to discern. An important target of research in this field should be to clarify the new patterns of relationships that are emerging between the elements of the corporation, its business units, and affiliated and associated firms.

The domination of industries and regions by large organizations is not as apparent as it once was. There are a number of reasons for this. Many large British corporations are taking steps to change their spheres of operation both geographically and in terms of their activities. Usually as part of a policy of finding and exploiting new markets, firms are progressively detaching themselves from their traditional involvement in the UK economy. As they reduce their levels of activity and investment and spread their assets across more locations, large British firms are outsourcing many of the things they formerly did for themselves at home and are changing their relationships with smaller firms. At the same time, foreign multinationals are increasingly setting up operations and introducing new activities in this country. Thus we are witnessing the increasing penetration of the British economy by the business units of foreign multinationals; but they too are not entirely self-sufficient and are establishing new patterns of relationships with small British firms. Traditionally in Britain, there is an absence of strongly interconnected relationships between firms (Lane 1995). While firms are necessarily working together, there is little sense of spontaneous cooperation. There are indications of central coordination and control by dominant business groups (Whitley 1999).

The connections between large and small firms are significant in shaping the path of economic development. There are complex patterns of change which involve the disassembly of the traditional organizational structures and the development of new patterns of interorganizational relations led by changes in the spatial location of large firms—both British and foreign. The metaphor of the symphony orchestra is attractive as a way of illustrating some of the features of what is happening here. The conductor of the symphony orchestra does not control the activity of the players, but they do follow the score and take their cue from the conductor's directions. The different sections of the orchestra also have leaders who help to coordinate activities.

7.2 Proposals for the new organization

The extent to which capital-extensive firms appear to be influential varies a great deal. At one end of the scale, there are strongly connected and somewhat insular networked organizations, which cooperate with firms belonging to them and a long-standing but limited set of associates and affiliates. Such structures, which are deeply embedded, exist in Germany (Lawrence 1980; Lane 1995) and Japan (Morishima 1982) and their influence is obvious. At the other end of the scale there is the British economy, where large firms have moved capacity abroad and the relations between firms are less formal and may be transient. In such situations, large firms seem to have lost their distinctiveness as economic aggregations exercising significant power. This perception is largely illusory, and there are reasons for thinking that the influence of large firms is still decisive in shaping relationships between firms and their activities. Among the evidence for this is the variation in the organizational structures adopted by firms and business units within groups. Any variation in internal organization of small firms, as discussed in Chapter 5, is explained by the need to adapt to their relationships with particular dominant partners.

One size does not fit all

Against the background of widespread organizational change, in which there is a great deal of variation in organizational forms, it is not helpful to think of the main task of organization studies as being to identify the one new and distinctive organizational type that fits most observable examples. Yet this is precisely what many writers on organizations today conceive as their task. They wish to assume the mantle of Max Weber, and identify *the* new dominant organizational form.

In the 1970s, with the beginnings of these processes, it was plausible to think that what was happening was the reorganization of bureaucratic types of organization towards something more flexible and adaptable (Kanter 1983, 1989). Today, it is widely realized that something more fundamental is occurring, but there is still a tendency to think in terms of the new organization being an inversion of the traditional bureaucracy. The idea that underlies this thinking is often nothing more sophisticated than the notion that—since bureaucracy is bad—the new organization must simply negate the features of bureaucracy. This idea gives the impression that all a management needs to do is to make sure to act against the bureaucracy and all will be well. This sort of account of the new organization is given in Table 7.1.

There is no reason to think that this bundle of attributes is a viable model for an organization. The extent to which real organizations share all the attributes listed in Table 7.1 has not been established and, considered in principle, the number displaying all of them is likely to be low. Research shows there are wide variations in organizational structure, even within the same general industrial sector. There is nothing specified here about how these features vary in their incidence, yet clearly the extent to which some organizations exhibit these attributes is negligible. For example, the idea that the high-surveillance firm allows 'spontaneity' or genuinely empowers employees is clearly wrong. More generally, lists of this sort suggest nothing at all about the relative importance of the attributes, and it is difficult to say which, if any, are essential, and which may be most clearly related to the causes of change. For these reasons, the listing in Table 7.1 is of value as a general statement of

able 7.1 The new organization as inversion of the qualities of bureaucracy

Old (Bureaucracy)	New (Post-Bureaucracy)
stability	disorganization
rationality	charisma, values
planning	spontaneity
control	empowerment
command	participation
centralization	decentralization/disaggregation
formal/inflexible	informal/flexible
large	downsized
hierarchical	delayered
individual jobs	team work

Adapted from Thompson and McHugh (2001).

tendencies. At best we can see that many contemporary organizations do have some of these attributes.

7.3 The post-bureaucracy

The work of Heckscher and Donnellon (1994), on the post-bureaucracy argues that the new organizational form, the 'post-bureaucratic' organization is emerging, rather than already here. These writers claim that organizations of this pattern will eventually be widespread if not universal. However, they recognize that there is a problem with defining the new organization as the opposite or negation of the most authoritative historical model. They can see that more must be said about the positive features of the new organization, and the reasons why it is developing. To this end, Heckscher and Donnellon present a number of arguments that are subtle but, in the end, unsatisfactory. For example, to explain why the post-bureaucracy may be difficult to describe exactly at the moment they argue that: 'The discussion of the post-bureaucratic organization is complicated by the fact that it does not exist . . . there is no concrete example that truly exemplifies the type . . . The notion of a post-bureaucratic type is drawn from a set of (largely partial and short-lived) examples that seem deliberately to violate bureaucratic principles' (1994: 17).

By arguing that the new organization is not yet an accomplished fact Heckscher and Donnellon avoid the problem of recognizing the wide variation in the form of organizations today. Because it is not yet quite apparent, both what is central to it and causing it are also not yet clear. They recognize, quite correctly, that there are ways of moving away from bureaucracy that do not change its fundamental character. This is a point made to good effect by other critics of the 'new organization' (Thompson and McHugh 2001). However, Heckscher and Donnellon pin their hopes for establishing the post-bureaucratic organization as something new and different on the claim that it has some novel basic characteristics. They claim that, in the post-bureaucratic organizational type, influence replaces power; and hence, the need to persuade participants—rather than direct them—becomes more salient for managers. Such practices are preferable to participants. In addition, these authors also suggest that, in the new organization, there has to be trust and a sense of mission, the sharing of information relevant to the mission, participative decision-making, solidarity, and identification. Information and ideas allegedly flow in many directions and not mainly from the top down. According to Heckscher and Donnellon, a better label for the post-bureaucracy would be 'the interactive organization', because such organizations allegedly involve more intense interaction and are not founded on authority as much as institutionalized dialogue.

It is difficult to see why dialogue negates or denies the existence of authority. There has always been dialogue in organizations. Influence may be thought of as describing a degree of power. From the view of the organization

---

BOX 7.1 Innovation through dialogue

Capacity to transform social situations is also a function of resources of two forms: 'allocative', which facilitate command over raw materials, production methods and products, and 'authoritative', yielding command over persons. But it is neither necessary nor sufficient to have formal authority. The narratives [studied in this research] revealed that only about six of the thirty innovators interviewed were able to implement the innovation within the sphere of their own authority. The remainder seemed to feel constrained to consult and negotiate with some set of peers, bosses and external agencies.

Even those who had direct authority to command resources consulted or negotiated with those over whom they had nominal command. This behaviour may have been part of an 'education strategy' intended to overcome resistance. It is also consistent with two other arguments: that the managerial role can be legitimised only through cooperation, or that followers can make a contribution to effective leadership. In general our data suggest a greater incidence of co-operation and joint contribution strategies. . .

The narratives are replete with stories of a great variety of social interactions within which the focal managers and others used their intrinsic and acquired capability to transform situations. Many refer to meetings, regular and irregular, formal and informal, including those related to the procedures managers had to follow in order for their project to be sanctioned by others.

Coopey et al. (1997: 236)

and its structure used in this book, the structure of the organization itself is an emergent property that arises from the interaction of groups. The organizational structure embodies the balance of power between the parties in an organization: it is difficult to imagine negotiation without dialogue. An organization that works entirely by people having their activities dictated for them is unrealistic. Although management has at times sought (and secured) extensive condign power over people at work through, for example, 'direct control' of their work performance (Friedman 1977), it has never taken away all discretion and precluded all dialogue. If this is so, the position of Heckscher and Donnellon amounts to little more than the idea that, in some managerial regimes, the operation of authority involves more dialogue, and is more subtle, than in others. Authority does not have to be overtly expressed or asserted, and may work more effectively (though less obviously) if there is dialogue. In the interactive organization we still have one group of people working for another and differential rewards coming to different stakeholders.

Interaction and cooperation as system requirements

Heckscher and Donnellon emphasize the idea that the new organization involves new levels of cooperativeness and communication from employees. But we should note that this is not sought from employees without limit. The opportunity for cooperativeness and communication is actually required to the degree that it is necessary and facilitative for the operation of the business. Indeed, the creativity and team-working capacities of individuals are not required for the benefit of employees themselves, nor because they are in some way generally beneficial, but only to the extent that they contribute to the objectives of the organization.

The value of team working, self-organization, and cooperation are constantly emphasized by authors. Team-working is seen to be an obviously superior mode of organization to traditional forms. At an early point Drucker (1988) came up with a prescription for the new organization based on cooperative teams. He proposed the new organization as defined by the way it utilizes the cooperative skills of people and their capacity to work together in teams. He, like Heckscher and Donnellon, sees this as a basic feature of the 'new organization'. In teams, Drucker proposes, people coordinate organizational activities economically and effectively. There is some truth in this. But it also is the case that these capacities have been frequently ignored as a way of organizing and motivating work for much of the time since the Industrial Revolution. Industrial regimes particularly have relied on strategies of control which entail the suppression of initiative and group cooperation. In view of this, the question arises: why is the value of team-working and cooperation being discovered and celebrated at this time?

The answer concerns the requirements of the new organization of businesses. Powerful though they are, management information systems do not cover every eventuality, and there is a high requirement for awareness of the possibility of emergent problems and opportunities on the part of employees. Such human capacities are made even more important because IT allows the numbers of staff to be drastically reduced. Effectively programmed, IT is good at the logical sequencing of tasks and activities that hitherto had been a main function of the organizational structure. Hence IT replaces many of the sequencing, work allocation, and coordinating activities that used to be central to the organizational hierarchy. In particular, the flow of information from the bottom of organizations, where the necessary work is done, to the top, where decisions are made about what to do, has been hugely facilitated and the activities of the organization can be accomplished with fewer staff. Furthermore, where production depends on the cooperation of large numbers of businesses, the requirement for awareness and likelihood of problems arising is at a premium.

The electronic organizational structure

In this book it is argued that organizational structures must be understood as political systems as much as functioning entities: structure is an emergent property of the relationships between individuals and groups. IT has usually been employed in ways which allow large reductions in the numbers of people

---

BOX 7.2 **Psychological and motivational requirements of network organisations**

Network organisations *require* managers and staff to change their assumptions and behaviours. Instead of developing plans and strategies independently, planning needs to be co-ordinated and even shared with other participants in the network. Information therefore must not be hoarded and protected, but shared to allow joint problem solving. Moreover, measurement and auditing systems need to be co-ordinated. Organizational members therefore need to adjust their mind-sets so that the well-being of the whole value chain is kept in mind and enhanced. For example . . . [Firms collaborate] with key suppliers. Together they can plan for and respond more quickly to changes in the production schedules. An organization may be considered well linked into its value chain if it scores high on a set of measures of joint development in marketing plans, product development planning, production and inventory planning, distribution planning and information systems planning. And for the management of resources and capabilities the indicators would be shared resources as opposed to separate resources in the areas of technical expertise, financial expertise, management skills, information systems and training, and development.

Mabey *et al.* (2001: 181), emphasis added

in the organization (especially supervisors and middle managers) as well as restructuring the jobs of many employees. Because of this, it is not just the technical capacity of management-information systems (MIS) that makes IT a powerful resource for those controlling company policy. New technology ensures that the traditional politics of organizations can be fundamentally changed. The extensive use of IT also explains how large organizations can be more radically dispersed and made up of large numbers of small elements whose activities are monitored, coordinated, and overseen by a small headquarters staff.

Generally, the work roles that remain in organizations after the introduction of advanced IT systems augment and support technically efficient information flows. To understand what they are doing and how they can contribute to complex processes requires that employees adopt an outward orientation and cooperative demeanour. One account of the contemporary corporation which uses this idea, though buried in a welter of other material, is the work of Davidow and Malone (1992) on 'the virtual corporation'. Here a central idea is that computer coordination becomes so important to an organization that the organizational structure is actually changed from being a set of processes coordinated by human beings (which technology supports) to one coordinated by technology (which human beings support). A virtual organization has a structure constituted by effective MIS. Adoption of MIS is not optional but required by intense competition. Once in place, however, the technological basis of the organization allows an effective system of production to work with fewer staff. The remaining staff must have much broader roles and a more adequate sense of corporate responsibility.

One of the main concerns of Davidow and Malone is manufacturing industry. The effectiveness of standard production technologies can, they argue, be greatly enhanced by information technology—if people are prepared to work in appropriate ways with the technology. Coordination is secured by IT, but since there will be gaps arising in information flows, especially if the activities of a firm have to be changed, one obvious solution to potential problems is to delegate detailed organizational activities to employees themselves. The emphasis on cooperation is in essence, therefore, explained by system needs; in particular the need is for the redistribution of supervisory and coordination functions. Crudely put, if supervision is taken out, there is no other recourse but to encourage employees to coordinate themselves. With minimal management hierarchy, suggest Davidow and Malone, there will be spontaneous reorganization as the remaining employees anticipate problems and form project groups to deal with the emerging problems their organization faces. In this view, the need for cooperation is not a chance discovery of a better way of organizing, or the benign expression of goodwill of employers, but a requirement that arises because of the use of information technology.

BOX 7.3 **Virtual corporation and MIS**

One of these . . . the computer based management information system (MIS) has been part of most large businesses for several decades. MIS have become vital to coping with the flattening organisation . . . With layers of management condensed and the system dispersed throughout the corporation [MIS] offer flexibility and market-response times that preserve options. And in a time of business and general economic uncertainty, that can be a priceless edge.

Technology will help with coordination and performance measurement challenges. Some companies are already implementing networks for just such a purpose. . . .

MIS, traditionally a means of quickly getting sales, inventory, and production infor- mation to decision makers, must expand until it integrates the entire corporation. Electronic technology must be used to transfer data back and forth between sales offices, the finance department, factories, and corporate headquarters. Unless the computer can shoulder some of the work, managers will never be able to deal with the load placed upon them by the wider reporting structures. This evolution, already under way, has been reflected in nomenclature changes, as MIS becomes simply IS (informa- tion systems) to show that the passage of information is no longer unidirectional, and as portions of MIS are referred to as ESSs (executive support systems) to reflect their role in top management decision making. Also, electronic data interchange (EDI) can do much to ease the manager's burden of interacting with suppliers, customers and other groups within the same organisations.

W. H. Davidow and M. Malone (1992: 64–5)

On this account, extensive new IT systems such as integrated MIS should head the list of the attributes of the post-bureaucratic organization. Without this, the extensive reorganization of work as described by the attributes in Table 7.1, especially the greater responsibility and 'empowerment' attributed to employees, would be difficult to imagine.

7.4 Connecting workplace change with corporate change

It is important to connect change at the level of the workplace with change at the level of the organization. There are models of the organization that envis- age equally radical ideas about structural change, but do not obscure the fact that authority is still there and essential to organizational functioning. Indeed, what we now consider are ideas that focus on the new large organization and its pattern of development.

Hedlund (1994) has proposed the 'N' form of organization, which he sees as a development beyond the 'M' form. Hedlund's model involves the extreme extension of operating autonomy to business units in a group whether they are branch offices or subsidiaries. Other writers with similar ideas are Solvell and Zander (1995), who suggest that the extreme devolution involved in such arrangements amounts to the development of a 'heterarchy'. This term means different forms of rule, and can be contrasted with autarchy (absolute rule) and hierarchy (rule by successive grades). Thus, the possibility of different forms of control existing within a structure of semi-autonomous units is envisaged.

For these writers the key problem is to understand the complex pattern of autonomy and control that exists within the same organization. They emphasize that the large corporation is both larger and decentred. So much power to make decisions is delegated that it can appear that little remains to be controlled or in control by the centre. True, branches of this type of organization are sometimes expected to act entrepreneurially—to meet new business opportunities—without being instructed to do so. Each branch is, therefore, treated to some extent as a separate business. However, such elements are not entirely free to act as they decide, but will be called to account for cost and profit performance. Hierarchy, in the sense of continuous supervision of all activities is removed. But even if responsibility for aspects of the basic managerial functions is devolved this does not mean all control and direction has disappeared. Monitoring and control of key variables relating to performance, such as the levels of sales, stock turnover, and profitability continues.

The myth of the occluded centre

It is a mistake to think that corporate groups will ever be entirely without a centre. As long as they are recognizable as corporations and groups of firms in common ownership, there will be power exerted over one part of the organization by another. To sustain itself as a group and a distinctive structure, there have to be elements of hierarchy in an organization. Such things as preferential access to information and the capacity for control based on it are indicators of this. In all firms, large or small, centralized or decentred, there are individuals and groups with power and the willingness to exercise it. Some individuals (and groups) can buy and sell elements of an organization or otherwise restructure them, for example, and hire and fire individuals. Almost invariably people with such powers are retained at the organizational centre; indeed those that have these powers tend to define the centre. Many writers, looking at the extent of decentring emphasize the autonomy of the periphery.

Solvell and Zander (1995) so emphasize autonomy at the periphery of modern organizations that they tend to forget that the autonomy remains relative. They write of the 'the firm as a brain model' having superseded the idea of the structure in which the HQ is the 'brain of the firm'. But, although this is a neat inversion and a provocative idea, it is to take the idea of decentring much too far. Though a centre may act on what is overseen quite seldom, the capacity for acting remains. Other writers are quite well aware that information technology makes possible more sophisticated control mechanisms based on continuous monitoring of activity at the periphery; and that such potentiality is the strength of the supposedly decentred organization. Tapscott and Caston (1993) writing about the effect of IT on organizational control use precisely the same metaphor as Solvell and Zander but draw a different conclusion. They write of the sophisticated IT and decision support system itself as 'the brain of the network'. Again there is emphasis placed on IT in general and MIS to supplant the human organizational structure. This time however the concern is the operation of such systems at the level of the corporate group which is the topic of interest. It is the implication of this work that the systems that comprise the command and control functions formerly undertaken by the management hierarchy are now frequently global in scope and perform their regulatory activities for the most part unobtrusively and automatically. But this does not mean that nobody is actually in control; such systems are constituted in the first place by the desire for control and achieving control is an important motivation of the senior management of the firm. This group has privileged access to, and ultimate control of, the MIS or 'brain of the network'.

Many British companies are now made up of a large number of smaller business units, whose activities are coordinated and controlled from a relatively small head office which stands at the hub of a powerful information transfer and handling system. A large multinational manufacturing company, for example, will have hundreds of plants and offices in numerous countries, similar numbers of subsidiary and associated or affiliated companies. The extent to which a structure like this is in the complete control of the corporate centre can be exaggerated, but this should not be taken as evidence for the absence of control. Writers seem to have taken the theoretical point that the end of a process of decentring is the random array of points, for the idea that this is necessarily where the organizations will end up. This is unrealistic and exaggerates the possibilities for the loss of hierarchy and central control in large firms. Certainly the few studies that there are which actually look for evidence of the extent of change come up with the conclusion that there has been less change than is suggested by theorists and management pundits (Ezzamel and Willmott 1998).

Decentring as a business strategy

An interesting argument about organizations and organizing is based on an idea of radical decentring (Sabel 1991). Sabel describes the large corporation,

---

BOX 7.4 Power struggles within the multinational enterprise

In a formulation of headquarters–subsidiary relationships based on the network approach, it has been observed that clear differences exist in local network contexts of foreign subsidiaries. It is also suggested that headquarters' limited knowledge about these contexts is an important determinant of the degree of control that can be exercised.

As the foreign unit accumulates in-depth and unique knowledge of the local network context it gains access to resources and capabilities which makes it independent and more difficult to control from headquarters.

O. Solvell and I. Zander (1998: 411)

---

as a 'Moebius strip organization'. The Moebius strip is itself badly named. A better name would be Moebius loop or band. To make one of these, take a flat ribbon or strip of paper. Make a loop from it by joining the ends, but, instead of making a simple loop, turn one end over by 180 degrees before joining it up. You now have a loop with a twist in it, which has a paradoxical feature. If you locate what is the inside of this loop and then move along it, you move onto the outside. With this loop you cannot tell which side is the inside and which is the outside. Sabel proposes this as a model for a corporate organization. In the course of his argument he identifies what he calls 'new production structures', which are large groups of organizations.

Sabel restricts his argument to the consideration of certain areas within manufacturing. In this account, the idea of the Moebius organization is used more generally to make a point. Suppose that a group of organizations in common ownership is allowed sufficient autonomy at the periphery to develop new lines of activity: the organization will perhaps develop in unexpected directions as it will undertake new activities. In some cases these new activities may well become important as sources of earnings and employment for the group. Similarly another possibility is for a different part of the same group to reduce some formerly important activities because they are now unprofitable. If both these processes of diversification and contraction take place simultaneously, then there may be, at the level of the organization as a whole, a structural shift of momentous dimensions. What was formerly central to the organization becomes peripheral; what was formerly peripheral becomes central. In this way, a new structure may, in some ways, mimic the paradoxical properties of the Moebius strip.

Clearly these properties of flexibility arising from decentring might be deliberately improved and developed. Organizations can be developed by strategies utilizing elements of decentring, and exploit the capacity of the periphery to respond to circumstances. In this way, organizations hedge their risks not by diversification into unrelated activities but by learning to move rapidly from declining markets or segments to prosperous ones in related industries. In such a strategy development costs and times have to be reduced, and product runs become short. Manufacturing has to be flexible and the technologies reused several times in short time-scales. This necessitates administrative decentralization—design, manufacture, and sale of a narrowly defined range of products is assigned to quasi-independent operating units. Thus corporate headquarters has less to do with overall strategy, though it might raise capital and allocate it amongst operating units, whilst continuously monitoring general performance.

It is possible that, in some variants of this decentred corporate group, central offices become very small. Corporate planning, accounting, research, and technical staffs are cut to the bone, if not disbanded at corporate level. So what we have is a federation of almost independent companies. According to Sabel, manufacturing in this pattern makes sustained development possible which can, through accumulated effort, produce a breakthrough to dramatic growth. Whether this is so is questionable, and Sabel has in mind a small number of examples in manufacturing industry. However, there is much in the above description—the pursuit of new markets, the replication of old activities in new markets, and so on—that describes the strategies of large British firms. Also, many British companies do seem to be adopting a loosely federated pattern.

It is a large step to take, to move from the idea that the corporation may have an interest in decentring, and even that it undertakes and develops such strategies, to the idea that it has no interests as a whole and it is, for all purposes, decentred. The extent to which innovation is allowed at the periphery can easily be exaggerated. The examples of large British organizations presented as illustrations in this text (Cable and Wireless, page 89; Spirent, page 97; Marconi, page 142; Kingfisher, page 159) do not indicate a loss of interest in directing corporate strategy.

The boundaryless corporation

Another idea is to describe the new organization as being 'boundaryless' (Ashkenas *et al.* 1995). As large firms have pared down the operations, and entered into external relations with other firms and subcontractors, so the boundary between the corporate group and what is outside of it becomes less distinct. We saw as early as Chapter 2 the extent to which business services firms and consultancies are proliferating in this country. These days, a large group may subcontract a great deal of its management, including such functions as information systems and the administration of human resources. Similarly, a company may draw components and supplies from a subsidiary or from an affiliate or on the open market. If we draw the boundary of the

---

BOX 7.5 **The boundaryless organization: breaking the chains of organizational structure**

Ashkenas, Ulrich, Jick, and Kerr argue that in the 'emerging organization' of the twenty-first century 'behaviour patterns that are highly conditioned by boundaries between levels, functions, and other constructs will be replaced by patterns of free movement across those same boundaries. No longer will organizations use boundaries to separate people, tasks, processes and places; instead, they will focus on how to permeate those boundaries—to move ideas, information, decisions, talent, rewards and actions where they are most needed' (1995: 2–3).

---

organization legally—and define it in terms of the assets it can call its own—we run the risk of greatly underestimating the scope of its activities and the extent of its influence.

It would be illegitimate to include all of the firms in the supply chain providing goods to Tesco or Sainsbury's, or the companies supplying parts to Ford or Honda, as being part of these organizations. Firms in the supply chains will not necessarily supply only one firm. Indeed, firms supplying final users are sometimes themselves large. Lots of small firms supply Tesco and Sainsbury's—but so too do Heinz and Nestlé which are multinationals. Similarly, major British firms participate in the supply chains of foreign multinational producers. One thinks of GKN (providing high-tech automotive components) or Pilkington (supplying windscreens and toughened auto-glass) to the car assemblers, or Rolls-Royce supplying aero engines to aeroplane makers. On the other hand, we must think of the influence of major companies extending way beyond their boundaries as conventionally defined.

7.5 **The network**

In the work we have considered so far, the attention of writers is confined to the consideration of the business unit or the company. True, in the last section the organizations under scrutiny have been large, and constitute business groups with large numbers of separate business units, yet they are still recognizable as corporations. But perhaps the largest body of writing about organizational change does not focus on single organizations at all but on wider groupings of organizations defined by their activities

Many writers agree on a newly emergent phenomenon in the development of loosely connected groups of firms that come into association to reach common objectives. Many writers (Williamson 1985; Sengenberger et al. 1990; Sayer and Walker 1992; Harrison 1994; Castells 1996; Dunning 1997) suggest that new organized relationships are emerging which are more inclusive than large corporations or corporate groups. These wider patterns connect the business units of large groups as well as independent firms in large-scale cooperative alliances. Here we are not looking at organizations in a legal sense. The most commonly used term to describe these emergent structures is 'network'. When networks become objects of study, such entities suggest the relative unimportance of the boundaries between different businesses.

There have been several attempts to describe and to classify network structures; but all networks involve the articulation of a large number of business units (whether belonging to the same firm or not) in some collective purpose or purposes. There are obvious advantages in such an arrangement in the production of complex products. In a network a large number of firms may contribute to the extended 'supply chain' producing parts and components for complex products like cars, which are then finally assembled at a separate location. The large and inflexible Fordist company cannot be reconfigured to produce a range of different products nearly so readily as a set of small business units and firms, supplying components to an assembler. It does not put large concentrations of capital investment at risk. But unlike physical nets, there are gathering points given various labels—'nodes', 'hubs', and 'multiple links' which indicate points of coordination and control of the whole structure.

These structures are different from the other forms of economic coordination. Before this, we have had firms (which are hierarchies coordinated by authority) and, surrounding and interacting with these, there have been markets—which are coordinated by contractual relationships (Williamson 1975, 1995; Rowlinson 1997). By contrast with both markets and hierarchies, networks are supposed to be structures intermediate between these and are indeed highly distinctive in their own right. As Powell suggests, the network is 'neither hierarchy nor market' (Thorelli, 1986; Powell 1991: 265) but something unique in between (see also Thompson *et al.* 1991). Clearly, networks can be thought of as something broader—and less structured—than a business and also more directed and controlled than any market. As such the network is, to many, a new mode of coordination for business organization. However, that there are hubs, i.e. points of 'radiating influence' suggests that networks are recognizably decentred modes of organization.

The question is open as to whether the network is something different or simply comprises novel combinations or mixtures of market and hierarchical modes of coordination. It is possible to stand this argument on its head and argue that everything is a network. From this point of view, market and hierarchy, as systematic sets of relations, are just peculiar types of networks (see Knoke and Kuklinski 1982; Knoke 1990). The debate here turns on whether the consideration of emergent phenomena such as networks yields

---

BOX 7.6 Applying network analysis to organizations

One important area in which the idea of networks has surfaced in recent years concerns the contemporary restructuring and reorganization of manufacturing activity in advanced industrial countries. . . . under contemporary conditions there may be a trend working in the opposite direction (from integration to disintegration). Because of the increased uncertainty associated with the rapidity of technological advance and changes in the demand and market characteristics of modern economic activity, hastened by the break-up of traditional aggregate economic regulatory mechanisms (the demise of Keynesianism and indicative planning, broadly speaking), the modern corporation's reaction has been to begin divesting peripheral activities, concentrating once again on core activities only and thus beginning to 'dis-integrate'. Alongside this, new networks of essentially small and medium scale, localized enterprises have emerged that form robust subcontracting supply networks for the main businesses with which they are linked.

The outcome is twofold: on the one hand an internal reorganization of the big corporation to allow a renewed flexibility and less bureaucratic style of operation, with semi-autonomous departments and divisions contracting amongst themselves in a network framework; on the other hand a re-emphasis on external flexibility with respect to supply contracting associated again with network structures.

Thompson *et al.* (1991: 15–16)

---

more and better insights than working without the concept. Thus it is necessary to examine the idea of networks more closely. Three different and influential ways of understanding networks can be distinguished.

Cooperative networks

The core feature of a network is the presence of large numbers of reciprocal relationships. For this reason it is often believed that these structures are beneficial to all participants; and this marks them out as a new kind of economic phenomenon. By dividing tasks between organizations, there is less sense of coercion and more reason to think that the individual's contributions do make a difference. In network forms of resource allocation, individual units survive not by themselves alone, because of their effective handling of their own internal transformation processes and response to the environment, but because of where they stand in relation to other units. There is a broadened concern for the fate of other groups with which a collaborator is in cooperation. Thompson and his colleagues argue

Cooperation thus emerges out of mutual interests and behaviour based on standards that no one individual can determine alone. Trust is thereby generated. Trust is, as Arrow (1974) has noted, a remarkably efficient lubricant to economic exchange. In trusting another party, one treats as certain those aspects of life which modernity rendered uncertain (Luhmann 1979). Trust reduces complex realities far more quickly and economically than prediction, authority or bargaining. (Thompson *et al.* 1991: 273)

It may be that communication is greatly improved in such structures. The information passed in networks is likely to be richer than information exchanged in market relations. Some people say it will be less contaminated with the language of control than communications in a hierarchy; for this reason too there is considerable appeal in network relationships.

For some writers, the importance of recognizing networks is the symptomatic discovery of the age. Castells (1996: 3) makes the following statement near the start of his monumental, three-volume study of contemporary social change: 'Our societies are increasingly structured around a bipolar opposition between the net and the self.' Castells argues that change towards the development of networks was initiated by corporations and their policies. He coins the concept 'the network enterprise' to explore the connection between organizational and social change, arguing that the development of new economic structures led to the development of new forms of interpersonal relations. These, he argues, have introduced new and pervasive forms of social relations, which have domesticated and transformed economic relations. Changes within firms, such as the adoption and development of IT, brought about more general changes in economic and social relations. So significant are these collective developments, Castells argues, that, taken together, the basis of social relations has been fundamentally changed. Thus it is that 'the rise of the network society' has ultimately tamed and domesticated relations within firms.

It is obviously inaccurate to characterize networks solely in terms of collaboration and concord. Each point of contact in a network can be a source of conflict as well as harmony. Networks 'commonly involve aspects of dependency and particularism' (Thompson *et al.* 1991: 271–2). Firms in a network will be of different sizes and have different resources available to them. It is difficult to think of situations where firms are even approximately equal participants in exchange relations. They would have to have equal competences and resources, and equal dependency on the other for participation to benefit participants equally. In many networks—one thinks of the suppliers to large retailers in Britain for example—there is little equality and reciprocity between suppliers and purchasers. Some networks are dominated by large businesses. Indeed, networks which large businesses control or direct are prevalent. In sum, because of the superior resources that large organizations mobilize, they often benefit disproportionately from the relations they have in networks, and it is easy to see that this may motivate them to enter such relationships.

It is true that large corporations are often not self-contained and self-sufficient these days, as was the case when large-scale Fordist enterprises

---

BOX 7.7 **The problem of resource dependency**

Since the others on whom an organization depends may not be dependable, Its effectiveness is indicated more by how well it balances these dependencies than by internal measures of efficiency of a financial or similar nature. To Pfeffer and Salancik the possible strategies that an organization may use to balance its dependencies are of four kinds. It may: 1, adapt to or alter constraints; 2, alter the interdependencies by merger, diversification, or growth; 3, negotiate its environment by interlocking directorships or joint ventures with other organizations or by other associations; 4, change the legality or legitimacy of its environment by political action.

D. S. Pugh and D. J. Hickson (1989: 58)

---

dominated regions and national economies, but this does not mean that participants enter business relationships within networks on a similar footing. Indeed, in many circumstances, supposedly independent firms are in highly dependent relationships with these larger players. The resource dependency organization approach to organizations (Pfeffer and Salancik 1978; Pfeffer 1981; Aldrich 1992) which suggests that each of these organizations controls resources such as capital, personnel, and knowledge, and achieves benefits from its relations in proportion to its dependency, is clearly applicable to the consideration of networks.

Functional networks

The most popular ideas for classifying networks relate them to what they supposedly accomplish. Thus, Ernst (1994) considers five kinds of network as follows: supplier, producer, customer, technology cooperation networks, and standards coalitions.

Ernst's classification is based on a common-sense notion of the production or other transformation processes that used to be thought about as taking place exclusively within firms. It is an analysis which echoes the functionalist analysis of firms, but transposes this functionality to the consideration of sets of organizations or organizational networks. Thus Ernst considers first networks which contribute to the supply of goods and services to assemblers and producers. Secondly, he distinguishes networks which combine producers into alliances, as in a cartel. Thirdly, he considers what happens after goods are produced, by looking at networks in relation to customers/consumers. The two remaining kinds of networks do not map simply over this sequence, because they are not primarily concerned with the production/transformation process, but relate to the attempts of particular groups of organizations to manipulate the conditions under which they produce or consume. Ernst argues that producer groups provide the most significant examples of networks and that electronics and automobiles are the most advanced industries in the diffusion of this network pattern of organization. In support of this it is certainly the case that the supply chains for these industries are now large, they span the globe, and implicate thousands of business units world-wide. They also happen to be industries in which some of the largest companies in the world are actively involved.

Another classification of networks, which suggests they are primarily functional, has been put forward by Cravens *et al.* (1996). In this analysis, the different kinds of network are related to features of their external conditions, and there is an explicit appeal to contingency ideas when setting out the alleged differences between kinds of networks. Here again modes of reasoning formerly applied at the level of the firm are being reapplied at the level of the network. The analysis by Cravens and his colleagues is interesting because it explicitly suggests that organizations in a network will usually be of different types, rather than predominantly similar as is implied by Ernst (1994). They also suggest that networks involve hierarchy, and, by implication want little truck with the idea that they are inherently egalitarian. Networks are, on this understanding, quasi-firms or groups of firms that have greatly extended their size and functionality by adopting a network arrangement.

Cravens *et al.* classify network organizations using the dimensions of volatility of environmental change on the one hand, and the type of relationships among network members (which ranges from 'collaborative' to 'transactional') on the other. This leads to the proposal that there are four basic types of network. These are given the following labels: hollow, flexible, value-added, and virtual network organizations. There are some puzzles about the distinction between these types, and there is little attempt on the part of these authors to distinguish which of these structures is alleged to be the most prevalent and/or the most effective. The value-added network is alleged to occur in situations in which the environment is not turbulent, and the relationship between network members is primarily market-based (i.e. 'transactional'). Examples of large firms are linked with this variant. But stable market conditions are often associated with the development of large centralized and bureaucratic organizations, so the puzzle here is why any degree of networking is preferred to traditional forms of organization.

A more plausible combination is where market conditions are turbulent, and yet these are combined with collaborative relations in the network, a combination these authors label the 'flexible network'. This allegedly makes sense as a viable combination because it is an effective response to increasing competition. In this, some of the costs of innovation are borne by the network collaborators and not by the core firm alone. But, again, in situations of increasing competition, it is usual for firms to reduce their margins and not to

---

BOX 7.8 **Networks as functional organizational forms**

Turbulence and rapid change in the business environment have been associated for some time with the development of new network organizational forms which put various types of strategic alliance and other inter-organisational collaborations into effect. This paper traces the rationale for the formation of such networks and the associated vertical, disaggregation of functions and implications for internal organizational design. This leads to the proposal of a classification framework for network forms. Using the dimensions of volatility of environmental change on the one hand, and the type of inter-organizational relationship involved (collaborative or transactional) on the other hand, network forms are classified as hollow networks, flexible networks, value-added networks and virtual networks. In each case it is possible *to identify the environmental and organizational contingencies* most likely to be associated with the emergence and adoption of a particular type of network arrangement. This argument leads to the identification of a new research agenda which has the goals of developing more robust conceptualisations of network characteristics; better understanding the *contingencies surrounding the emergence of network forms* and their relative efficiencies and specifying some of the major implications of network formation *for internal organizational design.* In parallel, the paper identifies a number of managerial implications for setting strategic priorities and developing appropriate management systems in these new organizational contexts.

Cravens *et al.* (1996: 303), emphases added

---

be generous in their dealings with business partners, conditions that could easily lead to the collapse of collaboration. In short, different combinations of market and other external conditions are not sufficient to explain why networks—as opposed to different variations in the form of corporations—are called into existence.

Networks as fields of power

As sites of considerable wealth and power, business groups may be considered as networks of power (Scott 1986, 1991). What they do is often formative of changes in their environment (Morgan 1988) and society, as Castells (1996) among others has suggested. It is not the case as contingency theorists allege that the environment of organizations always shapes them. Indeed, quality of life in British society today has been profoundly affected by the strategic decisions that big British organizations and business groups made ten or twenty years ago. There is a danger that if we do not look with an eye for the general picture at changes in the organization of business, we may misunderstand the character of emergent processes and structures. Hence it is appropriate to continue to be primarily concerned with the activities of businesses and business groups.

BOX 7.9 **Power in intercorporate networks**

Power in intercorporate networks is based on at least three distinct kinds of intercorpo-rate relation: personal, capital, and commercial. Personal and capital relations can, together, be seen as the principal *control relations* that surround enterprises. *Personal relations* are those links between agents that involve direct connections between people, or that involve the sharing or exchange of personnel. The most important types of personal relations in business are interlocking directorships and the kinship relations among the individuals involved in various corporations. Also of importance are such personal relations as those of friendship, acquaintance, and neighbouring. *Capital relations* are the links between business agents that result from shareholdings and from the granting or withholding of credit. Families that invest in two or more enterprises, and banks that lend to two or more industrial corporations, for example, create capital relations between the enterprises involved. The third type of intercorporate relation, *commercial relations*, involves the trading links that arise through the normal buying and selling of goods and services on the market.

Each of these types of relation can be studied at any one of three levels of analysis: people, enterprises, or sectors.

John Scott (1991: 184)

The move towards more dense types of relationships between contracting firms does not necessarily imply the emergence of distinctively new structures. In this sense, networks need not involve significant departures from older patterns of business organization. The decentred firm is a special kind of network in which significant power is retained by the hub. To the extent that a business grants autonomy from direct control to its parts, and lets the market decide on the viability of branches and subsidiaries, it allows the market to penetrate its formerly unitary structure. What are seen as networks are actu-ally often networked forms of corporation, or practical arrangements through which such corporations extend their spheres of interest and control without bearing the full costs of ownership. A large decentred firm may dominate a whole network of firms. This would obviously be the case with the firms that call supply chains into existence by issuing contracts for the manufacture of parts. Clearly, developing market-type relations within hierarchies is not always a radical departure from the principle of hierarchical control.

There are several things that make the tentacles of power less obvious when they operate through the dense interactions of networks. Networks allow more autonomy to constituent firms in some areas. But this is mainly because the controllers of business groups have come to see distinct advantages in a decentred strategy, perhaps even extending to letting the overall policy for the development of a group emerge from the choices made by the units com-prised by it. If the Moebius model of Sabel is realistic (see pages 177–9), senior management has, to a significant extent, given up responsibility for deciding

BOX 7.10 **How to become the hub of a network**

How and why does a company become a core organization in a network's value chain?
The main identifying feature of a core organization is that it 'manages the network'—a role that is not, however, legally recognized. The actual process of managing such a network is a difficult one and it requires skills for which, as yet, little or no formal training is usually offered. Boyle (1993) examines the role of the core as a user organization, as the provider and/or user of goods and services, and as the link organization. He sees the possibility of the role of the core organization changing over time as exemplified by Esso's shift away from being a petrol station franchiser to becoming a link organization by moving into forecourt convenience stores

[T]he capacity to command and co-ordinate service activities, supplier networks and contract relations has become an important strategic weapon and scale economy for many successful enterprises. Because the role of service technology in providing added value is becoming predominant, strategies are increasingly being built around core service skills, rather than products.

Mabey *et al.* (2001: 181)

where the organization as a whole is going. This is yet another difference from the most advanced organizational designs envisaged by the functionalists (the 'M' form organization) where overall strategy-making is centralized. But there is a difference between suspending the exercise of control over aspects of activity including the formation of strategy and giving up control in all its aspects.

In some circumstances, such as market turbulence, the decentred strategy could make a great deal of sense as a way of finding out what customers want and meeting demand in economical ways. There is no reason to think that the business group has ceased to be a significant structure of power in consequence. Some functions remain centralized and the potentiality of directing activities, of buying and selling subsidiaries and branches, has not changed. It is easy to exaggerate the generality of the tendency to decentre. Indeed, the tendency to decentre is more apparent than real. What is actually happening is that it is the policy of large corporations not to be dependent on any one national economy, and to reproduce their most profitable lines of activity in many locations. When they do this, large companies are forced to spread their assets more thinly and to subcontract many of their activities. This is a policy of expedient collaboration, rather than a policy motivated towards decentring as such. In many circumstances, business groups remain highly potent economic and political phenomena, even though they participate in collaborative relationships.

7.6 **Conclusions**

Debate about organizational change is often conducted without systematic consideration of the organizational structures that are emerging, or the motivations and strategies that are necessarily associated with them. This is true of much of the literature reviewed in this chapter.

To the extent that motivations are discussed, it is often taken as self-evident that post-bureaucratic organizations are being adopted because of their benefits for employees. Workplaces with these features would seem to be more congenial places in which to work by comparison with traditional bureaucratic structures. However, why such workplaces should have appeared is often not considered, leaving the suggestion that they have appeared because employees find them congenial. When we examine them, the attributes of the new organization are either proposed because they appeal to common sense (it is obvious that bureaucracy must be removed) or humanistic ideas (to do with the value of creativity and self-expression). There is a consistently optimistic humanism in many accounts. Commentators can be found arguing, for example, that both improvements in performance by business groups and better human relations are to be found almost everywhere. At their most sophisticated, as in the explanations of the network ideas advanced by Cravens *et al.* and Ernst, what we find are recycled functionalist ideas.

In this chapter it has been argued that there is an alternative and more convincing account of change, driven by the pursuit of higher levels of productivity and the desire to participate in different markets by large firms. This is realized, in the overall structure of a business, by reorganization in which the human coordination of activities is replaced by machine coordination using IT. This that allows the employment of fewer staff in the management and coordination of activities and thereby the achievement of higher levels of productivity and profitability with smaller inputs. At the same time, it changes the input required from employees, and increases the saliency of cooperativeness. Because of the need to spread out the available assets, at the level of the corporation also there is a good deal of disaggregation and decentring and a tendency for a lot of autonomy to be dispersed to the periphery (even for such things as deciding on strategic development).

But the overall pattern is not towards the loss of authority and control at the centre. Large organizations are becoming hubs of large networks whilst they are apparently disappearing as significant agents or sites of concentrated power. At the level of the individual business heavy emphasis has also been laid on the increased use of IT and the possibilities that this provides for delayering management structures. At this level, delayering is accompanied by the need for self-supervision by work groups (sometimes called their empowerment). The need for cooperation in activities at the level of the work group is therefore a system requirement and is not appropriately attributed to the discovery of the need for humane management policies. In interesting minor ways, the shift in the balance of power has not been entirely in the direction of the employer. The new technology has allowed whole tiers of management to be swept away, but the corporations are highly dependent on the alertness and sense of responsibility of those that remain.

The disappearance of full-time secure employment (especially in its highly skilled traditional forms) and the increasing profitability of large business suggest that the reasons for change probably have little to do with humanism. The main reason for change is that organizations have set out—with the help of new technology and powerful MIS—to do more with less input of resources. This applies in particular to less input in the forms of staff power. The most convincing accounts of change concern the way in which large organizations are reconfiguring themselves to become the hub of organizational networks, though in the case of many British organizations these are no longer located wholly or even mainly in the domestic economy. As the hubs of international networks, major companies form spheres of influence and power over numbers of affiliated and collaborating business units. Such organizations may be delayered internally, but they are not depowered either internally or externally. Our ability to explain this behaviour of firms is highly deficient, and likely to remain so if we continue to focus our attention on individual organizations, or on networks that are assumed to be benign.

Most of the literature we have reviewed here is, apart from the idea of the need for more competitiveness, strangely silent concerning the possible reasons for the strategies that businesses are adopting. They make insufficient acknowledgement that, if patterns of organization are changing dramatically, then this will be reflected in the changed motives and policies of corporate elites. Yet there is much that could be noted here. Until fairly recently most firms—even very large ones—saw themselves as being anchored in their economy of origin. They fixed their policy in relation to that of the home market and home government. In a direct sense, business had a share in government in this situation. This era is now over. If we want to understand the behaviour of business and the motives of its managers and directors, we must look in other directions. These days the strategy of major companies— and a surprising number of SMEs—is orientated outwards towards their international relationships, rather than inwards towards Britain. British businesses are entering into collaborative relations at home, because by doing so they can use the resources they save to expand abroad.

Whilst not significantly reducing their profits at home, they have substantially reduced their obligations to the society in which they emerged. British companies have moved further and faster in exporting their capital abroad and show least allegiance to their home state, policy decisions that are closely related to the decline of the ability of the government to tax them effectively and the rapid decline of the welfare state.

8

A national context for business organization

The models featured in the last chapter describe their subjects as detached from a specific social or economic context. The main purpose of these models is to clarify the supposed characteristics of some new organizational forms, but there are limitations in approaching things in this way. Using this approach, it can be assumed that to understand change all the analyst has to do is to study organizations and to ignore where they are located and the history of their development.

A more revealing perspective in many ways is one that recognizes that organizations and business systems develop in the context of specific social, economic, and political relationships. Three sets of ideas will be discussed in this chapter which do this. The first will be labelled the institutional approach. The designation 'institutionalism' has been attached to the work of many groups of writers. We have considered some of the ideas of American institutionalists at the end of Chapter 4, for example. In this discussion, however, attention will be limited to the work of a relatively small number of British and European writers, of whom the leading figures are Whitley (1992, 1999; Whitley and Kristensen 1997) and Lane (1995). This work is considered first not because it is the most long-standing or the most persuasive, but because it can be used to provide a general outline of the character of the institutional features of British business. As well as being of interest in its own right, it serves as a reference point. Two other general accounts of business, which operate at the level of the nation and/or the region, will also be considered.

The second and third groups of writings make the explanation of organizational change central. Institutionalist writings, despite their merits, do not explain why the pace of change varies a lot from time to time. There are periods in the history of advanced societies when organizational change is gradual and those in which it is more rapid and widespread. We are in a period of rapid and widespread change today. To illuminate these periodicities, two theories which account for them will be considered. Hence, we will briefly introduce and discuss what will be identified as a 'new or neo-liberal' account of change, one which draws on the work of such writers as Piore and Sabel (1984) and other scholars who have been influenced by them, people who have applied this type of analysis to Britain. Finally, this type of work will be contrasted with the more radical analysis identified as the 'regulationist school'.

8.1 The institutional approach to business

The idea of institution contains a number of interesting connotations. An institution is a set of practices that are customary or habitual, and have come to exist over long periods of time. Marriage is an institution as is professionalism. These are relationships which reproduce a pattern. Institutions typically endure: they persist in roughly the same configuration, changing gradually over time. As we have seen, Braudel (1983) analyses the corporation in this way. Business more generally may be seen as a specific set of related institutions that have acquired distinctive features. In this approach, however, it is not just business that is analysed. Business organizations are located within a set of related institutions. The position that writers such as Whitley (1992, 1999), Lane (1995), and a number of other writers share is that business organizations in different countries have distinctive characteristics.

Business becomes institutionalized in particular patterns for several reasons. Firstly, there is a point about continuity: business practices evolve from different starting points, and contemporary organizations often retain elements that derive from their origins. If, for example, kinship relations are strong and distinctive in the pre-industrial epoch, unless they actually hinder development, they are likely to be carried forward in their distinctive form. Secondly, there is situational reproduction. Behaviour in one institution is not confined there but carried over and reproduced in another. Thirdly, there is mutual adjustment which occurs because different types of institutions transact with each other. As they do so, they adjust to each other to form a highly distinctive set, conditioned to work in conjunction. These sets of distinctive institutions may be described as 'business systems' (Whitley 1992, 1999). Note that this kind of business system includes not only firms and their relations with other firms but other parts of the economy and polity as well. In these writers' views, contemporary organizations are thought of as being embedded within (and shaped by) their connections with other institutions.

In this approach, a given system shapes the organizations found and much about the characteristic outlook and strategy of their managers. Much of the discussion in Chapters 3, 4, and 5 can be seen to be consistent with the institutional approach. Although there was no attempt in these chapters to set

---

BOX 8.1 **The institutional context**

These points . . . suggest that the development and success of different kinds of managerial structures and practices in different contexts require explanation in terms of those contexts rather than being reduced to a single economic logic or it being assumed that market competition will, in some mysterious way, select the *most efficient* pattern of economic organisation. Equally, the search for some set of universal correlations between abstract contingencies and effective organisation structures across all market economies seems of limited value when it is realised that the effectiveness of particular forms of business organisation is institutionally relative, so that structures which are successful in one context may not be effective in others. Instead, I suggest that a key task in the analysis of market economies and organisations is to understand how distinctive patterns of economic organisation become established and effective in different societies and how they change in relation to their institutional contexts.

These patterns concern the nature of economic activities that are coordinated through managerial hierarchies and how these hierarchies organise their cooperative and competitive relations through markets. They can thus be summarised as configurations of hierarchy–market relations that become institutionalised in different market economies in different ways as the result of variations in dominant institutions. The systematic study of these configurations and how they become established is here termed the comparative analysis of business systems. Initially, I outline the major components of business systems as distinct ways of organising economic activities in market societies and identify their major characteristics which vary between institutional contexts. Next, the dominant institutions which help to explain these variations are discussed and some of the ways in which they impinge upon hierarchy-market relations are identified. Finally, I briefly consider the relations between business systems and national boundaries and the consequences of variations in their degree of integration and distinctiveness within and between nation states.

Richard Whitley (1992: 5–6)

---

out the character of the British business system in its entirety, there has been recognition of the peculiarity of British arrangements for doing business in a range of areas which may be seen as institutional adaptations. In the discussions of the pattern of relationships found in British companies in Chapter 4, for example, it was emphasized that the British management cadre is generalist rather than specialist in outlook, and indeed tends to lack formal education. Similarly, when considering the structural configurations of small or large firms in Chapters 5 and 6, it was clear that there are distinctive organizational structures to be found in this country, the influence of the form of capital supply being seen as particularly formative. The institutional approach of Whitley and others offers a way of drawing these features together and summarizing them.

Institutionalists argue that it is not a matter of chance that business organizations found in different countries have distinctive features. Business

organizations themselves form a central part of a wider pattern of institutional relationships. Hence, they have features that are distinctive. Within
the economy, for example, businesses in production sectors have to accommodate themselves to the institutional framework that exists when they seek
more capital for expansion, or when they employ labour. Similarly, the state is
another institution with a characteristic stance towards business which tends
to be formative of business practices. Thus the institutions of the economy,
the state and the polity, taken together, form a set of relations which surround
organizations and tend to induce conformity to a particular pattern. Whitley
originally used the idea of 'business recipes' as a way of describing the set of
conventions and practices typically followed by the businesses in particular
countries. He and others broadened this concept, and developed an idea of
'business systems'.

Business systems need to be distinguished from other applications of system ideas, some of which have been treated already. These authors do not
mean to designate a precisely delineated type of system (such as we might
have in mind using the idea of MIS). It is even broader than the system ideas
used by the contingency writers whose work was discussed and criticized in
Chapter 4. The boundaries of the 'business system' defined by the institutionalists are set wider than the organization itself. In contingency theory, the
organization was conceived as being a system which was subjected to pressures generally 'in the environment', the prevailing technology, current market conditions, and so on. But, in the approach being considered now, we are
looking at sets of business and other organizations. Clearly this involves a
different conception of the environment for firms than that envisaged by functional contingency writers. Here we move away from a set of externalities
conceived of as discrete variables exerting pressure to an idea that any organization is surrounded by other organizations (and which may control the
resources they need) and therefore exerts influences and pressures. In one way
or another, these external institutions are powerful in producing conformity.
There is no expectation that business systems will be similar or produce
similar organizational types. Indeed the opposite is assumed: different—
indeed divergent—kinds of business system will develop (Whitley 1999).

Businesses of every kind have to secure capital and labour, but these only
come in distinctive forms. It is a key insight of these writers that the factors of
production companies require to undertake activities are supplied by institutions of particular types. Thus, even big businesses have to face the fact that
capital is usually available from particular kinds of institutions and not others.
Similarly, there are distinctive kinds of policies towards manufacturing industry typically adopted by the state of the country concerned. Hence, the kinds
of external relations that businesses are constrained to make with external
agencies are fairly specific and highly formative. This approach, if intelligently

handled, does not eliminate any scope for the agency of groups of actors. However, it does suggest ways in which even powerful groups of agents may be significantly constrained. In institutional thinking, manufacturing industry, for example, develops in the context of a set of institutions of a particular kind which shape its development. Hence, the institutional approach is compatible with the basic ideas set out in Chapter 4. In the hands of Whitley (1992, 1999), and as used by some of the analysts that have broadly utilized his approach (Rasanen and Whipp 1992; Lane 1995; Kristensen 1997), the analysis is highly persuasive as an explanation of the particular features of British institutions.

8.2 The institutionalist account of Britain

There are particularly important relationships between businesses and those who supply capital. In Britain, there is a lack of specialist banks supplying long-term, low-interest loans. As we have seen British banks tend to supply short-term loan facilities only, and, more generally, to supply a small proportion of the investment capital for industry. As an alternative, firms may raise money by selling equity on the Stock Exchange. Because the stock market is highly developed in Britain, firms have to expect that investors may withdraw if the price of the stock falls, placing pressure on managers to make profits on a regular basis. If they do not, the price of their stock will not remain stable, and the organization may become vulnerable to takeover. The high proportion of funds that come from the market and the high proportion of stock held by institutional investors of one kind or another (who are interested in consistent profitability), focuses the attention of managers on their six-monthly reports. Although commentators may dispute the precise role of the stock market in perpetuating the demand for high returns in the short term, there is no doubt that the conditions of capital supply are influential in dictating the high-profit policy found in many companies.

Summing up the characteristics of the British business system, Lane (1995: 3) suggests that: 'The British model remains that of financier-dominated capitalism, characterized by voluntarism, arm's length relationships and by a high degree of fragmentation and diversity' (see Box 8.1). One of the many features of financier domination she goes on to mention is a lack of involvement in the banks (or groups of investors with a stable long-term attachment to particular industries) and the lack of coordinated programmes to restructure industries arising from such interests. It is because of their financial exposure then that even the larger British firms tend to be loosely federated, unintegrated, and technologically relatively underdeveloped. By such forms of argument,

---

BOX 8.2 **The British institutional pattern**

Britain and Germany can be presented as polar types on most aspects of industrial organization whereas France is much more difficult to typify in such terms. The British model remains that of financier-dominated capitalism, characterized by voluntarism, 'arm's-length' relationships and by a high degree of fragmentation and diversity. Firms are loose associations of lowly committed actors which, moreover, are exceptionally socially isolated. Unable to share risks, they undertake mainly short-term and low-risk investments in both fixed capital expenditure and human resources development.

The absence of collectivistic orientations at the level of the firm is replicated at the level of industries, due to the absence of either self-regulation or significant state inter-vention. The low degree of embeddedness and of formal regulation, together with highly individualistic orientations among the main actors, permit flexible and often innovative responses to new challenges while, at the same time, impeding their effect-ive implementation. Although the traditional adversarial approach to conflict resolution within and between firms is now becoming less marked, it has not yet been replaced with a stance of active involvement and co-operation.

Christel Lane (1995: 3)

Lane moves from discussing the character of the financial sector to a brief description of the organizational structures adopted by major companies

The pattern within the economy

The particular conditions attaching to the supply of capital to major business and its consequences is noted by these writers. Whitley refers to this pattern as involving 'Market or arm's length portfolio control' (Whitley 1999: 35) in which owner involvement in and knowledge of the business in which they have invested is 'very low'. He notes, however, the possibility of institutional control of strategy through the 'control over shares by portfolio managers'. In a similar vein Lane writes that British businesses are largely free from control by banks, but this is coupled with 'a considerable degree of indirect control [by the stock market] over management decision-making which, in the end, limits their manoeuvring space more than the German version of bank control' (1995: 50). This works in the following way:

Every major financial decision has to be taken with an eye on the movement of the stock market. Quick returns on investment and high dividends have to be achieved to keep the confidence of shareholders. Reinvestment of earnings is significantly lower than in France and even more so than in Germany. Industrial managers complain that stock market pricing does not adequately reflect expenditures for innovation and future profits and thus inhibits relevant investment. The ultimate sanction is the threat of hostile takeover which, in the British financial system, is relatively easy and frequent: in the 1980s three out of four takeover bids in the EC occurred in the UK. (Lane 1995: 50–1)

For the same reasons British businesses tend to be more flexible and adaptable than those found in many other countries. Lane has it that they are 'weakly embedded in the matrix of other organizations', and for there to be an absence of formal regulation. An upside of this is that, together with highly individualistic orientations amongst the main actors within companies, flexible and often innovative responses to new challenges are permitted. The British firm, being already decentralized, and 'loosely federated', has thus readily adopted the decentralized patterns that business pundits are apt to suggest should be adopted. Large British businesses—which are made up of large numbers of small constituent parts—are therefore more adaptive and, in this sense, more advanced than German ones. They are capable of creating new network relations, but these are rather unlikely to persist, in keeping with the idea that British businesses are more agile than those from other European countries. Whitley writes:

[M]arket forms of owner control are unlikely to encourage inter-firm alliances and cooperation, since they are typically associated with capital market-based financial systems that develop strong markets in corporate control and hence unstable owner-firm connections. Establishing long-term and wide-ranging alliances with business partners is riskier and more difficult in this situation than in economies where owners are more committed to the future of particular enterprises. (Whitley 1999: 38)

Institutionalist writers are not content to consider business systems in terms of the characteristic forms and relationships between elements of the economy. Two other kinds of institutions are discussed, firstly, the institutions of the state, and, secondly, the system of industrial relations, including consideration of the arrangements for education and training of labour.

The place of the state

The policies of the British state are distinctive. State policy is traditionally centralized in economic policy-making, regulating the economy by general interventions in monetary and fiscal policy. It is traditionally 'hands off' in its attitude to detailed policy interventions; and, except for periodic forays into state control of particular large-scale projects, with which it has a rather poor track record, the government leaves industry to its own devices. Some argue that the origin of this policy comes from the state being strongly orientated towards the needs of finance capital and the City of London, which is more concerned with international commerce than manufacture. Such institutions benefit from a *laissez-faire* policy, while productive industry does not. As we saw earlier, there is a problematic connection with productive industry, which is reinforced by state policy. Nor does the British state generally rely on or attempt to foster industry-based or regional institutions for the coordination and development of productive industry. These are prevalent in other European countries. In this country there is a lack of significant state intervention and little commitment to the oversight of either the development of new industries or the rationalization of the old. In these areas, the British business system does show remarkable continuity.

The shape of industrial relations

By contrast in other areas there is less to support the notion of institutional continuity. The area of industrial relations is a case in point. During the 1950s and 1960s, it was thought that Britain, like the continental powers, had developed a form of government that included, and not merely consulted, organized labour. The powerful trade unions, often as represented by the Trade Union Congress (TUC) were involved in policy-making at every level of government. However the level of industrial unrest remained high, despite the general rise of prosperity, and the inclusion of organized labour in policymaking was increasingly questioned. A trend towards decentralized bargaining was already established in the 1970s and the change to a right-wing government in 1979 introduced a deregulation in the economy and a disbanding of the 'tripartite' approach to policy-making (Purcell 1993). The power of the trade unions all but collapsed during the 1980s, as deregulation took effect, and employers made their own agreements with local unions. By the end of the 1980s, the traditional demand for skilled labour was declining rapidly, the system of industrial training by apprenticeship which supported it (Gospel 1995) had been abandoned, and strike rates were at the lowest point since records began. Such changes are precipitate. They are problematic for institutionalists to explain and arguably they do not explain them very well (Brown 1993).

BOX 8.3 **The collapse of demand for traditional forms of labour**

In 1954 Britain's 700 000 coal miners accounted for approximately three quarters of all recorded strikes. In 1974 a national strike by the Coal Board's 300 000 miners helped to bring down a government. By 1994 the coal mining industry had been reduced to a rump of sixteen pits and about 10 000 miners.

John Kelly (1998: 1)

What is striking about the recent history of British trade unions is its discontinuity and the fact that over a short span of twenty-five years the trade union movement has experienced rapid swings in its fortunes and equally rapid shifts in policymaking and styles of organization. Trends in aggregate union membership bear this out. Unions grew rapidly between 1969 and 1979 and have declined equally precipitously since.

Edmund Heery (1996: 196)

Criticisms of institutionalism

It is characteristic of this analysis to make comparative lists of the presence or absence of particular institutional features. What one business system has strongly developed, another economy has only weakly represented. Related to this, in making general assessments of any single business system, there is a tendency to draw up lists of attributes that balance points of strength with points of weakness, and to list factors conducing to change with factors that inhibit it. In her discussion of Britain, Lane suggests that the loosely embedded pattern of organization is seen as responsive to changing economic conditions. Whilst acknowledging this, Lane follows up with the suggestion that, while the British economy is responsive, our businesses are unable to produce effective implementation in the medium to long term. Whether there is sufficient recognition in this work of the dramatic changes already introduced by major British companies, as set out at the end of Chapter 6, is doubtful. In Germany, Lane argues, the institutions of the productive economy are more firmly embedded, and so slower to reorganize. However, change, when it does occur, is thorough. Whether this analysis produces a penetrating assessment of the differences in economic organization (as opposed to a systematic one) is not clear. Such analysis neglects the important problem of which factor or factors from the list are really decisive in deciding the directions of change.

Most importantly there is only a weakly developed sense in some institutionalist writing that the present period of history is really extraordinary in terms of the pace and extent of organizational change, especially in Britain. An emphasis on the institutional features of business systems, almost inevitably brings along the idea of gradual change and inhibits any notion that change might be epochal in some times and places. If change is extensive, as many able and persuasive thinkers (Aglietta 1979; Piore and Sabel 1984; Castells 1996) suggest it is, the writing we have just considered gives little sense that this is so and why. To illuminate this, we will have to look at accounts of organizational change that are even more broadly cast.

8.3 What about epochal change?

A crisis of continuity

Much of the twentieth century can be understood as a period of slow consolidation of a distinctive pattern of institutions in the advanced societies. In Britain, after the Second World War ended in 1945, the economy developed steadily, although the process was punctuated by periods of economic

difficulty in which development faltered. During this time there was a continuation of the movement towards the domination of large organizations in
the economy. There were other associated developments, such as the slow but
steady emergence of a larger middle class. One element of this was constituted
by a professional (in the sense of salaried) managerial cadre, another was the
groups of professionals employed within the welfare state. The first group
were people who earned their living by staffing the large organizations of the
private sector that were becoming increasingly prevalent. The second groups
were employed in the welfare state, which was founded in the aftermath of the
Second World War. The organizations that comprised this were also large. In
short, what we are discussing here is the establishment of the institutional
infrastructure of a particular kind of society based on big business and professional bureaucracies. Such a society has been given many names, such as the
affluent society (Galbraith 1958), the post-industrial society (Bell 1976), the
organizational society (Presthus 1979), and organized capitalism (Lash and
Urry 1987), but here it will be called the mass-production-mass-consumption
society.

This type of society had a high degree of state involvement in the management of the economy. Politically such societies were relatively stable, with
widespread agreement among parties of either political colour that the management of the economy in favour of business stability and sustaining full
employment were central. The economics of Keynes, which involved governments actively adjusting the level of economic activity, was also utilized by
government for the management of the economy. Trade unions were typically
strongly developed and were also regularly consulted over economic policy.
Then, quite suddenly in historical terms, in the middle of the 1970s, there was
the onset of massive and fundamental change, originating in the economy,
but radiating out to affect the institutions of the state and society as well.
Among other things, as we have seen, the trend towards larger organizations
was reversed, especially in manufacturing (Lash and Urry 1987: 105). Large
companies began to be more interested in changing their patterns of
organization and exporting their capital overseas. The shake-out from the
reorganization of the productive economy was massive during the 1980s;
nowhere more so than in Britain. There was the collapse of effective union
organization (Purcell 1993; Brown 1993). Then there was also a huge and
continuing reconstruction of the welfare state, undertaken in Britain initially
by right-wing governments in the same decade (Glennerster and Hills 1998).
Here again, new patterns of organization pioneered in the private sector were
widely introduced.

In the furore and excitement about the supposed need for change in all
organizations at the present time, to which management consultants and not a
few management academics are contributing, it seems to be overlooked how

---

BOX 8.4 **The need for disorganizing British capitalism**

We will want in the future to break these [large] organisations down into their separate business units and to give those units freedom to compete in their particular markets. Large corporations will become more like federations of small enterprises—not because small is beautiful, but because big is expensive and inflexible . . . I would expect tomorrow's companies to concentrate on the core activities of their business, relying for everything else on specialised suppliers who would compete for their custom.

Sir Adrian Cadbury, *Guardian*, 9 December 1981. Quoted by Lash and Urry (1987: 106)

---

effective the institutions of the mass-production-mass-consumption society were. The mass production of goods provided for a general increase in prosperity in the post-war period that was hitherto historically unprecedented; and indeed, substantial improvement in the standard of living extended itself to the bulk of the population. At the root of this was the increase in industrial productivity made possible by new techniques of production, which could and did drive down prices in a spectacular way. Not only was the unit cost of cars and other consumer durables progressively brought down, but also progressively up went the volume of sales and profits of large corporations. Given the scale of profits, the wages paid to employees could increase as well, allowing ordinary people to buy the products pouring out of the factories.

Thus the mass-production-mass-consumption society gave a huge boost to national wealth, which—for the first time in history—extended relative affluence to the lower levels of the population. In addition, in Western Europe, the welfare state, in which education, health care, and pensions were provided to the mass of the people, created conditions for social stability. The trade unions were integrated into both industry and government, at least offering the prospects for emerging cooperation. In short, the mass-production society delivered the goods: in more senses than one. The question is, why did all this have to change, as it did, increasingly rapidly, from the middle of the 1970s onwards? The institutions of mass-production society were disassembled as were the institutions of the welfare state. What caused this epochal change? Why has it gone much further and faster in Britain than almost any other advanced society? After all, Britain is not the most developed economy in the West.

8.4 The neo-liberal account of epochal change

Piore and Charles Sabel published an important book in the early 1980s (Piore and Sabel 1984) which says little about Britain except historically, but the basic ideas of these writers have been developed and applied to the economy of Britain by a number of others. Sabel and Zeitlin (1985), Hirst and Zeitlin (1988), and Zeitlin (1992), are amongst the key contributors.

Central to these ideas is that any developed economy can be expected to pass through periods of rapid change. What is happening today is simply the latest in a series of epochal economic shifts. In this account relatively long periods of economic stability alternate with periods of rapid transition as the economy attempts to reorganize itself. Hence, Piore and Sabel (1984) point to at least one other period of rapid change, similar to the present, in the

---

BOX 8.5 **Industrial districts, technology, and skilled labour**

Small firms in . . . industrial districts (the term is Alfred Marshall's, who applied it to Lancashire and Sheffield) often developed or exploited new technologies without becoming larger; large firms that from the start used sophisticated technology did not produce standardized goods. The technological dynamism of both these large and small firms defies the notion that craft production must be either a traditional or a subordinate form of economic activity. It suggests, instead, that there is a craft alternative to mass production as a model of technological advance. . . .

These districts were defined by three mutually dependent characteristics. The first, most obvious characteristic was the districts' relation to the market. The districts produced a wide range of products for the highly differentiated regional markets at home and abroad; but—more important—they also constantly altered the goods, partly in response to changing tastes, partly to change tastes, in order to open new markets. . . . This relation to the market encouraged and depended upon the second and third characteristics of the industrial districts: their flexible use of increasingly productive, widely applicable technology and their creation of regional institutions that balanced cooperation and competition among firms, so as to encourage permanent innovation. . . . Technology had to be flexible in both a narrow and a broad sense. It had to permit quick, inexpensive shifts from one product to another within a family of goods, and it had to permit a constant expansion in the range of materials worked and operations performed, in order to facilitate the transition from one whole family of products to another. Institutions had to create an environment in which skills and capital equipment could be constantly recombined in order to produce a rapidly shifting assortment of goods. As a precondition of this, firms were discouraged from competition in the form of wage and price reduction, as opposed to competition through the innovation of products and processes. . . .

Similar experimentation with flexible techniques and new materials occurred in the metalworking districts. The Birmingham hardware trades, for example, pioneered the development and application of metal stamps and presses, draw benches, electroplating, and die sinking, while they learned to work iron and then copper, brass, steel, and enamel into products that ranged from buttons to bedsteads to bicycles to small arms. In Sheffield, the cutlery industry developed silver-plating and led the way—together with the Remscheid firms in the edge-tool industry—in the production of crucible and specialty steels and the industrial use of electric arc furnaces.

M. J. Piore and C. Sabel (1984: 28–31)

historical record. These periods of transition are described as 'industrial divides', which explains the title of their 1984 book, which is called *The Second Industrial Divide*. An industrial divide marks a point at which an economy changes direction and, instead of continuing as before, development takes a new path. According to these writers, modern capitalism has passed through at least two long periods of stability, and two divides.

Piore and Sabel argue that industrial capitalism was initially established as a network of small firms, densely concentrated in what Marshall called 'industrial districts'. This was the pattern of organization consolidated through much of the nineteenth century in the industrial heartlands of Britain. In this pattern, there were a large number of areas of specialized production based in small, independent firms. There was a long period of relative stability and increasing prosperity based on this form of small capitalism. The system of production in industrial districts was labour-intensive by comparison with what came later. It depended on large numbers of skilled (and relatively highly paid) workers being available. It produced high levels of manufactured output, but it is easy for us to think that it was not efficient. However, in some ways it was a remarkable pattern of organization. It was flexible in the sense of being capable of rapid expansion. During this time, it was relatively easy for skilled workmen to become small capitalists themselves, as sufficient capital to set up in production could be accumulated from subcontracting. Hence the scale of output could grow rapidly. The fact is that this system not only supplied the rapidly growing home market for manufactures fairly effectively but Britain was—in the famous phrase—'the workshop of the world'. Economic growth was not a problem.

The first industrial divide

The challenge to this pattern of industrial capitalism came from the discovery of mass production in the USA at the end of the nineteenth century. This utilized higher concentrations of capital investment in the shape of machines, machine tools, and material handling equipment, but produced goods in higher volumes. Mass production was actually less labour-intensive, in the sense that it called for a lower ratio of employees to capital. It could also utilize cheap labour. This American system of manufacture ushered in a period of transition, identified as the 'first industrial divide'. This occurred in the USA in the period 1880 to 1910, and coincided with application of mass-production techniques to the production of consumer durables for the first time. This was the period of the establishment of the mass production of cars pioneered by Ford. The argument is that the organization of manufacture in the USA could have continued to be developed along the lines of industrial districts, but instead development took a decisive new direction. In the USA then, because of some chance conjunctures, such as the availability of a truly huge market, the ready availability of capital, and an abundance of cheap (though unskilled) labour, production takes a fundamentally different trajectory. This is because the mass-production system pioneered by Ford in America turned out to be a great deal more effective as a way of manufacturing complex products.

It took the other advanced countries longer than the USA to develop viable approximations to the US systems of mass production. In Britain the process was particularly protracted and painful. There are various reasons for this, amongst them, paradoxically, the abundance of highly skilled labour in this country, which, by the beginning of the twentieth century, was effectively unionized. Arguably, not until after the Second World War might Britain and other European countries be said to have developed something equivalent to the American system of manufacture. Even then, Europe, and particularly Britain, did not have mass manufacture on the scale of the American model. There were features of the British pattern of organization for production that were quite unique. High use was made of skilled labour until a relatively late stage, and, in many areas of production, large firms (which were not simply imperfectly integrated collections of small firms under holding companies) were slow to develop. In core areas of production, and particularly cars, the final producers were generally smaller and less well integrated than their major suppliers of components (Ackroyd and Lawrenson 1996).

In the process of transition and through into the period of stability following it, Britain lost its standing as a world leader in manufacture, and its industry seemed to be poorly equipped to cope with competition from abroad. Yet, belatedly, a form of large-scale production for manufactured products (on which our continued prosperity and standing as a world power is based) was established here.

The second divide

According to Piore and Sabel (1984), we are currently witnessing another transition through an industrial divide, and moving from one kind of socio-economic order to another. For this reason, change is occurring across the range of institutions and has an epochal or all-encompassing character. The answer to the question why things had to change fundamentally is first, there were some shocks—both internal and external—to the developed world. Social unrest re-emerged, then there were oil crises and world recession. The underlying problem for these authors, however, was with markets. The market for standardized products became increasingly saturated; most households had acquired cars and the other manufactured products, such as TVs and domestic appliances (Piore and Sabel 1984: 184). The productive capacity of mass-production facilities became such that these markets were oversupplied and no longer profitable for companies. Increasing competition, arising from the penetration of formerly secure home markets by overseas multinational companies, meant declining profits for mass-production firms.

In this second industrial divide, Piore and Sabel (1984) suggest that the combined effects of the availability of new technologies and the fragmentation of market demand has allowed the new forms of profitable relationships between productive organizations to emerge. The core phenomenon that they identify—and propose as a way forward—is a system of production based on flexible specialization (FS). In these arrangements, allegedly, large firms are once again less important. Where they exist they must become 'federated enterprises' (1984: 267). Economic output is secured by the activity of small firms and the way that they interrelate. Both of these are featured: it is not simply that there must be many small and differently organized firms, but it is also the development of interfirm networks and non-market support agencies, which make the whole structure effective as an aggregate. Here Piore and Sabel refer to 'regional conglomerations' (1984: 266). These concepts—of the federated enterprise and the regional conglomeration—are ways of describing the new organizational forms and the network discussed in the last chapter. This account makes such things indicators of the development of a whole new productive system.

FS not only covers the new pattern of relationship between small firms, it includes also characteristic forms of labour market and new ways of organizing production. As in the period before the first divide, the spontaneous development of new organizational forms, the development of interfirm networks, and the re-emergence of multi-skilled labour in high densities, are seen as essential elements of the new production paradigm. People who have the skills necessary for accomplishing the range of tasks involved in producing technically advanced products or services become in high demand. In these respects, there are some obvious parallels between FS and the business districts that were at their peak in Britain in the late nineteenth century. However, with regard to the use of labour, what is implied by FS is obviously in some ways greatly different from the nineteenth-century model. For example, there is the proposition that highly skilled labour will not need to be managed much, nor will firms have management hierarchies any more. Finding undersupplied and potentially lucrative niche markets for their firm's products is part of the package of skills that workers under FS will supposedly need. There are many similarities with other prescriptions about the ways new organizations will utilize labour. One thinks, for example, of the Atkinson model of the flexible firm (see Chapter 4 above). However, the neo-liberal writing we are now discussing contains optimistic accounts of conditions of work under FS, by comparison with other ideas. This optimism has been widely criticized.

BOX 8.6 **Choosing the directions of change**

Which of these possible worlds should we try to realize [managed mass production or flexible specialisation]? This is not merely a question of economic reorganization. It invites debate as well about the just distribution of power in industrial society—a debate complicated by the fact that it is not clear which world would benefit which groups most. . . .

The balance of power between labor and capital under either flexible specialization or multinational Keynesianism will thus have to be fought out country by country. It seems likely, for instance, that the spread of flexible specialization in the United States would weaken the labor. . . .

But choosing between the two systems is not so simple as picking the one most propitious to the side you favor in the contest between labor and capital. The two systems can both be instantiated in more or less comprehensive forms, so their relative attraction, to us at least, depends on whom they include and exclude.

M. J. Piore and C. Sabel (1984: 28-31)

What makes this account recognizably liberal in character is the emphasis placed on the importance of local initiatives and entrepreneurship in bringing about change. Where conditions are conducive, and where the necessary entrepreneurial will is supported by an appropriate regional infrastructure, it was found to be possible to make significant profits by making new kinds of products and services in greater variety at higher quality. Hence, for neo-liberal writers, a great deal of change in businesses can be understood precisely as arising from the effective solution of the problem of profitable production. If what they say is true, there was an acute challenge to the profitability—and therefore the continued existence—of large firms. This places considerable pressure on such firms to reorganize themselves into smaller units connected in federated structures, and so to approximate the structures of the new effective small firms. In this account, large firms follow rather than lead sequences of change and reorganization, as they are no longer the leading edge of organizational development. This does not square with the situation in Britain where large businesses are the originators of change rather than followers.

The limited distribution of FS

Piore and Sabel argue (1984) that there are few regions in the world that approximate FS. This is because the emergence of this system depends on the simultaneous appearance of particular requirements—the necessary skilled labour, the right kind of finance, an appropriate level of entrepreneurship for example. In addition, according to Piore and Sabel, if it is to develop rapidly as a system of production, FS needs a certain amount of support and encouragement as well. FS requires 'micro-economic regulation', in which, among other things, the local state is seen to give support to local industrial activities. Support for such things as appropriate education in localities and the fostering of marketing cooperatives would be appropriate. It is certainly true that these sorts of support for local industries are generally not forthcoming in this country, and perhaps this is part of the reason why Britain is not seen to be remotely in the running to develop FS. Those who have attempted to apply the idea of FS to Britain, such as Zeitlin (1992) and Hirst and Zeitlin (1988), portray this country as being particularly slow in developing the new arrangements. It might be argued that this is curious, since Britain retained many of the features of its early system of production based on industrial districts, which clearly influenced ideas about FS. The loosely federated elements of businesses and the relatively high use of skilled labour are features that might give the British a lead. The alleged responsiveness of the market-based British economy ought, also, presumably, be allowing the relatively rapid adoption of flexible specialization.

Commenting on the reasons why Britain has been slow in developing towards FS, Hirst and Zeitlin (1988) put forward a number of reasons. Although there were in Britain, historically, numerous industrial districts which were both specialized and flexible, these were effectively destroyed. One important factor here was the development of large-scale business through mergers. These mergers consolidated firms into common ownership. We may add that, after firms were merged, they were rationalized, though not necessarily quickly. They were only gradually developed into firms capable of large batch production. There was a belief in the desirability of large-scale production in Britain, but this was combined with the inability to raise sufficient finance to bring it about in an efficient manner. The British managerial cadre was poorly educated and had neither the foresight nor the capital to see the way forward to large-scale operations. The tragedy of the British system is that the old industrial districts were abolished slowly in favour of an undercapitalized and inefficient version of mass production. However, this was introduced, against concerted opposition, in the 1950s and 1960s. The British heritage of small firms was then finally removed only a short time before it might have become the basis for a new paradigm of production based on FS. As far as Hirst and Zeitlin (1988) are concerned, many of the inadequate features of British organization and management that have been considered before are now invoked as the reason both for the late introduction of mass production, and for the difficulty of moving on.

Few would suggest that the British economy is not undergoing massive change. It is further forward in the processes of change than many other countries. What is happening here does not fit the pattern of movement described by the development of flexible specialization. However, the kind of approach developed by Piore and Sabel is valuable because it recognizes and seeks to explain epochal change. It points to the fact that if change is to occur it depends on groups of people exerting their agency in effective ways, so as to overcome the inertial drag exerted by an existing pattern of institutions.

8.5 The regulationist account of change

The other approach to epochal change is 'regulation theory' which was originally developed by European Marxist writers, and retains characteristics of Marxist thinking. It takes its name from the idea that capitalism is an inherently unstable socio-economic system, and needs to be regulated. Even then, capitalism will have a tendency to crisis which is only resolved by periodic reorganization. The founding father of the approach is usually taken to be Aglietta who wrote *The Theory of Capitalist Regulation* in 1979. This and an influential work by Palloix (1976) take the development of capitalism in America as a basic reference point. However, there are now many writers regarded as being regulationist in general outlook including Lipietz (1987), Boyer (1988), Leborgne and Lipietz (1992), and a clutch of influential British writers such as Jessop (1994) and Peck and Tickell (1994). Their concern is with other countries including Britain.

These writers postulate that the productive economy develops on its own path and drives social development. In the normal course of events, as the capitalist economy develops, there is a build up of tensions between the economy and the rest of the society. In the original formulation by Marx, these are tensions which the structure ultimately cannot resolve, and will cause the capitalist society to be transformed into socialism by way of violent revolution. Historically, this process explains the transformation of society in Europe from feudalism to capitalism and potentially explains its future transformation from capitalism. However, the idea of fundamental or final transformation is now discarded; but what we have instead is the idea that capitalism is a lot more resilient than was originally thought. It is not the importance of tensions that has been overestimated, so much as the capacity for them to be absorbed and regulated that has been underestimated. In support of this idea, labour is more accommodating to the capitalist regime than was thought possible by Marx and his early followers—not least through the formation of reformist parties and trade unions. Corporations and managements are more adaptive and capable of absorbing conflict than was thought possible too.

BOX 8.7 Early regulationism

The aim of the early French regulationists was to develop a theoretical framework which could encapsulate and explain the paradox within capitalism between its inherent tendency towards instability, crisis and change, and its ability to coalesce and stabilize around a set of institutions, rules and norms which serve to secure a relatively long period of economic stability. This conceptual effort was underpinned by the observation that the stagnation of growth in the world economy after the mid-1970s amounted to much more than a cyclical lull, symbolizing a generalized crisis of the institutional forms that had come to guide the post-war world economy.

Ash Amin (1994: 7)

Regulationists argue that development of the capitalist economy to more elaborate forms produces significant tensions which cause change in a good deal of the rest of the society or 'social formation'. It is as if capitalism periodically breaks out of its existing regulatory shell, at which point the institutions of society are regrouped around the new economic forms. Much of the latter change is concerned with containment and regulation of the system as a whole. Indeed, this approach makes two kinds of contribution: one is to shift the emphasis in the explanation of change to developments in the capitalist economy; the other is to consider developments in other areas of organized social life as being related to (and to some extent functional for) the capitalist economy. Thus, at the heart of this approach is a set of propositions about historical transformations, which are, superficially at any rate, similar to the proposals of Piore and Sabel (1984). However, in this analysis, it is clear that what causes transformations in the first place are developments in capitalism, as corporations seek profitability.

Fordism/neo-Fordism/post-Fordism

Aglietta argues for five phases in the development of the US economy up to the end of the 1960s. These are: capital expansion (to 1875); extensive institutional build up (1875 to 1920); transition—mass production without mass consumption (1920 to 1945); Fordist accumulation—with collective-bargaining and the interventionist state (1945 to 1966); neo-Fordism/post-Fordism (1970 onwards). The effort to place capitalist activity at the centre of the analysis is suggested by the use of the label 'Fordism' to identify the latest stage of development. However, the notion of Fordism here refers to a much broader set of institutions than car factories themselves. Fordism, in this designation, is applied to the mass-production-mass-consumption society generally, where there is both the production of durables and their mass consumption along a range of state services (education, welfare, and health care provision, pensions, income support, and the like) not to mention the management of the economy. This group of writers is particularly keen on implicating the state and its policies in the relationships. Hence, the concept 'Fordism' as used here is offered as a description of the entire 'regime of accumulation', as it is called by regulationists.

Briefly, what is the accumulation regime (AR) and how is it seen to relate to other aspects of organized social life? The AR is the whole system of institutions involved in production and consumption prevailing at the time. It is analysed as being made up of two parts: the accumulation system (AS) and the mode of social regulation (MR). Both are highly abstract notions, but the AS can be seen as almost exclusively economic and takes in the labour process (the ways of organizing productive work activity itself, including the design of jobs), the broader system of production (the technology and management system typically employed in plants, of which the mass-production factory would be an example), and the macro-economic structure (referring to the relation of the elements in the economy including the flows of capital). The AS covers the development of new forms of industrial administration. In this account, Taylorism and other rationalized forms of early management are key stages in the development of the accumulation system. Fordism (as a factory regime) is a later stage of accumulation involving large batches of standardized products, extensive division of labour, layered hierarchies of control, and high wages. The accumulation system has a tendency to extend itself, and in particular to link the 'sphere of production' with the 'sphere of consumption' in relatively stable relationships. We can see how the AS is regulatory in some sense. Important though these are, they are by no means the most important form of regulation.

Developments in the AS are the first stage in the emergence of a general regulatory system of institutions. Stability and development, which particularly characterize the stage of Fordist mass production, are not secured through the accumulation system alone, but also the mode of regulation which grows up around it. The mode of (social) regulation (MR) then refers to general patterns of institutions which form a supporting or regulatory framework of institutions (of banks, small firms servicing big firms, worker organizations as well as the institutions of the state), which practise economic management. The mode of social regulation is essentially a broader institutional framework within which management of the economy takes place. It includes institutions such as trade unions, political parties, and the various arms of the state. Undoubtedly the most important institution or network of institutions is the state, the welfare state in particular. The availability of social security, education, and health services reconciles people to staying within the confines of the system. However, regulationists define the content of MR widely to include some abstract features of the economy such as the wage form, the monetary

---

BOX 8.8 Analysing Fordism

Fordism itself can be analysed on four levels.

As a distinctive type of labour process [or industrial paradigm], it involves mass production based on moving assembly-line techniques operated with the semi-skilled labour of the mass worker. Not all branches nor workers will be directly involved in mass production in a Fordist economy, of course: the important point is that mass production is the main source of its dynamism.

As a stable mode of macroeconomic growth [regime of accumulation], Fordism involves a virtuous circle of growth based on mass production, rising productivity based on economies of scale, rising incomes linked to productivity, increased mass demand due to rising wages, increased profits based on full utilisation of capacity, and increased investment in improved mass production equipment and techniques.

As a mode of social and economic regulation [mode of regulation], Fordism involves the separation of ownership and control in large corporations with a distinctive multi-divisional, decentralised organisation subject to central controls [Taylorist division of labour]; monopoly pricing; union recognition and collective bargaining; wages indexed to productivity growth and retail price inflation; and monetary emission and credit policies orientated to securing effective aggregate demand. In this context the key wage bargains will be struck in the mass production industries; the going rate will then spread through comparability claims among the employed and through the indexation of welfare benefits financed through progressive taxation for those not economically active. This pattern need not mean the demise of dual labour markets or non-unionised firms or sectors as long as mass demand rises in line with productivity.

And, fourthly, Fordism can be seen as a general pattern of social organisation ('societalisation'). In this context it involves the consumption of standardised, mass commodities in nuclear family households and provision of standardised, collective goods and services by the bureaucratic state. The latter also has a key role in managing the conflicts between capital and labour over both the individual and social wage. These latter features are clearly linked to the rise of Keynesian economic management and the universalist welfare state but neither element is essential for the growth of Fordism.

Bob Jessop, 'The Politics of Flexibility', 1991, reprinted in Amin (1994: 136–7)

---

form, the organizational form, and the market structure and the state. This constellation of interdependent elements regulates in some sort of way the working of the accumulation system. They do not, however, entirely stabilize the accumulation system, which, being capitalist, is inherently unstable.

How was Britain regulated?

What is the value of all this for the analyst of the institutions of contemporary Britain? Firstly, there is the general account of the widespread changes that occur after perhaps decades of seeming order and relative stability. Periodically, this theory suggests, there will be a crisis of accumulation and there will be a need for the accumulation system (AS) to reconstruct itself. At such times, there will also be widespread change in the supporting structure of the MR. When this happens, change will begin occurring in many areas of social institutions at the same time. So widespread will change be that, amongst other things, the social and economic expectations of people may also be destabilized (regarding such things as employment, welfare, lifestyle, and consumption patterns). However, it is the accumulation system (AS) and mode of regulation (MR), taken together, which must be considered, so that changes in the MR can be expected to be in some degree related to the changes in the AS, because the overall formation is taken to be more or less stable and functional. For this reason we can expect present change to stabilize around a new accumulation system. Considered in these terms, what we have seen, first in the USA at the end of the 1960s, and then beginning in Britain in the late 1970s, is a situation of increasing tension between the AS and the MR, which has resulted in the development of the AR as a whole.

In general these changes can be summed up as the reconstruction of Fordism and construction of something with new systemic properties. A large number of proposals have been made: post-Fordism or neo-Fordism are the most frequently cited labels for the regime of accumulation. Regulationist writers who have applied these ideas have aimed at connecting the particular features of the AS and the MR in different countries and comparatively. There are many insights flowing from this work and the ideas have been applied in a surprising range of ways (Amin 1994). In general, however, it is not for any agreed aggregate of insights that the approach has to be valued. There is a great deal of confusion about such key things as the nature of the emergent accumulation system, and a variety of terminology is used. Most writers seem to be agreed that new flexible forms of organization are necessary, especially in production; and for some observers the point is not to clarify one emergent form of organization for production so much as several. Many writers propose that there will be several versions of neo-Fordism, co-opting concepts from other traditions of research. Boyer (1988), for example, has proposed that Piore and Sabel's concept of flexible specialization can be regarded as one of the emergent forms of the accumulation system. Almost all writers suggest that in most areas of production and commerce, there have to be more decentred and flexible modes of manufacture. Understood at the level of insights into contemporary institutional change, what the regulationists say is hardly much advance on the ideas held by other analysts.

On the other hand, this has to be thought of as the most systematic and far-reaching attempt to clarify the nature of contemporary events. There are three things that seem worth emphasizing as positive features of the regulationist approach. The first is that it places in the foreground the idea that it is the capitalist economy which has shaped and is shaping the overall path of change. The idea of Fordism is, however, a liability in many ways. It would be easy to exaggerate the importance of a particular mode of mass manufacture in itself and as something shaping the rest of society in recent times. The Ford Company was well past its point of undisputed importance to the American economy in the period 1945–70. Fordist practices in manufacture were not approximated in many countries, and certainly not in Britain in this period. The term is now used to apply to the state, as in the phrases 'Fordist state' and 'Fordist welfare state', and here too it seems to be of doubtful value. The best that can be said for it is that this concept acknowledges that large firms are important elements within capitalism at the highest points of its development.

The second point of value lies in the suggestion that changes in other institutions are systematically related to change in the underlying economic movements. The break-up of traditional systems of labour recruitment and training, or changes in the provision of welfare services, are not random events on this account, but part of wider processes of change prompted from within the capitalist economy. On this view, it is not mysterious why the industrial relations system was rapidly disassembled, despite the supposed pressures for continuity, which feature so strongly in institutional accounts of change. Thirdly, there is a point that much of the change we are currently observing is related to the internationalization (or globalization) of capitalism. In sum, large capital in pursuit of global markets is the driver of the current phase of change and expansion. This is a factor of obvious importance that other accounts of change either do not mention, or give too little emphasis.

The question that regulation theorists are currently concerned with is: what is happening now? All seem agreed that we are going through another stage of transition, from Fordism to something else, variously described as post-Fordism or implying a refurbishment and extension of a basically similar

---

BOX 8.9 **Searching for a new institutional fix**

(I)t is premature to talk about a post-Fordist regime of accumulation because, while some significant experiments are under way in the production sphere, a coherent post-Keynesian mode of social regulation has yet to stabilize. Thus, it is only possible at present to talk about post-Fordism in the negative sense. The institutional and political conditions for a renewed period of sustained economic growth remain elusive. Given the existence of severe reservations about the sustainability of flexible accumulation, it is impossible to make any conclusive statements about the spatial logics of post-Fordism. There are, to be sure, substantial shifts in the spatial ordering of the world economy under way at present. But rather than in terms of the language of a new global-local order, they are perhaps best understood in terms of accelerating uneven development.

Jamie Peck and Adam Tickell (1994: 307)

regime, and neo-Fordism, implying that Fordism has been superseded by something new. Neo-Fordism places emphasis on the continuity of basic features of Fordist mass production, with large firms and their managements dominating economy and polity. The movement to multi-site manufacture in this perspective represents an extension of management control over several sites, the exportation of Fordist manufacturing capacity. Post-Fordism emphasizes the dramatic change to new technologies and the complete disassembly of Fordism.

8.6 Conclusions

All three accounts of change, the institutionalist, the neo-liberal, and the regulationist, discuss the patterning of institutions in the British economy. The second two of these have much in common. All three approaches imply that it is likely to be of only limited value to analyse organizations as phenomena in their own right, things that may be considered as separate entities and designed as such—for example in the manner of Mintzberg (1979, 1993). All this writing and research suggests that organizations are embedded in relationships with other types of institutions, and that there are systemic properties which make them adopt their particular forms. For this reason they are difficult to change. There is less agreement between the approaches over the extent of change—the way in which change is pulling the existing configurations apart and the extent to which they are being replaced. The question is, then, where does change come from, what are the limitations on it, and how can it be contained?

For the institutionalists, change is mainly from the outside (exogenous) rather than from the inside (indigenous). The need for change is coming from the development of international activities, whilst the existing pattern of institutions tends to reproduce itself. Hence, whether they like it or not, business people are being forced to decide how to reorientate their business systems to meet intensified foreign competition, both within home markets and in the world. Much of the weight of evidence from this group points to the notion that change is both likely to be slow and will have to take place in particular ways. Whitley argues that any convergence between distinctive patterns of institutions is unlikely, and the forces tending to bring this about have been exaggerated (Whitley 1999). According to these writers, any change will have differential effects because of special features of particular institutional systems. Hence, according to Lane (1995), because British businesses are market-orientated and only weakly embedded in the institutional fabric, they can be responsive in a way that is not possible for businesses in other countries. However, also because they are weakly embedded, the activities of businesses are not supported by other institutions. Hence, what they do is unlikely to be thorough and therefore less likely to be effective in the medium to long term. There are undoubtedly institutional patterns of the kind described by institutional writers, but they overemphasize their importance in explaining the trend of events.

For the neo-liberals, by contrast, the proposition that, when it comes, change originates mainly from the inside of particular countries is strongly supported. These authors suggest that the lack of change in normal times is explained much in the way that it is by the institutionalists: entrepreneurs carry on in the same way, attempting to innovate using best practice. When it is clear that conditions for doing business have changed (consumer markets have become saturated) they will be forced to behave in new ways, but these will not always be successful. Where favourable conjunctures of factors of production occur, however, then business may well discover new and effective patterns of organization. In many of the examples of the beginnings of flexible specialization (FS) described by Piore and Sabel (1984), the most important factors that they argue need to be present seem to be the existence of small specialist firms and pools of highly skilled and knowledgeable labour. If these are present, then FS may arise spontaneously; if it does not, then it still may be possible to kick-start it by sensitive local policies. The supporters of the analysis think that fostering local concentrations of small businesses is the way forward, and, as applied in Britain, people influenced by this thinking have been in favour of local policies rather than national ones. Big business is not seen as important in this approach, and this is a considerable failing. In some other ways, however, the neo-liberal analysis has a close similarity with the approach being made here, especially in the way that it points to the effective agency of particular groups as the source of change. In this account we point to the policies and practices of the controllers of big businesses as the effective agents of change.

The regulationist school argues that what is driving change is the capitalist economy and its associated institutions. Recent writing from this point of view places heavy emphasis on the development of the international economy. These writers emphasize the centrality of the need to generate surpluses within capitalism as a central motor of change, but they mostly focus on the properties of the system of institutions that constitute capitalist society. Until recently, they have paid insufficient attention to the way that international relations are affecting events. There have been several attempts to think about the relationship between the national and the global economy within this approach. Boyer (1988: 74), for example, speculates about 'the mode of adhesion to the international regime'. This approach does give central place to the spontaneous movements of elements of capital. But the expectation is for some regulatory network to develop. Historically such tendencies have been apparent. It is also clear that, as they move increasingly into international relations, capitalist firms may be escaping any significant regulation.

Although there seems to be little doubt that development within the economy is being driven by innovation by large business as it reconstitutes itself, there is insufficient recognition by any group of writers that decisive steps away from effective regulation are being taken by large business. The capacity for a surrounding shell of regulatory institutions to re-establish itself as capitalism adopts new forms of accumulation seems likely to be relatively weak, as businesses move to international operations. Outside the jurisdiction of the nation state there are few regulatory agencies, and the idea that they may be quickly established is dubious. In such circumstances the possibility that capitalist organizations may become substantially unregulated is fairly obvious. The extent to which the global financial system is regulated, for example, is limited. In these circumstances the possibility exists for quite a lot of variation to occur within the institutional structures of capitalism.

British business seems to have escaped regulation in obvious ways, and this is a key feature that has to be taken into account if we wish to understand the changes being experienced not only in the economy but in the social life of the country.

9

British business and globalization

9.1 Introduction

Any attempt to analyse the world as a whole is confronting a potentially large task, and it might be thought that undertaking the analysis of such a topic is daunting. Indeed there is a wealth of academic writing on this subject but, thankfully, much is not relevant to our concerns. Much recent writing, for example, is about the supposed effects of globalization on the outlook of people, their values, and culture. There is an emerging academic specialism considering the alleged emergence of global culture, for example (Feather-stone 1995). In this discussion, however, we will remain focused on theories concerned with structures and consider the extent to which British companies are participating in the emergence of a global economy, and the extent to which this accounts for changes in the organization of British business.

It is widely believed that there is a process of globalization going on today (Axford 1995; Spyby 1995; Albrow 1996; Scholte 2000). If this is so, it may well be important for the present argument. It has been suggested that British firms are only weakly embedded in their society by comparison with firms in other countries and that they have moved a lot of capacity abroad. Perhaps they are aiming to globalize? Moreover, perhaps British firms have, because of some fortuitous circumstances of their history, found unexpected advantages in the new global context for business and are moving ahead of the competition. If this is so, recognizing the processes of globalization may well be an important key to understanding contemporary change. Perhaps we need look no further for an explanation of epochal change in British society: major companies are leading a move towards globalization, to become leading world companies. If this is so, perhaps the problems the British economy is experiencing might be seen in a different light. It can be argued that it is only to be expected that companies will take this kind of expansionist path, and they should not be impeded. Indeed, as big businesses adapt to their new context, there may be some considerable dislocation in their economy of origin. These governments should ignore for the greater good.

In this chapter a different set of propositions is developed. There are three aspects. Firstly, it is not the case that British companies are actually motivated to become global in scale. What companies are doing is moving into wider international relations. To make this point, ideas about the character and strategy of British companies will be considered. British companies are not undertaking globalization, but internationalization. This point can be generalized: genuinely global companies from any region of the world are difficult to find. Secondly, and more generally, globalization is not taking place in the way that many think, and, to the extent that it is actually occurring, globalization does not have the characteristics and implications that are widely assumed. Ideas derived from national development are often unreflectively used as the source of models for globalization: such thinking is misleading. A third and final point is that the development of international involvement by British companies does not and should not put them beyond the reach of policy.

The first two issues are addressed in this chapter, whilst the question of policy will be considered in our concluding chapter. It has been suggested here that major British companies are moving some of their assets overseas whilst reducing their exposure in this country. This is especially so in terms of the reduction of the numbers employed by large British companies in this country. A study of a sample of the largest British manufacturers undertaken by the author, for example, showed that, in the twenty years between the beginning of the 1980s and the end of the 1990s, the proportion of overseas employees doubled from just over 30 per cent to 60 per cent of their total employees. If major defence contractors are excluded (these firms must retain a large number of British employees, for reasons of security), then the figure for overseas employees increases to nearly 80 per cent for the sample. However, by doing this sort of thing, it is not obvious that British businesses are trying to become global players. The policies of British companies are about profitable survival rather than growth. Although they operate in many countries, such companies transact the great majority of their business with only a few regions in the world. As we shall see, world commerce itself is largely restricted to trading between the developed parts of the world.

9.2 The structure and strategy of British multinational companies

Large British companies do not typically seek to occupy whole sectors of the economy in which they operate. British multinationals tend to proceed on a more piecemeal basis than many of their rivals. They identify their most profitable lines of activity and consolidate around them; they may also expand into adjacent areas and acquire competitors. The internationalization projects in which they are engaged are often little more than an extension of their domestic policies and practices to other countries. British firms are not blind to the value of securing market power either through monopoly (if you are the only producer, then buyers must pay your price) or monopsony (if you are the only buyer of sub-assemblies or of manufactured products you have significant power over your suppliers) and do achieve such positions. But, because it is likely to require high levels of investment, there is no aspiration to dominate a whole industrial sector. Instead, there is the aim of being good in particular product markets, and, if possible, to earn high profits from monopolizing supply in lucrative niche markets.

Although subject to similar pressures, British companies retain important differences in organization and outlook from American companies. We have noted already that British companies were slow to adopt the US originated 'M' form of company, preferring versions of the holding (or 'H' form) of company structure. They seem less concerned about having consistent management policies and practices than the Americans. British firms are more willing to buy into new areas of activity—whether they are strictly related to their core business or not—and to move their assets about in pursuit of profit. This makes them more mobile and tolerant of local conditions than companies from many other countries. If these features define the 'footloose' company, British businesses qualify as among the most market orientated and footloose in the world. This is easy to confuse with a policy aimed at developing a company by increasing its assets and global involvement.

Some examples may be helpful. Before it was broken up recently, United Biscuits (UB), a British multinational food producer, made the decision to withdraw from the US market, where competition was intense, by selling off its plants and subsidiary businesses there. At roughly the same time, the decision was made by the UB board to expand in South-East Asia and Australasia. Before long UB had, among other new businesses, an expanding manufacturing operation in China, where sales of digestive biscuits were said to be buoyant. Another example is GKN, which is one of the few remaining large British engineering companies. GKN is heavily involved in the manufacture of components for the automotive industry. Here a decision was made some years ago to invest strongly in the development of advanced braking systems, hoping to become the preferred and long-term supplier to a number of car manufacturers worldwide. At one point in the recent past, BTR (now part of Invensys) attempted to become the world's major producer of certain kinds of industrial seals, which meant taking over the foreign suppliers of these items. The CEO of Spirent speaks of occupying a 'sweet spot in the telecoms market' (see Box 4.8).

BOX 9.1 **The extent of capital export by British companies**

Thus, Multi-National Companies [MNCs] in a cross section of industries arose at the end of the 19th century when Britain had the largest volume of outward foreign direct investment (FDI), placed mainly in Commonwealth countries. Since the Second World War, the USA has overtaken Britain as the biggest outward investor. Despite some narrowing of the gap between Britain and the larger European countries in the stock of FDI, Britain remains second in the international league table.

For a large number of MNCs, FDI has been a more important strategy of internationalization than exporting for much of the post-war period. FDI of UK companies consistently has been in a wide range of industries but has concentrated heavily on the more standardised, lower-technology end of production, with a heavy concentration on packaged, branded consumer goods. But the more technology and knowledge-intensive industries of oil and pharmaceuticals have also been important. Britain's imperial history meant that a large proportion of FDI was initially placed in Commonwealth countries, but since the mid-1960s a reallocation has taken place. Although there is now a concentration on the USA and Western Europe as investment sites, the pattern of FDI remains marked by Britain's imperial legacy. British MNCs retain a much more extensive geographical spread of operations than their German counterparts. . . .

Among the large UK MNCs . . . a significantly smaller proportion of assets and activities remains concentrated in the home country. A look at figures on sales, investment and employment for some of the largest MNCs can readily illustrate the contrast. Thus in 1995, ICI had about 33 per cent of net operating assets located in Britain, realised just under 50 per cent of its turnover in the UK, but employed only around 35 per cent of its work force at home, and for Glaxo UK sales amounted to 8 per cent of the total, employment to around 33 per cent and capital expenditure was lower at home than abroad. BTR, a manufacturing conglomerate, had left only 21 per cent of sales, 14 per cent of investment and only just over a third of employment in the UK, and Grand Metropolitan, the foods and drinks company, has a much stronger focus on the US than the UK in terms of turnover, profits and net assets.

Christel Lane (1998: 469 and 474)

The place of companies in other economies

We may contrast these policies, and particularly the weak allegiance to the British economy, with the strategies of large Japanese companies. These are typically engaged in all areas of activity in a given industrial sector, and show stronger attachment to their home. If we look at the main Japanese *kieretsus* (sometimes still called *zaibatsus*), which are the groups of affiliated companies that form the heart of the Japanese economy, then they seem to be involved in all conceivable areas of activity from banking and insurance through trading, shipping, and all kinds of manufacture. There is hardly a manufactured product that the Mitsubishi Corporation, or one of several sister companies or numerous subsidiaries, does not make. Although they are smaller, the Korean *chaebols*—such as LG or Samsung—also aspire to make all products and supply all services in the same sort of way. Many commentators have recognized this kind of difference, and it is for this reason that Japanese capitalism has been seen highly organized. In some extreme evaluations, Japanese industrial policies are seen as an extension of state policy—Japan Inc as the country has been described by American critics. The same criticism, though formulated with more subtlety, lies behind the idea that Japanese capitalism is imperialism in another form (Kahn 1970).

There are few, if any, European businesses which have the aspiration to make everything in this Asian way. However, many of them share some of this outlook, in that they are committed to expansion and, if possible, securing a dominant position in their chosen sector. The German car companies, BMW and Mercedes-Benz, for example, which made their names by producing quality products, were not content to remain the leading producers in that end of the market. BMW's disastrous purchase of Rover Group was motivated by the aim of becoming a broad-spectrum car company and a long-term player in the global automotive market. Mercedes' joint venture with Chrysler has a similar motivation. British companies, with the possible exception of some pharmaceutical firms, do not have this aim in view in any shape or form. In sum, British companies are not engaged in globalization, though they may be seeking to find and exploit markets for their products in many countries of the world. Although such companies are in more economies and markets than twenty years ago, because they are not seeking forms of development that will

---

BOX 9.2 **Business groups in the Japanese economy**

The Japanese economy is . . . dominated by a very small number of giant combines which determine the direction of the entire economy. These combines are surrounded by a proliferation of smaller enterprises which usually depend on them directly or indirectly. They wield relatively little countervailing power.

Concentration is the first feature of imperialism. In Japan this takes the form of oligopoly rather than monopoly. The situation is . . . 'one of oligopolistic competition between the zaibatsu over a wide range of industries, with a fringe of small, specialised companies (often subcontractors for the zaibatsu enterprises) clustered around them'. . . . Six groups qualify as zaibatsu: the Mitsubishi, Mitsui, Sumitomo, Fuyo, Dai-Ichi Kangyo and Sanwa groups. In addition, there are seven other major groups which can conveniently be referred to as 'konzerns', mainly non-financial companies characterized by integrated operations, usually within a single industry or within several related industries. The seven are: Nippon Steel, Toshiba-IHI, Hitachi, Toyota, Nissan, Matsushita and Tokyu. The konzerns are not purely 'industrial' combines, but, unlike the zaibatsu, they do not have a bank or other central financial institution within the group.

Jon Halliday (1975: 273)

make them dominant companies in the world, they are simply engaging in increased internationalization.

9.3 In search of the global company

But if British firms do not approximate to it, there may be, nonetheless, a distinctive global firm emerging. A number of commentators believe this and suggestions have been put forward which take the view that multinational companies will develop into global companies with a recognizable organizational structure. The ideas of authors who argue this thesis have been considered in Chapter 7. Here we shall discuss models that are relevant to the issue of globalization (Perlmutter 1969; Bartlett and Ghoshal 1989; Hedlund 1994; Solvell and Zander 1995).

An early set of proposals was put forward by Perlmutter (1969) who argued for three different types of multinational company. They were called the 'ethnocentric', the 'polycentric', and the 'geocentric' forms. The idea here is that there is a process of development through which multinational organizations will pass, and, in the course of which, they become less nationalistic and more cosmopolitan. In the early stages of multinational operations, firms are likely to retain the characteristics of the country of origin and to be orientated towards the customs and practices of that place, they will be 'ethnocentric'. Almost as a natural development, it is reasonable to expect that the branches of a firm's operations will adapt to the diverse situations in which they find themselves. Contingency theory would certainly predict this, as the branches of the multinationals cannot expect to be more than partially sheltered from the environments in which they operate. Thus, from ethnocentricity, firms are expected to develop much higher degrees of 'polycentricity'. Perlmutter's suggestion amounts to a proposal that there will be an evolutionary process, the end point of which is the development of the truly global company, with no residual territorial or other allegiances.

The typology of Bartlett and Ghoshal (1989) is arguably also of this kind, although it does not imply a linear path of development. They propose that multinational organizations must solve the problems of how to decentralize (so as to gain maximum advantage from serving local markets) without also losing the advantages of size—such as securing economies of scale and scope. On the one hand, there are companies which retain centralization of core functions and competencies, but which try to be sensitive to local conditions, called by Bartlett and Ghoshal 'international companies'. On the other hand, there are 'multinational companies' which are more highly sensitive to local conditions but which could sacrifice overall integration as a result. (This type

approximates to Perlmutter's polycentric type of company.) For these analysts, most provocatively of all, there are already some very large companies
which qualify as global companies in terms of the markets they supply, but
which fall short in other ways. Such firms clearly can produce very cheaply in
almost any place as a result of retaining central plans and processes; however,
they lack sensitivity to the needs of localities and would be better for being
much more dispersed. According to these authors, the truly effective global
company (called by them the transnational company) has not yet fully
emerged. When it does so, however, it will be both dispersed and sensitive to
local conditions.

There are interesting parallels between the work of Bartlett and Ghoshal
(1989) and other writers already encountered in this book. These authors'
ideas have some similarities to those of Hedlund (1994) and Solvell and Zander (1995), discussed in Chapter 7. Hedlund *et al.* also tend to see the high
point of development of new organizational forms in terms of the achievement of a high degree of decentralization, in which operational autonomy is
granted to the constituent elements of large firms. Hedlund refers to the
development of the 'heterarchy', suggesting a diversity of forms and kinds of
regulation. This type of structure supposedly has many locations in which
there will be a number of different patterns of organization. Hence, the range
of relationships between units in the company as well as in relation to outside
organizations and groups will increase in variety (Hedlund 1986: 22–4). Subsidiary managers are, in effect, delegated the strategic role for the multinational company as a whole, because their initiatives, taken as a whole, are
what passes for group policy.

This proposal about structure has many correspondences with certain of the
network structures also outlined in Chapter 7. In a later development of
the approach of Bartlett and Ghoshal (1989), these researchers have renamed
the transnational company, which was their name for the most highly
developed form of international company, the 'differentiated network'
(Nohria and Ghoshal 1997). The differentiated network is 'composed of distributed resources linked through different types of relations, the local linkages within each national subsidiary, the linkages between headquarters and
the subsidiaries and the linkages between subsidiaries themselves' (Nohria
and Ghoshal 1997: 4). This complex and multifaceted pattern of relationships
is seen as providing the company with the means rapidly to innovate for new
products and services for national, regional, and global markets as well as to
maximize the efficiency of its operations by locating production, R&D, and
marketing/sales efforts wherever is most appropriate. This kind of argument is
sometimes combined with the idea that the whole company finally relin-
quishes any national allegiance; no longer based anywhere, it is 'footloose',
and truly global.

BOX 9.3 Towards the structure of the transnational company?

The most important source of international economic exchange is no longer the flow of trade between countries but the multinational company or MNC. According to the influential views of Robert Reich—a global web of companies is replacing the nationally specific firm. Observers in the labour movement have expressed concern at the ability of the transnationals to switch production between sites and to seek out countries with low labour costs.

The purpose . . . [here] is . . . to focus on one specific issue: the supposed evolution of the firm from being nationally specific, through stages variously labelled multinational and polycentric, to the true transnational enterprise. . . . The 'transnational solution' has been canvassed most thoroughly by Bartlett and Ghoshal. They contrast it with three prior approaches to cross-country operations. What they term multinationals build a strong local presence in each country. Such firms stress the ability to operate in each local market and thus tend to be decentralised groupings with little strategic direction from headquarters. Global companies have a more centralised and global-level approach to markets; the head office has a strong role in laying down policy for subsidiaries. International companies exploit parent company skills through world-wide adaptation rather than centralised imposition; they have a more federal structure in which the centre co-ordinates rather than instructs. All these structures are felt to have difficulty in handling the grouping complexity of global markets. The fourth type, the transnational, is seen as the coming solution to this problem. Writers such as Hedlund (1986) also argue, firms need to move away from hierarchical organisation towards a more flexible structure. The transnational is characterised by differentiated contributions from each national team, with knowledge being shared and responsibility dispersed. Instead of centralised command, responsibility is devolved, and co-ordination is attained not through instruction and monitoring but through co-operation, team work and shared values

There are some critics of the transnational model. Hu has argued that there are really very few transnationals: most firms are rooted in a particular national base on which they depend for their basic operating style, and national financial regimes prevent the rise of the truly stateless corporation. Porter similarly argues that firms gain competitive advantage from their location in specific national contexts.

P. K. Edwards *et al.* (1996: 40–2)

The limitations of the idea of polycentricity

Many aspects of this thesis are questionable. It is questionable how far decentralization actually is appropriate or functional for organizations; and the extent to which it is actually adopted. We may begin by assuming it is unlikely that global corporations will be extremely decentred unless there are compelling reasons why they should be, as there are many benefits, especially for corporate elites, from remaining centralized. The need to adapt to local conditions is the reason often given for decentring and 'polycentricity' and is unpersuasive in at least one sense: often there is no compelling need to adapt to local consumer tastes. It is characteristic of large companies that they shape the environments in which they operate, rather than adapt to them. One of the reasons is that they offer goods and services not otherwise available, or not otherwise available at the same quality and price. To what extent do Coca Cola, McDonald's, and Ford adapt to local environments? The same is true of chemical, oil, and pharmaceutical companies. True, large British retail-related manufacturers such as the Diageo, Six Continents, and Allied Domecq own local brands, from which they obtain much of their sales in particular localities, but they use the same production and distribution methods everywhere.

If extreme decentralization was indeed highly functional, one might expect that supply could quite well be achieved by independent small firms, or sets of them working together. In addition, authors such as Bartlett and Ghoshal (1989) and Solvell and Zander (1995) seem to have passed over the possibility that, if decentralization has been adopted by multinational concerns, it may have been so for expedient reasons as much as, if not more than, for reasons of alleged efficiency. As has been suggested before, even the largest companies do not have enough capital to undertake all the functions they might wish to in all the countries in which they operate. This obliges them very often to make the strategic choice between a lack of involvement in a particular country and reducing the scale of the commitment of their own assets in that place. By decentralizing and reliance on local partners and affiliations, such problems are avoided.

There is little evidence to demonstrate the existence of the truly global corporation as defined by the above ideas, despite the weight of support for the idea of the decentred or otherwise 'footloose' global corporation (Ohmae 1990, 1995). According to Edwards *et al.* (1996) there have been a few attempts to test the validity of the proposals of Bartlett and Ghoshal (1989) but they have been 'at best inconclusive'. On the other hand, there is both evidence and argument to the effect that, when they move into international operations, large companies retain their identity and national affiliations (Whitley 1999). As has been argued, whatever operational autonomy is allowed at the periphery, tight control of certain operational variables, such as, for British companies, financial performance monitoring (Morgan 1998) will usually be present. Indeed, the largest organizations in the world—if all affiliated companies are counted—are Japanese. Japanese companies are among the most firmly rooted in their home institutions and culture (Elger and Smith 1994; Hirst and Thompson 1999). It seems that the interest in profitability that is a feature of British companies does not weaken when organizations become extensive multinational corporations, or capital-extensive firms (CEFs) as they were called at the end of Chapter 6.

BOX 9.4 **The global reach of multinationals**

1. Market structure. Multi-national companies have tended to invest in oligopolistic markets in host Third World countries and have contributed to increased market concentration.

2. Monopoly profits. The market power of multinationals enables them to earn monopoly profits in host countries. These profits, however, do not always appear in the tax returns of the foreign subsidiaries because of various accounting procedures and particularly transfer pricing.

3. Abuse of market power and restrictive business practices. Multinationals restrict competition both individually and collectively. Individually they impose restrictive clauses on subsidiaries and licensees through technology contracts. These include tying inputs of raw materials, parts and machinery to the multinational supplier and restricting exports in order to divide world markets. Collectively they form cartels or collude through market sharing agreements, pricing policies and the allocation of spheres of influence.

4. Demand creation. Multinationals use their market power to create demand for their products rather than responding to consumer preferences expressed through the market. This leads to 'taste transfer' through the multinational and the expansion of the market for products which are inappropriate for local conditions. The beverage 'Coca Cola' has normally been seen as a prime example of such an inappropriate product.

5. Factor displacements. The package nature of foreign direct investment and the monopoly power of the multinationals lead to situations where part of the package displaces local inputs. Imports of capital and management can also displace local capital and entrepreneurship. The extension of control by foreign subsidiaries leads to what is termed the 'de-nationalization' of local industry.

Summarized by Robert Gwynne (1990: 125–6)

The persistence of national characteristics

Against the argument that there is an emergent form for the global company as a decentred, footloose international network, it is proposed that there are different forms of capital extensive firm, with different degrees and kinds of organization according to their country of origin. These vary greatly in their organization: the Japanese business groups being quite different from the American or the British. It can be argued that British firms have little commitment to a particular mode of organizing, and display quite a lot of diversity because they make expedient adaptations to local conditions. By comparison, the Japanese import senior management and their own business systems (Morgan 1998) as do the Germans (Whitley 1999). The subsidiaries of the large firms are differentially involved in local networks in the economic regions in which they operate. Again this argument has many points of similarity with those of the institutionalists (such as Lane, Whitley, and Morgan) who have considered the international operations of large firms.

BOX 9.5 The lack of internationalization

Our key general points are firstly that patterns of internationalisation are linked to national systems of firm governance, structure and strategy. The way in which firms develop their multinational operations will be through drawing on their existing competencies and expertise; as these differ across forms of capitalism, patterns of internationalisation will also vary according to country of origin.

Richard Whitley (1999)

Whitley is particularly strong in his support for the proposition that the multinationals continue to display the characteristics of their economy of origin (Whitley 1999).

According to this argument, pre-existing patterns of business organization lead to particular sorts of division of labour within the multinational corporation. These are partly reflected in the formal organization structure of subsidiaries and divisions but more importantly in the degree to which power is distributed around the corporation and how various points in the corporation seek to develop and extend their power. The multinational corporation is too complex an entity to be understood in terms of a single source of dynamic power. It is therefore important to examine how its structure (based on its original national business system-based competences) 'opens up various spaces for the exercise of power as it is extended into a specific geographical matrix of multinational relationships' (Whitley 1999). This concedes a good deal to the idea that multinationals, whatever their place of origin, will be affected by local conditions. But they will not necessarily adapt thoroughly, nor will they be able to, should they want to, adapt totally.

In *Divergent Capitalisms* (1999) Whitley suggests that the distinctive patterns of business systems he and his co-researchers have distinguished are likely to persist even though large companies extend activities to many other countries. Whitley argues for six distinctive kinds of business system, and the British system (seen to have many similarities with the American) is described as being 'compartmentalized', because he thinks the capacity for coordination of business activities other than by ownership—through such things as collaboration between competitors and alliances in production chains—is limited. Cooperative activity tends to be compartmentalized into clusters of organizations in the ownership of or otherwise dominated by particular large firms. The most distinctive feature of this system is the 'arm's length' control of companies by their nominal owners, the shareholders, which, nonetheless, leads to high control of production chains.

Convergence through the spread of global financial institutions?

An important question to be considered is whether, as they become larger and operate in a larger number of countries, multinationals will be able to escape from the formative effects of the institutions in their place of origin, and, in particular, from the effects of the conditions attached to capital supply. It might be thought that the largest multinational corporations are so large that they constitute a mode of coordination between finance capital and industrial capital. But even very large companies cannot rely entirely on accumulated profits and have to work with other institutions for raising capital. In his work, Whitley identifies the form of capital supply as shaping differences in the structure and strategy of business organizations. He draws a distinction between 'capital market-based financial systems' and 'credit-based financial systems' and suggests that the British institutional pattern is the former. To this extent, his argument is similar to ideas put forward earlier in this book, and points to the continuing relevance of such matters.

It does seem clear that, at the beginning of the twenty-first century, major British companies are still strongly tied into the Stock Exchange as the source of capital, and the mode of control through profitability that this brings with it. Arguably, however, there is increasing similarity between this system and that of the United States; indeed the finance capital system seems to have globalized quite extensively already, using common modes of organizing, based on Anglo-American institutions. The use of US financial reporting and accounting standards is also spreading as the largest firms of financial accountants and advisers (Stevens 1991; Rose and Hinings 1999) have themselves become organizations with a global spread. If it is true that such involvement is conducive to the adoption and spread of a particular pattern of organization, it can be argued that British companies ought to be amongst the world leaders because they are thoroughly adapted to these institutions. Hence, the persistence (or lack of persistence) of traditional patterns of organizations might be seen as a critical test of the thesis that global financial institutions will produce a standard form of multinational company.

Hence, a convergence in the adoption of a standard form of the multinational company might be produced by the gradual extension of the standard form of international finance capital. In support of this idea, the area in which the global economy has developed most strongly is in the sphere of finance capital. Trillions of dollars move around the world every day, searching for a fraction of a percentage point in rates of return. Such is the amount of money involved in these movements that they can quite easily destabilize small countries. Increasingly too, the rules governing the availability of finance, such as

---

BOX 9.6 Business-system characteristics

The effects of internationalizing financial flows on business-system characteristics could be considerable under certain conditions. If, for instance, most of the leading firms in credit-based financial systems were to raise the bulk of their external finance from international capital markets instead of relying on their usual business partners, this could alter the strategic priorities of these firms and eventually affect the nature of their domestic business system. Since these international markets are typically Anglo-Saxon in their governance norms and priorities, we could expect a general move to market-based relations between large shareholders and individual firms, more adversarial relations between firms and between employers and employees, and more emphasis on profits than growth goals.

However, this sort of change implies considerable shifts in established institutional arrangements, as well as in the relative influence and ability of interest groups and organizations to control key resources. It, therefore, seems unlikely to occur without substantial debate and conflict. Competing groups within both the firms concerned and their financial partners, as well as those elsewhere in the economy and society more broadly, can be expected to conflict over the desirable direction of changes to established financial structures and relationships. The outcomes of such conflicts will, of course, depend on the resources and legitimacy of different interest groups in different political economies and can by no means be assumed to converge on the dominance of Anglo-Saxon capital market rationalities.

Richard Whitley (1999: 129)

---

they are, are distinctive. The global finance capital system does seem to be increasingly dominated by Anglo-Saxon institutions, conventions, and practices. If such processes are in motion, they are likely already to be exerting pressure for conformity in the structures and forms adopted by major multinational companies. As there are more huge cross-national mergers with European and British or American companies (such as the takeover of Mannesmann by Vodafone, or the merger between Mercedes and Chrysler) units of European capital will be subjected to Anglo-Saxon institutions and their associated standards of conduct. Governments are also making reforms towards the Anglo-Saxon pattern of institutions. However, there is still scope for arguing that the full integration of companies within a uniform international system of finance capital is not likely to be achieved quickly.

Whitley (1999) argues strongly for the persistence of distinctive company forms in many parts of the world. In support of his argument, there are substantial centres of economic development that are outside of the sphere of influence of Anglo-Saxon institutions, namely Europe and the developed parts of East Asia. If homogeneity is to be secured by the extension of Anglo-Saxon finance capital institutions, it may be a long time coming.

BOX 9.7 **Reforms set to further reshape German capitalism**

For Germany, . . . next year is no ordinary year. Not only is it the year when Euro banknotes and coins replace the D-Mark, marking the final transition to a new era of European integration and sharper competition. Next year will also see the introduction of some of the most far-reaching reforms to Germany's taxation system, stock market regulations and methods of personal saving.

All these changes hold the potential to transform Germany's financial markets, enliven its corporate culture and improve its medium term macroeconomic performance. . . .

Even economic recession is unlikely to halt, let alone reverse, the steady re-shaping of the German capitalism and the move to an equity culture that have been taking place since the mid 1990s. . . .

A new law allows companies to make tax free sales of their shareholdings in other companies. In effect it opens the door to a complete reorganisation of German industry as banks, insurers and utilities put on the market equity stakes they have held for decades. The reforms also offer an opportunity for all Germany's leading financial and industrial groups to restructure themselves, concentrate on their core businesses and deliver better value to their shareholders.

Tony Barber, *Financial Times*, 15 September 2001, pp i and iv.

9.4 Arguments about economic globalization

Of course, the global economy could develop without anybody intending it. Whether the major companies of Britain (and/or those of other countries) are aiming to be global companies or not, the sheer density of international transactions might produce activity larger than that occurring within countries. Local economies need not dissolve into a world economy, the world economy may bypass or otherwise supersede them. Sooner or later, by one route or another, the global economy could become much more central to our concerns.

For some writers, economic globalization understood in this kind of way has arrived and its appearance is of major importance (Reich 1992; Ohmae 1995). For such people, there have been increases in the volume of international trade and the interpenetration of the economies of the world in recent years, to such an extent that the emergent global economy is the most salient frame of reference within which to consider events. Even if there is no statistical basis for a claim that the amount of international trading has become significant, for many the emergence of the world economy is inevitable in the longer term. In the longer term, the emerging global economy will be larger, more productive, and more efficient than anything that has existed before, and hence, we should not be too concerned about the overall benefit of the development. Thus, although there may be some initial problems in particular localities—such as the losses of manufacturing employment in the UK, the demise of trade unions, and the restructuring of the welfare state—in the medium to long term, the outcome will be beneficial. But, the problems of advanced economies such as Britain which seem to be losing out in the process of globalization as they exist are tiny by comparison with the fate of whole regions of the world that are not included in the supposed globalization process in any significant way.

It will be argued that what we take for globalization is a highly uneven process of development, in which wealth is concentrated in the control of major companies, and this actively excludes and systematically disadvantages huge tracts of territory and large numbers of people in the world. Actually, the majority of the wealth in the world is produced by large companies. These mostly are rooted in the economically advanced regions. It has been estimated that over 50 per cent of the value of world production is made by very large firms (Hirst and Thompson 1999). Other estimates suggest that two-thirds of world GNP is produced by the hundred largest companies (WTO 1995). It seems unlikely that such a pattern of wealth creation will spontaneously develop so as to include underdeveloped regions and peoples. In practice, globalization has not involved the elimination of barriers to trade and investment, the growth of international exchange, and international economic relations, to the improvement and diffusion of technology, except within restricted enclaves of the developed regions of the world. What we are now seeing is the limited development of commercial relations between those developed regions. The vast majority of transactions remain within the developed regions.

Globalization as a seamless development

A common assumption about global economic development is that it has taken place evenly and gradually, and will continue in this way. Although development may experience some minor bumps, the growth of the international economy is likely to be, as it supposedly has been in the past, steady and incremental. If the pace of change is now increasing, it is simply the culmination of a process, the general outlines of which are firmly established and of long standing. As it has been in the development of particular economies towards industrialization and developed economy status, so it will be with the world economy. There is no reason to think that development will be any less dynamic or that it will not occur in the same way. Such ideas about the process of development are expressed or implied in many general accounts of globalization (Spyby 1995; Axford 1995; Waters 1995). According to this view, what we are seeing today is nothing more than the intensification of

---

BOX 9.8 **Globalization—a necessary myth?**

Globalization has become a fashionable concept in the social sciences, a core dictum in the prescriptions of management gurus, and a catch-phrase for journalists and politicians of every stripe. It is widely asserted that we live in an era in which the greater part of social life is determined by global processes, in which national cultures, national economies and national borders are dissolving. Central to this perception is the notion of a rapid and recent process of economic globalization. A truly global economy is claimed to have emerged or to be in the process of emerging, in which distinct national economies and, therefore, domestic strategies of national economic management are increasingly irrelevant. The world economy has internationalized in its basic dynamics, it is dominated by uncontrollable market forces, and it has as its principal economic actors and major agents of change truly transnational corporations that owe allegiance to no nation state and locate wherever on the globe market advantage dictates.

This image is so powerful that it has mesmerized analysts and captured political imaginations. But is it the case?

Paul Hirst and Grahame Thompson (1999: 1)

---

processes set in motion a great many years before. As we have seen, Braudel (1983) traces the origin of trading companies from the eleventh century in Europe. This might be taken as indicating a gradual process of economic development taking place over centuries. Trading relations across the world are certainly of long standing, and they have simply become so prominent now that they are more important than the activity in national economies.

Hence, there is a common view that although there may be a quickening in the pace of development, what we are seeing is the extension of the process of gradual and incremental development of the world economy. It is true that, in these developments, certain centres and countries will lead, but the extension of Western economic institutions will be inexorable. There is a tendency here to generalize from the example of European development to the emerging world system, in that at some point supposedly in the quickening process of development, there will be 'take-off' to sustained economic growth—to use the influential concept developed by Rostow (1963). If the pace of change is currently quickening, it has to do with the final stages of rapid development leading to self-sustaining global development. Multinational companies and their activities do not constitute a problem in this perspective; they may be important engines of global development. Without them, however, there would not be much global development at all, and hence little in the way of a global economic system.

The *laissez-faire* approach to world development

The view that an acceptable form of global development will occur spontaneously is strongly supported by some academics. According to the Japanese writer Ohmae (1990, 1995), for example, the globalized economy is one where distinct national economies are subsumed and rearticulated into the global system by international transactions which are growing in volume and importance. The multinational company is important in bringing this about, but, in order to do so effectively, it will have to develop further and be free of regulation. As we have seen, the claim that there are such things as true multinationals is dubious. Nevertheless Ohmae builds his view of the emergent global economy around the idea of 'genuinely footloose capital, without national identification and with an internationalized management' (Ohmae 1995). Such firms are, apparently, willing to locate and relocate anywhere in the globe to obtain the most secure or the highest returns. According to Ohmae (1990), in a truly globalized economy, transactions would be directed by market forces, without reference to national fiscal or monetary policies. The system has to be substantially unregulated because 'interdependence would ... readily promote disintegration, i.e. competition and conflict— between regulatory agencies at different levels.' Under such a system, manufacturing organizations would be centred on those parts of the world where labour is both most competent and most tractable, leading to the economic development of underdeveloped regions. On this view, there is no need for state power to act as the regulator of economic processes.

The reality of regulation

There is, arguably, much wishful thinking in this type of account. It is unlikely that an effective system of global regulation will arise spontaneously. In addition, however, it is surely Utopian to think that there will be little need for regulation. It is very unlikely that even development will be produced with minimum interference. It has not been possible in the past to develop an economic order outside a framework of national and international regulation. However much liberals may deny the necessity for it, capitalism has, without exception hitherto, developed alongside nationalism and national systems of regulation. To this extent the regulation theorists are correct. There is a strong correlation between economic success and the development of effective national systems of economic protection and regulation. The world system, as it has existed, has also worked within the interstices of a pattern of international rivalries, in which, during the last 150 years there has also been a dominant economic power. When the capacity of the British state to be the dominant economy in the world palpably failed in the early decades of the twentieth century, there was a decline in the extent of international trade until American hegemony was firmly established.

There are different views about the importance of regulating global economic processes. Firstly, there are writers who think that, in the medium to long term, as was the case in the economic development of nations, economic institutions will become gradually regulated by an emerging structure of global regulation. Just as business developed within a national system of law and of governmental institutions, so we can see the beginnings of a system of international law and international courts. In addition, the beginnings of regulating international bodies—analogous to those which developed in individual states—are already developing in the shape of such bodies as the World Trade Organization, the International Labour Organization, and the International Monetary Fund. This emerging framework of institutions, it is argued, will tie big business down and regulate global economic development. Potentially at least the global economy may be managed in much the same way as, until quite recently, all national economies have been managed. It is possible to envisage 'global Keynesianism', referring to the system of economic ideas used to regulate post-war domestic economies, and the possibility of such a system being transferred to the global level (cf. Jessop 1994).

To use the national economy as a model for development for the world economy is misleading. Economic development in the world as a whole is much more uneven than it was in any industrializing national economy as it approached the point of sustained growth. The world is also demarcated into

---

BOX 9.9 **The relations of accumulation**

Benjamin Franklin, testifying to a committee of the British House of Commons in 1766, explained further how his Pennsylvania could import £500 000 worth of goods from Britain each year while exporting only £40 000 in return as he answered the question, 'How then do you pay the balance?'

'The balance is paid by our produce carried to the West Indies, and sold in our own islands, or to the French, Spaniards, Danes and Dutch; by the same carried to other colonies in North America, as to New England, Nova Scotia, Newfoundland, Carolina and Georgia, by the same carried to different parts of Europe, as Spain, Portugal and Italy. In all which places we receive either money, bills of exchange, or commodities that suit for remittance to Britain; which together with all the profits on the industry of our merchants and mariners, arising in those circuitous voyages, and the freights made by their ships, center finally in Britain, to discharge the balance, and pay for British manufactures continually used in the province, or sold to foreigners by our traders'.

Andre Gunder Frank (1978: 196)

different geopolitical areas that prevent or promote economic development (Wallerstein and Hopkins 1996). Many areas of the world are lacking economic resources and are unable to promote economic development politically. Africa is an example of a huge territory which is substantially detached from all of the main economic blocs. It is no accident that it contains some of the most impoverished countries in the world (Evans 1995; Woodiwiss 1996). African countries are unable to connect themselves to centres of economic development and so to be drawn into cycles of improvement. The fact is that the vast majority of production activities, and the majority of value creation is concentrated in the developed parts of the world. Given the importance of multinational corporations to economic development, this suggests that, although multinational corporations operate in many countries, their main contribution is in the context of areas of high economic development.

Large firms do generate a high proportion of added value, but they do so mainly from within those parts of the world that are already economically developed. The vast majority of manufactured products are produced within—and traded between—the limited enclaves of the developed world.

9.5 Geopolitical blocs and regulation

Challenges to the gradualist view of the development of the world economy have been mounted in a number of ways. There is no single example of a state, including Britain, in which the economy grew without some sort of regulation. State apparatuses grew up at the same time as the developing economy in most advanced countries and, in different ways and to different degrees, supported and regulated economic development. Nationalism, and strong national cultures, linked the state and the institutions of the economy in a strong bond. In some cases—Japan and Germany are examples—the economy was to some extent the deliberate construction of state policy, so that it is not really possible for the economy to become detached from the polity. Multinationals have grown up and become immensely powerful and though, in some states, of which Britain is an example, they have substantially escaped from the control of government, they remain located in specific territories and are in characteristic ways formed by their relationship with other institutions. In this account the importance of financial institutions for British companies has been emphasized. Multinational corporations are not noticeably in a process of development towards the heterogeneous world system. They remain embedded within and are contingently dependent on local infrastructure.

In his path-breaking account of the development of the world economy, Wallerstein (1984) emphasizes the importance of geopolitical relations in shaping the development of the world system. According to Wallerstein, the modern economic development of Europe was at first a response to medieval Western Europe finding itself in a position of relative economic under-development in relation to China in the East. Certainly the European economy at that time was dependent for all sorts of luxury items on China. According to Wallerstein and his adherents (Wallerstein and Hopkins 1996), the impulse to trading and creativity within Europe is not understandable outside this pattern of international relations, and what we are seeing today is the passing of US economic dominance, in favour of the dominance of the Far Eastern bloc of countries, led by Japan. Whether this is right or wrong, it does seem to be the case that the impulse to trading within Europe and the world is not understandable outside of competitive relations between geopolitical blocs.

BOX 9.10 **The geopolitical basis of world accumulation**

The process of accumulating capital on a world scale required the continual develop-ment of the world's forces and means of production.

This process was a very uneven one, and thereby continually reproduced and deep-ened what we call the core-periphery zonal organization of world production, the basis of the axial division and integration of labour processes. The construction historically of the capitalist world economy as world-system has entailed the establishment of com-modity chains of production extending backwards from the organizing centres, at first all in Western Europe, into what were areas (and peoples) initially external to the relational processes and structures forming the growing world-system. This systemic and ongoing peripheralization, within the capitalist world-economy, of most of the world's peoples and production processes and the location of core processes in a few centres accounts in our view for the massive and ongoing inequalities of well-being among and within the state jurisdictions of the system.

Accordingly, just as there have been stronger and weaker states (gauged by military strength and political efficacy), so there have been core zones that have tended, by definition, to monopolize the high profit monopolies while the peripheral zones housed production processes operating within truly competitive markets and hence character-ized by truly low-profit activities. This relational inequality underlay the continuing political tensions among and within the states of the system. It is not one that can ever be overcome as long as the endless accumulation of capital remains the primary goal, since the endless accumulation of capital requires the existence of high profit (necessar-ily largely monopolized) economic activities. To the extent that everyone would seek to engage simultaneously in these high-profit activities, the boat would become 'over-loaded' and accumulation would dry up. Hence the uneven distribution of rewards has been the necessary pendant of capital accumulation, and is fundamental to the system.

I. Wallerstein and T. K. Hopkins (1997: 4)

Globalization as a myth

The contribution of multinational companies to the global sum of value added—usually measured as the global gross national product (GGNP) but which now ought to be relabelled the gross world product (GWP)—has been differentially estimated. For Hirst and Thompson slightly more than 50 per cent of GWP is produced by the largest firms. Such data should not only be seen as indicating the importance of the multinational corporations, but also the economic exclusion of many parts of the world. This sort of observation has led Hirst and Thompson (1996, 1999) to question whether globalization is the best way of trying to understand contemporary economic development. They refer to globalization as a 'myth' (1999: 1–18) and argue instead for what they call an international economy. They argue that 'An international economy is one in which the principal entities are national economies. Trade and investment produce growing interconnection between these national economies' (Hirst and Thompson 1999: 8). So far, trade is most noticeable between developed countries. Trade relations, as a result, tend to be between developed regions. The importance of trade is, however, that it is progressively replaced by the centrality of investment relations between nations, which increasingly act as the organizing principle of the system. The form of interdependence between nations remains, however, strategic and ought to be understood as being undertaken in pursuit of national interests.

According to Hirst and Thompson, the period of this international economic system which dominates the developed world—and therefore the world as a whole—is typified by the rise and maturity of the multinational corporation (MNC). The important aspect of the MNC is that it retains a home base, with national regulation. Manufactured products and certain kinds of services do enter into international trade more generally than this, though important volumes of trade occur mainly through trading relations between the developed parts of the world; that is, between the EU and North America and Japan. Thus it can be argued that what is happening, considered economically, is not globalization so much as an extension of traditional patterns of development but with increased international dimensions. Wallerstein suggests (1984) economic power develops within geopolitical structures. Followers of Wallerstein, bringing this analysis up to date (Wallerstein and Hopkins 1996), have argued that the international economy is being developed today in the context of the decline from undisputed status as the dominant geopolitical power of the USA to a situation in which there is rivalry between three blocs: the USA, Europe, and Japan. Ikeda (1996) argues along this line that, on the basis of some indicators of economic importance, such as changes in the location of the world's largest companies over the last twenty-five years, the USA has been in decline, whilst the importance of Europe has remained static and Japan's importance has moved sharply upwards.

Geopolitical blocs

Hirst and Thompson (1999) go some way towards analysing world trade in terms of competing international economic blocs. In this view, what has emerged is a system of three economic blocs in the world, sometimes referred to as the 'Triad' (Ohmae 1990). To develop this approach, it can be argued there is a dominant economy controlling each bloc, but the blocs themselves are more complex. Within each there is the following: an economically dominant region—which usually does not correspond precisely to the national boundaries of the leading state—some satellite economies, and a relatively underdeveloped hinterland or captured trade area. Thus a bloc provides for the continued protection of a developed area, emergent satellite areas, and captured markets including relatively underdeveloped but dependent regions. Thus, for the American bloc, parts of the USA are economically dominant, but it has satellite areas within the USA itself, as well as in Canada and Mexico, whilst the whole of South America and much of the adjacent Pacific is the relatively underdeveloped hinterland. Rivalling this structure on one side is the united states of Europe (or Euroland), which has the golden triangle between London, Paris, and Berlin as its core and other parts of Europe as its satellites. The underdeveloped former communist counties of Eastern Europe and Russia form the underdeveloped hinterland. The last bloc is in East Asia, with the core economy in Japan. Korea, Hong Kong, and Singapore are its important satellites and China and other developing economies of East Asia its hinterland.

From this perspective, many of the problems of the British economy and the particular pattern of development of its multinational corporations, arise from the historical alignments of the British economy to other blocs. At one time, towards the end of the nineteenth century, Britain was the dominant world power. Its satellite economies and hinterland were not in adjacent territories—where there were strong economic rivalries developing—but in the world in the British colonies and other dependent territories. The British financial sector serviced world trade as well as exporting capital in large amounts to contribute to economic development. As this hegemony faded, from the turn of the twentieth century, Britain sought a closer relationship with the USA as the new dominant power in the world. The trading and other links between the British and the US economies have always been important, and remain so today. However, following the grant of independence to the colonies and final collapse of nationalistic rivalries in Europe after 1945, there is a need to realign the British economy with the European bloc and for economic development to take place as part of this bloc. The problem with this is, of course, that British institutions are unlike those of continental Europe. Although there are differences between the institutions of Germany and France, these are less than the differences between these two and Britain. As a result, the British economy lacks integration with Euroland. British firms are more willing to operate internationally than firms from continental Europe, having the colonial experience and access to supportive institutions. The British economy has the highest proportion of foreign direct investment (FDI) in relation to its size in the world (Dunning 1997; Hirst and Thompson 1999).

MNCs within blocs

In favour of the thesis that economic blocs are important is the fact that trading and economic interconnectedness generally is much stronger within than between economic blocs. Within blocs, markets—particularly for consumer goods—are dominated by the multinationals of the dominant economy. There is, of course, trading between the blocs. Japanese companies are the most active in developing a world presence. The flows of foreign direct investment (FDI) have been highest from the Asian to other blocs in recent years, though historically the North American bloc was the most important. Japan also has the largest companies and those that are most strongly attached to the nation state. Despite the volume of Japanese exports and the extent of the Japanese invasion of Britain and other places by Japanese transplants, as measured by the tendency for Japanese companies to keep their assets at home, and the small numbers of foreign executives at the highest levels of these companies, Japanese firms remain strongly located within their own economic bloc. European companies (other than Britain) show less tendency to operate multinationally than the Japanese. The countries of Europe also continue to be strongly nationalistic as well—especially the French. Indeed, whether Euroland can be recognized as in a unified bloc is arguable.

[T]he internationalization of production and trading activity remains extremely unequally distributed, with a domination of the *Triad* countries and a few favoured rapidly expanding less developed economies. The vast bulk of the world's population is heavily disadvantaged, and almost ignored by these developments. Income distribution is also severely unequal, with little sign that this is changing.

Paul Hirst and Grahame Thompson (1999: 95)

Hirst and Thompson test their model of the international economy (based on the idea of developed regions) and that of the undifferentiated global economy against a range of evidence. The international economy emerges a more plausible than the globalized one against the data. A crucial observation is that multinational companies that are not located in particular territories appear to be very rare. Most companies are nationally based and trade multinationally on the strength of the location of the bulk of their assets in a particular bloc. They also mostly repatriate to their home countries the majority of their profits. Hirst and Thompson show for example that more than 70 per cent of the profit made by German multinationals is declared at home and more than 60 per cent of profit made by US firms is declared in North America. The comparable figure for British firms is less than 50 per cent (Hirst and Thompson 1999: 83). Hirst and Thompson also consider but reject the hybridization model wherein 'the globalized economy would encompass and subsume the international economy . . . (rearticulating) many of the features of the international economy, transforming them as it reinforced them.' Chief amongst Hirst and Thompson's reasons for rejecting such hybridization as a description of current conditions is the 'weak development of TNCs and the salience of MNCs and also the ongoing dominance of the advanced countries in both trade and FDI' (Hirst and Thompson 1999).

Hirst and Thompson are correct to argue for the internationalized economy but to note its severe limitations in allowing true globalization to emerge. They suggest that, as an international regime it is less open than previous ones, such as that established by Britain as the (waning) world power. They write that:

The present highly internationalized economy is not unprecedented: it is one of a number of distinct conjunctures or states of the international economy that have existed since an economy based on modern industrial technology began to be generalized from the 1960s. In some respects the current international economy is less open and integrated that the regime that prevailed from 1870–1914. (Hirst and Thompson 1999: 2)

As some of the extreme advocates of globalization do not sufficiently recognize, at present the world economy is far from being genuinely 'global'. Rather, trade, investment, and financial flows are concentrated in the triad of Europe, Japan, and North America and this dominance seems set to continue. Capital mobility notwithstanding, there is not a massive shift of investment and employment from the advanced to the developing countries in the manner Ohmae (1995) suggests will occur. Rather, foreign direct investment (FDI) is highly concentrated among the advanced industrial economies and the Third World remains marginal in both investment and trade.

9.6 **Conclusions**

In sum, British companies are moving into international operations in that they are setting up a subsidiaries abroad and, where possible, buying related businesses in other countries. However, this is not to be equated with genuine globalization in the economic sphere, and the extent of this has been exaggerated. In addition, the openness of the British economy, and the belief in market forces has allowed the intensification of foreign competition in the domestic market to take hold more rapidly than elsewhere. The pressures in the British institutional environment, in particular the supply of capital, remain. This has prompted British companies to seek profit abroad. By doing so, they have escaped governmental control much more completely than is apparent in almost any other country. A case can be made that British firms have moved more rapidly and more adroitly into a particular type of internationalization than companies based in many other countries. But this should not be confused with policies of globalization.

British companies are not adopting effective new patterns of organizing and they are not developing in a way that other corporations are. It seems that, when they move into international operations, the forms adopted by British firms are developments from patterns they have adopted in the past. As we have argued previously, the British multinational firm is a distinctive form of small capital-extensive firm or CEF (see the end of Chapter 6). It has a loosely federated structure in which similar activities to those undertaken in the UK are reproduced in other locations, and in which there may be considerable adaptation to local business conditions. If this is so, then many British firms do approximate to the organizational forms put forward by writers on the global company. However, we should not infer from this that British multinational firms lead the world in terms of effective organizational design for effective global operations. The British firm is a form of capital-extensive structure. Any approximation to the form advocated by exponents of the alleged transnational company is fortuitous.

We can add to this that commonly promoted ideas about the emerging pattern of the global economy are at least questionable if not wrong. Far from gradually developing towards a homogeneous world which is evenly developed, the world economy is developing along lines which are heavily influenced by existing geopolitical alignments. While we should realize that these are not beyond the reach of policy, the task of influencing such trajectories of development will not be easy. Major economic powers have the capacity, especially if they coordinate policy, to exert powerful governance pressures over financial markets and other economic institutions. To quote Hirst and

Thompson (1999: 3): 'Global markets are thus by no means beyond regulation and control, even though the current scope and objectives of economic governance are limited by the divergent interests of the great powers and the economic doctrines prevalent among the elites.' Whether this is true will be considered more fully in the final chapter when questions of policy are considered.

10

Towards industrial policy

10.1 Introduction

The aim is to conclude this book with the consideration of questions of policy. The subject of industrial policy has seldom been more neglected than it is today. There are, of course, many who are sceptical of the very idea of industrial policy because it suggests the need for an attempt to influence or guide economic development. In the thinking of many, there should be few attempts to direct or regulate the economy. Thus, the institutions of the economy and their typical activities are the measure of what should be done and, as such, they are beyond criticism. It is a measure of how far we have moved towards the dominance of *laissez-faire* thinking in politics that the need to consider such questions is often ruled out in principle (though see Coates 1996; Suneja 2001).

Yet when the changes in the organization of the economy considered in this book are related to each other and their major social consequences are clarified, it seems fairly obvious that the need for industrial policy should be reviewed. At various points in this book it has been suggested that reorganization is taking place in many British businesses in terms of organizational structures. These changes have to do with the export of capital and productive capacity by major firms, the reduction of the numbers employed in this country in many branches of industry, with concomitant changes in the amounts and kinds of labour required and their typical conditions of employment. Considered in the context of the national economy, the policies being pursued amount to fairly systematic deindustrialization. The exodus of British firms, and their associated jobs, is not exactly matched by the influx of foreign firms and the employment they bring with them. But even if it were, the demands being made on our people and the returns to the economy, in terms of profit, earnings from investments, and so on are by no means the same. Consistent with this there are other commentators who conclude, in the manner of this book, that the formulation of a coherent industrial policy is both required and urgent.

BOX 10.1 A window of opportunity?

In a world of global economic forces and consolidating trade blocs, the space for national programmes of industrial reconstruction is progressively more difficult to find. Neither time nor market forces are on our side. But industrial recovery and social justice can still go together, if the political will and social forces are there to insist upon the link. The task is paramount and it is urgent: because in its absence, the future of employment, prosperity and welfare rights in the UK will be bleak indeed.

David Coates, Centre for Industrial Policy and Performance, Bulletin No 2, 1993

One of the tasks of this chapter, then, is to argue that the changes discussed in the book are connected and have a mutually reinforcing pattern. This tends to intensify the tendency to deindustrialization and to increase the demands on the welfare state. However, another task is to argue that the only way to reverse these trends is to formulate and put in place policies that will have the required effect. If left alone, the effects of the tendency for large businesses to accelerate their withdrawal from the domestic economy—and the related inability of the government to raise sufficient taxation even for ameliorative policies to soften the social effects of secular economic decline—will become progressively more obvious and more difficult to respond to politically. Similarly, it is becoming increasingly obvious that the *laissez-faire* path towards industrialization was not an option for any but the first industrializing nations.

Before confronting questions of industrial policy directly, it is necessary to summarize the arguments of the book which have policy relevance. This is most economically done by looking again at the ideas that have underwritten this review of the organizational infrastructure of the economy.

BOX 10.2 Not whether to intervene, but how

For any state seeking to industrialize today, it is, as Peter Evans has recently argued, not a question of whether the state should intervene in economic development, so much as how much. Evans writes:

Sterile debates about 'how much' states intervene have to be replaced with arguments about different kinds of involvement and their effects. Contrasts between 'dirigiste' and 'liberal' or 'interventionist' and 'non-interventionist' states focus attention on degrees of departure from ideal—typical competitive markets. They confuse the basic issue. In the contemporary world, withdrawal and involvement are not the alternatives. State involvement is a given. The appropriate question is not 'how much' but 'what kind' (Evans 1995: 10).

Such judgements should be borne in mind by those having charge of developed countries slipping in the rankings.

10.2 Theoretical reprise

The theoretical approach utilized in this book has not been formally invoked often in the course of the main substantive chapters. After the initial theoretical building blocks were set out in Chapter 4, however, the account of structures deployed in that chapter has been utilized implicitly in much of the book. It was argued formally in Chapter 4 that what happens in organizations can be attributed to the groups that are active agents exercising the powers they have—which in turn flow from whatever resources they control. The result of their interaction is, among other things, the structure of the organization. The structure expresses the balance of power between the parties to the organization. Clearly, however, the resulting structure that collective activity creates is the context in which further action and interaction takes place. Considered in terms of their internal dynamics, there is a strong tendency for organizations to reproduce themselves in roughly the same form over long periods of time. The exercise of authority—which has to take particular forms to work at all—and other forces—such as the mimetic tendency of organizations to copy the forms adopted by other organizations—means that the normal tendency is for the structures to reproduce themselves.

If we are now seeing widespread change in the structures of organizations, which there is much evidence to support, it must be because the traditional balance of power in the organization has shifted considerably. Theoretically speaking, there are number of possible reasons for this. It could be that some new alliance between previously distinct groups altered things, but in this analysis the thrust of the argument has been to say it is management which has acquired access to a new set of resources, now being able to control other groups more effectively. Thus change is best understood in terms of groups within management acquiring new powers with which to act, and being allowed to exercise them by influential representatives of the owners in the shape of institutional shareholders. Specifically, it has been argued that access to new and much more effective IT systems has been combined in the UK with a new and unprecedented freedom for management to act. These things together have allowed some really important changes in organizational structures to be engineered. Among the most important are: within any organizational unit for there to be fewer levels of hierarchy and for there to be many more organizational units. However, the general character of these changes has been widely misconstrued as the increase in cooperative structures and the removal of the need for authority and control. The thrust of the argument here is, of course, that these are not alternatives: increased cooperation is a system requirement, but this is not to be equated with the removal of authority or the loss of central control.

The flattening of organizational hierarchies—which is a widespread feature of organizational change—is often taken to be evidence of the opposite of what it is. It is, by definition, the removal of a structure formally graded into many uniform levels of authority. This is not to be equated with the removal of all authority. To some extent the removal of differences in influence and importance is cosmetic rather than real. In the new situation there may be some new formal equality of status, but this is not to be confused with the complete removal of differences in conditions of work or contracts of employment. Engineers in a factory or other plant—who are employed for their ability to keep the machinery running—are not paid the same as manual workers, who are employed to work with the machinery when it is running. This continues to be true, irrespective of whether they wear the same overalls and use the same facilities to eat their lunch. To the extent that the removal of groups exercising authority is real rather than cosmetic, it represents the reduction of the privileged (and costly) grades of staff that are no longer essential to the effective running of organizations or keeping them in control. To this extent the removal of hierarchy is a levelling down more obviously than it is a levelling up. Removal of hierarchies also means removal of organizational careers, in the sense that organizations no longer generally offer an improving trajectory of status and earnings for long-serving employees. People cannot be promoted if there is no hierarchy within which to be promoted. The loss of careers in which even the probability of having a job is in doubt is a considerable loss emotionally and culturally (cf. Sennett 1998). Because of the widespread deskilling and removal of career possibilities involved in the removal of layers of management—not to mention the simplification and routinization of many tasks—the flattening of hierarchies can and perhaps should be thought of as being, to a considerable extent, the proletarianization of people in employment.

Yet there are a number of features in the contemporary organization of work that seem to point in precisely the opposite direction to proletarianization. One is the freedom from direct control of work performance, and the capacity now extended to many groups of workers to order their own work to some extent. Surely this is evidence of democratization rather than proletarianization? One important point to make here is that in many jobs—especially in some of the most technologically advanced sectors—the extent of self-organization and empowerment is trivial. Information technology has so programmed some jobs using information technology—one thinks of call centres, for example—that the discretion allowed to the worker is small (Taylor and Bain 1999). The human powers that employees are called upon to utilize amount to nothing more than to activate their voice at the designated time and in the designated ways—this entails not deviating from the script or proceeding either faster or slower than is required by the instruction manual (Thompson and Warhurst 1998; Taylor and Bain 1999). For those jobs where there does seem to be a more substantial element of real empowerment, the point is that the extent of the discretion is usually limited to the requirements of the work system. Despite its sophistication, even in its most developed forms, information technology is not so seamless that it can do without human input entirely. People are needed to input information and to interpret it, to fill in gaps left in the information flows, or to respond to enquiries from the public; in short, to utilize human powers and skills at key points to make up for what information technology lacks.

This point has been argued in the body of the text by suggesting that the remaining elements of human discretion in work systems are system requirements. Their inclusion in the design of work systems is not to be confused with the proposition that managers have learned to trust their employees or the value of allowing human discretion. The crucial point to notice is the limitation invariably placed on the extent of the discretion and 'empowerment' allowed to employees. Employees are usually required to exercise their discretion in limited ways over limited issues. It is strange to claim that this sort of thing can be understood as democratization. To make the point graphically, employees' ideas about the strategy of the company are not commonly taken into account, and employees are not typically empowered to do anything about company policy if they do not approve of it. If we consider this against the measure of the degree of political democratization typically seen in Western states, what we see in organizations is difficult to see as the extension of democracy at work. The fact is that the degree of empowerment extended to the average employee is extremely limited and extends just as far as the employer deems it valuable. More generally, although the acquisition of IT and, in particular, powerful management information systems, has greatly increased the powers of managers in respect of ordinary employees, it has not entirely removed the need for them, and, in some ways it has actually increased the dependency of employers on their few remaining employees. The amount of investment at risk puts a premium on responsibility, for example. Similarly the likely loss in the event of process malfunction requires employees to be alert and willing to act promptly and responsibly.

Archer's account of agents

In her discussion of similar theoretical ideas, Archer draws a helpful distinction between 'corporate' and 'primary' agents (Archer 1995: 258). By 'corporate agents' she means not that groups are organized as corporations, but that they are constituted so that they are capable of acting in a unified or 'corporate' way in pursuit of their interests. Citing Bentley's dictum 'when the groups are stated, everything is stated' (Bentley 1967: 200) with qualified approval, Archer goes on to point out the different powers of groups.

Corporate agents, with the capacity to alter the terms of interaction, are distinguished by Archer from 'primary agents'. Primary agents are groups or collectives distinguished by the lack of much capacity to induce change in their circumstances, but who nonetheless continue to reproduce their own circumstances. This inability to effect change is best understood in terms of limitations on their agency, which is restricted to the ability to reproduce the context in which they find themselves. Archer writes (1995: 258):

In short, the prior social context delineates collectivities in the same position . . . and within this context they have to carry on . . . Those in this category are termed 'Primary Agents'. They are distinguished from 'Corporate Agents' at any given time by lacking a say in structural or cultural modelling. At that time they neither express interests nor organize for their strategic pursuit.

Archer's consideration of different agents is coloured by the fact that she is discussing groups (corporate agents) in society rather than within the corporation. However, to adapt these ideas to the context of the corporation throws up interesting contrasts. One is that *all* the groups internal to the organizations discussed here—managers, owners, professionals, and workers—*traditionally* have been corporate agents in Archer's terms. All of them were able to affect outcomes within the organization to some extent—and many of them to a considerable extent. They were certainly considered in that way in Chapter 4. The definition of organizational structure used in that chapter—that the organizational structure embodies the balance of power between groups—is an explicit admission of this. In support of this idea, all these groups also constitute themselves as agents in the wider society.

As they exist within the corporation, these groups have drawn power inside the corporation from that fact they are also constituted as corporate agents outside the organization. As we have seen the powers of owners are often

---

BOX 10.3 **The distinction between 'corporate' and 'primary' agents**

Organised interest groups are indeed special and they pack a very special punch as systemic stability and change are concerned. For those (groups) who are aware of what they want, can articulate it to themselves and others and have organised themselves to get it, can engage in concerted action to reshape or retain the structural . . . feature in question. These are termed 'corporate agents': they include self-conscious vested interest groups, promotive interest groups, social movements and defensive associations. Their common denominators are articulation and organisation.

Margaret Archer (1995: 258)

augmented by the fact that some of them are effectively tied to and can claim to represent socio-economic elites through kinship or other social affiliations. Something similar is obvious for the established professions. They have professional organizations that secure some control over the markets for their labour. Through the licensing of practitioners and other devices, professions limit the numbers of their own members and so increase the scarcity of their skills (Larson 1977; Abbott 1988). Indeed, it would be an inadequate account of the organizational behaviour of ordinary employees that omits any discussion of their ability to act against the power of managers. Organization outside the corporation in the form of unions is one reason for this. There is also informal organization of employees of various kinds (discussed, for example, in Ackroyd and Thompson 1999). There is an interesting asymmetry between managers and other groups in this respect in that they are, by and large, not formally organized outside the workplace, having no significant external professional organization, though they are unrivalled as corporate agents inside the corporation. By comparison, the power of all subordinated groups within organizations is limited.

To use Archer's terminology, contemporary organizational changes have entailed the reduction of the corporate agency of subordinated groups outside the organization as well as inside it. The reduction in the proportion of the population that the major corporations employ and to whom they will pay premium wages are the most important aspects of this. Hence, the most significant wider change in the organization of the groups we have distinguished within the corporation has been the emasculation of organized labour. But, by being able to remove much middle management, there is no doubt that the other groups have been coercively reconstituted as well. Only the professions have been able to withstand having their position radically weakened within the organizational structure of corporations (Ackroyd 1996). It is going too far to say that contemporary organizational change has removed the capacity of subordinated groups to be corporate agents within organizations, because it does allow them to have some influence on their immediate circumstances. On the other hand, it has reduced the powers of all the groups identified in Chapter 4 as the main internal stakeholders, other than senior managers, in the modern corporation: professionals and owners as well as ordinary employees.

The loss of the powers of stakeholder groups (corporate groups in Archer's terms) within the organization is significant for a number of reasons, but the main one concerns the properties of the new economy now emerging. This matter will be dealt with more fully below. At this point it is relevant to consider the increase in the importance of economic, as opposed to political or civil, institutions in shaping the life chances of people. To put the point bluntly: the importance of economic organizations as institutions shaping social outcomes and processes is increasing while that of states is decreasing. If this is so, the ability of the majority of people to influence outcomes—even those that affect them—is steadily diminishing. As citizens they have some powers as corporate agents within the state (Marshall 1950). By contrast, as employees they have little capacity to alter the policies of the companies that employ them. This is especially true for those who are part of the permanently unemployed or the 'underclass' as it is sometimes called, who are excluded from employment on a permanent basis (Murray 1990; Mann 1992). It is sharply ironic that the hard won democratic freedoms of citizens—to be represented and so to have some sort of influence on policy—have been achieved in time to find that the real locus of power in society has shifted to institutions over which ordinary people have an almost complete lack of influence (Hertz 2000)

This is not to say that the only change in the position of the corporate groups in and around organizations—other than managers—has been uniformly towards weakening. There are some groups whose position has been improved by contemporary organizational change. Two of the most important groups here are business consultants and information system specialists, whose improving fortunes have been considered briefly at various points in this book. It is interesting, however, that these 'corporate agents' have been successful not by remaining as employees within the corporation, or by adopting professional modes of organization, but by becoming separate businesses supplying services to large corporations. This discussion brings us naturally to

---

BOX 10.4 **Structural unemployment**

By 1987, nearly a third of the unemployed had been on the register for over a year and in the North, the North West, and West Midlands, roughly half of those unemployed had been unable to find work within a year. The unemployed rate also varied widely, with a rate of 8.5 per cent in the South East, but 16.9 per cent in the North, 14.3 per cent in the North West and 13.8 per cent in Yorkshire and Humberside. Even in these areas, however, unemployment was variable. Thus Sunderland had a rate of 21.4 per cent, whereas Kendal had only 8.3 per cent unemployment, despite the fact that both are classified as the North. Even within Sunderland, unemployment was concentrated in particular areas. . . . When it is borne in mind that the value of social security has fallen in relation to earnings and the retail price index, it is clear that the poor were worse off in the 1980s than they were in the 1970s. Not only were they poorer, but they have been poorer for longer periods of time. . . . For some working-class households, owner-occupation has been a traumatic experience rather than a privilege. In 1988, 37 000 people were more than 6 months in arrears with their mortgage, which is four times as many as in 1979. Moreover, 16 150 properties were repossessed compared with 2500 in 1979.

K. Mann (1992)

the consideration of interorganizational relations and how theory might account for these.

10.3 The emergent properties of interorganizational relations

In this book, the proposition that the massive reorganization of business that has been taking place is not something that can be considered by looking at organizations in isolation emerged early. The importance of interfirm relations was encountered first in Chapter 2 which argued that the properties of the economy are relevant to the question of what is happening to sectors of the economy and to organizations.

After the theoretical discussion of Chapters 3 and 4, in Chapter 5 it was argued that organizational change amongst SMEs was not being driven primarily by the entrepreneurship of independent small firms. There was every indication of an apparent paradox that the number of small organizations was proliferating, but economic change was not being driven by an increase in the extent or the effectiveness of primary entrepreneurship. The paradox is resolved only when the connection is made between changes in the form of small organizations and the restructuring of large businesses. The structural forms of many small businesses are not to be understood uniquely as the result of the interaction of the corporate groups found within them. On the contrary, they are forms adopted mainly because of the constraints constituted by their relations with large businesses.

Such things are to be understood by looking at the emergent properties of systems of interfirm relations, and the argument in subsequent chapters was about the actual structures it is appropriate to see emerging within the reconstructed economy. The position adopted in this book is that the new economy has distinctive properties, which have a considerable effect on the structure and function of all the economic institutions within it. The difference between this approach and the orthodox contingency theory, which it seeks to replace, is that the properties of the emergent system are not seen to be given for large and small firms alike. As was suggested in the criticism of contingency theory, the environment does not bear on large firms in the same way. With their superior resources, for example, large firms are in a position to decide what arenas they wish to operate within, and often also salient features of the economic environment itself. Many of the features of the economic system as a whole are enacted (i.e. brought into existence) by the activities of large firms. These activities can often be seen to set the context for the activities of smaller firms.

Against the network as a distinctive emergent structure

The distinctive forms of emergent interfirm relationships have to be carefully assessed. For some writers, Castells (1996) and Thompson *et al.* (1991) among them, what has emerged is something new and distinctive between market and hierarchy called 'the network'. The problem with this is the idea that authority and control have been removed from the equation. On careful examination, what we see in most instances of interfirm relations are hierarchies of firms. True, these do not have a simple hierarchical quality, and can be understood as the penetration of hierarchy by market relations. But hierarchy is still present either because power is retained through rights of ownership or through such things as the practical control of access to resources and the ability to withhold or grant economic preferment or other advantages. In many cases of interorganizational relations, the idea of reticulation is less valid as a description than is imbrication: the former suggests equality between points connected by lines of equal weight and importance, as in a net; whereas the latter suggests one entity being partly overlain and controlled by other entities, as in the tiles on a roof. To understand an imbricated structure it has to be the right way up.

Again Archer's concepts are useful here. Archer (1995: 259) argues that 'A Primary Agent in one domain may be a Corporate Agent in another at any specific T(ime).' This proposition helps us to see the nested quality of the relations between firms. Looking up the hierarchy of organizations, the point that needs to be made to explicate the relationship between large and small firms is the opposite of Archer's actual formulation. If we consider the roles of the managements of independent firms they are, in their own organization the pre-eminent corporate agents. It is they who decide what work is undertaken and who gets employed and paid and so on. However, in their relationships with the controllers of large firms, they are more like primary agents, in that they have little say as to policy and whether they will be given the contracts or other preferment they need to continue in business. It was argued in Chapter 5 that the typical form of many firms is powerfully shaped by their relationships with larger companies. What were identified as the new flexible firm and the high-surveillance firm respectively were organized differently because of their relations with different kinds of large companies. These are good examples of the way the relationships between firms can exert powerful controls from the outside.

The formative role of big business

Almost all firms these days are not independent in that they do not produce and sell finished goods on the open market. They earn their surplus by contributing goods or services to the supply chains or by buying and selling goods commercially; that is, they frequently have other organizations as clients. They are part of complex structures in which many firms are implicated. But what is difficult to accept is that the outcomes from these cooperative relations are—as is often implied—somehow equal, fair, and free from conflict. Such propositions are countered by the proposition that often these relationships are orchestrated, if not otherwise more directly imposed and controlled, by large organizations. Often activities of small firms—and their organizational forms—can be related directly to their relations with large companies. Whether or not they are owned by larger organizations, the independence of small firms operating in supply chains is significantly constrained by the requirements for work dictated to them by larger companies higher up the chain.

Increasingly, big businesses are the prime movers in contemporary organizational change. What large businesses do are so often key parts of the context

---

BOX 10.5 Dependency in a subcontracting network

In 1985 I began a study of the introduction of new technology in small and medium French engineering firms . . . preliminary visits to firms with 200 to 500 employees revealed that most *had substantially reduced their employment levels* since 1980. The value of their sales, however, had in most cases increased after a dip in 1982–3. This could be explained in part by improvements in their productivity, but also by a substantial increase in their use of subcontracting for intermediate component production.

To some extent, of course, the firms had used subcontracting before; few were of sufficient scale in their operations to warrant investing in plant for such specialized tasks as gear grinding or heat treatment. And they all made use of subcontracting to meet temporary capacity constraints. What I was observing, however, was different. It was a shift to subcontracting on a permanent basis for such standard operations as turning, milling and drilling. It allowed the firms to avoid making investments in up-to-date machine tools and was frequently the occasion for a reduction in capacity, with some existing plant being sold off. While the general type of operation subcontracted was not specialized or specific to the particular firm in question, *the design and specifications of the components were.* Thus it was not a case of substituting in-house production for standardized components available in the market: rather, components were being machined (turned, milled, and so on) by subcontractors *according to firm-specific plans produced in the design offices of the client firm.*

Edward Lorenz (1989: 196), reprinted in Thompson *et al.* (1991), emphases added

in which small businesses find themselves. While what is happening in business units and small businesses are related effects, by and large small businesses are responding to the initiatives of large businesses, rather than leading change. To understand the patterning of organizational change, we must see it in terms of the move of large companies to reduce their exposure in this country and to place more of their capacity overseas. There is evidence to show that large British companies have been more willing and more able to reorganize themselves to exploit overseas markets. Multinationals originating in the rest of Europe have been slower to reorganize for international operations. Indeed, in the process of recent change, British companies have moved more of their productive capacity than many observers would think necessary or desirable. The considerable effects of the export of British capital have been masked to some extent by the movement into this country of multinationals based overseas.

The distinctive policies of large British businesses

The basic cause of the changed activities of large businesses is a matter of debate. In recent history it has been characteristic of large British businesses to alternate between policies of diversification and focus. For long periods, the activities of major companies were diverse. They did not follow a policy of trying to develop a broad spectrum of activities within the same market sector as the idea of the 'M' form company suggests is appropriate: they are content to have different lines of activity in sometimes widely dispersed sectors being undertaken by firms which were part of the same company. As was noted in Chapter 6, there is a tendency for large British companies to acquire small businesses in order to boost their profitability and to sell off businesses at other times for the same reason. Subsequently, businesses that are judged not to be central to core activities will be periodically divested. In this way, using the device of acquiring and divesting subsidiary companies, the policy of large companies has alternated between diversification and focusing.

The current phase of change is an interesting combination of these historical tendencies, combining focusing with a high degree of internationalization. Today, the policy of many British companies is to think about reproducing their core activities in many other markets, principally in the developed world. Much reorganization of large British businesses—and the distinctive policy of focusing on highly profitable activities—is to do with a refusal to have their prosperity tied strongly to home markets. The ill-fated reorganization of Marconi had this rationale. This example is drawn to our attention because of the poor choice that was made about what activities to focus upon; but it is otherwise not particularly exceptional. This example does draw attention—in a dramatic way—to the importance of the pursuit of profits by major companies and the way they characteristically decide to seek it at the present time by adjustments to their structure. The policy of the Kingfisher group is not essentially dissimilar in that central to it is a high degree of focusing. The policy aims to reproduce highly profitable lines of retailing in Europe, whilst divesting less profitable areas of retailing in the UK.

Large British business is not usually trying to contract, although there are many examples where the net effect of divestment activities is to produce smaller companies than there were before. They are though, above everything else, trying to become more profitable. In this there is another paradox: British businesses are among the most mobile and dynamic in the world. They are leading the field when it comes to the speed and extent of their international-ization. But it is implausible to think that because of this British companies will form the leading players in an emerging global economy. Their strategic policies are too little concerned about the growth of productive capacity and market share to make such ambitions realistic. It is often not the active push of intensifying foreign competition in home markets that impels their move-ment, so much as the pull of the possibility of earning high profits abroad. Growth in the scale and range of activities takes second place to profitability—always. It is this that explains the recurrent tendency for British businesses to abandon high value-added manufacture if it requires high levels of invest-ment, as it typically does. It is this that also explains that there is no ambition to undertake the full range of production in a given sector, or to seek growth of market share.

The effects of the activities of large British businesses in exporting their capital (British foreign direct investment is the highest per capita in the world) would have been more noticeable and far-reaching had it not been for the fact that foreign multinationals are investing in Britain on an unprecedented scale. Between the two of these movements, the one outward the other inward, the patterns of causation behind change have been difficult to discern. Certainly the complexity of interfirm relations has encouraged the view that there is more openness in business relationships and opportunity for cooperative relations between large and small firms. To some extent this is true, but these points are not incompatible with the idea that interfirm relations are often controlling and even coercive.

The combined effects of British businesses moving out of their traditional markets and production sites and foreign firms moving in has led to British labour markets experiencing deep changes. The effects of the changes in organizations and changed patterns of employment in them have produced some profound changes in contemporary British society. Thus it can be argued that much contemporary social change can be traced to the changed policies and activities of big businesses. But before looking at the social con-sequences of organizational change, we should look briefly at the implications

> **BOX 10.6 Distinctive policies of large British companies in the 1980s**
>
> The most important of these opposing forces is the giant British firm which operates its own anti-industrial policy. There is little doubt that, in a deflationary environment, Lords Wienstock and Hanson or Professor Smith can destroy jobs and reduce exports faster than they can be created by local networks of Japanese newcomers. This point is proved by the record of the nineteen eighties; as we have seen, over the last decade, the top 25 British-owned firms destroyed 200 000 British manufacturing jobs and acquired or created a similar number overseas, while all the Japanese newcomers created just 25 000 manufacturing jobs. The anti-industrial policy of giant British firms is an acute problem that will not go away because the highly concentrated structure of British manufacturing puts so much economic power into the hands of a small number of giant firms. If we consider the 100 British-owned manufacturing companies with the largest stock market capitalisation, our rough calculations suggest that the home and overseas sales turnover of these companies adds up to a sum equal to 45 per cent of the total output of manufacturing industry in Britain. In other national economies, industrial policy can concentrate on positive tasks; in Britain it is equally important to address the issue of damage limitation by neutralising the anti-industrial policies of our giant firms.
>
> Williams *et al.* (1990*a*: 481)

of the above analysis for the different activities undertaken in the British economy.

10.4 Continuity in some basic patterns of economic activity

It is not the case that there is nothing in common between British industry and industry in other parts of the developed world. It is part of the common pattern even today for multinational companies to locate most overseas activity in the developed world and certainly to restrict most of their commercial relations (in their buying and selling of goods and services) between close neighbours and a relatively small number of trading partners worldwide. The extent to which there are truly global companies and a truly global economy is highly limited. British companies are not alone in undertaking internationalization as opposed to globalization. Hence, although there has been profound change in some areas, the sectoral composition of the economy has changed little. British firms have given up certain areas of manufacture—cars for example—but cars are still made in large number in the UK. Numerous foreign firms—Ford, GM, Nissan, Honda, and Toyota—have manufacturing plants, not to mention numerous subsidiaries and affiliates. Some major British firms are important participants in the supply chains of this industry: GKN, Invensys, and Pilkington, for example. As we have seen, at the end of the last century, there were still more than sixty very large British firms heavily engaged in manufacturing. True, they were diversified and strongly orientated to manufacturing goods for retailing, but this is a bias of long-standing.

Although there is a tendency for cheap wage economies in the Third World to be dumped with low value-added manufacturing, the extent to which agile production has occurred is greatly exaggerated in Britain and much of the rest of Europe. For most complex products the supply chains are too complicated to expect the entire manufacturing process to be exported. More generally, the idea that there has been a radical departure from the economy of manufacture remains doubtful. British companies have progressively withdrawn from certain areas of manufacture, and have periodically focused themselves on particular areas of activity, but they show little sign of giving up manufacture and changing their character entirely. Thus the idea that there might be radical change over time in the areas of activity in which major firms are involved—in the manner implied by some models of highly decentred business groups—is implausible. Although they may both diversify and focus at different times, with only few exceptions, British firms have tended to stick with the businesses they know best.

The continued importance of the economy of manufacture

The small extent of the move away from manufacture is partially hidden in the case of British companies by the way that the figures relating to sector activities are compiled. Among the points to be aware of here is the extent to which activities—including many managerial functions—have been externalized. As indicated by Table 2.2. the decline in the size of the manufacturing and commercial sectors of the economy is more or less matched by the rise of the business services sector. True there were many workers (such as administrators, marketing, and systems analysts) in the old bureaucratic types of organizational structure, who would have been classified as production workers in the past simply because they worked for production companies. Arguably this was inaccurate, especially if the purpose of the figures is to establish the kind of work people do. On the other hand, it is equally an error to infer that all of the business services workers are simply administrative workers (or that the size of the workforce devoted to production has massively diminished) if many of them are actually providing business services to companies whose business is production.

As has been argued also, the rise of employment in retailing and leisure is small, and there is a reduction in the proportion of organizations in these sectors of the economy. The technological displacement of services is a long-standing process that has been much studied (Bell 1976; Gershunny 1978). Arguments for the importance of retailing and services in the economy thus have to rely on the financial or other indicators of the importance of these sectors in the economy. The extent of the displacement of the economy of manufacture by the service economy has been greatly exaggerated. Further, the extent that the service economy can replace the wealth-creating productive economy has been misunderstood. Similar points can be made concerning the shift to the knowledge economy. One of the most obvious symptomatic changes in organizational structures has been the firms associated with business services. The emergence of business consultancy companies and their role in restructuring the corporate economy was indicated in outline in Chapter 2. Many business consultancy companies and information technology suppliers have their origins in servicing the new corporate forms that have emerged in traditional sectors of the economy. In Chapter 5 the distinctive type of organization—the knowledge intensive firm (the KIF)—was identified. The knowledge companies are not in any sense supplanting the traditional sectors but are dependent on them to continue to exist. As the suppliers of services that companies either had no need of before new technology—or which they supplied for themselves—such firms are best seen as a redistribution of the specialist labour required by traditional areas of economic activity.

The problem of the British economy is now much what it always was: it is not that it does not manufacture, but that it manufactures the wrong sorts of things (low value-added goods) in inefficient ways (undercapitalized plants which rely too greatly on the contributions from labour which is not well educated or trained). The added complication is that the traditional patterns of manufacture—which rely on high inputs of traditionally skilled labour—have been replaced by new patterns that rely on semi-skilled, part-time, and temporary workers. Foreign multinationals operating here—although likely to be more highly capitalized than British firms—certainly do not employ large numbers of traditionally skilled workers. Many have been identified as 'screwdriver plants', implying that no skill more complicated than that required to work a screwdriver to fix components is required (Williams *et al.* 1992).

10.5 **What has precipitated change?**

Given the emphasis that has been laid on the importance of access of the managerial cadre to new resources in the explanation of change, it might be thought that the present account is like the neo-liberal theory of economic transformation offered by the likes of Piore and Sabel (1984). In their account, emphasis was placed on the elements of chance in the way that factors of production came together in the USA at the 'first industrial divide' in the combinations that made new ways possible. There is recognition of chance variations being sometimes of considerable importance in the direction of change. It has been argued here, for example, that because of institutional factors, British business is more sensitive to downturn in profit levels than many foreign companies. This, combined with other factors such as the increased freedom that corporate executives have engineered for themselves, explains why British companies have moved further and faster than those found in continental Europe. The long history of international mobility has also led British industry to be more mobile in moving productive capacity abroad and seeking to replicate weakly capitalized but profitable lines of business in overseas markets.

Though there is some acceptance of the influence of institutional factors in this account of organizational change, such that it does seem that British capital is following a distinct trajectory even as it internationalizes, it is not assumed that the cause of change is chance differences. It is certainly not suggested that the main reason for change can be reduced to the activities of corporate managers. The theory in use here is not basically voluntaristic. To identify the key source of change as being the innovatory behaviour of the elite cadre of corporate executives is to point clearly and decisively to the importance of power in the initiation of change. True, the power exercised by such people is not so obvious as that exercised by the corporate leaders of an earlier generation. Large firms do not dominate regions and dictate policies to governments so obviously as they did in the recent past. The power of the leaders of large companies is now exerted as much by proxy as by direct effects, through the contracts they offer to subsidiaries and affiliates as much as their own activities.

There is no escaping the realization that corporate executives wield awesome power. In deciding which companies to buy and sell, or how to reorganize the businesses they control, they shape what Weber called the 'life chances' of hundreds of thousands of employees. However, this is not all there is to consider. A key question for the theorist is how far these most powerful 'corporate agents' are themselves constrained to act, and indeed are the agents of forces outside of themselves. The answer is that executives of the largest businesses are constrained to some extent by some features of their circumstances: they still have to raise capital and declare profits. But there is a deeper question here most acutely posed by regulation theorists, who argue that the periodicity of general economic change must be related to the structure of capitalism, which is driven along by the unfolding dynamics of the capitalist mode of production. One of the many differences between the views of the neo-liberal theorists such as Piore and Sabel and the neo-Marxist regulationist theorists is precisely the extent to which they see discretion being exercised in shaping institutional patterns in different phases of capitalist development. How far do the demands of the capitalist economy shape the political and cultural superstructure?

The regulationist argument is that there is a logic to the development of capitalism, and the pattern of institutions surrounding the economy itself will be profoundly shaped by the trajectory of the capitalist development. In regulationist analyses, the institutions of the economy and those of society are so deeply interconnected that it is difficult to pick them apart; but they retain attachment to the view that change begins with economic processes. But how far the regulation of the economy is necessary to the continued development of capitalism is far from clear. Regulationism and institutionalism suggest that capitalism is capable of being shaped into a variety of different patterns. However, some patterns of capitalism show highly regulated features as they internationalize—Japanese capitalism is an example—but other national capitalisms show less tendency to sustain regulation. British capitalism is a case in point. Traditionally, British capitalism has been among the least regulated of capitalist patterns. The emergent European pattern falls between these extremes, being closer to the Japanese than the British pattern. But because capitalism has been regulated, does not mean it has to be regulated. Once having broken the shell of regulative institutions in the nation state, there is no inevitability about internationalized capitalism being regulated in the broader arenas it comes to inhabit.

Viewed in this way, the longer term, prospects for the British economy are not particularly good. Substantially detached from both the American and the European blocs, British capitalism is an unregulated fragment unlikely to be viable on its own. The question before British policy-makers is whether they wish to buy into the more regulated European system of capitalism. So far as the population of Britain is concerned, however, the need for some kind of regulation is clear. As Britain slips in the ranking of countries as measured by national income per head and as social services crumble to be comparable to those found in the poorest European countries, the policy of continuing to leave big business to its own devices becomes less convincing. The matter of industrial policies has broader relevance than might be appreciated. This is because the organization of the economy has a series of effects which ramify through the society.

10.6 Some social consequences of organizational change

It can be argued that many other changes in the contemporary economy—the decline of trade unionism, for example—can be traced to changes at the core of the economy. The withdrawal of British businesses from involvement in the production of complex products using traditional methods and the increasing penetration of our economy by foreign multinationals has ushered in profound changes in the shape of labour markets (Rubery 1989; Lovering 1990). Associated with these changes there has been a collapse of opportunities for relatively highly skilled and reasonably well-paid employment in manufacturing industry (jobs which were typically taken by men) and the rise of part-time and unskilled or semi-skilled jobs in this area of the economy (jobs which are increasingly taken by women). Gospel (1995) has shown, for example, that the traditional pattern for the recruitment and training of skilled labour for industry—the apprenticeship system—has all but collapsed. There has been the development of structural unemployment, which is hidden by the availability of large numbers of part-time temporary and poorly paid opportunities to work (Casey 1991; O'Reilly 1992; Emmott and Hutchinson 1998). The rise of what right-wing commentators called the underclass (Murray 1990, 1994; cf. Hutton 1996 and Mann 1992), that is, a large section of the population without the prospect of secure and reasonably well-paid employment which now depends on welfare for survival, can also be related to these economic movements.

General social changes related to changes in the organization of the economy have not featured centrally in this book; but they are important aspects of the context of change. It is easy to assume that change is just change: it is simply part of an inevitable process of modernization which nobody in particular initiated, and that, in the long run, will be beneficial for everyone. On the other hand, it seems there are some dramatic winners and losers arising from the processes that are now in motion; and it is not at all clear that the interests of the British economy or the people of Britain are being well served. It is one of the objectives of this book to contribute to a debate about the causes and consequences of contemporary change and to get the issue of influencing economic change back onto political agendas. Precisely because the organization of the economy affects so many areas of life it can be said that this book discusses some of the most momentous changes in social organization in recent times. For this reason alone they ought to be at the subject of political concern.

To illustrate the significance of economic change we only have to think about the kinds of jobs that are now available for the majority of people. Gone are the days when there was a great deal of manual industrial work to which traditionally trained (and predominantly male) workers were recruited. After more than 100 years during which jobs in manufacturing were the most common form of work in Britain, with 40 per cent or more of employed in this work, this kind of employment suddenly went into decline in the late 1970s. The numbers of such jobs fell steeply through much of the 1980s (Ackroyd and Whittaker 1990). The rate of loss eased in the 1990s, but the secular trend of decline remained clear. There have been some compensatory trends—the rise of service occupations and jobs created by developments of IT. For this reason we have not experienced quite such dire effects as so much loss of traditional jobs might have produced.

There has been little improvement even in conditions of work, to say nothing of the loss of job security (Sennett 1998). While it is possible for some few gifted and well-connected new graduates from universities in this country beginning their careers (working as consultancy interns, say, or as trainee merchant bankers) to enjoy starting salaries of £40 000 and to have the realistic prospect of enjoying interesting work as well as the probability of future advancement, the vast majority of jobs in the new economy are not like this. More typically, jobs in services are highly routinized, and are less secure and less well paid than even traditional industrial employment. A trained call-centre operative could earn less than a quarter of the salary of the lucky or well-connected graduate trainee, and, of course, will have few prospects of improvement in earnings or conditions of work in the medium term (Fernie and Metcalf 1997). Clearly, however, the effects of economic change on forms of employment and conditions of work are not the only things to consider.

The kinds of jobs on offer in the new economy have dramatically shifted the gender balance in employment, for example. The growth of employment in the services sector has involved disproportionate increases in the numbers of part-time and temporary jobs, jobs that are predominantly taken by women. Secular increases in the proportion of the female population in employment and the rise of long-term male unemployment have undoubtedly had a series of effects on the way families are constituted and what we might loosely call the politics of domesticity. No doubt there was already a movement towards more equality in the gender relations found in the household before any serious change in the economy set in, but it is a reasonable conjecture that this would have been given increased impetus by the changes under consideration

---

BOX 10.7 **The survival of the working class**

Most people in contemporary Britain work for a living; they have tiny savings, little countervailing power against their employer and are thus two or three monthly pay cheques away from living on income support if they lose their job. The men and women who live in those starter homes in the great big housing estates around our cities may not work in huge factories any more but they remain just as at risk to capitalism, employer power and loss of work as their forebears were. The working class remains; it is working in the service sector, wears suits and is harder to organise into trade unions. It may not be so solidaristic, but because it's harder to recognise we shouldn't dismiss its existence. Its relations to work and power are critically very similar to those of the old working class.

Capitalism is becoming much more interested in distribution, wholesaling, retailing and intellectual property rights than the location and management of the production process. If you are a large player you can finance and manage successful manufacturing anywhere in the world frankly; you do it where it's most cost-efficient. But this 'weight-lessness' does not transform the underlying tensions and motion of capitalism; rather it empowers [truly] knowledge-based workers over non-knowledge based workers. The new commanding heights of the economy may be the so-called symbolic analysts who manipulate information rather than blue-collar workers making steel—but all the difficulties about exploitation, private ownership and instability remain remarkably the same.

W. Hutton in Giddens and Hutton (eds) 2001: 25

---

here. To put the point bluntly: if a wife became the main earner when a husband could no longer find traditional manual employment, the balance of power in the home is likely to have changed irrevocably as a result. That such well-documented trends as the increased incidence of divorce and the visibility of domestic violence are related to such changes is, of course, highly likely.

The economic performance of the economy is a matter of considerable importance, of course, but, if the above observations are reliable, it should be clear that the efficiency of economic changes is not all that should be considered. Hence, it is contended here that what the economy is and what it does should not simply be studied in a factual and functional way and especially not to avoid a view that focuses on economic performance to the exclusion of other considerations. It is assumed in this book that it is important to consider economic change more broadly than is habitually done. Thus, we should not only consider changes in the types of jobs on offer in the economy, but also look at such questions as what has caused the widespread production of such jobs and whether—again broadly speaking—the net effects of change can be considered good or bad. In short, there should be some general accounting of the effects of change both inside and outside the workplace. The point is that economic change is a matter of too much importance to be safely left to business executives and economists. Their perspectives seldom consider more than what immediately concerns them: the profitability of their particular firms on the one hand and the general performance of the economy on the other.

Whatever the conclusion arrived at on the basis of economic considerations, then, there are strong social arguments for attempting new forms of industrial policy.

10.7 The problem of policy

It is not the case that the matters that are seen to be central problems in this book—and in need of concerted attention from reformers—have remained unidentified hitherto. Although it is unusual for such matters to be treated as important in books on organizational analysis, many of these issues have been confronted by those interested in questions of policy many times before. They have not only been identified before, but general diagnoses of the need for reform have been formulated. Policies to deal with the perceived problems of economic reform have also been devised. There is much that is potentially in need of discussion if the full range of problems is to be considered: the reform of the financial system should be addressed, including the policies and orientations of the banks. The operation of the Stock Exchange and other financial markets is an obvious priority for reform also. If this was not enough to be going on with, there is also the problem of the constitution of British firms and the need to reform their governance. There can be no full and adequate consideration of these matters in the space available. For those seeking more comprehensive accounts than it is possible to offer here, the reader is directed to the consideration of Will Hutton's writings (1996, 1997) and such sources as the bulletins issued by the Centre for Industrial Policy and Performance of the University of Leeds (CIPP 1993–2000). In this discussion the aim is to identify key problems that could fairly easily be the subject of legislative action.

The key role of pension funds

Lying behind the increased freedom to act in pursuit of profitability—and giving it a certain acceptability if not credence—is the desire of certain influential groups of large shareholders for continuing dividends. As has been suggested in the body of the text, institutional shareholders—insurance companies and, more important than these, pension funds—have become hugely influential in the formation of the policies of quoted British companies. Pension funds could hold the majority of their assets as government stocks and other fixed-rate stocks. As a hedge against inflation—and in pursuit of the

---

BOX 10.8 **A presciption for reform**

- The upgrading of the DTI as a strategic planning agency locked in dialogue with industry and labour on the long-term needs of the UK manufacturing base developing policy on how to sustain/phase out declining industries, nurture new ones and encourage the development and application of new technologies. To be effective, that debate will need to be an open and public one, with the DTI equipped both organisationally and financially to signal its preferences effectively to industry and the banks.

- New state institutions will also be needed—particularly a set of locally and regionally-rooted publicly owned investment banks, charged to work closely with small and medium size UK companies, and to do so within a long-term perspective: encouraged—that is to stay in and with local companies in periods of difficulty, to facilitate their restructuring rather than to preside over their demise.

- New sets of rules will have to be imposed at national level: new rules on pension funds to encourage long-term domestic industrial investment; new legislation on corporate governance, to give a voice to workers and consumers, and to reduce that of shareholders; and more generally, a new set of worker and trade union rights, to put a social base under industrial reconstruction.

- An effective industrial policy will also require the active development of regionally generated industrial districts consolidated by local decision-making between councils, chambers of commerce and unions—with strong central support and finance.

- Active monitoring of the investment decisions of large corporations will also be needed; with government aid tied to agreements on local sourcing, and with strong action at the European level to establish codes of behaviour for multinationals in areas as disparate as environmental pollution and worker rights.

- And finally there will have to be a strong European dimension to industrial policy— with the UK government initiating reform of the European competition rules (to allow the temporary nurturing of infant industries, and the restriction of capital flows for economies in deficit) and helping to design new and imaginative trade rules across the boundary of the Community itself.

From an Address to the National Conference of British Chambers of Commerce, by David Coates, Director, Centre for Industrial Policy and Performance, University of Leeds, 1993

---

legislative provisions which govern their operation—pension funds have become big holders of private equity. Pensions funds now typically hold more than 80 per cent of their assets as shares and, according to Hutton, more than 40 per cent of the shares of quoted companies are owned by such funds. Now dividends should be a return on investment which are only declared if the company concerned has done well. However, high dividends are expected and steady increases in the quoted price of shares are now routinely sought. So large are the holdings of such funds, in that the removal of their support is likely to

---

BOX 10.9 **The importance of pension funds**

Pension funds own nearly half the quoted shares in British companies. The question is what the law should insist should be the relationship and mutual responsibilities between those funds and the companies in which they invest. It is no longer adequate to say that they can turn up (if they want) once a year to an annual parliament of shareholders and sell their shares whenever they choose, especially if there is a hostile takeover bid. At the very least funds need to vote on key decisions, to play a part in setting commercial objectives and to ensure that executive pay is not excessive.

Will Hutton, in Giddens and Hutton (2001: 35)

---

do serious damage to the perceived value of a company, that they are highly motivated to continue to declare dividends whether their trading perform-ance justifies it or not.

Pension funds more than other kinds of institutional shareholders thus have power over the policies of companies without any of the obligations of ownership. It is the continuous need for the declaration of high profits that legitimates the high-handed policies of the new breed of corporate executives who claim the competence to manipulate company assets. The surprising fact is that the members of pension funds—as distinct from their managers—do not have the same interest in maximizing short-term income. The beneficiar-ies of pensions—considered as a totality—have an interest in the long-term viability of British industry. Similarly British citizens now and in the future have an interest in the long-term viability of British companies. If their inter-ests were more effectively and appropriately represented, it seems unlikely that pension funds would pursue the policies they do. Alternatively, changes in the priorities for pension funds could be enacted relatively easily. The democra-tization of the government of pension funds—so that the interests of mem-bers are properly represented in their policy formation—is a key practical expedient in changing the current behaviour of British companies which would be easy for a government to bring about.

Democratizing companies

A similar point could be made about the democratization of the control of British companies more generally. At present even those who are supposed to be able to influence company policy would have great trouble if they wanted to change policy away from the objective deemed important by the current dominant executive group. Some simple reforms seem likely to be effective in making companies more responsive to external influences on their activity. Insisting on more extensive disclosure of information about company activities—especially financial information—would obviously be beneficial.

At the least there should be completely independent auditing of company accounts and complete disclosure of the accounts to non-executive directors. Transparent and commonly accepted accounting guidelines ought to be automatically enforced. Such expedients would begin to break down the sovereign powers of the executives of major companies which are, under present arrangements, all but total.

One basic step in this direction would be making legislative provision to ensure that large institutional investors—especially insurance fund managers and the controllers of pension funds—recognize and exercise their obligations to vote at company AGMs. Too often such groups assume a correspondence between their interests and those of the companies in which they invest, when there is a correspondence between their short-term interests and those of corporate elites. Beyond this, however, putting in place some mechanisms allowing motions affecting company policy to be easily framed by groups of shareholders and other stakeholders, combined with obligatory procedures ensuring that such motions are heard and voted upon, would begin to place some checks on companies in the interests of owners and other stakeholders. Of course, more thorough democratization of company governance would be more effective and should be seriously considered by government. Companies should have members from stakeholder groups other than just owners, and the obvious candidates for inclusion here are representatives of employee groups. However, large debtors—such as companies' bankers—should be obliged to take more interest in the long-term survival of the companies to which they lend, and could be effectively induced to do so if their interests were more closely involved with such companies.

In many ways the social democratic capitalism found in Germany or Sweden, in which there is the inclusion of key stakeholders on the boards of companies, such as bankers or groups of employees, is a model which could be copied. The German system of supervisory boards—which are charged *inter alia* with concern for strategy and on which there are employee representatives—is perfectly workable. Such a form of constitution would serve as a check on the ill-considered policies of focusing and internationalization currently being undertaken by British companies. Such arrangements, as experience in continental Europe has shown, do not lead to the collapse of companies, but they do foster the development of cooperative enterprise and the gradual consolidation and development of companies.

Tackling the financial institutions

By the policy expedients set out above, many, and perhaps most, of the writers still interested in industrial policy think it is possible to produce some important changes in British capitalism even at this late stage. The largest unsolved

problem for the policy-makers, however, is what to do about financial institutions. Tackling the influence of financial institutions such as the banks and the
Stock Exchange directly—as opposed to indirectly as suggested in some of the
above ideas—is obviously a much tougher proposition than making some
modest changes in company governance structures and regulations. The question of the feasibility of undertaking reforms of financial institutions has been
considered for many years. When, as sometimes occurs, agreement is reached
that something should be done—no small achievement in itself—policy has
foundered because of the resistance of the vested interests involved.

This has led many interested in industrial policy to the conviction that a
system of special banks and other institutions to support long-term investment, in which either the national or the local stake has a considerable stake,
will be required if there is a serious intention of reversing current trends. As
time has gone on, however, such proposals seem increasingly implausible; the
inability of governments themselves to raise capital is leading them to be
increasingly dependent on private finance even for the support of public-
sector institutions. There seems to be very little indication that this aspect of
policy is now taken seriously. As the scale of the global finance system has
grown—on an average day, currency transactions amounting to greatly more
than the annual British GNP take place—the likelihood of even modest local
change in capital supply orchestrated by the state is remote. However, there is
still a considerable range of variation in the form adopted by international
financial institutions and they still bear the mark of the economic systems
from which they have originated. The world financial system has not yet
coalesced around any particular set of institutions, however common the
assumption that the dominant pattern will be some variant of the American
system. For the moment, then, there is, at least in theory, the opportunity to
attempt to develop a better-regulated set of finance capital institutions.

BOX 10.10 **Global finance as 'casino capitalism'**

Not everyone involved in this debate would agree with Erdman—or Grieder and
Schumann—that the [financial] markets have simply 'outgrown' governments. Some
would argue that though governments have been left behind, they can always catch up,
given the will to do so. . . . For the moment, the point is only that the liveliness of this
debate over globalisation in international finance at the very least suggests that it is
indeed an issue of some importance. My personal conviction—and my motivation
for returning to the themes of Casino Capitalism—is that it is the prime issue of
international politics and economics.

Susan Strange (1998: 18)

Bibliography

ABBOTT, A. (1988) *The System of Professions*. Chicago: University of Chicago Press.

ACAS (Advisory Conciliation and Arbitration Service) (1988) *Labour Flexibility in Britain: The 1987 ACAS Survey*, Occasional Paper 41, London: ACAS.

ACKROYD, S. (1995) 'On the Structure and Dynamics of Small UK Based Information Technology Firms', *Journal of Management Studies*, 32 (2): 141–61.

—— (1996) 'Organisation Contra Organisations: Professions and Organisational Change in the United Kingdom', *Organisation Studies*, 17 (4): 599–621.

—— (2000) 'The Challenge of Business Consultancy Firms', paper to the 16th EGOS Colloquium, Helsinki, Finland.

—— BURRELL, G., HUGHES, M., and WHITAKER, A. (1989) 'The Japanization of British Industry?' *Industrial Relations Journal*, 19(1): 11–23.

—— and FLEETWOOD (2000) *Realist Perspectives on Management and Organisation*. London: Routledge.

—— and LAWRENSON, D. (1995) 'Manufacturing Decline and the Managerial Division of Labour in Britain: The Case of Vehicles', in I. Glover and M. Hughes (eds), *The Professional-Managerial Class*. Aldershot: Avebury.

—— —— (1996) 'Knowledge-Work and Organisational Transformation', in R. Fincham (ed.), *New Relationships in the Organised Professions*. Aldershot: Avebury, 149–70.

—— and PROCTER, S. (1998) 'British Manufacturing Organization and Workplace Industrial Relations: Some Attributes of the New Flexible Firm', *British Journal of Industrial Relations*, 36(2): 163–83

—— and THOMPSON, P. (1999) *Organisational Misbehaviour*. London: Sage.

—— and WHITAKER, A. (1990) 'Manufacturing Decline and the Organisation of Manufacture in Britain', in P. Stewart, P. Crowther, and P. Garrahan (eds), *Restructuring for Economic Flexibility*. Aldershot: Avebury, 9–32.

AGLIETTA, M. (1979) *A Theory of Capitalist Regulation*. London: New Left Books.

ALBROW, M. (1996) *The Global Age*. Cambridge: Polity Press.

ALDRICH, H. (1979) *Organisations and Environments*. Englewood Cliffs, NJ: Prentice-Hall.

—— (1992) 'Incommensurate Paradigms: Vital Signs from Three Perspectives', in M. Reed and M. Hughes (eds), *Rethinking Organisations, New Directions in Organisational Analysis*. London: Sage.

ALFORD, H. (1994) 'Cellular Manufacturing: The Development of the Idea and its Application', *New Technology, Work and Employment*, 9: 3–18.

ALLEN, J., and MASSEY, D. (1989) *Restructuring Britain: The Economy in Question*. London: Sage.

ALLETZHAUSER, A. (1990) *The House of Nomura*. London: Bloomsbury.

ALVESSON, M. (1995) *The Management of Knowledge Intensive Companies*. Berlin: Walter de Gruyter

AMIN, A. (ed.) (1994) *Post Fordism: a Reader*. Oxford: Blackwell.

ANDERSON, S., and CAVANAGH, J. (2000) *Field Guide to the Global Economy*. New York: New Press.

ARCHER, M. (1995) *Realist Social Theory: The Morphogenic Approach*. Cambridge: Cambridge University Press

ARMSTRONG, P. (1984) 'Competition between Organisational Professionals and the Evolution of Managerial Control', in G. Thompson (ed.), *Work, Employment and Unemployment*. Milton Keynes: Open University Press, 97–120

—— (1985) 'Changing Control Strategies: The Role of Competition between Accounting and Other Organisational Professions', *Accounting, Organisations and Society*, 9 (2): 129–48

—— (1986) 'Management Control Strategies and Interprofessional Competition: The Case of Accountancy and Personnel Management', in D. Knights *et al.* (eds) *Managing the Labour Process*, Aldershot: Gower, 25–46.

—— (1987a) 'Engineers, Managers and Trust', *Work, Employment and Society*, 1(4): 421–40.

—— (1987b) 'The Rise of Accounting Controls in British Capitalist Enterprises', *Accounting, Organisations and Society*, 12(5): 415–36.

—— (1989) 'Limits and Possibilities for HRM in an Age of Management Accountancy', in J. Storey (ed.), *New Perspectives on Human Resource Management*. London: Routledge, 154–66.

—— MARGINSON, P., EDWARDS, P., and PURCELL, J. (1996) 'Budgetary Control and the Labour Force: Findings from a Survey of Large British Companies', *Management Accounting Research*, 7(1): 1–23.

ARROW, K. J. (1974) *The Limits of Organisation*. New York: W. W. Norton.

ASHKENAS, R., ULRICH, D., JICK, T., and KERR, S. (1995) *The Boundaryless Organisation*. San Francisco, Calif.: Jossey-Bass.

ATKINSON, J. (1984) 'Manpower Strategies for Flexible Organisations', *Personnel Management*, Aug., 28–31.

—— and MEAGER, N. (1986) 'Is Flexibility Just a Flash in the Pan?' *Personnel Management*, Sept., 26– 9.

AXFORD, B. (1995) *The Global System*. Cambridge: Polity Press.

BACON, R., and ELTIS, W. (1976) *Britain's Economic Problem: Too Few Producers*. London: Macmillan.

BARNETT, C. (1985) *The Audit of War*. London: Macmillan.

BARTLETT C. A., and GHOSHAL, S. (1989) *Managing Across Borders: The Transnational Solution*. Hutchinson: London.

BASSETT, P. (1986) *Strike Free: New Industrial Relations in Britain*. London: Macmillan.

BELL, D. (1961) *The End of Ideology*. New York: Collier Macmillan.

—— (1976) *The Coming of Post-Industrial Society*. New York: Basic Books.

BENDERS, J., and VAN HOOTEGEM, G. (1999) 'Teams and their Context: Moving the Team Discussion beyond Dichotomies', *Journal of Management Studies*, 36(5): 609–28

BENTLEY, A. F. (1967) *The Process of Government*. Cambridge, Mass.: Harvard University Press.

BERLE, A. A., and MEANS, G. C. (1947) *The Modern Corporation and Private Property*. New York: Macmillan.

BLACKABY, F. (ed.) (1979) *Deindustrialisation*. London: Heinemann.

BLACKLER, F. (1995) 'Knowledge, Knowledge Work and Organisations', *Organisation Studies*, 16 (6): 1021–46.

—— REED, M., and WHITAKER, A. (1993) 'Knowledge Workers and Contemporary Organisations', *Journal of Management Studies*, 30 (6): 851–62.

BLAU, P. (1955) *The Dynamics of Bureaucracy*. Chicago: University of Chicago Press.

—— and Scott, W. (1963) *Formal Organisations: A Comparative Approach*. Routledge: London.

BOER, H. (1994) 'Flexible Manufacturing Systems', in J. Storey (ed.), *New Wave Manufacturing Strategies*. London: Paul Chapman, 80–102.

Boston Consulting Group (1970) *The Product Portfolio Concept*. Boston: Boston Consulting Group Inc.

—— (1975) *Strategy Alternatives for the British Motorcycle Industry*, London: HMSO.

BOWER T. (1993) *Tiny Rowland: a Rebel Tycoon*. London: Heinemann.

BOYER, R. (1988) *The Search for Labour Market Flexibility*. Oxford: Clarendon Press.

BRAUDEL, F. (1983) *The Wheels of Commerce*. London: William Collins.

BRAVERMAN, H. (1974) *Labour and Monopoly Capital: The Degradation of Work in the Twentieth Century*. New York: Monthly Review Press.

BROCK, D., POWELL, M., and HININGS, C. R., (1999) *Restructuring the Professional Organisation*. London: Routledge.

BROWN, R. (1992) *Understanding Industrial Organisations*. London: Routledge.

BROWN, W. (1993) 'The Contraction of Collective Bargaining in Britain', *British Journal of Industrial Relations*, 31: 189–200.

—— and Walsh, J. (1991) 'Pay Determination in Britain in the 1980s: the Anatomy of Decentralisation', *Oxford Review of Economic Policy*, 7, 44–59.

BRUMMER, A., and COWE, R. (1994) *Hanson, A Biography*. London: Fourth Estate.

BUCHANAN, D. (1994) 'Cellular Manufacture and the Role of Teams', in J. Storey (ed.), *New Wave Manufacturing Strategies*. London: Paul Chapman.

—— and HUCZYNSKI, A. (1997) *Organisational Behaviour*. London: Prentice Hall

—— and BADHAM, R (1999) *Power, Politics and Organizational Change: Winning the Turf Game*. London: Sage.

BURNS, T., and STALKER, G. M. (1961) *The Management of Innovation*. London: Tavistock.

BURRAGE, M., and TORSTENDHAL, R. (eds) (1990) *Professions in Theory and History*. London: Sage.

CAMPAGNAC, E., and WINCH, G. (1997) 'The Social Regulation of Technical Expertise: The Corps and Profession in France and Great Britain', in R. Whitley and P. H. Kristensen (eds), *Governance at Work: The Social Regulation of Economic Relations* Oxford: Oxford University Press.

CARLSON, S. (1951) *Executive Behaviour: A Study of the Workload and the Working Methods of Managing Directors*. Stockholm: Strombergs.

CASEY, B. (1991) 'Survey Evidence on Trends in "Non-Standard" Employment', in A. Pollert (ed.), *Farewell to Flexibility*. Oxford: Blackwell, 171–99.

CASEY, C. (1995) *Work, Self and Society: After Industrialism*. London: Routledge.

CASTELLS, M. (1996) *The Rise of the Network Society (The Information Age: Economy, Society and Culture*. Vol. 1). Oxford: Blackwell.

CHANDLER, A. D. (1962) *Strategy and Structure.* Boston: MIT Press.

—— (1977) *The Visible Hand: The Managerial Revolution in American Business.* Cambridge, Mass.: Harvard University Press.

—— (1990) *Scale and Scope: the Dynamics of Industrial Capitalism.* Boston: Harvard University Press.

—— and DEAMS, H. (1980) *Managerial Hierarchies: Comparative Perspectives on the Rise of the Modern.* Boston: Harvard University Press.

—— HAGSTROM, P., and SOLVELL, O. (1999) *The Dynamic Firm.* Oxford: Oxford University Press.

CHANNON, D. (1982) 'Industrial Structure', *Long Range Planning,* 15(5): 3–17.

CHARKHAM, J. (1994) *Keeping Good Company: A Study of Corporate Governance in Five Countries.* Oxford: Oxford University Press.

CHILD, J. (1969) *British Management Thought.* London: Allen & Unwin.

—— (1972) 'Organisational Structure, Environment and Performance: The Role of Strategic Choice', *Sociology,* 6(1):1–22.

—— (1977) *Organisations: Guide to Problems and Practice,* London: Harper Row.

—— (1984) *Organisations: Guide to Problems and Practice,* 2nd edn. London: Paul Chapman.

—— and KEISER, A. (1979) 'Organisation and Managerial Roles in British and West German Companies', in Lammers *et al.* (eds), *Organisations Alike and Unlike.* Routledge.

CHURCH, R. (1986) 'Family Firms and Managerial Capitalism', *Business History,* 28(2): 165–80.

—— (1994) *The Rise and Decline of the British Motor Industry.* Basingstoke: Macmillan.

CIPP (1993–2000) Bulletins of the Centre for Industrial Policy and Performance, 1–14, University of Leeds.

CLARK, I. (1996) 'The State and New Industrial Relations', in I. Beardwell (ed.), *Contemporary Industrial Relations: A Critical Analysis.* Oxford: Oxford University Press.

CLARK, J. (1995) *Managing Innovation and Change: People, Technology and Strategy.* London: Sage.

CLEGG, S. (1989) *Frameworks of Power.* London: Sage.

—— and DUNKERLEY, D. (1980) *Organisations, Class and Control.* London: Routledge.

COATES, D. (1994) *The Question of UK Decline: The Economy, State and Society.* Brighton: Harvester Wheatsheaf.

—— (ed.) (1996) *Industrial Policy in Britain.* London: Macmillan.

CONGDON, T. (1991) 'Does the City Help or Hinder British Industry?', *Business and Economics Review,* 6: 3–10.

CONSTABLE, J., and McCORMICK, R. (1987) *The Making of British Managers.* Corby: British Institute of Management.

CONTI, R., and WARNER, M. (1993) 'Taylorism, Teams and Technology in "Re-engineering" Work Organisation', *New Technology, Work and Employment,* 8: 31–46.

COOPEY, J., KEEGAN, O., and EMLER, N. (1997) 'Managers' Innovations and the Structuring of Organisations', *Journal of Management Studies,* 35 (3): 263–84.

COWE, R. (1993) *The Guardian Guide to the UK's Top Companies.* Cambridge: Cambridge University Press.

CRAVENS, D. W., PIERCY, N. F., and SHIPP, S. H. (1996) 'New Organisational Forms for Competing in Highly Dynamic Environments: the Network Paradigm', *British Journal of Management*, Vol.7.

—— SHIPP, S. F., and CRAVENS, K. S. (1994) 'Reforming the Traditional Organisation: The Mandate for Developing Networks', *Business Horizons*, 5(1): 19–28.

DAVIDOW, W. H., and MALONE, M. S. (1992) *The Virtual Corporation*. London: Harper Collins.

DELBRIDGE, R. (1998) *Life on the Line in Contemporary Manufacturing: The Workplace Experience of Lean Production and the Japanese Model*. Oxford: Oxford University Press.

—— TURNBULL, P., and WILKINSON, B. (1992) 'Pushing Back the Frontiers: Management Control and Work Intensification under JIT/TQM Factory Regimes', *New Technology, Work and Employment*, 7(2): 97–106.

DIGGLE, B. (1990) Hanson, A Report by the Credit Suisse Bank. First Boston, London.

DONALDSON, L. (1985) *In Defence of Organization Theory*. London: Sage.

—— (1995) *American Anti-management Theories of Organization*. Cambridge: Cambridge University Press.

—— (1996) *For Positivist Organization Theory*. London: Sage.

DONNELLON, A., and SCULLY, M. (1994) 'Teams, Performance and Rewards: Will the Post Bureaucratic Organization be a Post Meritocratic Organisation', in C. Heckscher and A. Donnellon (eds), *The Post Bureaucratic Organisation*. London: Sage.

DORE, R. (1985) 'Financial Structures and the Long-Term View', *Policy Studies*, 10–29

DORF, R (1983) *Robotics and Automatic Manufacturing*, Reston, Va.: Reston Publishing.

DRUCKER, P. (1974) 'New Templates for Today's Organisations', *Harvard Business Review*, 74 (1): 50–5

—— (1988) 'The Coming of the New Organisation', *Harvard Business Review*, 88 (1): 45–53

DU GAY, P. (1996) *Consumption and Identity at Work*. London: Sage.

—— (2000) *In Praise of Bureaucracy*. London: Sage.

DUNNING, J. H. (1997) *Alliance Capitalism and Global Business*. London: Routledge.

EDQUIST, C., and JACOBSSON, S. (1988) *Flexible Automation: The Global Diffusion of New Technology in the Engineering Industry*. Oxford: Blackwell.

EDWARDS, P. (1987) *Managing the Factory: a Survey of General Managers*. Oxford: Blackwell.

—— (1995) 'Assessment: Markets and Managerialism', in P. Edwards (ed.), *Industrial Relations: Theory and Practice in Britain*. Oxford: Blackwell.

—— ARMSTONG, P., MARGINSON, P., and PURCELL, J. (1996) 'Towards the Transnational Company? The Global Structure and Organisation of Multinational Firms', in R. Crompton, D. Gallie, and K. Purcell (eds), *Changing Forms of Employment*. London: Routledge.

ELBAUM, B., and LAZONICK, W. (1986) *The Decline of the British Economy*. Oxford: Oxford University Press

ELGER, T. (1991) 'Task Flexibility and the Intensification of Labour in UK Manufacturing in the 1980s', in A. Pollert (ed.), *Farewell to Flexibility?* Oxford: Blackwell, 46–66.

—— and SMITH, C. (eds.) (1994) *Global Japanization: The Transnational Transformation of the Labour Process*. London: Routledge.

Emmott, M., and Hutchinson S. (1998) 'Employment Flexibility: Threat or Promise?', in P. Sparrow and M. Marchington (eds), *Human Resource Management: The New Agenda*. London: Financial Times Pitman, 229 44.

Ernst, D. (1994) *Inter-firm Networks and Market Structure*. Berkeley, Califa University of California Press.

Evans, P. (1995) *Embedded Autonomy, States and Industrial Transformation*. Princeton, NJ: Princeton University Press.

Ezzamel, M., and Willmott, H. (1998) 'Accounting for Teamwork: A Critical Study of Group-based Systems of Organizational Control', *Administrative Science Quarterly*, 43: 358–96.

—— Lilley, S., and Willmott, H. (1996) 'The View from the Top: Senior Executives' Perceptions of Changing Management Practices in UK Companies', *British Journal of Management*, 7(2): 155–68.

Fallon, I. (1991) *Billionaire: The Life and Times of Sir James Goldsmith*. London: Hutchinson.

Featherstone, M. (ed.) (1995) *Global Culture*. London: Sage.

Fernie, S., and Metcalf, D. (1997) *(Not) Hanging on the Telephone: Payment Systems in the New Sweatshops*. Centre for Economic Performance: London School of Economics.

Fidler, J. (1981) *The British Business Elite*. London: Routledge.

Fjermestad, J., and Chakrabarti, A. (1993) 'Survey of the Computer-Integrated Manufacturing Literature: A Framework of Strategy, Implementation and Innovation', *Technology, Analysis and Strategic Management*, 5(3): 251–71.

Fligstein, N. (1990) *The Transformation of Corporate Control*. Boston: Harvard University Press.

Frank, A. G. (1978) *World Accumulation, 1492–1798*. London: Macmillan.

Friedman, A. (1977) *Industry and Labor*. London: Macmillan.

Galbraith, J. K. (1958) *The Affluent Society*. London: Hamish Hamilton.

—— (1977) *The Age of Uncertainty*. London: André Deutsch.

—— (1983) *The Anatomy of Power*. London: Sphere Books.

Gallie, D. (1991) 'Patterns of Skill Change: Upskilling, Deskilling or the Polarization of Skills', *Work, Employment and Society*, 5(3): 319–51.

Gerschenkron, A. (1962), *Economic Backwardness in Historical Perspective*. Cambridge: Mass.: Belknap.

Gershunny, J. (1978) *After Industrial Society?* London: Macmillan.

—— and Miles, I. (1983) *The New Service Economy*. London: Francis Pinter.

—— —— (1992) *Towards a Service Society*. London: Francis Pinter.

Gerwin, D. (1987) 'An Agenda for Research on the Flexibility of Manufacturing Processes', *International Journal of Operations and Production Management*, 7(1): 38–49.

Giddens, A. (1979) *Central Problems in Social Theory, Action, Structure and Contradiction in Social Analysis*. London: Macmillan Press.

—— and Hutton, W. (2001) *On The Edge: Living with Global Capitalism*. London: Vintage.

Glennerster, H., and Hills, J. (1998) *The State of Welfare*. London: Oxford University Press.

GOFFEE, R., and SCASE, R. (1995) *Corporate Realities: Dynamics of Large and Small Organisations*. London: Routledge.

GOOLD, M., and CAMPBELL, A. (1987) *Strategies and Styles: the Role of the Centre in Managing Diversified Corporations*. Oxford: Blackwell.

GOSPEL, H. (1995) 'The Decline in Apprenticeship Training in Britain', *Industrial Relations Journal*, 26 (1): 32–44.

GOULDNER, A. (1954) *Wildcat Strike*. London: Routledge & Kegan Paul.

—— (1954) *Patterns of Industrial Bureaucracy*. Glencoe, Ill.: Free Press.

GOWLER, D., and LEGGE, K. (1983) 'The Meaning of Management and the Management of Meaning: A View from Social Anthropology', in M. J. Earl (ed.), *Perspectives on Management: A Multidisciplinary Analysis*. Oxford: Oxford University Press.

GWYNNE, R. N. (1990) *New Horizons? Third World Industrialisation in an International Framework*. Harlow: Longman.

HAKIM, C. (1990) 'Core and Periphery in Employers' Workplace Strategies: Evidence from the 1987 ELUS Survey', *Work, Employment and Society*, 4(2): 157–188.

HALES, C. P. (1986) 'What Do Managers Do? A Critical Review of the Evidence', *Journal of Management Studies*, 23. 1.

HALLIDAY, J. (1975) *A Political History of Japanese Capitalism*. Monthly Review Press.

HANDY, C. (1987) *The Making of Managers: A Report on Management Education, Training and Development in the USA, Western Germany, France, Japan and the UK*. MSC/NEDC/BIM.

HANNAH, L. (ed.) (1976) *Management Strategy and Business Development*. Macmillan: London.

—— (1980) 'Visible and Invisible Hands in Great Britain', in A. D. Chandler and H. Deams (eds.), *Managerial Hierarchies*. Cambridge, Mass.: Harvard University Press.

—— (1983) *The Rise of the Corporate Economy*. London: Methuen.

HARRISON, B. (1994) *Lean and Mean: The Changing Landscape of Corporate Power in the Age of Flexibility*. New York: Basic Books.

HART, P. E., UTTON, M., and WALSHE, G. (1973) *Mergers and Concentration in British Industry*. Cambridge: Cambridge University Press.

HARTLEY, J. (1983) *Robots at Work: A Practical Guide for Engineers and Managers*. Bedford: IFS Publications.

HECKSCHER, C., and DONNELLON, A. (eds) (1994) *The Post-Bureaucratic Organisation: New Perspectives on Organisational Change*. London: Sage.

HEDLUND, G. (1986) 'The Hypermodern NMC-A Heterachy?', *Human Resource Management*, 25 (1): 9–35.

—— (1994) 'A Model of Knowledge Management and the N Form Corporation', *Strategic Management Journal*, 73–90.

—— and RIDDERSTRALE, J. (1992) 'Towards the 'N' Form Organisation: Exploitation and Creation in the NMC', in B. Toyne and D. Nigh (eds), *Perspectives on International Business Theory, Research and Institutional Arrangements*. Columbia, SC: University of South Carolina Press.

HEERY, E. (1996) 'The New Unionism', in I. Beardwell (ed.), *Contemporary Industrial Relations: A Critical Analysis*. Oxford: Oxford University Press.

HERTZ, N. (2000) *The Silent Takeover: Global Capitalism and the Death of Democracy*. London: Heinemann.

HIGGINS, W., and CLEGG, S. (1988) 'Enterprise Calculation and Manufacturing Decline', *Organisation Studies*, 9 (1): 69–90.

HILFERDING, R. (1910) *Finance Capital*, published in translation by Routledge, London 1981.

HILL, T. (1991) *Production/Operations Management*, 2nd edn. Englewood Cliffs, NJ: Prentice-Hall.

HININGS, R., and GREENWOOD, R. (1988) *The Dynamics of Strategic Change*. Oxford: Blackwell.

—— and LEE, L. (1971) 'Dimensions of Organisation, Structure and Their Context', *Sociology* V: 83–93.

HIRST, P., and THOMPSON, G. (1996) *Globalization in Question* 1st edn., Cambridge: Polity Press.

—— —— (1999) *Globalization in Question* 2nd edn., Cambridge: Polity Press.

—— and ZEITLIN, J. (eds.) (1988), *Reversing Industrial Decline*. Oxford: Blackwell.

HOBSBAWM, E. (1968) *Industry and Empire*. Harmonsworth: Penguin.

—— (1975) *The Age of Capital*. London: Weidenfeld & Nicholson.

HUCZYNSKI, A., and BUCHANAN, D. (2000) *Organisational Behaviour*. London: Financial Times/Pitman.

HUTTON, W. (1996) *The State We're In*. London: Vintage.

—— (1997) *The State to Come*. London: Vintage.

—— and GIDDENS A. (eds), (2001) *On the Edge: Living with Global Capitalism*. London: Vintage.

IKEDA, S. (1996) 'World Production', ch. 3 in I. Wallerstein, and T. Hopkins, *The Age of Transition: Trajectory of the World System 1945–2025*. London: Pluto Press.

Ingersoll Engineers (1990) *Competitive Manufacturing: The Quiet Revolution*. Rugby: Ingersoll Engineers.

—— (1994) *The Quiet Revolution Continues*. Rugby: Ingersoll Engineers.

INGHAM, G. K. (1984) *Capitalism Divided: The City and Industry in British Development*. London: Macmillan.

JACQUES, E. (1990) 'In Praise of Hierarchy', *Harvard Business Review*, Jan./Feb. 70(1).

JAIKUMAR, R. (1986) 'Postindustrial Manufacturing', *Harvard Business Review*, 64(6): 69–76.

JARILLO, J. C. (1993) *Strategic Networks*. Oxford: Butterworth-Heinemann.

JESSOP, R. (1994) 'Post-Fordism and the State', in A. Amin (ed.), *Post Fordism: A Reader*. Oxford: Blackwell.

JONES, B. (1988) 'Work and Flexible Automation in Britain: A Review of Developments and Possibilities,' *Work, Employment and Society*, 2(4): 451–86.

—— (1989) 'Flexible Automation and Factory Politics: The United Kingdom in Current Perspective', in P. Hirst and J. Zeitlin (eds), *Reversing Industrial Decline?*, Oxford: Berg, 95–121.

—— (1991) 'Technological Convergence and Limits to Managerial Control: Flexible Manufacturing Systems in Britain, the USA and Japan', in S. Tolliday and J. Zeitlin (eds.), *The Power to Manage?* London: Routledge, 231–55.

KAHN, H. (1970) *The Emerging Japanese Superstate*. New York: Macmillan.

KHANDWALLA, P. N. (1977) *The Design of Organizations*, New York: Harcourt Brace Jovanovich.

KANTER, R. M. (1983) *The Change Masters*. London: Unwin.

—— (1989) *When Giants Learn to Dance*. London: Unwin.

KEEP, E., and RAINBIRD, H. (1995) 'Training', in P. Edwards (ed.), *Industrial Relations: Theory and Practice in Britain*. Oxford: Blackwell, 515–42.

KELLY, J. (1998) *Rethinking Industrial Relations: Mobilisation, Collectivisation and Long Waves*. London: Routledge.

KENNEDY, W. P. (1987) *Industrial Structure, Capital Markets and the Origins of British Economic Decline*. Cambridge: Cambridge University Press.

KERBO, H., and McKINSTRY, J. (1995) *Who Rules Japan? The Inner Circles of Economic and Political Power*. Westport, Conn.: Praeger.

KEYNES, J. M. (1936) *General Theory of Employment Interest and Money*. London: Macmillan.

KIPPING, M. (2001) 'Trapped in Their Wave: The Evolution of Management Consultancies', in T. Clark and R. Fincham, *Critical Consulting: New Perspectives on the Management Advice Industry*. London: Routledge.

KIRBY, M. W. (1992) 'Institutional Rigidities and Economic Decline: Reflections on the British Experience', *Economic History Review*, 45 (4): 637–60.

KNOKE, D. (1990) *Political Networks: The Structural Perspective*. Cambridge: Cambridge University Press.

—— and KUKLINSKI, J. (1982) *Network Analysis*. Beverly Hills, Calif.: Sage.

KOTTER, J. P. (1999) *John Kotter on What Leaders Really Do*. Boston: Harvard Business Press.

—— and LAWRENCE, P. C. (1974) *Managers in Action*. New York: Free Press.

KRISTENSEN, P. H. (1997), 'National Systems of Governance and Managerial Prerogative in the Evolution of Work Systems: England Germany and Denmark Compared', in R. Whitley and P. H. Kristensen (eds), *Governance at Work: the Social Regulation of Economic Relations*. Oxford: Oxford University Press.

KUNDA, G. (1992) *Engineering Culture: Control and Commitment in a High Tech Corporation*, Philadelphia: Temple University Press.

LANDES, D. S. (1969) *The Unbound Prometheus: Technical Change and Industrial Development in Western Europe from 1750*. Cambridge: Cambridge University Press.

LANE, C. (1988) 'Industrial Change in Europe: The Pursuit of Flexible Specialisation in Britain and West Germany', *Work, Employment and Society*, 2: 141–68.

—— (1995) *Industry and Society in Europe: Stability and Change in Britain, Germany and France*. Aldershot: Edward Elgar.

—— (1998) 'Between Globalisation and Localisation: A Comparison of Internationalisation Strategies of British and German MNCs', *Economy and Society*, 27 (4): 462–85.

LARSON, M. (1977) *The Rise of Professionalism: A Sociological Analysis*. Berkeley: University of California Press

LASH, S., and URRY, J. (1987) *The End of Organised Capitalism*. Cambridge: Polity Press.

—— and URRY, J. (1994) *Economies of Signs and Space*. London: Sage.

LAWRENCE, P. (1980) *Managers and Management in Western Germany*. London: Croom Helm.

LAZONICK, W. (1990) *Competitive Advantage on the Shop Floor*. Cambridge, Mass.: Harvard University Press.

—— (1991) *Business Organisation and the Myth of the Market Economy*. Cambridge: Cambridge University Press.

LEBORGNE, D. A., and LIPIETZ, A. (1992) 'Conceptual Fallacies and Open Questions on Post Fordism', in M. Storper and A. J. Scott (eds), *Pathways to Industrialisation*. London: Routledge.

LEGGE, K (1998) 'Flexibility: The Gift-wrapping on Employment Degradation?' in P. Sparrow and M. Marchington (eds), *Human Resource Management: The New Agenda*. London: Financial Times/Pitman, 286–95.

LIPIETZ, A. (1987) *Mirages and Miracles: the Crises of Global Fordism*. London Verso.

LITTLER, C. (1982) *The Development of the Labour Process in Capitalist Societies*. London: Heinemann.

LONGSTRETH, F. (1979) 'The City, Industry and the State', in C. Crouch (ed.), *State and Economy in Contemporary Capitalism*. London: Croom Helm.

LORENZ, E. H. (1991) 'Neither Friends nor Strangers: Informal Networks of Subcontracting in French Industry', in G. Thompson, G. Frances, J. Levacic, and J. Mitchell (eds.), *Markets, Hierarchies and Networks*. London: Sage.

LOVERING, J. (1990) 'A Perfunctory Kind of Fordism', *Work, Employment and Society*,

LUHMANN, N. (1979) *Trust and Power*. Chichester: Wiley.

MCLOUGHLIN, I. (1990) 'Management, Work Organization and CAD: Towards Flexible Automation?' *Work, Employment and Society*, 4(2): 217–37.

MABEY, C., SALAMAN, G., and STOREY, J. (2001) 'The End of Classical Organisational Forms?', ch. 12 of G. Salaman (ed.), *Understanding Business Organisations*, London: Routledge.

MANN, K. (1992) *The Making of an English 'Underclass'?* Buckingham: Open University Press.

MARGINSON, P. (1991) 'Change and Continuity in the Employment Structures of Large Companies', in A. Pollert (ed.), *Farewell to Flexibility?* Oxford: Blackwell.

—— ARMSTRONG, P., EDWARDS, P., PURCELL, J., and SISSON, K. (1988), *Beyond the Workplace: Managing Industrial Relations in the Multi-Establishment Enterprise*. London: Blackwell.

—— —— —— —— with HUBBARD, N. (1993), *The Control of Industrial Relations in Large Companies: An Initial Analysis of the Second Company Level Industrial Relations Survey*, Warwick Papers in Industrial Relations, no. 45, Industrial Relations Research Unit, University of Warwick.

MARSHALL, A. (1890) *Principles of Economics*. London: Macmillan.

MARSHALL, T. (1950) *Citizenship and Social Class and Other Essays*. Cambridge: Cambridge University Press.

MAYER, C. (1987) *New Issues in Corporate Finance*. London: CEPR Discussion Paper 181.

MEEKS, G. (1977) *Disappointing Marriage: A Study of the Gains from Mergers*. Cambridge: Cambridge University Press

MERTON, R. (1949) *Social Theory and Social Structure*. Glencoe Ill.: Free Press.

MEYER, M. W., and ZUCKER, L. G. (1989) *Permanently Failing Organisations*. Newbury Park, Calif.: Sage.

MILLER, D., and FRIESEN, P. (1982) 'Structural Change and Performance: Quantum versus Piecemeal—Incremental Approaches', *Academy of Management Journal*, 31(3). 544–69.

MILLER, J. (1979) *British Management vs. German Management*. Farnborough: Saxon House.

MINTZBERG, H. (1973) *The Nature of Managerial Work*. New York: Harper & Row.

—— (1978) 'Patterns in Strategy Formation', *Management Science*, 24(9): 934–48.

—— (1979) *The Structuring of Organizations, A Synthesis of Research*. London: Prentice Hall International.

—— (1993) *Structure in Fives: Designing Effective Organizations*. London: Prentice Hall.

MORGAN, G. (1986) *Images of Organization*. London: Sage.

—— (1988) *Creative Organization Theory*. London: Sage.

—— (1998) 'Varieties of Capitalism and the Institutional Embeddedness of International Economic Co-operation', Paper for Work, Employment and Society Conference, Sept. 1998.

MORISHIMA, T. (1982) *Why Has Japan Succeeded?* Cambridge: Cambridge University Press.

MURRAY, C. (1990) *The Emerging British Underclass*. London: Institute of Economic Affairs.

NACAB (National Association of Citizens' Advice Bureaux) (1997) *Flexibility Abused: A CAB Evidence Report on Conditions in the Labour Market*. London: NACAB.

NEDO (National Economic Development Office) (1986) *Changing Working Patterns: How Companies Achieve Flexibility to Meet New Needs*. London: NEDO.

NEWMAN, A. D., and ROWBOTTOM, R. W. (1968) *Organisational Analysis: A Guide to Better Understanding of the Stuctural Problems of Organisations*. London: Heinemann.

NICHOLS, T. (1986) *The British Worker Question: A New Look at Workers and Productivity in Manufacturing*. London: Routledge & Kegan Paul.

NOHRIA, N., and GHOSHAL, S. (1997) *The Differentiated Network*. San Francisco: Jossey-Bass.

OHMAE, K. (1990) *The Borderless World*. London: Collins.

—— (1995) 'Putting Global Knowledge First', *Harvard Business Review*, Jan–Feb., 119–25.

OLIVER, N., and WILKINSON, B. (1992) *The Japanization of British Industry*, 2nd edn.. Oxford: Blackwell.

O'REILLY, J. (1992) 'Where do you Draw the Line? Functional Flexibility, Training and Skill in Britain and France', *Work, Employment and Society* 6: 369–96.

OWEN, G. (1999) *From Empire to Europe: The Decline and Revival of British Industry since the Second World War*. London: HarperCollins.

PACEY, A. (1983) *The Culture of Technology*. Oxford: Blackwell.

PALLOIX, C. (1976) 'The Labour Process from Fordism to Neo-Fordism', in *The Labour Process and Class Struggle*. London: Lawrence & Wishart.

PAYNE, P. (1984) 'Family Business in Britain: An Historical and Analytical Survey', in Okochi and Yasuoka (eds), *Family Business in an Era of Industrial Growth*. Tokyo: University of Tokyo Press.

PECK, J. (1998) *Work Place: The Social Regulation of Labour Markets*. New York: Guilford Press.

—— and TICKELL, A. (1994) 'Searching for a New Institutional Fix: The After Fordist Crisis', in A. Amin (ed.), *Post Fordism: A Reader*. Oxford. Blackwell.

PERLMUTTER, H. V. (1969) 'The Tortuous Evolution of the Multi National Corporation', *Columbia Journal of World Business*, 4 (1): 9–18.

PETTIGREW, A. M. (1985) *The Awakening Giant*. Oxford: Blackwell.

PFEFFER, J. (1981) *Power in Organisations*. London: Pitman.

—— (1992) *Managing with Power: Politics and Influence in Organizations*, Boston: Harvard University Press.

—— and SALANCIK, G. R. (1978) *The External Control of Organisations*. New York: Harper Row.

PHILLIMORE, A. J. (1990) 'Flexible Specialisation, Work Organization and Skills: Approaching the "Second Industrial Divide" ', *New Technology, Work and Employment*, 4(2): 79–91.

PIKE, R., SHARP, I., and PRICE, D. (1989) 'AMT Investment in the Larger UK Firm', *International Journal of Operations and Production Management*, 9(2): 13–26.

PIORE, M., and SABEL, C. (1984) *The Second Industrial Divide: Possibilities for Prosperity*. New York: Basic Books.

POLLARD, S. (1982) *The Wasting of the British Economy*. Aldershot: Croom Helm.

—— (1992) *The Development of the British Economy*. London: Edward Arnold.

POLLERT, A. (1988) 'The Flexible Firm: Fixation or Fact?', *Work, Employment and Society*, 2: 281–316.

POOLE, M., and JENKINS, G. (1998) 'Human Resource Management and the theory of Rewards: Evidence from a National survey', *British Journal of Industrial Relations*, Vol 36(2): 227–47.

—— (ed.) (1991) *Farewell to Flexibility?* Oxford: Blackwell.

POWELL, W. W. (1991) 'Neither Market nor Hierarchy: Network Forms of Organization', ch. 22 in G. Thompson, J. Frances, R. Levacic, and J. Mitchell (eds), *Markets, Hierarchies and Networks*. London: Sage.

—— and DiMAGGIO, P. (eds) (1991) *The New Institutionalism in Organizational Analysis*. Chicago: University of Chicago Press.

PRAIS, S. (1976) *The Evolution of Giant Firms in Britain*. Cambridge: Cambridge University Press.

PRESTHUS, R. (1979) *The Organizational Society*. London: Macmillan.

PROCTER, S. (1995) 'The Extent of Just-in-Time Manufacturing in the UK: Evidence from Aggregate Economic Data', *Integrated Manufacturing Systems*, 6 (4): 16–25.

—— and ACKROYD, S. (1998) 'Against Japanization: Understanding the Reorganization of British Manufacturing', *Employee Relations*, 20(3): 237–47.

—— HASSARD, J., and ROWLINSON, M. (1995) 'Introducing Cellular Manufacturing: Operations, Human Resources and Trust Dynamics', *Human Resource Management Journal*, 5: 46–64.

—— and MUELLER, F. (2000) 'Team-working: Strategy, Structure, Systems and Culture', in S. Procter and F. Mueller (eds), *Team-working*. London: Macmillan, 3–24.

—— ROWLINSON, M., MCARDLE, L., HASSARD, J., and FORRESTER, P. (1994), 'Flexibility, Politics and Strategy: In Defence of the Model of the Flexible Firm', *Work, Employment and Society*, 8: 221–42.

PROWSE, S. (1994) *Corporate Governance in an International Perspective*. Basle: Bank for International Settlements.

PUGH, D., and HICKSON, D. (1976) *Organisational Structure in its Context: The Aston Programme I*. Farnborough: Saxon House.

—— and HININGS, R. (1976) *Organisational Structure: The Aston Programme II*. Farnborough: Saxon House.

—— —— (1989) *Writers on Organisations*. Harmonsworth: Penguin.

PUNCH, M. (1996) *Dirty Business: Exploring Corporate Misconduct*. London: Sage.

PURCELL, J. (1987) 'Mapping Management Styles in Employee Relations', *Journal of Management Studies*, 24: 533–48.

—— (1989) 'The Impact of Corporate Strategy on Human Resource Management', in J. Storey (ed.), *New Perspectives on Human Resource Management*. London: Routledge.

—— (1993) 'The End of Institutional Industrial Relations', *Political Quarterly*, 64: 6–23.

—— and AHLSTRAND, B. (1994) *Human Resource Management in the Multi-Divisional Company*. Oxford: Oxford University Press.

RAELIN, J. (1986) *The Clash of Cultures: Managers and Professionals*. Boston: Harvard University Press.

RASANEN, K., and WHIPP, R. (1992) *National Business Recipes, A Sector Perspective*. London: Sage.

REED, M. (1996), 'Expert Power and Control in Late Modernity', *Organisation Studies*, 17 (4): 573–597.

—— and ANTHONY, P. (1992) 'Professionalizing Management and Managing Professionalization: British Management in the 1980s', *Journal of Management Studies*, 25 (5): 591–613.

REICH, R. (1992) *The Work of Nations*. London: Simon & Schuster.

RENNER, K. (1904) *Institutions of Private Law and their Social Function*, published in translation by Routledge 1949.

ROSE, T., and HININGS. C. R. (1999) 'Global Clients Demands Driving Change in Global Business Advisory Firms', in D. Brock, M. Powell, and C. R. Hinings (eds), *Restructuring the Professional Organisation*. London: Routledge.

ROSTOW, W. W. (1963) *Stages of Economic Growth: A Non-Communist Manifesto*. Cambridge: Cambridge University Press.

ROWLINSON, M. (1997) *Organisations and Institutions: Perspectives in Economics and Sociology*. London: Macmillan.

RUBENSTEIN, W. D. (1993) *Capitalism Culture and Decline in Britain 1750–1990*. London: Routledge.

RUBERY, J. (1989) 'Precarious Forms of Work in the United Kingdom', in G. Rogers and J. Rogers (eds.), *Precarious Jobs in Labour Market Regulation*. Brussels: International Institute for Labour Studies.

RUSH, H., and BESSANT, J. (1992) 'Revolution in Three-quarter Time: Lessons from the Diffusion of Advanced Manufacturing Technologies', *Technology, Analysis and Strategic Management*, 4(1): 3–19.

SABEL, C. (1991) 'Moebius Strip Organisations and Open Labour Markets: Some Consequence of the Reintegration of Conception and Execution in a Volatile Economy', in P. Bourdieu and J. Coleman (eds.), *Social Theory for a Changing Society*. Colorado: Westview Press.

—— and ZEITLIN, J. (1985) 'Historical Alternatives to Mass Production: Politics, Markets and Technology in Nineteenth-Century Industrialisation', *Past and Present*, 108 (3): 133–76.

SAVAGE, M., BARLOW, J., DICKENS, P., and FIELDING, T. (1992) *Property, Bureaucracy and Culture*. London: Routledge.

SAYER, A., and WALKER, R. (1992) *The New Social Economy: Reworking the Division of Labor*. Oxford: Blackwell.

SCARBOROUGH, M., and TERRY, M. (1998) 'Forget Japan: The Very British Response to Lean Production', *Employee Relations*, 20 (3): 224–36.

SCHOLTE, J. A. (2000) *Globalization: A Critical Introduction*. London: Palgrave.

SCOTT, J. (1986) *Capitalist Property and Financial Power*. Hassocks: Wheatsheaf.

—— (1991) 'Networks of Corporate Power: A Comparative Assessment', *Annual Review of Sociology*, 17 (2): 181–203.

—— (1996) *Stratification and Power: Structures of Class, Status and Command*. Cambridge: Polity Press.

—— (1997) *Corporate Business and Capitalist Classes*. Oxford: Oxford University Press.

—— and GRIFF, J. (1984) *Directors of British Industry: The British Corporate Network*. Cambridge: Polity Press.

SCOTT, W. R. (1995) *Institutions and Organisations*. London: Sage.

—— MEYER, J.W., (1994) *Institutional Environments and Organizations, Structural Complexity and Individualism*. London: Sage.

SELZNICK, P. (1949) *TVA and the Grass Roots*. Berkley, Calif.: University of California Press.

SENGENBERGER, W., LOVEMAN, G., and PIORE, M. (1990) *The Re-Emergence of Small Enterprises*. Geneva: Institute of Labour Studies.

SENNETT, R. (1998) *The Corrosion of Character*. New York and London: Norton.

SEWELL, G., and WILKINSON, B. (1992) 'Someone to Watch over Me: Surveillance, Discipline and the Just in Time Labour Process', *Sociology*, 26(2): 271–89.

SHUTT, J., and WHITTINGTON, R. (1987) 'Fragmentation Strategies and the Rise of Small Units', *Regional Studies*, 19.

SILVERMAN, D. (1970) *The Theory of Organisations*. London: Heinemann.

SLACK, N. (1983) 'Flexibility as a Manufacturing Objective', in C. Voss (ed.), *Research in Production/Operations Management*. Aldershot: Gower, 101–19.

—— (1987) 'The Flexibility of Manufacturing Systems', *International Journal of Operations and Production Management*, 7(4): 35–45.

SLAPPER, G., and TOMBS, S. (1999) *Corporate Crime*. Harlow: Longmans.

SMITH, C., and THOMPSON, P. (1992) *Labour in Transition: The Labour Process in Eastern Europe and China*. London: Routledge.

SOLVELL, O., and ZANDER L. (1995) 'Organization of the Dynamic Multinational Enterprise', *International Studies of Management and Organization*, 25 (1): 17–38.

—— —— (1998) 'International Diffusion of Knowledge, Isolating Mechanisms and the Role of the Multi-National Enterprise', in A. Chandler, P. Hagstrom, and O. Solvell (eds) (1999), *The Dynamic Firm*. Oxford: Oxford University Press.

SPYBY, T. (1995) *Gobalisation and World Society*. Cambridge: Polity Press.

STARBUCK, W. (1993) 'Learning by Knowledge-Intensive Firms', *Journal of Mangement Studies*, 29 (6): 713–40.

STEARNS, L. (1990) 'Capital Market Effects on External Control of Corporations', in S. Zukin and P. DiMaggio, *Structures of Capital*. Cambridge: Cambridge University Press.

STEVENS, M. (1991) *The Big Six*. New York: Macmillan.

STEWART, R. (1964) *Managers and Their Jobs*. Maidenhead: McGraw Hill.

—— (1976) *Contrasts in Management*. Maidenhead: McGraw Hill.

—— (1982) *Choices for the Manager*. Maidenhead: McGraw Hill.

STRANGE, S, (1986) *Casino Capitalism*. Oxford: Blackwell.

—— (1998) *Mad Money*. Manchester: University of Manchester Press.

SUNEJA, V. (2001) *Policy Issues for Business*. London: Sage.

TAPSCOTT, D., and CASTON A. (1993) *Paradigm Shift: The New Promise of Information Technology*. New York: McGraw-Hill.

TAYLOR, F. W. (1911) *The Principles of Scientific Management*. New York: Harper

TAYLOR, P., and BAIN, P. (1999) 'An Assembly Line in the Head: Work and Employee Relations in the Call Centre', *Industrial Relations Journal*, 30 (2): 101–17.

THOMPSON, G., FRANCES, J., LEVACIC, R., and MITCHELL, J. (eds.) (1991) *Markets, Hierarchies and Networks*. London: Sage.

THOMPSON, P. (1984) *The Nature of Work*. London: Macmillan.

—— and ACKROYD, S. (1995) 'All Quiet on the Workplace Front? A Critique of Recent Trends in British Industrial Sociology', *Sociology*, 29(4): 615–33.

—— and McHUGH, D. (2001) *Work Organisations: A Critical Introduction*. London: Palgrave.

—— and WARHURST, C. (1998) *Workplaces of the Future*. London: Macmillan.

THORELLI, H. B. (1986) 'Networks: Between Markets and Hierarchies', *Strategic Management Journal*, 7 (1): 37–51.

TIDD, J. (1991) *Flexible Manufacturing Technologies and International Competitiveness*. London: Pinter.

Times 1000 (1998) *The Definitive Guide to Business Today*. London: Times Books.

TOURAINE, A. (1974) *Post-Industrial Society*. London: Wildwood House.

TRIST, E., HIGGIN, G., MURRAY, H., and POLLOCK, A. (1963) *Organizational Choice: Capabilities of Groups at the Coal Face under Changing Technologies: the Loss, Rediscovery and Transformation of a Work Tradition*. London: Tavistock.

TSOUKAS, H. (1994) 'What is Management? The Outline of a Metatheory', *British Journal of Management*, 5 (2): 289–301.

TURNBULL, P. (1988) 'The Limits to Japanization: Just-in-time, Labour Relations and the UK Automotive Industry', *Industrial Relations Journal*, 17(3): 193–206.

TWISS, B., and WEINSHALL, T. (1980) *Managing Industrial Organisations*, London: Pitman.

URRY, J. (1990) *The Tourist Gaze*. London: Sage.

VOLBERDA, H. W. (1998) *Building the Flexible Firm: How to Remain Competitive.* Oxford: Oxford University Press.

WALLERSTEIN, I. (1984) *The Politics of the World Economy: The States, the Movements and the Civilisations.* Cambridge: Cambridge University Press.

—— and HOPKINS, T. (1996) *The Age of Transition: Trajectory of the World System 1945–2025.* London: Pluto Press.

WARD, I., and CADDELL, L. (1987) *Great British Bikes.* London: MacDonald & Co.

WATERS, M. (1995) *Globalisation.* London: Routledge.

WATTERSON, D. (1993) *The Gods of Ancient Egypt.* London: B. T. Batsford.

WEBER, M. (1968) *Economy and Society.* London: Bedminster Press.

WEICK, K. (1969) *The Social Psychology of Organising.* Reading, Mass.: Addison Wesley.

WEITZ, E., and SHENAV, Y. (2000) 'A Longitudinal Analysis of Technical and Organizational Uncertainty in Management Theory', *Organization Studies,* 21 (1): 243–265.

WHITLEY, R. (1989) 'On the Nature of Management Tasks and Skills: Their Distinguishing Characteristics and Organisation', *Journal of Management Studies,* 26 (3): 210–24.

—— (ed.) (1992) *European Business Systems.* London: Sage.

—— (1999) *Divergent Capitalisms: the Social Structuring and Change of Business Systems.* Oxford: Oxford University Press.

—— and KRISTENSEN, P. H. (eds) (1997) *Governance at Work: the Social Regulation of Economic Relations.* Oxford: Oxford University Press.

WICKENS, P. (1996) *The Ascendant Organisation.* London: HarperCollins.

WIENER, M. J. (1981) *English Culture and the Decline of the Industrial Spirit 1850–1980.* Cambridge: Cambridge University Press.

WILLIAMS, K., HASLAM, C., WILLIAMS J., and CUTLER, T. (1992) 'Against Lean Production', *Economy and Society,* 21 (3): 321–4.

—— WILLIAMS, J., and THOMAS, D. (1983) *Why are the British Bad at Manufacturing?* London: Routledge.

—— —— and HASLAM, C. (1990*a*) 'The Hollowing Out of British Manufacturing and its Implications for Policy', *Economy and Society,* 19: 456–70.

—— —— —— (1990*b*) 'Facing up to Manufacturing Failure', (eds), in P. Hirst and J. Zeitlin, (eds). *Reversing Industrial Decline.* Oxford: Blackwell.

—— HASLAM, C., WILLIAMS, J., ADCROFT, A., and JOHAL S. (1992) *Factories or Warehouses: Japanese Foreign Direct Investment in the UK and USA,* Polytechnic of East London Occasional Papers on Business, Economy and Society, 6.

WILLIAMSON, O. (1975) *Markets and Hierarchies: Analysis and Antitrust Implications.* New York: Free Press.

—— (1985) *The Economic Institutions of Capitalism.* New York: Free Press.

—— (1995) *Organisation Theory: From Chester Barnard to the Present and Beyond.* New York: Oxford University Press.

WILLMOTT, H. (1993) 'Strength is Ignorance, Freedom is Slavery: Managing Culture in Modern Organisations', *Journal of Mangement Studies,* 30 (4): 515–52.

WILSON, D., and ROSENFELD, F. (1990) *Managing Organizations: Text Readings and Cases.* London: McGraw-Hill.

WOMACK, J., JONES, D., and ROOS, D. (1990) *The Machine that Changed the World*. New York: Collier-Macmillan.

WOOD, D., and SMITH, P. (1989) *Employers' Labour Use Strategies: First Report of the 1987 Survey*, Department of Employment Research Paper 63. London: Department of Employment.

WOOD, S. (1995) 'The Four Pillars of HRM: Are they Connected?' *Human Resource Management Journal*, 5: 49–59.

WOODIWISS, A. (1996) 'Searching for Signs of Globalisation', *Sociology*, 30 (4): 799–810.

WOODWARD. J. (1958) *Industrial Organisation: Management and Technology*. London: HMSO.

WRIGHT, M., CHIPLIN, B., and COYNE, J. (1989) 'The Market for Corporate Control: The Divestment Option', in J. Fairburn and J. Kay (eds) *Mergers and Merger Policy*. London: Oxford University Press.

WTO (1995) *International Trade: Trends and Statistics*. Geneva: World Trade Organization.

ZEITLIN, J. (1992) 'Industrial Districts and Local Economic Regeneration', in F. Pyke and W. Sengenberger (eds), *Industrial Districts and Local Economic Regeneration*. Geneva: International Institute of Labour Studies, ILO.

ZEITLIN, M. (ed.) (1970) *American Society Inc*. Chicago: Markham.

—— (1974) 'Corporate Ownership and Control: The Large Corporation and the Capitalist Class', *American Journal of Sociology*, 79.

—— (1976) 'On Class Theory of the Large Corporation', *American Journal of Sociology*, 81.

ZUKIN, S., and DIMAGGIO, P. (1990) *Structures of Capital*. Cambridge: Cambridge University Press.

ZYSMAN, J. (1983) *Governments, Markets and Growth: Financial Systems and the Politics of Industrial Change*. London: Martin Robertson.

Index